HEALTH IN AGING

Russell A. Ward, Ph.D., is Associate Professor of Sociology at the State University of New York at Albany. His research has focused on informal support networks of older persons and factors affecting health behavior. Recent publications include *The Aging Experience* and *The Environment for Aging*.

Sheldon S. Tobin, Ph.D., is Director of the Ringel Institute of Gerontology and Professor in the School of Social Welfare at the State University of New York at Albany. He is Editor-in-Chief of *The Gerontologist* and the author of numerous publications that have focused primarily on psychosocial aspects of aging and services for the elderly. Recent books include *Enabling the Elderly, The Experience of Aging, Last Home for the Aged,* and *Current Gerontology: Long Term Care*.

HEALTH IN AGING
Sociological Issues and Policy Directions

Russell A. Ward
Sheldon S. Tobin

Editors

SPRINGER PUBLISHING COMPANY
New York

Springer Publishing Company, Inc.
536 Broadway
New York, NY 10012

87 88 89 90 91 / 5 4 3 2 1

Library of Congress Cataloging-in-Publication Data

Health in aging.

   Includes bibliographies and index.
   1. Aged—Health and hygiene—United States.
2. Aged—Medical care—United States.   3. Aged—Long
term care—United States.   I. Ward, Russell A.
II. Tobin, Sheldon S.   [DNLM: 1. Aged. 2. Health
Policy—United States.   3. Health Services for the
Aged—United States.   WT 30 H4346]
RA564.8.H427   1987   362.1'6   87-16352
ISBN 0-8261-6130-8

Printed in the United States of America

Contents

75194   v

Foreword

The focus of this volume on social factors in health and health care is of central importance to the well-being of older people, and hence of central interest to all of us at the National Institute on Aging. Many of the contributors and participants have been and many still are NIA grantees. As invited by the Editors of this volume, we are delighted to make a few observations on behalf of NIA. Together with the Introduction, our observations may make some small contribution to use by readers of a book addressing topics on which we ourselves have often written (as in our *Beyond Ageism: Postponing the Onset of Disability*).

Much has been learned about how health relates to the life course, especially toward its end. (Incidentally, we prefer to think of "aging" not as a process characterized by some arbitrary marker of "old age." Rather, we often speak and write about "aging from birth to death.") But *what* have we learned? We shall mention only two of the areas in which progress has been made: preventive measures and interventions.

Despite the fact that the great majority of older Americans live in their own homes and are quite able to perform activities of daily living without help from others, we know that older people are more likely than younger people to need the services of physicians and to utilize extensively the facilities provided by hospitals, nursing homes, and home care programs. Given the twentieth-century triumph of extension of life, the development of high-quality health care appropriate to the needs of older persons is imperative. We know from countless studies and surveys the dismal facts about the costs involved. We also know that the bulk of care for older people continues to be provided through self-care and informal care—though these forms of care need wider recognition in both professional practice and public policy.

But we know too that the only sure way of containing health care costs—both public and private—is to keep people healthy. It is becoming increasingly obvious that social and behavioral factors are relevant not only to the design of high-quality health care, but also to the maintenance of health and effective functioning in the middle and later years. As our NIA program announcements note, for some older people aging means healthy, effective, fulfilling lives, while for others aging means chronic ill health, prolonged disability, loneliness, and disengagement from affairs. Such differences in the ways people age are influenced not only by biology, but also by the social environments they grow old in—by the work they do, the people they interact with, the household and community they live in. Social factors influence individuals' perceptions of illness and their behavioral responses.

Furthermore, there is growing awareness in the biomedical community that social and psychological factors are strategically important in maintaining health and in influencing the aging process itself. The Surgeon General has pointed out that perhaps as much as half of all United States mortality has a significant social and behavioral component. More recently, we have learned that traditional behavioral and social risk factors continue to be important for predicting mortality even among those aged 70 and over. At the National Institutes of Health, the Working Group on Health and Behavior is highlighting and encouraging research on prevention and on the ways health and behavior are related, and nearly every Institute is fostering research in this area. Health care systems and other social institutions, such as work organizations, are beginning to apply this knowledge by emphasizing prevention of health problems.

Although much more needs to be known, recent research is also pointing to promising directions for intervention once disabilities have set in or deficits are experienced. For example, we know that behavioral modification techniques can be used by family members to increase positive behaviors such as self-care, adherence to medical regimens, exercise, and involvement in social activities among older people with behavioral problems. Intellectual decline with aging (when it occurs) can often be slowed or reversed by relatively simple training interventions. Older people can often learn to compensate for declines in reaction time, memory, and other age-related deficits through mnemonic strategies, care, and persistence. Reaction time itself, formerly believed to be biologically constrained, can be improved under fostering social conditions. Particular styles and sizes of type can facilitate reading, and improved environmental design can offset inability to see large objects in low contrast. Food can be adapted to the age-related changes in taste and smell that influence eating behaviors to combat the serious malnutrition problem of many older people. Under specified conditions, older patients can learn to exercise a higher degree of behavioral control over EEG through biofeedback (they learn this more readily than younger patients). Among the frail elderly, even those in nursing homes, a heightened sense of personal control exerts an influence on immune functioning, active participation, and perhaps even on mortality.

In short, the evidence is mounting to show that modification in attitudes, behaviors, social relationships, and environments can often prevent, postpone, or reverse disabilities currently associated with the later years. There is clear evidence that prevention efforts are not wasted on older people, that compensation for deficits can be trained, and that curative and palliative medical care should be pursued. The older population has tremendous capacities for engagement in social activity and high levels of health and functioning. Through continued research, we need to specify further the ways in which to enhance these capacities.

Prevention and intervention are just two of the research areas about which we now have some firm understandings. The gaps in knowledge of the relationship between aging processes and health obviously are still large. Quite properly, the editors of this volume do not claim to provide firm answers to the major research or policy issues we all face. They have, nevertheless, taken some long steps toward clarifying our understanding of how research may optimally be translated into policy and how, in turn, policy issues may be used to stimulate new and imaginative research designs.

The editors speak of "frontiers." From our vantage point, there are and will continue to be many frontiers in the still uncharted areas of age and aging. Indeed, when in 1983 we edited *Aging in Society: Selected Reviews of Recent Research*, we too talked about "frontiers" and "leading edges." This new work on *Health in Aging* is a welcome addition to our common enterprise.

Matilda White Riley
Kathleen Bond
National Institute on Aging
November, 1986

Contributors

Vern L. Bengtson, Ph.D., is Director of the Andrus Center Gerontology Research Institute and Professor of Sociology at the University of Southern California in Los Angeles. He is Chair of the Section on Aging of the American Sociological Association and was previously Chair of the Behavioral and Social Sciences Section of the Gerontological Society of America. His research and publications in gerontology have focused on intergenerational family relationships, socialization, and ethnicity.

Laurence G. Branch, Ph.D., is Professor of Public Health and Chief of the Health Services Section at the Boston University School of Public Health and was formerly Associate Professor of Health Policy at Harvard Medical School and an Associate Director of the West Roxbury V. A. Geriatric Research, Education, and Clinical Center. He has published extensively on health policy for older people, the development of disability, and alternatives within long-term care.

Neena L. Chappell, Ph.D., is Director of the Centre on Aging and Associate Professor in the Departments of Sociology and of Social and Preventive Medicine at the University of Manitoba in Canada. A National Health Research Scholar, she has done research on informal and formal health care.

Rodney M. Coe, Ph.D., is Professor in the Department of Community Medicine, St. Louis University School of Medicine, and Education Coordinator for the Geriatric Research, Education, and Clinical Center of the St. Louis V. A. Medical Center. A former President of the Midwest Council for Social Research on Aging, he has written extensively in the area of medical sociology, with particular emphasis on issues in gerontology and geriatrics.

Diana Coupard, B.A., is a medical student at the University of Pennsylvania. She was previously a research assistant at the Brookings Institution.

Dale Dannefer, Ph.D., is Associate Professor of Education and Sociology at the University of Rochester, and in 1985–1986 was a Fellow at the Andrew Norman Institute for Advanced Study in Geriatrics and Gerontology in Los Angeles and the University of Southern California. He has written numerous articles on the state of theory in the study of aging and human development. His current interests center on intracohort variability over the life course and the processes that regulate it, and the relation between cultural assumptions about aging and the scientific study of aging.

Linda K. George, Ph.D., is Associate Director of the Duke University Center for the Study of Aging and Human Development, as well as Professor of Psychiatry and Sociology. She is the author of numerous publications on social and psychological aspects of aging. Her major research interests include the impact of chronic disease on individuals and families, the epidemiology of psychiatric disorders, and the determinants of help-seeking for physical and psychiatric illnesses.

Ray Hanley, M.P.A., is a Senior Research Analyst at the Brookings Institution, where he specializes in research on long-term care for the elderly. He previously worked for the Office of the Assistant Secretary for Planning and Evaluation, U. S. Department of Health and Human Services, and at the University of Washington.

Charles F. Longino, Jr., Ph.D., is Director of the Center for Social Research in Aging and Professor of Sociology at the University of Miami. His research projects have included the Midwestern Retirement Community Study, the Retirement Migration Project, and the Oldest Americans Study. His publications have focused especially on the topics of retirement communities, migration, and gerontological theory.

Kyriakos S. Markides, Ph.D., is Associate Professor in the Department of Preventive Medicine and Community Health, University of Texas Medical Branch in Galveston. His research interests are primarily in the areas of health and intergenerational relations. He is currently analyzing data from his longitudinal study of Mexican-Americans and Anglos and his three-generations study of Mexican-Americans.

Victor W. Marshall, Ph.D., is Professor of Behavioural Science and of Sociology at the University of Toronto. A National Health Scientist, he is Editor-in-Chief of *The Canadian Journal on Aging* and the recipient of the Laidlaw Foundation Award. He has published extensively in the sociology of aging and of health, including *Last Chapters: A Sociology of Aging and Dying* and *Aging in Canada*.

Allan R. Meyers, Ph.D., is Associate Professor of Public Health (Health Services) at the Boston University School of Public Health. His research interests include the organization and funding of long-term care, social studies of alcohol use, and the interface between public health and public policy.

Ray R. Mosely II, M.A., is a doctoral candidate in the Department of Sociology at Southern Illinois University at Carbondale. His dissertation focuses on occupational status effects on the use of health services.

Alan Sager, Ph.D., is an Associate Professor at the Boston University School of Public Health. His current research interests include urban hospital closings and financial distress, preventive health practices for older citizens, and the sources of inequity in health services. He is the author of *Planning Home Care with the Elderly.*

Beth J. Soldo, Ph.D., is Chair and Associate Professor in the Department of Demography, Georgetown University. She is also a Senior Research Scholar at the Center for Population Research and the Kennedy Institute of Ethics at Georgetown. Her research and publications have focused on the effects of the demographic imperative for age-related public policy questions, notably the structure of long-term care in the United States.

Denise Spence, M.S.P.H., is a Senior Research Analyst at the Brookings Institution, where she specializes in research on long-term care for the elderly. She previously worked at Project Hope.

Lois M. Verbrugge, Ph.D., is a social demographer at the University of Michigan. Her research centers on sex differences in health status, health behavior, and mortality, with special interest in middle-aged and older persons. She has a Research Career Development Award from the National Institute of Child Health and Human Development to pursue her work on sex and social role differentials in health and mortality.

Joshua M. Wiener, Ph.D., is a Senior Fellow at the Brookings Institution, where he specializes in research on long-term care and Medicaid. He previously worked at the Health Care Financing Administration, U. S. Department of Health and Human Services, the Massachusetts Department of Public Health, the U. S. Congressional Budget Office, the New York State Moreland Act Commission on Nursing Homes and Residential Facilities, and the New York City Department of Health.

Fredric D. Wolinsky, Ph.D., is Associate Professor of Sociology at Texas A&M University, where he continues his work on modeling the health and illness behavior of the elderly with the support of a Research Career Development Award from the National Institute on Aging. He is about to embark on another NIA-funded study of utilization differences among aged Anglo, Black, Mexican-American, Cuban-American, and Puerto-Rican Americans.

CONFERENCE DISCUSSANTS

Mary Jo Bane, Ed.D., is Executive Deputy Commissioner of the New York State Department of Social Services and in the Spring of 1987 will return to Harvard University as Professor of Public Policy in the John F. Kennedy School of Government. She is the author of several books in the area of human services and public policy, including *The State and the Poor in the 1980's* and *Here to Stay: American Families in the Twentieth Century.*

James J. Callahan, Jr., Ph.D., is Director of Mental Health Training and

Senior Research Associate at the Heller School, Brandeis University. He has served as Director of the Medicaid Program, Secretary of Elder Affairs, and Commissioner of the Department of Mental Health in Massachusetts.

Alfred Gellhorn, M.D., is Director of Medical Affairs for the New York State Department of Health. His career in academic medicine has included basic biomedical research and clinical medicine at Columbia University, Dean of the Medical School and Director of the Medical Center at the University of Pennsylvania, and founder and first Director of the Sophie Davis School for Biomedical Education at the City University of New York.

Rose Campbell Gibson, Ph.D., is Associate Professor of Social Work and Faculty Associate of the Institute for Social Research at the University of Michigan. A former U. S. Public Health Service Fellow, she has published numerous articles and monographs on aging and family relations in the black population.

Marie R. Haug, Ph.D., is Professor Emerita of Sociology and Director Emerita of the Center on Aging and Health at Case Western Reserve University in Cleveland, Ohio. She has published widely on issues of aging and health, including books on *Elderly Patients and Their Doctors* and *Consumerism in Medicine.*

George L. Maddox, Ph.D., is Professor of Sociology and of Medical Sociology (Psychiatry) and chairs the University Council on Aging and Human Development at Duke University. He has served as Secretary General and Vice-President of the International Association of Gerontology, Chair of the Section on Aging of the American Sociological Association, and President of the Gerontological Society of America. In 1983 he was co-recipient of the Sandoz International Prize for Research in Aging; in 1985 he received the Distinguished Contribution to Aging Award of the American Sociological Association and the Kleemeier Research Award of the Gerontological Society of America. He is the Editor-in-Chief of the *Encyclopedia of Aging.*

Mildred B. Shapiro, M.A., is Associate Commissioner of the New York State Department of Social Services, Division of Medical Assistance (Medicaid), and Adjunct Professor at Union College in health economics. She has been Director of Economics Analysis in the New York State Department of Health, Associate Director of the New York State Health Planning Commission, and Commissioner of the New York State Commission on Quality of Care for the Mentally Disabled. Her articles and publications focus on the field of labor and health economics.

HEALTH IN AGING

Introduction

Population aging is one of the dominant trends of the twentieth century. This is an international phenomenon, as all regions of the world are experiencing increases in both the absolute and relative sizes of the older population. In the United States, the 65+ population has grown from 3 million persons and 4% of the total population in 1900, to over 25 million persons and 11% of the total population in 1980. Over that same time, life expectancy at birth has risen from less than 50 years to over 70.

This aging trend will continue into the future. It has been estimated that the 65+ population of the United States in the year 2030 will include over 64 million persons, representing 21% of the total population (U.S. Senate Special Committee on Aging, 1985). This dramatic increase in the size of the older population reflects the aging of the post-World War II baby boom. It also, however, reflects continuing improvement in health and medical care. Improvements in life expectancy over most of this century have largely been attributable to reduction of mortality early in the life cycle; but mortality reductions have also been evident at the oldest ages, particularly in recent decades. Indeed, the 75+ population is now the fastest-growing segment of the population.

These demographic patterns have numerous implications for both individuals and societies. Life extension alters the rhythm of the life cycle for individuals, as new stages, such as retirement and grandparenthood, become typical experiences. Life extension also presents challenges to the social institutions of society. Patterns of education, work, and family life must adapt to altered age structures. Social policies must also adapt, in part due to the increasing dependency ratio of old to young. This is evident, for example, in recent debates over pension policy.

Linkages between aging and health have a clear relevance to the context we have described. Health-related changes are perhaps the most obvious accompaniments of aging, with implications for both individuals and societies. For the individual, physical health is central to well-being, affecting morale, ability to engage in routine activities of daily living, and adequate performance of social roles. Societies experiencing population aging, in turn, must develop services and policies to address changing health patterns and assistance needs of older persons. Rising public expenditures are illustrative of the challenges confronting modern societies. Medicare expenditures, for example, rose from about $7 billion in 1970 to more than $50 billion in 1983. Thus, as Shanas and Maddox (1985) have noted, "physical and psychological well-being are matters of social as well as personal concern" (p. 696).

Although aging and health are clearly related, the nature and implications of their relationship are not straightforward. Aging in the latter half of life is obviously associated with increasing morbidity and mortality, reflecting intrinsic biological processes of senescence as well as the accumulated effects of extrinsic factors such as diet and lifestyle. It is difficult, however, to provide a clear portrait of the health of older people. Indeed, it is unwise to attempt a simple description.

Health may be defined and measured in many ways, including the presence of disease or symptomatology, the level of functioning in the activities of daily life, and subjective feelings of healthiness or well-being (Shanas & Maddox, 1985). Different definitions permit the health status of the elderly to be described in many ways, some pessimistic and some optimistic. On the one hand, a large majority of older people have one or more chronic health conditions; for example, nearly one-half have arthritis, more than one-third, hypertension, and more than one-fourth, hearing impairments and heart conditions (U.S. Senate Special Committee on Aging, 1985). As a consequence, older people place heavy demand on the health care system; for example, they account for about one-fourth of all physician office visits and nearly one-third of all hospital rounds (Iglehart, 1985). On the other hand, despite chronic illness and use of health care, only a small minority of older people are unable to carry on normal activities, and most define their health as good or excellent. Adding to the complexity, utilization data often hide the skewed nature of service use, as a small minority of older persons account for the bulk of health care utilization and expenditures.

Health in aging is similarly perplexing at the societal level. Projections into the future are particularly fraught with uncertainties. Witness the recent debates over the possibility of a "compression of morbidity." Fries (1983) has argued that "rectangularization of the survival curve," an expression used to characterize the graph showing that death is occurring very late in life for all but a small percentage of the population, can also be interpreted as a shortening of the period of infirmity and disability before death. This optimistic view, however, is countered with a more pessimistic alternative in which the preterminal period of morbidity and frailty may lengthen as ill and disabled older people survive for longer periods of time, potentially lowering the aggregate health status of the elderly (Manton,

1982; Verbrugge, 1984). Different assumptions lead to different scenarios that have very different implications for social programs and policies.

The linkages between aging and health encompass the full range of disciplines and policy domains. The particular focus of this volume is on a sociological understanding of health in aging that goes beyond chronology and biology to an awareness of age as a social construct and aging as a social process. Indeed, the experience of aging is complex, varied, and changing because the social context within which it occurs differs across individuals and over time. The life course of any individual reflects the intersection of history, social change, and specific biographical experiences (Elder, 1981). Similarly, the nature and implications of health patterns over the life cycle reflect social processes and social structure.

We do not seek to address all relationships between aging and health. It would not be possible to do so in a single volume. Thus, we do not directly address the biology of aging, except as deterioration is reflected in patterns of morbidity and mortality; nor do we address psychological issues such as differential vulnerability to age-associated stressors or the covert processes used to cope with deterioration in aging. Rather, our essential goal is to understand the sociological processes related to health and effective functioning in later life, as well as to encompass major policy implications of those processes.

The relevant sociological processes are both social-psychological and structural and include individual, organizational, and societal levels of analysis. We need to understand the factors that shape individual responses to health and illness. We also need to understand organizational responses to the health needs of individuals and to the constraints of the surrounding social structure. Finally, aging and health must be viewed within the larger context of changes in the age structure of the population, in patterns of morbidity and mortality, and in social policies and social institutions.

ORIGINS OF THE BOOK

This book grew out of the sixth in a series of annual conferences on diverse topics sponsored by the Department of Sociology at the State University of New York at Albany. That conference, held in April of 1986, was co-sponsored by the Ringel Institute of Gerontology. Its focus on health issues related to aging reflected the experiences and interests of its organizers (the editors of this book).

The conference had two broad objectives: to capture some of the complexity regarding social aspects of health in aging and to serve as a forum for discussion of the implications of this knowledge for social policy. A more specific objective of the participants, both presenters and listeners, was to share approaches to, as well as findings from, our research with a hope of clarifying complex phenomena and identifying needed research that would be undertaken by us or others. After establishing these objectives, we took an inductive approach to developing the specific content of the conference. That is, rather than first defining topics and then soliciting participants, we began by seeking out leading research scholars and asking them to present papers based on their current, ongoing research. We then grouped sets of speakers by the common issues in their work. Finally, we invited knowledgeable discussants to respond to sets of papers. This approach, we feel, provided the best opportunity to address those issues related to health in aging that are of current interest and significance. Biographical sketches of authors and discussants are provided at the beginning of the book.

This process has resulted in a collection of interrelated papers by active scholars working on the frontier of research. Many are reports of work in progress, and each represents a stage in the research process. Some papers are quite speculative in nature, having been prepared to guide future research. Other authors are wrestling with preliminary analyses of data from small pilot studies, seeking to clarify research questions. Other papers contain reports of studies that are at a more mature stage in the research process and include carefully constructed sampling designs, a comprehensive set of measures, and sophisticated analytic techniques to assess specific research hypotheses. Finally, some papers offer an integration of existing research knowledge that clarifies policy implications. All papers include material on future directions for research and policy. Inclusion of participants from both the United States and Canada also permits observations of similarities and contrasts in the experiences of societies with different populations and policies.

We sought to enliven the conference through inclusion of discussants who could successfully bridge the often substantial gap between empirical research and social policy. Two groups of discussants were invited: accomplished researchers who are attuned to policy issues (Marie Haug, George Maddox, and Rose Gibson) and senior policy administrators who are also productive scholars (James Callahan, Mary Jo Bane, Mildred Shapiro, and Alfred Gellhorn). In inviting members of the latter group of discussants, we took advantage of our favorable location in the capital of New York State. Comments of the discussants were consistently well-conceived and stimulating, contributing significantly to the success of the conference. Their comments will be cited in introductory sections of this volume.

PLAN OF THE BOOK

The papers have been grouped into four parts. Because each part will be introduced in more detail, here we will offer only brief synopses.

Part 1 provides an orientation to patterns of morbidity and mortality associated with age. Recognizing the complexity of those patterns, the contributors approach health from a multidimensional standpoint. The papers in this section introduce several themes that recur throughout the book; for example, the heterogeneity of aging and patterns of health, the implications of present patterns and trends for the future, and methodological issues in the study of health and aging.

Having assessed age-related patterns of health in the first part, we turn in Part 2 to patterns of health care. Assistance for the health-related needs of older people comes from a variety of sources: from oneself, from informal support networks of family and friends, and from formal health care services. Assistance also occurs in a variety of sites, including home, outpatient services, inpatient care within hospitals, and institutional care within nursing homes. Papers in this part address many gaps in our understanding of these care sources and sites.

The processes that shape health care utilization by the elderly are incompletely understood; Shanas and Maddox (1985), for example, note the "complex and imperfect way in which illness and the need for health care are translated by individuals into demand for and utilization of health services" (p. 697). We also know little about the nature and consequences of interactions between patients and providers within the health care system (Haug, 1981). The latter interactions are particularly important because of their implications for diagnosis, treatment, and subsequent health outcomes. Additionally, although we know that informal networks are a central source of assistance for older people, there is a continuing need to clarify the nature of that support and its outcomes for both the giver and receiver of support (Cantor & Little, 1985; Ward, 1985). In particular, there is a need to understand the strains associated with caregiving (Cantor, 1983) and to clarify the linkages between informal and formal supports (Litwak, 1985). These issues receive particular attention in the second part.

The focus of Part 2, and indeed of the book as a whole, is on older people who reside in the community, rather than in institutional settings. This selective focus is intentional, reflecting the reality that the relationships between health and aging are largely community issues. The majority of health-related assistance received by older people is provided informally by community residents (family, friends, and neighbors). Even the "frail elderly" are predominantly a noninstitutional population. Only 5% of the older (65+) population reside in nursing homes; even among persons aged 85 and over, only about one in five resides in a nursing home. Indeed, it has been estimated that older people in the community with extreme physical limitations outnumber those in institutions by two to one (Soldo, 1980).

Part 3 focuses on issues related to long-term care. Such issues have particular relevance for the elderly, whose health problems tend to be chronic, degenerative, and multiple. Aging of the population combines with inflation of health care costs to generate critical policy issues. Health care expenditures in the United States, which amounted to $12 billion or 4.6% of the GNP in 1950, are projected to reach $757.9 billion or 11.5% of the GNP in 1990, with long-term care services for chronic diseases and conditions representing one of the fastest growing components of these expenditures (Lawrence & Gaus, 1983). The private sector has been a major source of these funds, but both personal and public costs have been rising dramatically.

Shanas and Maddox (1985) have noted that current systems of health care are not oriented to long-term or community-based care, focusing instead on acute care and delivery of services in institutional settings. Medicare, for example, has spurred debates over its costliness, yet it covers less than one-half of the health care expenses of older persons and barely touches long-term care needs. Recommendations from the 1981 White House Conference on Aging emphasized the need for a community-based continuum of services as part of a comprehensive health care system, but also recognized the many unresolved issues related to financing, organization, and delivery of health care. There are many options for redressing the lack of support for chronic care (see, for example, Callahan & Wallack, 1981; Lawrence & Gaus, 1983). The papers contained here assess the viability of the major alternatives.

The final part of the book extends our attention more explicitly to the future. Recognition is given to the dynamic nature of aging for both individuals and societies. Riley (1982) has underscored the relevance of two interdependent dynamics: (1) cohort succession, or change in the size and characteristics of the older population, and (2) social change, or alteration of the social context within which aging takes place. She notes that these processes are never perfectly synchronized, thus creating strains and pressures on individuals and societies. In particular, "disordered cohort flow" (Waring, 1975) disrupts social institutions, while the quality of life of individuals is jeopardized by the failure of institutions such as work and family to accommodate to the aging of the population. The final paper includes speculation along these lines, analyzing trends associated with both cohort succession and social change.

SOME RECURRING THEMES

A number of themes are evident in this volume. Three in particular recur throughout the papers: the heterogeneity and variability of aging and of the linkages between health and aging, information needs and research design issues related to that heterogeneity and variability, and the complexities of the relationships between research and policy.

Heterogeneity and Variability of Aging

The diversity of aging and of the older population, reflecting both intracohort and intercohort heterogeneity, makes any simple statements about health status, health-related behaviors, and health care needs of "the elderly" unwarranted. Throughout this collection there are reminders of the variability found within the older population due to, for example, gender and ethnic differences. Gender differences occur in morbidity, disability, informal support, and so forth; and because older women outnumber older men by three to two, issues of income, housing, and health care are in many ways women's issues.

Social change is an additional source of heterogeneity and variability, reflecting the dynamic qualities of aging. This is evident in discussions of morbidity and disability, the functioning of informal support networks, and patterns of service access and utilization. It is also evident in speculations about the societal context for aging in the future. The papers recognize the multidimensionality of aging and the necessity of understanding the linkages between health and such other spheres as work and family.

Data and Design Issues

Recognition that aging is a dynamic and variable phenomenon has important methodological implications. One implication is the need to utilize both macro and micro data. Although data that summarize aggregate patterns and processes are needed, findings may lack sufficient specificity. George Maddox, in his comments at the conference, noted that health statistics and large-scale survey data provide a "view from 30,000 feet" that is difficult to translate to the lives of individuals. Such data must be complemented by an understanding of the ways in which individuals act and interact within the realities of their own worlds.

A second methodological implication of the diversity and variability of aging is the need to disentangle age, period, and cohort effects (Maddox & Campbell, 1985). The usual cross-sectional design, whereby data are gathered from different age groups at one time, does not allow clear differentiation between the effects of aging and the effects of the characteristics and experiences of particular cohorts; we can assess neither the stability of empirical patterns over time nor the extent to which cross-sectional data reflect unique factors operating only at that time period. These interpretive difficulties indicate the need for longitudinal research designs, in particular cohort analyses following several cohorts over time.

The authors of papers in this volume nicely address these issues. They make appropriate use of the most sophisticated forms of multivariate analysis, while avoiding naive interpretations and simplistic causal inferences. Both macro- and microlevel data are used, often in innovative ways, to clarify empirical issues of health and aging. Attention is paid to conceptual and analytical issues of cross-sectional and longitudinal designs. In sum, we are presented with state-of-the-art research that is also cognizant of unresolved issues that remain.

The Relationship Between Research and Policy

This volume, as did the conference that gave it life, addresses both research and policy issues related to health and aging. Health care policy is an area of growing visibility and debate that is not likely to subside in the foreseeable future. Policy related to health in aging is clearly a complex arena, with no shortage of issues or alternative avenues. The papers presented here take a selective view of those policy issues. They are oriented more clearly to research issues, attending to related policy issues but for the most part not having these issues as the central focus.

This can perhaps be understood as a function of the sociological orientation of the papers. Indeed, this was a topic of some discussion at the conference and was reflected in the comments of several discussants. Mary Jo Bane, for example, wished for clearer indications of "good" and "bad" patterns of health care, with guidelines for encouraging the former and discouraging the latter. James Callahan raised issues concerning the political "will" to implement policy and the potential consequences of political realignments. George Maddox also noted a failure to address political strategies for formulating policy and mobilizing support to implement beneficial social programs. More generally, he noted that sociologists tend to be uncomfortable when addressing policy formation and implementation. They tend to be guarded in giving advice to policymakers, viewing the policy arena as more political than scientific and shying away from specific recommendations because of their acute awareness of the multidimensionality of constructs and the heterogeneity of the population (as we have noted earlier).

Although the authors of papers in this volume give little attention to the formation and implementation of policy, their policy focus can be understood from the standpoint of policy analysis. Davis (1985) notes that policymaking is a political process and that "policy analysis assists in this process by delineating the nature and extent of problems to be addressed, and by analyzing major alternatives for action in terms of their benefits, costs, and consequences" (p. 730). This set of papers contributes to this analytic need in both implicit and explicit ways.

The heterogeneity of aging and of the older population complicates efforts to construct comprehensive policies. Variability in health care needs and in patterns of health care utilization requires similarly varied policy options and raises issues of equity across subgroups. Indeed, the heterogeneity of the older population raises questions about the advisability of using age *per se* as the basis for policy (Neugarten, 1982). Crystal (1986), for example, found substantial improvement in the relative economic status of older people, such that they could not be said to be disadvantaged as a group; yet Crystal also found a high level of inequality within the older population and suggested the need for a more selective focus on the needs of disadvantaged elderly. Rose Gibson, in her comments at the conference, also suggested that disadvantaged minorities may age more rapidly than whites, reflecting a quickening of critical life events (for example, childbirth, loss of spouse, and retirement) and earlier onset of disease, physical limitation, and mortality. Thus, the possibility of earlier vulnerability and dependency raises issues concerning the appropriateness of age-based policies for minorities.

These papers assist in clarifying the nature and sources of diversity in health and health care needs within the older population and, also, the need for multidimensional assessment of individuals and their environments. These clarifications are necessary steps in identifying appropriate targets for social policy. Yet findings must be presented so that, as George Maddox noted, they are both recognizable to policymakers and "actionable."

Social policy must also attend to the future, and the papers in this volume remind us of the problems inherent in making projections into the future. The variable and dynamic qualities of aging mean that predictions are fraught with uncertainty. Forecasts of health care utilization and service needs, for example, depend upon assumptions about population aging, cohort flow, and associated patterns of morbidity, disability, and mortality. Policy must be forged within the parameters of best- and worst-case scenarios. Both scenarios are evident in these papers, as is an attendant mixture of both optimism and pessimism about the future.

To conclude, our intent is neither to address all aspects of health in aging nor to provide the final answers to research and policy questions. Rather, the reader should view this volume as a reflection of the current state of research and related policy issues in selected areas and as a guide to salient aspects of conceptualization, research design, and policy analysis.

REFERENCES

Callahan, James, Jr., and Stanley Wallack (eds.). 1981. *Reforming the Long-Term-Care System: Financial and Organizational Options.* Lexington, MA: Lexington Books.

Cantor, Marjorie. 1983. "Strain Among Caregivers: A Study of Experience in The United States." *The Gerontologist* 23: 597–604.

Cantor, Marjorie and Virginia Little. 1985. "Aging and Social Care." In *Handbook of Aging and the Social Sciences,* edited by R. Binstock and E. Shanas. New York: Van Nostrand Reinhold.

Crystal, Stephen. 1986. "Measuring Income and Inequality Among the Elderly." *The Geronotologist* 26: 56–59.

Davis, Karen. 1985. "Health Care Policies and the Aged: Observations from the United States." In *Handbook of Aging and the Social Sciences,* edited by R. Binstock and E. Shanas. New York: Van Nostrand Reinhold.

Elder, Glen. 1981. "History and the Life Course." In *Biography and Society: The Life History Approach in the Social Sciences,* edited by D. Bertaux. Beverly Hills, CA: Sage.

Fries, James. 1983. "The Compression of Morbidity." *Milbank Memorial Fund Quarterly* 61: 397–419.

Haug, Marie (ed.). 1981. *Elderly Patients and Their Doctors.* New York: Springer.

Iglehart, John. 1985. "Medicare Turns to HMOs." *New England Journal of Medicine* 312(2): 132–136.

Lawrence, Diane and Clifton Gaus. 1983. "Long-term Care: Financing and Policy Issues." In *Handbook of Health, Health Care, and the Health Professions,* edited by D. Mechanic. New York: Free Press.

Litwak, Eugene. 1985. *Helping the Elderly.* New York: Guilford Press.

Maddox, George and Richard Campbell. 1985. "Scope, Concepts, and Methods in the Study of Aging." In *Handbook of Aging and the Social Sciences,* edited by R. Binstock and E. Shanas. New York: Van Nostrand Reinhold.

Manton, Kenneth. 1982. "Changing Concepts of Morbidity and Mortality in the Elderly Population." *Milbank Memorial Fund Quarterly* 60: 183–244.

Neugarten, Bernice. 1982. *Age or Need? Public Policies for Older People.* Beverly Hills, CA: Sage.

Riley, Matilda. 1982. "Aging and Social Change." In *Aging From Birth to Death: Sociotemporal Perspectives,* Vol. II, edited by M. Riley, R. Abeles, and M. Teitelbaum. Boulder, CO: Westview Press.

Shanas, Ethel and George Maddox. 1985. "Health, Health Resources, and the Utilization of Care." In *Handbook of Aging and the Social Sciences,* edited by R. Binstock and E. Shanas. New York: Van Nostrand Reinhold.

Soldo, Beth. 1980. "America's Elderly in the 1980's." *Population Bulletin* 35(4): 1–47.

U.S. Senate Special Committee on Aging. 1985. *Aging America: Trends and Projections.* Washington, DC: U.S. Government Printing Office.

Verbrugge, Lois. 1984. "Longer Life but Worsening Health? Trends in Health and Mortality of Middle-aged and Older Persons." *Milbank Memorial Fund Quarterly* 62: 475–519.

Ward, Russell. 1985. "Informal Networks and Well-Being in Later Life: A Research Agenda." *The Gerontologist* 25: 55–61.

Waring, Joan. 1975. "Social Replenishment and Social Change." *American Behavioral Scientist* 19: 237–256.

PART 1
Age-Related Health Patterns

Introduction

In this section different portraits are drawn of the health status of older persons through the use of a variety of health statistics. Recognition is given to the multidimensional nature of health and to the relevance for health of such other spheres as family and housing. These chapters also provide a context for thinking about the policy implications of health and aging and about the difficult task of projecting into the future.

Verbrugge begins by noting that the properties of health and illness are not easily captured by available health statistics. This is especially true of the daily symptoms and discomforts that constitute the majority of experiences of ill health. Verbrugge, however, provides an unusually clear and detailed assessment of the "iceberg of morbidity." Employing this construct, Verbrugge creatively analyzes changing patterns of health and health care utilization across age groups by examining health indicators from both national and community health surveys. She synthesizes her findings by developing a scenario of health stages along the course of morbidity, starting with daily symptoms and ending with death.

A distinction between rates and ranks proves very useful in clarifying general patterns of health change associated with age. Increases with age in chronic conditions and associated limitations reflect changes both in the rates of health problems and in the rankings of leading health problems. In contrast, rates of acute health conditions change with age, but rankings of those conditions are quite stable. The distinctively chronic character of health problems in later life underscores the importance of long-term care, the focus of Part 3. Verbrugge also finds, however, that change in the rankings of health problems is greater between youth and middle age than between middle age and older years. The precursors of health problems in late life typically appear in middle age and are not very visible in young adulthood—a statement that is intuitively reasonable but not previously demonstrated. This reminds us that aging is not synonymous with old age; rather, age-associated health and illness must be understood as a process of change over the life cycle.

Sex differences are evident in many of the papers in this volume, and Verbrugge's distinction between rates and ranks helps clarify the nature of sex differences in health status. She finds pervasive sex differences in rates of health problems, but similarity in ranks; that is, women have more health problems and use more services, but they suffer fundamentally the same kinds of health problems as men throughout the life course. Thus there is a need to distinguish between differences in frequency and in kind of health problems when sorting out variability in aging and among the older population.

Verbrugge also notes the need for better health statistics to uncover the morbidity "iceberg." In particular, existing data tell us little about day-to-day patterns of symptoms and self-care, a topic that is addressed in chapters by Chappell and George in Part 2. Unfortunately, there has been reduced federal support for such data-gathering efforts. Verbrugge's paper makes clear the need for data that more adequately reflect the multidimensional nature of health. She notes that each portrait of population health is valuable to different parties: consumers, providers, and policymakers. George Maddox, as noted earlier, commented that policymakers need adequate empirical data, which, as was also noted in the book's Introduction, is the first task of policy analysis; that is, "delineating the nature and extent of problems to be addressed."

This is easier said than done, since different statistics yield quite different portraits of health. Alfred Gellhorn commented at the conference that the use of health statistics such as daily symptoms involves some danger if those symptoms receive a "diagnosis" and become treated as a "disease." Indeed, Verbrugge notes that subjective health ratings by individuals decline less with age than one might expect, particularly given the dramatic increases in health problems. Maddox also commented that one can arrive at very different statistics depending upon the definition of "frailty." To influence policy, statistics must be translated into assessments of need for care and of resources available to meet those needs.

The chapter by Longino and Soldo provides a nice complement to Verbrugge's paper. Similar to Verbrugge, they note that the current fragmented approach to data collection is insufficient to examine fully the quantitative and qualitative dimensions of population aging. In particular, they indicate that effective planning requires attention to the qualitative aspects of aging. Their chapter contributes to this need in two ways. First, Verbrugge's analysis of symptoms and diseases is supplemented by a focus on functional dependency and quality of life. Second, health is viewed as an interaction between the individual and his or her environment, with specific recognition of social and physical environments that may either confound or ameliorate disability. They attend, for example, to informal caregiving and planned housing environments as dimensions of the responsiveness of the environment to the health-related needs of individuals. The importance of interventions to improve quality of life is relevant to later discussions; for example, this is noted as a primary goal of long-term care in Part 3.

Whereas Verbrugge analyzes patterns of health across broad age groups, Longino and Soldo attend more directly to heterogeneity within the older population. They note intracohort and intercohort differences in risk factors and the existence of diversity within levels of disability. Recognition of this heterogeneity is critical to effective policymaking and social forecasting. In particular, Longino and Soldo note that health care needs depend not only on the health status of older individuals, but also on the characteristics of their environment (for example, their living arrangements). We are again reminded of the futility of formulating policy for "the elderly" as if their needs were homogeneous.

Longino and Soldo also explore the linkages between health-related disability and other quality-of-life deficiencies. They indicate that the service needs of older people are not discrete, but rather clustered, because physical disabilities are often associated with multiple deficiencies in social and economic resources. Health needs in aging must be considered broadly and together with other needs, a topic that is given explicit attention in Bengtson and Dannefer's chapter in Part 4.

The analysis undertaken by Longino and Soldo leads them to give more explicit attention to policy issues. A clustering of needs indicates a need for integrated services that can intervene to slow the rate of decline into disability. To do so, Longino and Soldo indicate that we must modify services and environments, but that we obviously face difficult policy choices in a competitive context of finite resources. Orderly consideration of those choices requires the kind of policy analysis incorporated into the papers in this volume.

The first two chapters in combination raise a number of issues for the future. As we noted in the book's Introduction, projection is fraught with uncertainty. Both Verbrugge and Longino and Soldo emphasize the complexities inherent in constructing scenarios for the future. Increased survival of frail older persons may increase levels of morbidity and disability. Alternatively, medical advances may continue to reduce the impact of disease, thereby lessening disability. Projections are further complicated by the implications of cohort succession and potential changes in family structure, living arrangements, and lifestyle. As indicated in the chapters, different scenarios yield quite different projections, a message that is echoed in Bengtson and Dannefer's chapter in Part 4. Longino and Soldo also note, however, that even the most optimistic scenario for the future yields a substantial increase in the number of frail elderly, and they point to the necessity of modifying social and physical environments to enhance functional capacity.

The final chapter in this section represents a shift in focus, as Markides analyzes predictors of mortality and the implications of differential mortality for research design. As a sociologist, he investigates the role of social factors, extending the concept of risk factors in mortality beyond those traditionally analyzed by epidemiologists. Thus attitudes, behavior, and lifestyle must be added to genetics, biological aging, and health care as factors that underlie mortality statistics. The role of social factors in this regard often remains unclear. A case in point from Markides's chapter is the predictive value of subjective age.

The methodological orientation of Markides's chapter also has very general relevance to efforts to understand relationships between aging and health. In the book's Introduction we noted the problems inherent in cross-sectional research and the value of longitudinal research. Certainly there is no need to belabor the difficulties in translating cross-sectional findings into chains of cause and effect. Yet it is instructive to note that in one of the earliest large-scale cross-sectional studies of aging, the Kansas City Study of Adult Life, an association between greater interaction with family and lower life satisfaction was interpreted as family contact causing lower morale. The more obvious interpretation is that older persons become sick and experience reduced well-being, resulting in more frequent family visits and caregiving (informal supports will be addressed in the chapters in Part 2).

Although the benefits of longitudinal research are noted throughout the chapters in this collection, Markides cautions us that such research is no panacea. The dropout of subjects, thereby altering the composition of the study population over time, can lead to misleading interpretations even if this is interpreted as natural attrition. In particular, dropouts due to morbidity and mortality are likely to come disproportionately from the most disadvantaged groups in the sample. This is apropos to Maddox's comment that researchers often give too little attention to sampling, relying instead on sophisticated statistical analyses to overcome insurmountable problems in design.

Thus these initial chapters provide us with valuable information about the relationships between health and aging, but they also remind us of the difficulties in gathering and interpreting such information. Difficulties in sampling, in selecting appropriate indices of health and illness, and in interpreting longitudinal data are only some of the many methodological problems that confront researchers (and policymakers) with a formidable task when they wish to understand health in aging.

1

From Sneezes to Adieux: Stages of Health for American Men and Women*

Lois M. Verbrugge

Health is a decidedly dynamic affair for individuals. It is experienced and remembered as a day-by-day, year-to-year, and lifetime phenomenon. Symptoms come and go, levels of discomfort rise and fall, ailments are one-time events or reappear all too often, chronic conditions are held in check or progress or sometimes disappear. These experiences are monitored and evaluated, and they prompt decisions about role accommodations and therapeutic actions in short time frames and long ones. Severe or prolonged symptoms spur people to change their regular activities for several days or sometimes permanently. Self-care with drugs, home remedies, or first aid is applied to many symptoms, either initially or routinely. Especially bothersome or ambiguous symptoms are brought to physicians and other health professionals for diagnosis and care. The most serious episodes of trauma and disease propel individuals into hospitals for controlled therapy and surgical repair. Ultimately, one condition or a pernicious group of them brings an end to one's days by death.

A central purpose of health statistics is to measure the human experience of ill health—the levels of morbidity and its consequences in a population. Statistics are selective, usually being limited in two ways. First, statistical

*This chapter is modified from an article in and reprinted with permission from *Social Science and Medicine*, 22, Lois M. Verbrugge, "From Sneezes to Adieux: Stages of Health for American Men and Women," Copyright 1986, Pergamon Journals Ltd.

The principal difference is a new section here, "Future Health Profiles."

This chapter is dedicated to the author's father, Frank Verbrugge, who was an important mentor for her and who died in 1985, far too soon.

series truncate counts of morbidity events by using severity thresholds. And counts of health service contacts are truncated by excluding nonphysician care.[1] Second, and much more limiting for our knowledge of population health, series are entirely absent for symptoms and discomforts of daily life and for self-care activities, especially actual use of nonprescription and prescription drugs. These symptoms and actions are the majority of ill-health experience, not the minority.

A visual metaphor—the iceberg of morbidity—captures this situation. Above water is visible, or measured, morbidity: diseases and injuries that propel permanent limitations, medical services, and death. Below water is the larger expanse of unmeasured morbidity: day-to-day problems that prompt self-care or no care. Moving from bottom to top, one encounters more serious health problems and more intensive professional care. The iceberg metaphor has been used casually, simply to distinguish minor ailments of daily life from major ones that induce medical care and death (Alonzo, 1979; Dunnell & Cartwright, 1972; Wadsworth, Butterfield, & Blaney, 1971).[2] Rudimentary estimates of seen and unseen morbidity have been made by White, Williams, and Greenberg (1961), who do not employ the iceberg metaphor in their analysis, and by Last (1963).

A similar, but less visual, concept is "stages of health." The phrase was coined by Suchman (1965) and has been developed by others (Fabrega, 1973; Kasl & Cobb, 1966a, 1966b; McKinlay, 1972; Mechanic, 1972, 1978; Stoeckle, Zola, & Davidson, 1963; Zola, 1973). The stages reflect decision points along the course of morbidity: namely, whether or not people perceive discomforts; whether or not symptoms are labeled as illness and how severe they are judged to be; how symptoms influence role performance; and whether symptoms receive self-care, ambulatory medical care, or hospital care. The stages can be seen as filters; some symptoms get minor personal attention and accommodation, while others pass through to more public, expensive, and long-term consequences. Severity (degree of bother) and seriousness (life threat) are key determinants of people's re-

---

[1]For the United States, the National Health Interview Survey provides acute incidence and chronic prevalence rates. Incidence rates are based on only those problems that caused people to restrict activities or seek medical care. Until recently, chronic condition rates were based on health problems that inhibit performance of major (job, housework) or secondary (clubs, shopping, church attendance, etc.) activities. Now rates are based on simply the presence of a chronic disease or impairment. Frequency of visits to physicians and of hospital stays are also measured in the survey, but not contacts with other health professionals. For decades, mortality rates have been based on the principal, or underlying, cause of death, and co-morbidities were ignored. This situation is changing; the National Center for Health Statistics recently began to publish annual reports on multiple causes of death, and it also offers pertinent public-use tapes.

[2]A monograph titled *The Symptom Iceberg* (Hannay, 1979) seems relevant but uses the term very differently; namely, for symptoms that people consider severe or serious but nonetheless do not seek medical care. The term "symptom iceberg" refers only to this kind of symptom and nothing more.

sponses to symptoms. But demographic and psychosocial factors are also important, and medical sociologists study how they, too, affect cognitive evaluations of symptoms and trigger therapeutic actions.

The iceberg and stage concepts are heuristic, and they do not have fixed definitions or standard empirical uses. Their common substantive thread is to contrast personal and public facets of health. The iceberg notion arises from epidemiology, and its purpose is to describe population health. One way to operationalize it is to compare a variety of morbidity and health care rates, often drawn from independent sources. The stage notion is sociological, and its purpose is to understand individuals' decisions about therapeutic care. Operationally, researchers want to estimate probabilities that symptomatic people will be disabled or will obtain professional care. This requires a single data source, which queries symptoms and ensuing actions from the same people.

But, if one wishes, the notion of stages can be applied to population level analyses, too. Each statistical series—rates of symptoms, physician visits, hospital discharges, etc.—can be said to represent a stage of health. The rates measure cumulative events or actions taken by individuals. (Transition probabilities from symptoms to actions can be roughly estimated, but remain truly unknown.) We shall use the term "stage" in this manner.

This chapter traces health from daily symptoms to death for American (U.S.) men and women. What are the leading health problems at these different stages: daily symptoms; incidence and prevalence of diseases/injuries/impairments in a year's time; problems that induce long-term limitations in role performance; problems brought to office-based physicians for care; conditions that compel hospitalization; and, lastly, causes of death? In answering this, we will emphasize *ranks* of health problems rather than numerical *rates*. We will see that leading health problems shift, sometimes markedly, across stages of health. Changes in leading problems across life (age groups) and sex differences within each age group are also considered. The age spans analyzed are 17–44, 45–64, and 65+ (differing slightly from this in a few series). They are called young, middle-aged, and older adults, respectively.

Several prior analyses have a similar style to this one (Dingle, 1973; White, 1973). Their data are much more rudimentary than this chapter's, but they contain fine insights into population health.

DATA SOURCES

Age–sex–cause-specific rates for seven stages of health were secured from a variety of United States health surveys and vital statistics.

National Data

Six statistical series are national in scope. *Acute condition incidence* and *chronic condition prevalence* rates were computed from unpublished tabulations of the 1979 National Health Interview Survey.[3] Rates of *activity limitation due to chronic conditions* were computed from pooled 1979–1980 National Health Interview Survey data.[4] Detailed rates for *physician visits* based on the 1979 National Ambulatory Medical Care Survey and rates for *short-stay hospital episodes* based on the 1979 National Hospital Discharge Survey are published in Hing, Kovar, and Rice (1979). *Death* rates for the three broad age groups studied here are seldom published, and 1980 rates were obtained from the National Center for Health Statistics on request. Further details about the health survey designs are in issues of *Vital and Health Statistics,* Series 10 and 13, published by the National Center for Health Statistics.[5]

Data were obtained for the time period 1979–1980. Although cause-specific rates vary from year to year, their ranks are highly stable over time.[6] Since this analysis concentrates on ranks, results are as true now as for 1979–1980. Changes will occur only if current leading diseases/injuries are prevented or cured on a widespread basis, and thereby drop notably in rank. This is a possibility over the long run of decades, but not in the short run.

All of the statistical series use the International Classification of Diseases (ICD) as the basis for coding morbidity, but they vary in how the ICD codes are aggregated in final rates. Exact comparability of titles across the series is impossible, but high similarity is. Each series typically allows several levels of aggregation; we have chosen comparable levels so the number of titles used in all series here is similar. (Further details are in initial footnotes of Tables 1-1–1-4.)

In each series, the leading 15 titles were identified for each age-sex group. Rates and ranks for them are shown in tables here. Rates for other titles are

---

[3]Chronic prevalence rates can also be derived from the Medical History Questionnaire of the National Health and Nutrition Examination Survey (NHANES). But it contains only a limited set of titles, and we needed a full set spanning *all* chronic titles for this analysis. Age–sex-specific rates for the NHANES titles are available from the author on request or can be computed from public use tapes.

[4]Another important kind of limitation is mobility. From time to time, mobility problems have been queried in the National Health Interview Survey, but no age–sex–cause-specific rates are available.

[5]Residence rates for long-term care are not considered here. The population of nursing home residents is relatively small (about .5% for the total U.S. population and under 1% of adults) and mostly elderly (about three-fourths are 75+ years). Age–sex–cause-specific rates that identify the principal health problems of residents are published in National Center for Health Statistics, *Vital and Health Statistics,* Series 13, No. 51, Table 8. The foremost conditions for both sexes are cardiovascular diseases (heart disease and stroke) and mental disorders.

[6]The author has confirmed this by comparing results here with other years, some earlier and some later, available to her.

available from the author on request, or for two series are published in Hing et al. (1979), as noted above.

Rates from sample surveys have been evaluated for sampling error using National Center for Health Statistics procedures and criteria (relative standard error under 30%).

Despite their importance, age–sex–cause-specific rates are rarely published for the U.S. health surveys. This has inhibited detailed analyses of stages of health for Americans. Innovative aspects of this chapter are presentations of these specific rates and comparisons across the surveys. The tables included here are dense with information, and many facets of them will not be discussed. Readers may enjoy pursuing them hereafter.

Community Data

One series is community-level in scope. No national statistics exist for *daily symptoms,* and we have therefore chosen relevant data from the Health In Detroit Study. The study has a population-based sample of metropolitan Detroit white residents ages 18+. Respondents were interviewed first and then kept daily health records for six weeks in the fall of 1978. To date, it is the only general population survey in the United States to use prospective health diaries as a principal data source, rather than as a memory aid for later retrospective questioning or as an experimental device to test health survey methods (Verbrugge, 1980).

The health diaries yield age–sex–cause-specific rates of daily symptoms. We discuss 10 major groups of symptoms and also the top 10 specific symptoms. (The symptom classification used yields rates that are either more aggregated, or less so, than the other series studied here, so we have opted to report both levels.) Respondents also wrote down the causes of their symptoms, and we discuss the top 10. Rates are standardized to six weeks for all diary-keepers to adjust for age–sex variation in dropout (Verbrugge, 1984a).

The Detroit results will be compared with other community-level surveys that asked about recent morbidity in retrospective interviews.

YOUNG ADULTS

The principal *daily health problems* are very similar for young men and women (Table 1-1). Respiratory ailments stand out from all the rest. Second come musculoskeletal symptoms, followed by general (such as tiredness, edema, ache all over), nervous system (almost entirely headache), and then psychological (tension, nervousness) symptoms. After that point, genitourinary problems rank higher for women, and skin/nails/hair (mostly skin) problems for men.

TABLE 1-1 Leading Daily Symptoms for Detroit Men and Women[a, b]

Major groups of symptoms (Average no. of symptoms in 6-week period)[c]

Rank	Men 18–44	Women 18–44
1	Respiratory, 9.4 ($\bar{x}$)	Respiratory, 13.3 ($\bar{x}$)
2	Musculoskeletal, 5.2	Musculoskeletal, 6.2
3	General, 3.6	General, 5.4
4	Nervous system, 2.8	Nervous system, 5.0
5	Digestive, 1.8	Digestive, 4.3
6	Psychological[d], 1.3	Psychological, 2.4
7	Skin, nails, and hair, 0.6	Genitourinary, 2.1
8	Eyes and ears, 0.3	Eyes and ears, 1.7
9	Genitourinary, 0.1	Skin, nails, and hair, 1.0
10	Cardiovascular,*	Cardiovascular, 0.2
	(*N*=157 diary-keepers)	(*N*=213)

Rank	Men 45–64	Women 45–64
1	Musculoskeletal, 5.5 ($\bar{x}$)	Musculoskeletal, 16.5 ($\bar{x}$)
2	Respiratory, 4.8	Respiratory, 9.8
3	General, 2.2	Nervous system, 4.9
4	Nervous system, 2.2	General, 3.7
5	Digestive, 1.7	Digestive, 3.1
6	Skin, nails, and hair, 0.5	Psychological, 2.9
7	Psychological, 0.4	Eyes and ears, 1.7
8	Eyes and ears, 0.3	Genitourinary, 1.2
9	Cardiovascular,*; Genitourinary,*	Skin, nails, and hair, 0.5
10	——†	Cardiovascular, 0.2
	(*N*=59)	(*N*=98)

Rank	Men 65+	Women 65+
1	Musculoskeletal, 19.4 ($\bar{x}$)	Musculoskeletal, 13.7 ($\bar{x}$)
2	General, 6.3	Respiratory, 7.7
3	Skin, nails, and hair, 5.5	General, 4.8
4	Respiratory, 5.0	Eyes and ears, 3.6
5	Eyes and ears, 3.6	Nervous system, 3.2
6	Digestive, 3.1	Psychological, 2.3
7	Nervous system, 1.6	Cardiovascular, 1.9
8	Cardiovascular, 0.8	Digestive, 1.8
9	Genitourinary, 0.7	Genitourinary, 1.5
10	Psychological, 0.7	Skin, nails, and hair, 0.2
	(*N*=27)	(*N*=35)

Specific symptoms[e,f,g] (Percent of all symptoms)

Rank	Men 18–44		Women 18–44	
1	Headache, 13.3%	Nerv(210)	Headache, 12.7%	Nerv
2	Nasal congestion, 13.0	Resp(400)	Tiredness, 7.5	Gen
3	Tiredness, 8.7	Gen(015)	Nasal congestion, 7.1	Resp

Rank	Symptom	Code	Symptom	Code
4	Sore throat, 7.5	Resp(455)	Sinus problems, 6.3	Resp
5	Sinus problems, 7.0	Resp(410)	Tension/nervousness, 5.1	Psych
6	Back trouble (pain, stiffness), 5.4	Musc(905)	Back trouble, 4.9	Musc
7	Leg trouble, 5.3	Musc(920)	Cough, 4.5	Resp
8	Tension/nervousness, 4.9	Psych (100)	Sore throat, 2.8	Resp
9	Cough, 4.7	Resp(440)	Upset stomach (incl. nausea), 3.2	Dig(525)
10	Neck trouble, 4.7	Musc(900)	Menstrual pain, 3.0	Genito (745)
	(N = 2720 symptoms)		(N = 7283)	

Rank	Men 45–64	Code	Women 45–64	Code
1	Headache, 13.2%	Nerv	Headache, 9.7%	Nerv
2	Nasal congestion, 7.6	Resp	Back trouble, 6.7	Musc
3	Leg trouble, 7.1	Musc	Knee trouble, 5.5	Musc(925)
4	Tiredness, 7.0; Knee trouble, 7.0	Gen, Musc	Tension/nervousness, 5.4	Psych
5	Cough, 4.2		Joint pain, unspecified, 5.1	Musc (970)
6	Neck trouble, 4.0; Back trouble, 4.0	Musc(900), Musc	Sinus problems, 4.6; Leg trouble, 4.6	Resp, Musc
7	Sore throat, 3.4	Resp	Tiredness, 4.1	Gen
8	Generalized pain (ache all over), 2.3; Hand/finger trouble	Gen(060), Musc (960)	Nasal congestion, 4.1	Resp
9	Tension/nervousness, 2.2	Psych	Neck trouble, 3.9	Musc
10	——		Cough, 3.2	Resp
	(N = 919)		(N = 3818)	

Rank	Men 65+	Code	Women 65+	Code
1	Leg trouble, 11.0%	Musc	Knee trouble, 8.8%	Musc
2	Skin irritation (itching, pain), 8.0	Skin(870)	Leg trouble, 8.2	Musc
3	Hand/finger trouble, 6.9	Musc	Tiredness, 8.1	Gen
4	Generalized pain, 5.6	Gen	Back trouble, 7.4	Musc
5	Back trouble, 5.2	Musc	Tension/nervousness, 6.0	Psych
6	Foot/toe trouble, 5.1	Musc(935)	Nasal congestion, 5.6	Resp
7	Shoulder trouble, 4.4	Musc(940)	Circulation problems (pallor, flushed), 4.8	Circ(280)
8	Knee trouble, 4.1	Musc	Headache, 4.5	Nerv
9	Chest area pain (excl. heart), 4.0	Gen(050)	Shoulder trouble, 4.2	Musc
10	Hip trouble, 3.0	Musc(915)	Eye problems (allergy, swelling), 3.6	Eye(335)
	(N = 1218)		(N = 1256)	

(*continued*)

TABLE 1-1 (*continued*)

Attributed causes of symptoms[h] (Percent of all causes)

Rank	Men 18–44		Women 18–44	
1	Respiratory diseases[f], 25.7%	D	Respiratory diseases, 26.4%	D
2	Physical exertion (esp. job, household work, sports), 7.5	K	Sleep troubles, 11.2	K
3	Sleep troubles, 7.3	K	Gynecological/obstetrical troubles (esp. menstruation), 10.7	K
4	Physical environment (weather, season), 7.0	K	Physical exertion, 9.0	K
5	Adverse effects (esp.too much alcohol)[i], 7.0	J	Musculoskeletal diseases, 7.8	D
6	Too much work or stress, 5.9	K	Adverse effects, 7.5	J
7	Injury, type unspecified, 5.7	J	Too much work or stress, 5.8	K
8	Sprains and strains, 5.4	J	Medical treatments (esp. recent surgery), 5.4	K
9	Eating(esp. ate too much, rich food), 3.4	K	Physical environment, 5.2; Eating, 5.2	K, K
10	Musculoskeletal diseases, 3.3	D	Skin diseases, 3.1	D
	(*N* = 1793 causes)		(*N* = 2893)	

Rank	Men 45–64		Women 45–64	
1	Musculoskeletal diseases, 21.8%	D	Musculoskeletal diseases, 24.3%	D
2	Respiratory diseases, 19.7	D	Respiratory diseases, 15.1	D
3	Physical exertion, 7.5	K	Medical treatments (esp. old surgery), 5.1	K
4	Accident, injury unspecified, 6.9	J	Physical exertion, 5.0	K
5	Adverse effects, 4.8	J	Digestive diseases, 4.6	D
6	Sleep troubles, 4.6	K	Physical environment, 3.2	K
7	Physical environment, 4.3	K	Sprains and strains, 3.2	J
8	Too much work or stress, 3.6	K	Sleep troubles, 3.0	K
9	Digestive diseases, 3.3	D	Social problems (esp. with family/kin), 2.2	K
10	——		Circulatory diseases, 2.1	D
	(*N* = 670)		(*N* = 2345)	

Rank	Men 65+		Women 65+	
1	Musculoskeletal diseases, 38.4%	D	Medical treatments (esp. recent/old surgery), 14.2%	K
2	Respiratory diseases, 7.3	D	Respiratory diseases, 13.8	D
3	Circulatory diseases, 7.0	D	Musculoskeletal diseases, 9.1	D
4	Skin diseases, 6.7	D	Circulatory diseases, 7.6	D
5	Malignant neoplasms, 6.5	D	Eye diseases, 6.8	D
6	Physical exertion, 5.3	K	Physical environment, 6.4	K
7	Endocrine/metabolic diseases, 4.8	D	Injury, type unspecified, 5.2	J
8	Medical treatments, 4.6	K	Ear diseases, 4.4	D
9	Sleep troubles, 4.1	K	Genitourinary diseases, 4.3	D
10	Physical environment, 3.8 (N = 628)	K	Sleep troubles, 3.9 (N = 927)	K

GENERAL NOTE: Titles have the same rank only if their sample n's are identical.

*Less than 0.1.

†——=All further symptoms/causes have small n (less than 20 diary days).

aThe Health In Detroit Study had a representative sample of white adult (ages 18+) residents of the Detroit metropolitan area, who kept daily health records for six weeks in the fall of 1978.

bSymptoms were coded according to the Reason For Visit Classification developed for the National Ambulatory Medical Care Survey (Schneider, Appleton, and McLemore, 1979). Its Symptom Module (S) has 10 major groups, about 160 more specific symptoms (3 digit), and a further level (4th digit) as well. In this table, we rank the 10 major groups in Item 1 and the specific symptoms (3 digit) in Item 2.

cData are standardized to a six-week period for each diary-keeper. This adjusts for some dropout during the diary phase of the study (Verbrugge, 1984a).

dThe Detroit study concentrated on physical symptoms. Respondents rarely reported distinctly emotional ones such as anxiety or depression, but they did frequently report stress-related symptoms such as tension and nervousness. These physically felt, but psychologically toned, symptoms are classified in the Psychological group (Schneider et al., 1979).

eEach symptom's major group and 3-digit code are indicated on the right.

fThe symptom "cold" or "head cold" (S445) is removed from Item 2 and included as an attributed cause in Item 3. Most respondents with colds listed symptoms such as headache, cough, etc., and then named cold as the disease causing them. Colds are added into the disease "upper respiratory infections" (D600). (Note: This adjustment is not made in Item 1, so cold is included in the Respiratory group averages.)

gWe use the word "trouble" in Item 2 to indicate musculoskeletal pain, stiffness, aching, soreness, and spasms in the location named.

hAttributed causes may be diseases, injuries, or other reasons. The Disease Module (D) and Injury Module (J) of the Reason For Visit Classification were used, plus an Other Cause Module (K) designed specially for the Detroit study. The Other Cause Module covers environmental, behavioral, medical treatment, and some reproductive (menstruation, menopause, pregnancy) causes for symptoms. Ranks here are based on 37 groups (15 major groups of diseases, 12 subgroups of injuries/adverse effects, and 10 major groups of other causes). The most common specific causes are given in parentheses. The module type is indicated on the right.

iLess common are: air pollution, reaction to medication.

Reflecting this general picture, specific symptoms are also similar for the sexes. Respiratory symptoms and others associated with colds are at the top. These are headache, nasal congestion, tiredness, sinus problems, and sore throat, with cough further down the list. Musculoskeletal symptoms rank next for men, but not so strongly for women. Women have a greater diversity of daily symptoms than men do (only 57% of all women's symptoms are in the top 10, compared to 74% for men's).

When asked about the causes of their symptoms, young adults point first to upper respiratory infections. Most other causes named are injuries and behavior/environment factors rather than diseases. Men and women accord similar prominence to insufficient sleep, drinking, and overwork. Physical exertion, weather/season, and injuries rank higher in men's lives; menstruation and childbirth (called "recent surgery" in the code scheme) in women's.

The prominence of respiratory infections for young adults also appears in national data on *acute conditions*. Of all acute problems severe enough to prompt restricted activity or medical care, flu and colds are topmost for both sexes (Table 1-2). Rates for all other problems are much lower. Among them, injuries rank higher for men, and reproductive (includes menstrual) and urinary disorders for women. (Normal deliveries are included in the table, although they are a nonmorbidity title; see Table 1-2 footnote.)

Only small percents of young adults report having *chronic diseases or impairments* (Table 1-2). Respiratory disorders due largely to allergies (chronic sinusitis and hay fever) stand out from all other problems. Below them are chronic back conditions, hypertensive disease (this is hypertension without heart disease), hemorrhoids, and skin problems. The sexes have similar profiles, with just a few exceptions: Sensory and skeletal impairments are more prominent for men; but arthritis, chronic reproductive and urinary disorders, and migraine are more prominent for women. All of these except hypertension are nonfatal problems; that is, they rarely if ever cause death. Fatal diseases are seldom in the list for young adults, and those that appear rank low (heart conditions, asthma, bronchitis). (Hypertension can be classified either way. It is only occasionally fatal by itself, but acts as a powerful risk factor for heart and cerebrovascular diseases. We will class it as a fatal condition in this analysis.)

Limitations in job, housework, and other social activities due to chronic conditions are uncommon for young adults. When they do occur, back trouble is most frequent (Table 1-3). Next come asthma, other skeletal impairments, and musculoskeletal disorders (other than arthritis). Only a few fatal disease titles appear among the leading causes of limitation. Men's and women's lists are quite similar overall.

The acute incidence and chronic prevalence lists for young adults have some interesting parallels. In both domains, respiratory problems are foremost. Beyond that, injuries generate transient and persistent problems for men, while genitourinary problems bother women more. But the chronic prevalence and limitations lists differ greatly from each other. Note how the leading chronic diseases (such as sinusitis, hay fever, hypertension) seldom cause limitations, whereas rare ones (such as asthma, heart disease) ascend in that regard. And although disease titles dominate the prevalence lists for men and women, impairments share top ranks with diseases in the limitation lists. Both points mirror the fact that young adults typically have good health. Chronic diseases that do occur are usually not severe or life threatening, and they have minimal consequences for role involvement. This leaves an open field for the limitations list; the few limitations suffered come from enduring effects of injuries/deformities and occasional fatal diseases.

Reasons for *office visits* reflect the principal symptoms that young adults experience (Table 1-3). Respiratory problems propel visits most often for both sexes. Beyond that, effects of injuries are often leading diagnoses for men; these are superseded by reproductive disorders, urinary diseases, and weight problems for women. (Normal pregnancy and postpartum care are excluded from Table 1-3, being nonmorbidity titles. If included, pregnancy visits would rank first for young women.)

For office visits, mental distress also ranks very high as a diagnosis for both sexes. This might seem extremely high to some readers, since the title is absent from the incidence and prevalence lists. That is because the data source for these rates does not query frequency of mental problems. Consequently, we cannot compare the relative importance of experienced vs. treated mental problems from these statistical series.[7] By contrast, limitations statistics do encompass mental conditions. They appear in the leading titles lists for young men and women, but cause much less trouble for social activities than do physical ailments.

Hospitalizations are infrequent for young adults and do not center on their most common problems (Table 1-3). Respiratory conditions do not figure at all among the leading diagnoses, nor do young adults' other leading diseases. Instead, injuries prompt hospital stays most often for men, reproductive disorders for women, and atypical diseases (urinary system/ gallbladder diseases, alcoholism, hernia, appendicitis, neoplasms) for these ages. This reflects the efficacy of medical intervention for injuries and reproductive problems on one hand, and the nonserious nature of most chronic diseases that young adults suffer on the other. (Normal deliveries and sterilization procedures in the absence of diseases are excluded from Table 1-3, being nonmorbidity titles. If included, deliveries would rank first for young women.)

Lastly, *causes of death* show a still different picture for young adults (Table 1-4). Diseases and violent injuries, which rarely figure in daily

---

[7]What about mental symptoms in daily life? The Detroit survey focused on physical symptoms, and this was made clear during the initial interview and training for diary-keeping. Nevertheless, many psychologically toned symptoms, especially stress-related ones like tension, were reported. They are relatively common for women of all ages and for young men (Table 1-1). If mental distress had been solicited in the survey, more reports would certainly have occurred.

TABLE 1-2 Leading Acute and Chronic Conditions for American Men and Women

	Incidence of acute conditions (1979) (No. of conditions per 1,000 population per year)[a]		Prevalence of chronic conditions (1979) (No. of conditions per 1,000 population)[b]	
Rank	Men 25–44	Women 25–44	Men 17–44	Women 17–44
1	Influenza[c], 424.7	Influenza, 524.6	Chronic sinusitis, 119.6	Chronic sinusitis, 175.6
2	Common cold, 338.8	Common cold, 372.2	Hay fever, without asthma[e], 84.8	Hay fever, without asthma, 97.4
3	Sprains and strains, 135.3	Genitourinary disorders, 170.3	Impairments of back or spine[f], 61.6	Impairments of back or spine, 68.5
4	Open wounds & lacerations, 104.0	Other upper respiratory conds., 149.9	Hypertensive disease[g], 60.5	Arthritis, 58.1
5	Other upper respiratory conds., 85.1	Other infectious/parasitic diseases, 129.5	Hearing impairments, 56.3	Hypertensive disease, 57.1
6	Other infectious/parasitic diseases, 79.7	All other acute conds., 129.4	Hemorrhoids, 44.7	Hemorrhoids, 52.0
7	All other acute conds., 76.4	Virus NOS, 118.5	Diseases of sebaceous glands (acne), 41.8	Diseases of sebaceous glands (acne), 51.3
8	Other current injuries, 67.3	Deliveries and disorders of pregnancy/puerperium[d], 90.7	Visual impairments, 41.5	Eczema, dermatitis, and urticaria, 47.5; Migraine, 47.5
9	Virus NOS, 62.5	Sprains and strains, 73.6	Arthritis, 36.9	Diseases of urinary system, 42.4
10	Contusions & superficial injuries, 61.7	Musculoskeletal diseases, 61.2	Heart conditions, 33.5	Heart conditions, 41.2
11	Musculoskeletal diseases, 58.4	Other current injuries, 56.0	Impairments of lower extremity or hip[f], 26.8	Female troubles except breast[h], 35.0
12	Upper GI disorders, 49.5	Contusions & superficial injuries, 55.6	Eczema, dermatitis, and urticaria, 26.4	Chronic bronchitis, 34.9
13	Dental conditions, 49.3	Open wounds & lacerations, 44.5	Functional/symptomatic upper GI disorder, 24.5	Hearing impairments, 34.1

	Men 45–64	Women 45–64	Men 45–64	Women 45–64
14	Genitourinary disorders, 43.9	Upper GI disorders, 40.1	Diseases of nail, 22.8	Varicose veins, 31.8
15	Fractures & dislocations, 38.7	Bronchitis, 39.1	Asthma w/ or w/o hay fever, 22.1	Anemias, 27.0

	Men 45–64	Women 45–64	Men 45–64	Women 45–64
1	Influenza, 281.0	Influenza, 298.5	Hypertensive disease, 202.9	Arthritis, 311.5
2	Common cold, 257.4	Common cold, 239.7	Arthritis, 188.4	Hypertensive disease, 225.0
3	Virus NOS, 88.2	Virus NOS, 103.7	Chronic sinusitis, 164.1	Chronic sinusitis, 212.2
4	Other current injuries, 63.6	All other acute conds., 89.1	Hearing impairments, 147.8	Heart conditions, 125.5
5	Sprains and strains, 59.1	Other upper respiratory conds., 76.9	Heart conditions, 131.8	Hearing impairments, 93.1
6	Contusions & superficial injuries, 53.0	Genitourinary disorders, 73.9	Visual impairments, 74.4	Hay fever, without asthma, 79.2
7	All other acute conditions, 52.5	Contusions & superficial injuries, 71.7	Impairments of back or spine, 71.8	Impairments of back or spine, 77.1
8	Open wounds & lacerations, 51.5	Sprains and strains, 69.0	Hemorrhoids, 59.9	Varicose veins, 77.0
9	Other infectious/parasitic diseases, 49.9	Upper GI disorders, 57.8	Hay fever, without asthma, 58.5	Hemorrhoids, 69.1
10	Musculoskeletal diseases, 36.8	Other current injuries, 52.8	Diabetes, 56.0	Migraine, 63.1
11	Diseases of the ear, 36.6	Open wounds & lacerations, 47.8	Hernia of abdominal cavity, 49.8	Diabetes, 59.7
12	Other upper respiratory conds., 35.6	Other digestive system conds., 42.3	Synovitis, bursitis, and tenosynovitis, 46.0	Corns and callosities, 56.6
13	Upper GI disorders, 33.3	Musculoskeletal diseases, 40.6	Impairments of lower extremity or hip, 36.4	Synovitis, bursitis, and tenosynovitis, 56.2
14	Dental conditions, 25.9	Diseases of the ear, 30.6	Functional/symptomatic upper GI disorder, 36.2	Diseases of urinary system, 45.1
15	Fractures & dislocations, 25.3	Other infectious/parasitic diseases, 25.4	Ulcer of stomach and duodenum, 33.7	Eczema, dermatitis, and urticaria, 43.6

(continued)

TABLE 1-2 (*continued*)

	Men 65+	Women 65+	Men 65+	Women 65+
1	Common cold, 198.6	Common cold, 270.1	Arthritis, 354.6	Arthritis, 504.4
2	Influenza, 151.7	All other acute conds., 166.0	Hearing impairments, 327.2	Hypertensive disease, 434.2
3	All other acute conds., 114.8	Influenza, 160.3	Hypertensive disease, 315.0	Heart conditions, 280.6
4	Musculoskeletal diseases, 71.8	Genitourinary disorders, 72.6	Heart conditions, 265.7	Hearing impairments, 249.6
5	Other current injuries, 57.6	Other current injuries, 62.0	Chronic sinusitis, 135.4	Chronic sinusitis, 171.1
6	Contusions & superficial injuries, 39.5	Contusions & superficial injuries, 61.6	Arteriosclerosis, 121.5	Varicose veins, 126.3
7	Sprains and strains, 39.1	Fractures & dislocations, 48.2	Visual impairments, 119.7	Arteriosclerosis, 125.0
8	Genitourinary disorders, 38.5	Upper GI disorders, 45.8	Impairments of back or spine, 76.5	Visual impairments, 117.6
9	Pneumonia, 34.4	Musculoskeletal diseases, 44.9	Diabetes, 73.7	Impairments of back or spine, 109.0
10	Other upper respiratory conds., 33.9	Diseases of the ear, 37.2	Hernia of abdominal cavity, 71.3	Diabetes, 83.9
11	Other respiratory conds., 30.7	Virus NOS, 37.0	Emphysema, 68.2	Frequent constipation, 79.6
12	Other digestive system conds., 30.5	Other respiratory conditions, 36.2	Diseases of prostate[i], 58.0	Hemorrhoids, 75.8
13	Virus NOS, 30.4	Other upper respiratory conds., 29.8	Hemorrhoids, 52.3	Corns and callosities, 73.9
14	Fractures and dislocations, 29.2	Sprains and strains, 28.6	Impairments of lower extremity or hip, 48.1	Diseases of urinary system, 71.2
15	Other infectious/parasitic diseases, 27.6	Other infectious/parasitic diseases, 27.7	Hay fever, without asthma, 44.6	Impairments of lower extremity or hip, 61.6

aCounted only if they caused restricted activity or medical care. Ranks are based on 25 disease or injury subgroups (Diagnostic Recode #2, NCHS). They belong to five major groups: Infective and Parasitic Diseases (common childhood diseases, virus not otherwise specified, other infective and parasitic diseases), Respiratory Conditions (common cold, other upper respiratory conditions, influenza with digestive manifestations, other influenza, pneumonia, bronchitis, other respiratory conditions), Digestive System Conditions (dental conditions, functional and symptomatic upper gastrointestinal disorders not elsewhere classifiable, other digestive system conditions), Injuries (fractures and dislocations, sprains and strains, open wounds and lacerations, contusions and superficial injuries, other current injuries), and All Other Acute Conditions (diseases of the ear, headaches, genitourinary disorders, deliveries and disorders of pregnancy and the puerperium, diseases of the skin, diseases of the musculoskeletal system, all other acute conditions). The final subgroup includes diseases of the eye, acute circulatory conditions (such as arterial rupture, peripheral vascular symptoms, short term hypotension), and all others NEC (symptoms of unclear origin). Rates for the 25 subgroups are reported by age and also by sex in Vital and Health Statistics issues (see Series 10, Nos. 132, 136), but not for age-sex groups.

bRanks are based on 71 disease and impairment titles that encompass all chronic conditions in the International Classification of Diseases. The rates are based on questions about (a) specific diseases and impairments experienced in the past 12 months and (b) recent disability and medical care, and the conditions causing them.

cRate here combines influenza with digestive manifestations and other influenza. The first title is a small fraction of all influenza (typically 5–10%). If the two types are treated separately, other influenza continues to hold the rank shown.

dNormal childbirth typically involves some restricted activity and medical care. The event can be viewed as nonmorbidity and thus out of the scope of the analysis. But the raw data did not allow separation of deliveries, so the title is necessarily included.

eIncludes upper respiratory allergy.

fThese are deformities and orthopedic impairments. Excluded are absence and paralysis.

gHypertension without heart involvement. Commonly called high blood pressure.

hIncludes chronic inflammatory diseases, endometriosis, prolapse, fistula and cysts, menstrual and menopausal problems, infertility, and lesser titles.

iExcludes genital organ cancers, which are always classified as malignant neoplasms.

SOURCES: For acute conditions: Based on unpublished tabulations from the 1979 National Health Interview Survey, provided by the National Center for Health Statistics. For chronic conditions: Based on unpublished tabulations from the 1979 National Health Interview Survey, provided by the National Center for Health Statistics.

All rates shown here have low sampling error (relative standard error under 30%).

TABLE 1-3 Impact of Health Problems on American Men and Women

Limitation from chronic conditions (1979–1980)
(Persons with limitation in major or secondary activity due to condition/1,000 pop.[a])

Rank	Males Under 45[d]	Females Under 45
1	Back/spine impairment[e], 9.2	Back/spine impairment, 10.0
2	Lower extremity/hip impairment[e], 9.1	Asthma, 5.6
3	Other impairments[f], 7.0	Other musculoskeletal diseases, 5.0
4	Asthma[g], 6.6	Lower extremity/hip impairment, 5.0
5	Other musculoskeletal disorders[h], 5.9	Arthritis, 4.5
6	Upper extremity/shoulder imp.[e], 3.7	Other impairments, 4.3
7	Visual impairments, 3.2	Diseases of heart, 2.8
8	Diseases of heart, 3.2	Hypertensive disease, 2.4
9	Specific mental disorders[i], 3.0	Specific mental disorders, 1.9
10	Arthritis, 2.7; Hearing imp., 2.7	Diabetes, 1.8
11	Paralysis, 2.6	Visual impairments, 1.7
12	Hypertensive disease[j], 1.9	Paralysis, 1.7
13	Chronic/allergic skin diseases, 1.6	Mental symptoms, 1.7
14	Mental symptoms[i], 1.5	Upper extremity/shoulder imp., 1.6
15	Hay fever w/o asthma, 1.5	Hearing impairments, 1.5

Visits to office-based physicians (1979)
(Visits per 1,000 population) (Principal diagnosis[b])

	Men 15–44	Women 15–44
1	Acute upper resp. infections, 84.6	Acute upper resp. infections, 142.4
2	Fractures, 73.5	Anxiety states & other neuroses, 113.3
3	Anxiety states & other neuroses, 69.9	Diseases of female pelvic organs[n], 103.6
4	Sprains and strains of back, 51.2	Obesity, 86.7
5	Laceration and open wound, 50.3	Other female genital tract problems[n], 73.6
6	Essential hypertension[j], 38.8	Diseases of urinary system, 71.1
7	Bursitis and synovitis, 28.2	Sprains and strains of back, 52.5
8	Prostate & other male genital, 26.5	Menstruation disorders, 42.5
9	Bronchitis, 23.7	Diseases of breast, 42.0
10	Diseases of urinary system, 23.4	Complications of pregnancy, etc.[o], 38.0
11	Asthma, 17.0	Essential hypertension, 37.1
12	Dislocation w/o fracture, 15.0	Benign neoplasms, 33.7
13	Obesity, 13.9	Fractures, 26.5
14	Hemorrhoids, 13.4	Asthma, 26.4
15	Displaced intervertebral disc, 12.9	Laceration and open wound, 25.0

Hospital stays (1979)
(Discharges from short stay hospitals per 10,000 population) (Principal diagnosis[c])

	Men 15–44	Women 15–44
1	Fractures, 65.3	Pregnancy w/ abortive outcome, 94.9
2	Laceration and open wound, 38.1	Complications of pregnancy, etc., 88.4
3	Alcohol dependence syndrome, 36.7	Other female genital tract problems, 74.4
4	Diseases of urinary system, 36.6	Diseases of female pelvic organs, 71.4
5	Hernia of abdominal cavity, 31.0	Menstruation disorders, 69.1
6	Displaced intervertebral disc, 24.2	Benign neoplasms, 53.2
7	Sprains and strains of back, 23.9	Diseases of urinary system, 49.6
8	Dislocation w/o fracture, 22.9	Gallbladder diseases, 33.9
9	Intracranial injury[p], 22.7	Anxiety states & other neuroses, 30.9
10	Appendicitis, 19.8	Fractures, 23.6
11	Prostate & other male genital, 19.4	Chronic tonsils/adenoids disease, 23.0
12	Anxiety states & other neuroses, 17.2	Diseases of breast, 21.2
13	Malignant neoplasms, 15.1	Malignant neoplasms, 19.6
14	Diabetes mellitus, 13.4	Genital prolapse, 15.0
15	Gastritis and duodenitis, 12.6	Displaced intervertebral disc, 14.8

TABLE 1-3 *(continued)*

Limitation from chronic conditions (1979–1980)
(Persons with limitation in major or secondary activity due to condition/1,000 pop.[a])

Rank	Men 45–64	Women 45–64
1	Diseases of heart, 59.4	Arthritis, 59.0
2	Arthritis, 36.2	Diseases of heart, 38.2
3	Hypertensive disease, 26.5	Hypertensive disease, 33.9
4	Back/spine impairment, 25.1	Back/spine impairment, 22.0
5	Other musculoskeletal disorders, 23.9	Other musculoskeletal disorders, 21.4
6	Lower extremity/hip imp., 20.4	Diabetes, 17.2
7	Diabetes, 14.8	Lower extremity/hip imp., 13.9
8	Arteriosclerosis[k], 14.1	Arteriosclerosis, 9.8
9	Emphysema, 13.4	Malignant neoplasms, 9.6
10	Visual impairments, 8.9	Asthma, 8.4
11	Other respiratory diseases[l], 8.5	Mental symptoms, 7.9
12	Paralysis, 8.0	Other digestive diseases, 6.5
13	Upper extremity/shoulder imp., 7.7	Visual impairments, 6.4
14	Other digestive diseases[m], 7.5	Other impairments, 5.9
15	Hernia of abdominal cavity, 7.1	Emphysema, 5.3

Visits to office-based physicians (1979)
(Visits per 1,000 population) (Principal diagnosis[b])

	Men 45–64	Women 45–64
1	Essential hypertension, 227.4	Essential hypertension, 244.3
2	Ischemic heart disease, 118.9	Malignant neoplasms, 110.8
3	Diabetes mellitus, 98.4	Menopausal disorders, 96.1
4	Prostate & other male genital, 73.6	Acute upper resp. infections, 95.3
5	Bursitis and synovitis, 63.9	Obesity, 94.0
6	Acute upper resp. infections, 63.7	Diabetes mellitus, 92.9
7	Malignant neoplasms, 60.0	Anxiety states & other neuroses, 92.4
8	Anxiety states & other neuroses, 51.3	Diseases of urinary system, 84.1
9	Arthritis, 45.6	Arthritis, 81.2
10	Diseases of urinary system, 44.9	Fractures, 65.6
11	Fractures, 43.3	Sprains and strains of back, 55.1
12	Hernia of abdominal cavity, 39.1	Bursitis and synovitis, 54.9
13	Sprains and strains of back, 38.0	Benign neoplasms, 48.6
14	Bronchitis, 34.4	Diseases of breast, 44.8
15	Laceration and open wound, 32.6	Ischemic heart disease, 41.3

Hospital stays (1979)
(Discharges from short stay hospitals per 10,000 population) (Principal diagnosis[c])

	Men 45–64	Women 45–64
1	Malignant neoplasms, 139.9	Malignant neoplasms, 158.8
2	Ischemic heart disease, 116.3	Benign neoplasms, 71.1
3	Hernia of abdominal cavity, 84.6	Disease of urinary system, 67.1
4	Disease of urinary system, 78.6	Gallbladder diseases, 63.1
5	Alcohol dependence syndrome, 66.9	Diabetes mellitus, 58.0
6	Acute myocardial infarction, 64.6	Ischemic heart disease, 54.3
7	Prostate & other male genital, 62.7	Fractures, 47.4
8	Coronary atherosclerosis, 61.2	Other female genital tract problems, 44.6
9	Fractures, 51.6	Menstruation disorders, 41.4
10	Cerebrovascular disease, 42.5	Hernia of abdominal cavity, 34.7
11	Diabetes mellitus, 40.9	Breast diseases; Displaced disc, 34.5
12	Displaced intervertebral disc, 38.1	Cerebrovascular disease, 32.8
13	Ulcer of stomach and duodenum, 35.7	Essential hypertension, 31.4
14	Gallbladder diseases, 31.9	Genital prolapse, 30.0
15	Pneumonia, 30.9	Arthritis, 27.8

(continued)

TABLE 1-3 (*continued*)

Limitation from chronic conditions (1979–1980)
(Persons with limitation in major or secondary activity due to condition/1,000 pop.[a])

Rank	Men 65+	Women 65+
1	Diseases of heart, 135.0	Arthritis, 143.1
2	Arthritis, 82.4	Diseases of heart, 93.2
3	Hypertensive disease, 46.5	Hypertensive disease, 65.3
4	Emphysema, 39.0	Diabetes, 30.7
5	Arteriosclerosis, 34.9	Lower extremity/hip imp., 29.7
6	Visual impairments, 31.1	Visual impairments, 29.6
7	Diabetes, 27.7	Arteriosclerosis, 25.5
8	Lower extremity/hip imp., 25.1	Back/spine impairments, 20.5
9	Cerebrovascular disease, 24.5	Other musculoskeletal dis., 17.2
10	Paralysis, 21.0	Cerebrovascular disease, 15.0
11	Other musculoskeletal disorders, 18.4	Paralysis, 12.4
12	Back/spine impairments, 18.0	Malignant neoplasms, 12.4
13	Malignant neoplasms, 17.7	Other digestive diseases, 11.4
14	Other respiratory diseases, 17.3	Hearing impairments, 11.4
15	Hearing impairments, 14.3	Hernia of abdominal cavity, 9.2

Visits to office-based physicians (1979)
(Visits per 1,000 population) (Principal diagnosis[b])

	Men 65+	Women 65+
1	Essential hypertension, 275.1	Essential hypertension, 504.0
2	Ischemic heart disease, 264.1	Ischemic heart disease, 198.2
3	Malignant neoplasms, 178.6	Arthritis, 159.2
4	Diabetes mellitus, 166.2	Diabetes mellitus, 154.4
5	Prostate & other male genital, 111.1	Malignant neoplasms, 153.1
6	Diseases of urinary system, 90.1	Cataract, 140.4
7	Arthritis, 76.9	Diseases of urinary system, 116.5
8	Acute upper resp. infections, 74.0	Acute upper resp. infections, 107.1
9	Cataract, 69.9	Fractures, 97.7
10	Cerebrovascular disease, 59.7	Anxiety states & other neuroses, 62.1
11	Benign neoplasms, 51.8	Hypertensive heart disease, 51.7
12	Hernia of abdominal cavity, 47.3	Cerebrovascular disease, 51.1
13	Fractures, 41.3	Anemias, 50.6
14	Ulcer of stomach and duodenum, 40.7	Bursitis and synovitis, 50.1
15	Bronchitis, 40.4	Hernia of abdominal cavity, 42.8

Hospital stays (1979)
(Discharges from short stay hospitals per 10,000 population) (Principal diagnosis[c])

	Men 65+	Women 65+
1	Malignant neoplasms, 481.0	Malignant neoplasms, 306.2
2	Cerebrovascular disease, 244.3	Cerebrovascular disease, 232.0
3	Prostate & other male genital, 194.5	Fractures, 212.0
4	Disease of urinary system, 180.9	Coronary atherosclerosis, 155.8
5	Coronary atherosclerosis, 175.9	Cataract, 134.9
6	Ischemic heart disease, 144.5	Congestive heart failure, 123.4
7	Hernia of abdominal cavity, 140.4	Disease of urinary system, 115.5
8	Pneumonia, 135.4	Diabetes mellitus, 115.4
9	Congestive heart failure, 133.7	Ischemic heart disease, 106.2
10	Acute myocardial infarction, 118.2	Pneumonia, 91.4
11	Cataract, 103.0	Gallbladder diseases, 83.6
12	Fractures, 87.4	Acute myocardial infarction, 76.5
13	Cardiac dysrhythmias, 86.0	Cardiac dysrhythmias, 71.4
14	Gallbladder diseases, 73.0	Diverticula of intestine, 64.8
15	Diabetes mellitus, 72.1	Arthritis, 64.6

TABLE 1-3   (*continued*)

[a]A condition is considered chronic if it has lasted 3 or more months or is a problem always classified as chronic regardless of onset (e.g., diabetes, emphysema). Ranks are based on 53 disease and impairment titles (Diagnostic Recode #3, National Center for Health Statistics) that encompass all chronic conditions in the International Classification of Diseases. Major activity is job or housework; secondary activities are clubs, shopping, church attendance, etc. Ranks are rounded for presentation in this table; titles have the same rank only if their rates are identical at the second decimal place.

[b]Ranks are based on about 60 disease and injury titles, both acute and chronic, which encompass the International Classification of Diseases (ICD). Excluded are nonmorbidity visits (for vaccination, examination, contraception, normal pregnancy, postpartum care, etc.; these are V codes in the ICD). If normal pregnancy visits were included, they would rank first for women 15–44 (rate of 443.1). Reproductive titles shown exclude genital organ cancers, which are always classified as malignant neoplasms.

[c]Ranks are based on about 60 disease and injury titles, both acute and chronic, which encompass the International Classification of Disaeses (ICD). Excluded are nonmorbidity stays (for deliveries, sterilization procedures in absence of disease, renal dialysis, organ donation, etc.; these are V codes in the ICD). If normal deliveries were included, they would rank first for women 15–44 (rate of 710.8). All reproductive titles exclude genital organ cancers, which are always classified as malignant neoplasms. Patients can be alive or dead at time of discharge.

[d]Tabulations for ages 17–44 are not available. Rates for children (under 17) are very low for most conditions, so the ranks shown here pertain adequately to adults 17–44.

[e]This is deformities and orthopedic impairments. Excluded are absence and paralysis.

[f]A residual group: Excludes back/spine, upper extremity/shoulder, lower extremity/hip, and multiple impairments. Includes such problems as loss of smell/taste, learning disability, absence/loss of toes/fingers, ankle/foot/toe impairment, disfigurement of face area, and jaw/dentofacial anomalies.

[g]With or without hay fever.

[h]A residual group: Excludes arthritis. Includes such problems as chronic joint pain and stiffness, sacroiliitis, displacement of intervertebral disc, vertebrogenic pain syndrome (low back pain), osteomyelitis, and osteoporosis.

[i]Specific mental disorders are psychoses, neuroses, personality disorders, and mental retardation. Mental symptoms include such problems as depression, anxiety, nervousness, eating disorder, and sleep disturbance.

[j]Hypertension without heart involvement. Commonly called high blood pressure.

[k]Also called atherosclerosis.

[l]A residual group: Excludes chronic bronchitis, emphysema, asthma, hay fever, and chronic sinusitis. Includes such diseases as nasal polyp, chronic rhinitis, chronic laryngitis, bronchiectasis, and pneumoconioses/other lung diseases due to external agents.

[m]A residual group: Excludes ulcer of stomach and duodenum, hernia of abdominal cavity, and gallbladder diseases. Includes such diseases as esophagitis, gastritis, enteritis, colitis, diverticula of intestine, peritonitis, cirrhosis, and disease of teeth/gums/jaw/mouth.

[n]Diseases of female pelvic organs includes cervicitis, endocervicitis, salpingitis, endometriosis, and other inflammatory diseases. Other female genital tract problems includes fistula, cervical erosion, dysmenorrhea, premenstrual tension syndrome, infertility, and other noninflammatory disorders.

(*continued*)

TABLE 1-3 (*continued*)

ºThe full title is: Complications of pregnancy, childbirth, and the puerperium.
ᴾExcept those with skull fracture.
All rates shown here have low sampling error (relative standard error under 30%).
SOURCES: For limitations: Based on unpublished tabulations from the 1979 and 1980 National Health Interview Surveys, provided by the National Center for Health Statistics. Rates are calculated for pooled 1979–1980 data to increase their stability. For office visits and hospital stays: Vital and Health Statistics, Series 3, No. 24, Tables 6,9 (Hing et al., 1983). The office visit data are from the 1979 National Ambulatory Medical Care Survey. The hospital discharge data are from the 1979 National Hospital Discharge Survey.

symptoms, annual health, ambulatory care, and even hospital stays, now rank very high. Because common conditions in this age span do not kill, room is left for uncommon, often abrupt, events to take the lead as killers. The only strong parallel with prior stages is injuries, which rank high both in young men's lives and also their deaths.

MIDDLE-AGED ADULTS

Musculoskeletal problems are the uppermost *symptoms* of daily life for middle-aged people, standing out especially for women. Respiratory symptoms rank second. All the other symptom groups have distinctly lower rates.

The leading specific symptoms reflect this general picture, being almost exclusively from the musculoskeletal and respiratory domains. Headache, a symptom often but not solely linked to respiratory infections, is the top problem for both men and women. Pain and stiffness are common in many body sites and sometimes all over. Cold symptoms (nasal congestion, cough, sore throat), tiredness, and tension/nervousness are also common. Daily troubles are similarly concentrated on the top 10 titles for men and women (60% of all men's symptoms are in the list, and 54% of women's).

In contrast to young adults, the middle-aged name diseases as the main causes for daily symptoms. Musculoskeletal diseases (mostly arthritis) are at the top. Respiratory diseases are second—a mix of acute and chronic titles when we look at the specific ones named. For the lesser causes, both sexes note physical exertion, weather/season, and too little sleep. Men attribute symptoms to accidents and drinking relatively more than women do, and women name past surgery more.

Annual rates of *acute conditions,* serious enough to cause short-term disability or medical care, show that respiratory diseases are most frequent, with nonspecific viruses next. Injuries form the third tier for middle-

TABLE 1-4 Leading Causes of Death for American Men and Women[a]

Causes of death (1980) (No. of deaths per 100,000 population)

Rank	Men 25–44	Women 25–44
1	Accidents, 68.6	Malignant neoplasms, 30.1
2	Diseases of heart, 34.6	Accidents, 17.3
3	Homicide, 29.4	Diseases of heart, 11.9
4	Malignant neoplasms, 25.8	Suicide, 7.7
5	Suicide, 24.0	Homicide, 6.4
6	Chronic liver disease and cirrhosis, 10.3	Chronic liver disease and cirrhosis, 5.0
7	Cerebrovascular diseases, 5.1	Cerebrovascular diseases, 5.0
8	Pneumonia and influenza, 2.9	Diabetes mellitus, 2.0
9	Diabetes mellitus, 2.7	Pneumonia and influenza, 1.8
10	Congenital anomalies, 1.5	Congenital anomalies, 1.1
11	Nephritis and nephrosis, 1.2	Chronic obstructive pulmonary diseases, 0.9
12	Chronic obstructive pulmonary diseases, 1.0	Nephritis and nephrosis, 0.7
13	Benign neoplasms, 0.7	Benign neoplasms, 0.7
14	Septicemia, 0.6	Complications of pregnancy/childbirth/puerperium, 0.7
15	Ulcer of stomach and duodenum, 0.4	Septicemia, 0.6

Rank	Men 45–64	Women 45–64
1	Diseases of heart, 505.3	Malignant neoplasms, 265.8
2	Malignant neoplasms, 348.0	Diseases of heart, 177.3
3	Accidents, 61.9	Cerebrovascular diseases, 39.9
4	Chronic liver disease and cirrhosis, 50.5	Chronic liver disease and cirrhosis, 23.2
5	Cerebrovascular diseases, 50.0	Accidents, 21.6
6	Chronic obstructive pulmonary diseases, 35.0	Diabetes mellitus, 17.7
7	Suicide, 23.7	Chronic obstructive pulmonary diseases, 17.6
8	Diabetes mellitus, 18.2	Suicide, 8.9
9	Pneumonia and influenza, 17.8	Pneumonia and influenza, 8.7
10	Homicide, 15.4	Nephritis and nephrosis, 5.5
11	Nephritis and nephrosis, 7.1	Benign neoplasms, 3.4
12	Septicemia, 5.0	Homicide, 3.4
13	Ulcer of stomach and duodenum, 4.0	Septicemia, 3.2
14	Atherosclerosis, 4.0	Hypertension w/ or w/o renal disease, 2.5
15	Benign neoplasms, 3.8	Atherosclerosis, 2.0

(*continued*)

TABLE 1-4 *(continued)*

	Men 65+	Women 65+
1	Diseases of heart, 2778.6	Diseases of heart, 2027.5
2	Malignant neoplasms, 1371.6	Malignant neoplasms, 767.8
3	Cerebrovascular diseases, 557.0	Cerebrovascular diseases, 584.0
4	Chronic obstructive pulmonary diseases, 297.9	Pneumonia and influenza, 154.9
5	Pneumonia and influenza, 212.5	Atherosclerosis, 113.9
6	Accidents, 124.4	Diabetes mellitus, 102.7
7	Atherosclerosis, 104.0	Chronic obstructive pulmonary diseases, 84.5
8	Diabetes mellitus, 92.8	Accidents, 78.9
9	Nephritis and nephrosis, 63.6	Nephritis and nephrosis, 42.1
10	Chronic liver disease and cirrhosis, 56.0	Chronic liver disease and cirrhosis, 24.6
11	Suicide, 35.0	Septicemia, 24.0
12	Septicemia, 30.9	Hypertension w/ or w/o renal disease, 23.4
13	Hypertension w/ or w/o renal disease, 25.9	Hernia of abdominal cavity and intestinal obstruction, 17.9
14	Ulcer of stomach and duodenum, 23.2	Ulcer of stomach and duodenum, 14.6
15	Benign neoplasms, 16.2	Benign neoplasms, 13.9

[a]Ranks are based on 72 disease and injury titles that encompass the International Classification of Diseases. For titles with the same rate (at one decimal place), the relative ranking was determined from the number of deaths reported for them.
SOURCE: Unpublished rates from 1980 vital statistics, provided by the National Center for Health Statistics.

aged men, but they come after reproductive (including menopausal) and urinary disorders for middle-aged women.

Five *chronic conditions* stand out for middle-aged people of both sexes: arthritis, hypertensive disease, chronic sinusitis, heart conditions, and hearing impairments. The significant presence of cardiovascular problems at this stage, but not in daily symptoms, reflects their diagnosed but usually asymptomatic status at middle ages. Diseases are more prominent in the prevalence list of middle-aged, compared to young adults, and fatal diseases join nonfatal ones in the top-rank titles. Skeletal impairments descend in importance; sensory impairments rise and end up superseding skeletal ones. No reproductive problems make the list of leading chronic conditions in middle ages. Men's and women's lists are very similar (exceptions are higher ranks for hernia among men and for varicose veins and migraine among women).

The chief causes of *limitations* for middle-aged adults are diseases. Now the most prevalent diseases are the most limiting ones as well. Arthritis ranks first for women and second for men, up from its middle ranks at younger ages. Many fatal diseases now appear in the limitations list. Titles new to this age group are heart diseases, hypertensive disease, diabetes, arteriosclerosis, emphysema, and malignant neoplasms. Heart diseases take on striking prominence, being the chief limiter for men and in second place for women. Among the fatal titles are several low-prevalence diseases (emphysema, asthma, arteriosclerosis, malignant neoplasms); this signals their debilitating nature for middle-aged persons when they do occur. Among the impairments, skeletal titles surpass sensory ones. The key limiting conditions are very similar for men and women. (The only notable difference is the higher importance of neoplasms and mental problems for women; those titles are not in men's list.)

Office visits center on chronic diseases that are infrequently symptomatic for middle-aged people but stand to benefit from medical treatment and counsel. The leading reason for medical care is hypertension, and it is distinctly set apart from all other titles. Near the top are ischemic heart disease (for men), diabetes, and malignancies—all life-threatening conditions. Reproductive disorders rise in middle-aged men's, compared to young adults', list (prostate and other genital disorders). But they are less pervasive in middle-aged women's; two titles appear in contrast to five at younger ages. (Note that all reproductive titles exclude genital organ cancers, always classified with neoplasms.) Acute respiratory conditions, mental distress, and injuries (men) shift down to middle ranks, now supplanted by chronic physical diseases. The leading reasons for physician visits are generally similar for men and women. The exceptions are that ischemic heart disease is more prominent for men, whereas malignant neoplasms rank higher for women. This difference foreshadows causes of death, where heart disease ranks higher for men and malignant neoplasms for women. Weight problems are also more important in women's visits.

The leading reasons for *hospital stays* now closely parallel those for ambulatory care. Life-threatening diseases are preeminent for men (malignant neoplasms; cardiovascular diseases; alcoholism, a risk factor for liver disease; and diabetes). Women have a greater diversity of fatal diseases, reproductive disorders, and rarely-fatal diseases in their leading diagnoses for hospital care.

Deaths for middle-aged men and women are largely due to heart diseases and malignant neoplasms. Rates are markedly lower for violent injuries and other diseases. The leading killers are presaged in hospital stays, ambulatory care, and even limitations. But they remain very different from the symptoms of daily life.

OLDER ADULTS

The foremost *daily symptoms* for older adults are musculoskeletal, being over twice as frequent as any other kind. General symptoms (such as ache all over, fatigue, chest pain other than heart) rank close to the top. Leading specific symptoms also center on musculoskeletal troubles for both sexes. There is frequent discomfort in many body sites (leg, knee, back, hip, shoulder, foot/toe). About 90% of the musculoskeletal symptoms reported are of pain; the remainder are mostly stiffness. Tiredness and aching all over are also prominent specific symptoms. Respiratory and headache symptoms virtually disappear from the list, compared to other ages. Older men and women report a similar variety of daily symptoms (57% in their top 10 for men, and 61% for women).

Causes named for daily symptoms are largely diseases, especially arthritis. Circulatory diseases make their first appearance as a high-rank cause. Women commonly cite aftereffects of recent and past surgery as reasons for their aches and pains. Injuries and behavior/environment reasons now rank low compared to diseases.

Acute problems diminish sharply in frequency for older adults compared to younger ones. Nevertheless, colds and flu maintain the top ranks. "All other acute conditions" moves up from middle ranks in other ages and now vies with respiratory infections in frequency. This residual group is largely made up of transient, ambiguous troubles, discomforts whose origin is unclear. Lower in rank are injuries, genitourinary disorders, and musculo-skeletal inflammations. The lists of leading acute problems are very similar for men and women (but note that genitourinary problems continue to surpass injuries among women).

Four *chronic conditions* predominate at older ages for both sexes: arthritis, hypertensive disease, heart conditions, and hearing impairments. Among the cardiovascular titles, fatal diseases become more dominant (hypertensive disease, heart conditions, arteriosclerosis), and nonfatal ones less so (hemorrhoids, and relative rates for varicose veins). Several killer diseases make their debut as leading problems at older ages: arteriosclerosis for both sexes, and emphysema for men. Sensory impairments clearly outdistance skeletal ones in prevalence.[8] And for the first time, reproductive disorders (prostate problems) are in men's list of leading conditions.

Persistent *limitations* in work and leisure activities come mostly from three diseases: arthritis, heart conditions, and hypertensive disease. The nonfatal one (arthritis) tops the list for women but remains second to heart disease for men. The fatal diseases in the list are generally the same as at middle ages, but their ranks now rise, reflecting increasing severity at older ages. Visual impairments equal or exceed skeletal ones in causing

[8]Why are sensory problems so infrequent in older adults' health diaries, even though prevalence rates of hearing and vision conditions rise sharply with age? (This rise appears in Detroit interviews as well as national data.) Interviews with older people about yesterday's symptoms also yield low reporting of sensory symptoms (Brody & Kleban, 1983). Most likely, sensory problems are quite constant from day to day, so people may fail to count them as symptoms unless overtly queried.

limitations. The very high prevalence of hearing problems (Table 1-2) is not translated into many limitations. This is due to their nature—they do not prevent activities so much as diminish their enjoyment—and correction by hearing aids. The leading limiting conditions and their ranks are similar for men and women.

Physician visits for older people concentrate on fatal chronic diseases, distinctly more so than at middle ages. Hypertension continues to hold first rank. The next ranks go to ischemic heart disease, malignant neoplasms, and diabetes (with one exception for women). Further down are cerebrovascular diseases, bronchitis, and hypertensive heart disease. Accompanying this overall elevation of fatal diseases, one nonfatal one— arthritis—also rises in prominence as a propeller of medical care, especially for women. Cataracts appear in the list, paralleling the increased importance of visual problems in prevalence, limitations, and, as we soon see, hospital stays. Acute respiratory infections and mental distress fall in rank, and all injuries except fractures disappear from the list. Prostate problems continue to be a leading reason for men's visits, but reproductive troubles vanish altogether from women's array of leading diagnoses. The leading reasons for men's and women's visits are generally very similar (with exceptions of prostate problems for men, and higher ranks for arthritis and fractures for women).

The main reasons for *hospital stays* are almost entirely life-threatening diseases for both sexes. Malignant neoplasms top the list, cerebrovascular disease is second, and a variety of cardiovascular titles appear thereafter. Pneumonia appears for the first time, compared to earlier ages; although it is an acute condition with low incidence, it can be very serious for the frail elderly. Prostate problems rank very high for men, but reproductive titles now vanish from women's list. Fractures rank high for women, reflecting both more osteoporosis among females and also more frailty among women aged 65+ (because of their older age distribution than men aged 65+).

Heart diseases are the principal *cause of death* for older men and women, with cancer and stroke ranking second and third. Deaths from these diseases are usually no surprise. They have already prompted extensive health services and activity limitations, especially the heart problems, and their symptoms have stretched into daily life as well. Violent deaths come predominantly from accidents; suicide and homicide are less prominent at older ages than earlier ones.

ACROSS LIFE

How do the kinds of problems people suffer change with advancing age? Do young and older adults differ more in their daily symptoms than their causes of death?

TABLE 1-5 Short-Term Health Problems of Detroit Men and Women[a] (Based on Daily Health Records for Six Weeks)

	Men			Women		
	18–44	45–64	65+	18–44	45–64	65+
No. of symptomatic days (per person)[b]	13.1	11.2	17.9	17.6	18.5	18.1
No. of health problems (per person)[c]	16.3	13.0	31.0	25.8	28.7	31.0
No. of specific symptoms (per person)[d]	25.0	17.7	46.7	41.6	44.6	40.6
Daily physical well-being (from 1 = terrible to 10 = wonderful) (average)[e]	7.8	7.8	7.5	7.6	7.3	7.2
No. of diary-keepers (N)	157	59	27	213	98	35

[a]The Health In Detroit Study had a representative sample of white adult (ages 18+) residents of the Detroit metropolitan area, who kept daily health records for six weeks in Fall 1978. Figures here are based on the 589 persons who kept at least one week of records. Data are standardized to a 42-day period for each diary-keeper to adjust for some dropout during the diary phase of the study.

[b]Q2: "Did you have any symptoms or discomforts today?" Days with Yes checked are symptomatic ones.

[c]The daily health record had a Symptom Chart for each day. Respondents wrote down all symptoms of the day, grouping the ones they considered due to the same cause. Each such grouping is counted as a distinct health problem. If the same problem occurs on several days, it is counted each day it appears.

[d]Symptoms were coded according to the Symptom Module of the Reason For Visit Classification (Schneider et al., 1979). (See Note b of Table 1-1 for further details.)

[e]Q1: "How did you feel physically today?" Responses are on a 10-point scale, with 1 labeled terrible and 10 labeled wonderful.

We have noted some shifts from one age group to the next in prior sections. Now we take the entire span of adulthood and summarize changes across age. We will concentrate on how the ranks of morbidity titles change, with cursory attention to how rates change.[9]

The differentials we note are likely to be very stable over time, true for this decade and several to come. They will change only if risks and disease experience are very different for now-young cohorts across their lifetimes than they have been for now-old cohorts.

We begin with people's overall evaluation of their health status: *Physical well-being* declines with age for broad age groups. This appears both in the Detroit survey (Table 1-5) and national ones (Table 1-6). The decline across age is much gentler than we might expect, given the sharp increases in chronic health problems with advancing age.[10]

Does the *frequency of daily symptoms* increase with age? The Detroit study finds that symptom rates are quite constant across age for women. Men have a curvilinear pattern, with least symptom experience in mid-

TABLE 1-6 Self-Rated Health Status of American Men and Women[a]

	Men			Women		
	17–44	45–64	65+	17–44	45–64	65+
	(Percent distributions)					
Excellent	56.9%	39.6%	29.3%	48.5%	33.5%	27.5%
Good	36.0	39.5	39.9	41.6	44.2	42.5
Fair	5.8	14.5	21.1	8.4	16.7	22.1
Poor	1.3	6.4	9.7	1.5	5.6	7.9

[a]"Compared to other persons ___'s age, would you say that his health is excellent, good, fair, or poor?" Self-reports, rather than proxy reports, were secured for adults whenever possible. (The question was changed in 1982 and now reads "Would you say ___'s health in general is excellent, very good, good, fair, or poor?")

SOURCE: 1978 National Health Interview Survey. Computed from data published in Vital and Health Statistics, Series 10, No. 142, Table 2 (Ries, 1983). Persons with health status NA are excluded here.

[9]Overall rates of acute conditions, limitations, ambulatory care, hospital stays, and mortality by age are published in issues of *Vital and Health Statistics*, Series 10 and 13, and *Monthly Vital Statistics Report*, publications of the National Center for Health Statistics. A compilation of such statistics is in Hing et al. (1979). Health profiles of middle-aged people are analyzed in Nathanson and Lorenz (1982) and of older people in Kovar (1977a, 1977b), Shanas (1962), Siegel and Davidson (1984), and Verbrugge (1983, 1984c).

[10]When detailed age groups are used, surveys often find a curvilinear pattern across age instead—the very oldest groups (above age 75) having more positive assessments than adjacent groups (ages 60–75) (Cockerham, Sharp, & Wilcox, 1983; Ferraro, 1980; Linn & Linn, 1980; Ries, 1983; Stoller, 1984). Reasons proposed for this are: (1) the most ill elderly are institutionalized and thus not in the survey population, (2) the oldest group evaluates their health compared to decedent peers, (3) the oldest people have a lower standard of what constitutes good health, and (4) the oldest people are robust survivors and have genuinely better health with respect to fatal diseases and related symptoms than many slightly younger people.

dle ages and a pronounced rise at older ages (Table 1-5). There is little other research evidence on this point, and it shows diverse patterns: (1) An English study finds small increases in recent symptoms for men and women across broad age groups (number of symptoms in past two weeks; computed from Dunnell & Cartwright, 1972, p. 19). (2) A Scottish study of recent symptoms shows small steady increases with age for men, but peak rates in middle ages for women (number of symptoms in past two weeks; Hannay, 1979, p. 92). (3) A Baltimore sample shows a large jump in symptom rates for people aged 65+ compared to middle-aged and young adults, who have similar rates (percent with health problem in past 2 weeks; Kohn & White, 1976, Fig. 5.16). (4) Quite different from these, a study of Los Angeles adults finds a small negative association between recalled morbidity and age (repeated interviews over a year's time; Marcus, Seeman, & Telesky, 1983). This is attributed to the high incidence of such acute problems as colds, flu, and digestive upsets among young adults.[11]

Thus some very basic questions about daily health of contemporary adults are scarcely answered. How do rates of symptomatic days and of symptoms change with age? Do acute condition days diminish and chronic condition days increase, as we would expect? Do older people have more "multiplicity" of daily troubles than other age groups; that is, more bothersome conditions on symptomatic days and also more symptoms within each condition? (The Detroit data support the first, but not the second, point.) Are episodes of ill health longer for older adults? Do their chronic conditions flare up (thus, repeated episodes) more often?

Types of daily symptoms change markedly across ages. The Health In Detroit study shows the following: Respiratory problems and headaches dominate for young adults; they fall in incidence and rank in middle ages, and still further down at older ages. Musculoskeletal problems ascend in prominence across age, being increasingly due to arthritis and decreasingly to physical exertion and injuries. Sensory and cardiovascular symptoms rise in importance with age. Young adults frequently name injuries and behavior/environment factors as the causes of their symptoms; disease names become more common in middle ages; and they dominate the causes named by older people.

---

[11]Several surveys from earlier decades provide *sickness rates* over longer (months or years) periods for age–sex groups. Rates tend to increase with age for men and women (Collins, 1940; Collins, Trantham, & Lehmann, 1955; Dominion Bureau of Statistics, 1960; Logan & Brooke, 1957; Sydenstricker, 1928). A few statistics from these are republished in White et al. (1961, Tables 1, 2). Two other sources merit mention. Well-known studies from the 1950s in San Jose and California State have monthly rates of acute and chronic sicknesses, based on diaries and interviews, but rates are not shown by age (Allen, Breslow, Weissman, & Nisselson, 1954; Mooney, 1962). Similarly, an Illinois study yields monthly rates of days felt ill, based on diaries and interviews, but none by age (Sudman & Lannom, 1980). The three studies just cited classify rates by whether the sickness caused restricted activity or not.

Several other contemporary studies in the United States and Great Britain have details about recently experienced symptoms by age (Dunnell & Cartwright, 1972; Hammond, 1964; Marcus et al., 1983; Proprietary Association, 1984; Wadsworth et al., 1971) or only for older adults (Brody & Kleban, 1983; Shanas, 1962). None of them uses a prospective health diary like Detroit; instead, all have retrospective questions for a short, recent time interval or questions about current complaints.[12] Despite many differences across these surveys, they concur with the findings above for the Detroit diaries.[13] Thus, the differences by age that we noted are likely to be true for Americans and Britons as a whole.

Although rates of *acute conditions* fall sharply with age, the topmost problems stay constant; namely, respiratory infections. Injuries of many kinds rank next for young men and descend only a little in rank at middle and older ages. For women of all ages, reproductive and urinary disorders rank next after respiratory ones, and injuries thereafter. Ambiguous acute symptoms, not clearly due to a particular disease or injury, rise in prominence across age. The rankings of acute conditions are very stable across age; thus, the same basic problems recur through life although their frequency changes.

The likelihood of having *chronic conditions* rises sharply with age, and the leading ones change radically. Diseases ascend in importance, especially life-threatening ones. One nonfatal disease, arthritis, also ascends; it moves into first place for older adults, followed by a cluster of cardiovascular conditions. Chronic sinusitis, the key chronic problem for young adults, descends in rank across age as other diseases pass it. Skeletal impairments diminish in importance, while sensory impairments become more prominent. Chronic reproductive organ disorders are not frequent in any age group. Note how they appear in the young women's list but not thereafter, and enter the older men's list but not before.

Limitations due to chronic conditions increase with age. At young ages, they are typically due to skeletal impairments and asthma. The picture changes in middle ages, as arthritis and killer diseases appear and become severe for some people. Their domination in the limitations list becomes even more pronounced at older ages. Impairments do not disappear

---

[12]Symptom details are available from several *long-term* (one year or more) prospective studies, conducted with very selective samples, by Hinkle and colleagues (Christenson & Hinkle, 1961; Hinkle, Plummer, & Whitney, 1961; Hinkle, Redmont, Plummer, & Wolff, 1960) and by Dingle and colleagues (Dingle, Badger, & Jordan, 1964). The descriptive statistics are fascinating and inventive, even though they cannot be used for general population estimates.

[13]An exception is Shanas (1962). The survey finds different ranks for recent symptoms among older persons than the other surveys. This is due to coding rules that apparently assigned all symptoms *without* a specific disease name to a single (and thereby large) residual group.

but simply shift further down the list. Among them, visual impairments mount in importance as limiters of social activity, and they reach comparable status to the principal skeletal impairments.

Physician visit rates rise with age for both sexes, especially for men. Colds and flu dominate visits by young adults, with mental distress, injuries, and (for women) reproductive disorders taking up most other leading titles. In middle age, fatal chronic diseases displace all of these and take topmost ranks, and more such diseases appear in lower ranks as well. This becomes even more true at older ages. Physician visits for one nonkiller, arthritis, also gain prominence with age, especially for women. Although important at young ages, reproductive titles disappear from women's list by older ages. By contrast, prostate and other genital disorders maintain middle ranks for men throughout life.

Hospital stays increase in frequency with age for men and at older ages for women. In young adulthood, injuries are the leading reason for men's stays, and reproductive disorders for women. These give way to fatal chronic diseases (especially malignancies) and nonfatal chronic ones (especially digestive and urinary ones) in middle ages. By older ages, injuries and reproductive titles have almost left the list (with the important exceptions of fractures for both sexes and prostate disorders for men). Fatal diseases take up virtually all positions, with malignancies decisively at the top.

Death rates rise very rapidly across the three age groups. But the titles of leading causes are virtually invariant throughout life, being mostly degenerative chronic diseases and violent injuries. Their ranks shift, however. Injuries are very prominent for young adults, then decline in importance at later ages. Malignant neoplasms and heart diseases always head the disease titles. But with age, other cardiovascular diseases rise in rank, as do chronic obstructive pulmonary diseases (bronchitis, emphysema, asthma). Diabetes maintains middle ranks at all ages. Pneumonia/influenza appears at all ages but makes a noteworthy ascent in rank at older ages.[14]

Summing up, the leading problems change with age in every stage of health. That is, the *ranks* of given titles almost always change and the array of *titles* often changes, too. The shifts tend to be greater from young to middle ages than from middle to older ones. This is especially evident for chronic-condition prevalence and health services use, as fatal diseases make their appearance in middle age and progress from then on. Two stages show relatively great stability: Leading acute conditions tend to be similar across age; and, remarkably, the greatest stability of all is in mortality, whose ranks and component titles change less across age than any other health stage.

[14]Its role as a contributing cause of death, rather than principal one, also rises for older adults.

SEX DIFFERENCES

Are the health experiences of men and women vastly different, or do they actually tend to suffer the same kinds of health problems? We begin by noting sex differences in rates[15], then concentrate on how ranks of health problems differ for men and women.

Women experience more daily symptoms, higher incidence of all types of acute conditions (except injuries at young ages), higher prevalence of non-fatal chronic diseases, more physician visits per year, and more hospital stays (at young ages). These excesses persist even if reproductive events and disorders are removed. Men surpass women in only a few respects. They have higher prevalence of the principal fatal chronic diseases and most impairments, higher limitation rates from those problems and overall limitation rates, more hospitalization in older ages, and higher mortality rates for leading causes. Thus, despite popular notions, morbidity and mortality statistics are not contradictory about men: The health statistics show that they are more bothered by serious life-threatening diseases, and this culminates in higher death rates for them.

These sex differences in rates tend to be largest for young adults and smallest for older adults. (This is true even when all reproductive events or all sex-specific titles are removed.) In brief, women suffer more frequent but less serious morbidity than men. One sex tends to be sicker in the short run of life, but the other in the long run.

Now we consider ranks. Despite pervasive sex differences in rates, men and women tend to suffer from the same kinds of health problems. That is, the leading conditions (titles and ranks) at each stage of health are more similar than they are different. This becomes increasingly true at older ages.

Evidence abounds in Tables 1-1–1-4. Note that the foremost daily symptoms are similar for men and women in each age group. The top acute conditions are the same for them at all ages, and the whole lists of acute problems become more similar with age. Leading reasons for professional care also become more similar with age, as diseases rise and displace men's injuries and women's reproductive disorders. In each age group, the leading chronic conditions and limiting conditions are strongly similar for men and women, in both the component titles and their ranks. Lastly, the array of causes of death is similar, especially for middle-aged and older adults. Although readers will find many specific differences in data, and certainly important ones, they are surrounded by basic similarities.

---

[15]Sex differences in morbidity and mortality rates have been studied extensively and are reviewed in Hing et al. (1979), Nathanson (1977), Verbrugge (1976a, 1976b, 1982, 1985), Waldron (1982, 1983), and Wingard (1984).

Thus, what distinguishes men and women most is their *frequency* of illness, injury, health care, and mortality, not the *types* of morbidity they typically suffer. In brief, what differs most is the rates, not the ranks. This point has been missed heretofore in comparisons of contemporary men's and women's health.

CONNECTIONS ACROSS STAGES OF HEALTH

Do daily symptoms have much to do with visits to physicians and causes of death? Are there more such connections at older ages than younger ones?

For *young adults,* the most commonality appears at the initial stages of daily symptoms, annual health (the incidence and prevalence rates), and ambulatory care. Respiratory problems and acute ones dominate in these stages. Later stages are markedly different from them, and also from each other: Limitations are topped by impairments and nonfatal musculoskeletal troubles, as well as asthma. Hospital stays center on injuries for men, reproductive disorders for women, and low-prevalence diseases for both. Causes of death are atypical diseases and violent injuries.

At *middle ages,* more links begin to appear across the stages. They form most strongly at the terminal stages. Hospital stays involve the diseases that are leading causes of death. And those diseases also begin to penetrate ambulatory care (often in the form of the risk factor hypertension) and limitations, though they do not yet dominate those stages. A different set of links forms at earlier stages from arthritis. As it rises in prevalence, more limitations and daily symptoms due to it are reported. But overall, the endpoints of daily health versus causes of death still remain distinctly different.

Commonalities across stages are strongest at *older ages.* The leading causes of death stretch back into all prior stages. They take over most ranks for hospital stays and the top ones for ambulatory care. They vie with nonfatal diseases and impairments for prominence in limitation and pre-valence rates. And they are now manifest in daily symptoms—not the most frequent ones, but ones that are certainly present. Arthritis also establishes a greater hold. Aches and pains become the principal complaints of daily life, the most prevalent chronic problem, the top- or second-rank limiter, and a common reason for ambulatory care.

In sum, the health profile for young adults differs greatly depending on which stage we look at. More similarity develops in middle ages, and the profile is most consistent for older adults. The increasing connections mir-ror the growing penetration of fatal diseases and arthritis into all facets of health status and health care as people age.

ICEBERGS OF MORBIDITY

Visual images are economical, capable of summarizing abundant statistics. So let us return to the iceberg metaphor and elaborate it. Our aim in pursuing the image is not fanciful but instead scientific, to facilitate analyses of population health.

Imagine an iceberg with distinct *layers,* the boundaries between them being permeable. Each layer is a different accounting of health events. Daily symptoms are at the bottom, symptoms treated by oneself next, then problems that cause short-term restricted activity, conditions that cause long-term limitation next, visits to health professionals, hospital episodes, and then deaths at the top. These are stages of health. Layers above water are routinely measured facets of health; layers below water are facets seldom or never measured for a population.

Assume there is an iceberg for each age group. All icebergs have the same height and a simple overall shape. But the *diameters* of their layers, which reflect the overall rates of health events, vary greatly. Comparing diameters (actually volumes) of a certain layer across the icebergs indicates how rates change with age. Comparing diameters across the layers in one iceberg indicates how readily symptoms translate into disability and medical care. What would we see? From the young to middle to older iceberg, a given layer's diameter (such as daily symptoms) increases. Within icebergs, the young adult iceberg looks peaked, with relatively little professional care and few deaths compared to symptoms. But the older adult iceberg is broad-topped, with relatively frequent professional care and deaths compared to symptoms.

Within each layer are colored sections, representing rates for types of conditions. There are *colors* for seven basic types: (1) acute disease, (2) injury (acute conditions such as bruises, causes of death such as homicide), (3) nonfatal chronic disease (rarely or never causing death), (4) fatal chronic disease (degenerative disease that inherently progresses to death), (5) sensory impairment, (6) skeletal and other impairment, and (7) reproductive events and procedures (normal pregnancy/childbirth, sterilization in absence of disease). Reproductive disorders (complications of pregnancy/childbirth/puerperium and reproductive organ diseases other than cancer) are in sections (1) and (3). Section (7) is actually nonmorbidity, and it can be excluded from the iceberg if only morbidity conditions are desired. (We did this in Tables 1-2 and 1-3.) The relative size of color sections within a layer shows the ranks of conditions; for example, the importance of acute problems compared to chronic ones. Comparing the salience of a color across layers reveals how conditions penetrate through facets of daily life, health care, and death.

An inventive illustrator might also denote rates of sex-specific conditions by applying *gloss* to the relevant fraction of a section. Sex-specific morbidity is reproductive disorders (defined above) and reproductive organ cancers. It occurs in sections (1), (3), and (4). Sex-specific nonmorbidity is section (7), which if included is glossed completely. Such glossing would reveal the importance of reproductive problems for young women and older men.

Lastly, color *shading* can be used to indicate sex differences, the ratio of male-to-female rates. Using some standard shade for parity (sex ratio of 1.00) in all colors, deeper shades would mean higher male rates; and lighter shades, higher female rates.[16] We would see that lighter shades prevail in the bottom layers of icebergs, and deeper ones at the very top. The young adult iceberg has the largest gradations in shade from bottom to top (daily health being especially feminine, but death especially masculine), and the older adult iceberg has the smallest gradations.

Thus the iceberg metaphor allows analysis of rates, ranks, component diseases and injuries, reproductive disorders and events, sex differences, and age differences. It can serve either as a means of mentally organizing data or as a real pictorial device for showing them.

This chapter has focused on colors; that is, the ranks of conditions within a stage of health (layer) and also across stages, ages, and sex. We have used specific disease, injury, and impairment titles rather than collecting them into the seven basic types above. The leading causes for each stage (Tables 1-1–1-4) were drawn from complete sets of age–sex–cause-specific rates. Those causes make up the bulk of ill health in any stage, but one would nevertheless use the complete sets of rates to construct pictorial icebergs for the population.

FUTURE HEALTH PROFILES

Trying to see the iceberg of morbidity for current adult cohorts is hard, but envisioning it for the future is even harder. Population morbidity depends on age distribution; personal lifestyle behaviors from childhood to current age; medical ability to diagnose, prevent, control, and cure disease; efficacy of rehabilitation techniques and special aids; and social attitudes and economic incentives about illness. We can project quite well forthcoming trends in age distribution, but changes in the other factors are uncertain. Still, various possible scenarios of population health

---

[16]The frequency of sex-specific conditions will especially affect a section's overall shade. Darkest hues occur when male specific disorders are very common, and lightest hues when female specific disorders are.

can ·be laid out if we make clear and sensible assumptions about these factors.[17]

To illustrate the process, let us think about the health of *older* people in the future and focus on just *lifestyle* and *medical* inputs, as they pertain to chronic illnesses.

Scenario 1. The expertise of contemporary medicine is disease diagnosis and control. In addition, individuals' good health habits probably delay the onset of diseases and diminish their severity for many people, and may sometimes even prevent disease occurrence. Assuming that medical advances and lifestyle improvements continue in the same ways (i.e., control more than cure or prevention), then future older people may be just as likely to *acquire* diseases in their lifetimes as current people, but the *impact* of those diseases will be less severe. This shift toward mildness implies that prevalence rates and basic ("any") disability/limitation rates would remain stable over time, but indicators of severe disability and limitation would fall. However, if *mortality* is delayed by these medical and personal factors (this has apparently been the case for the past two decades and is likely for coming ones), then the situation is more complex. People rescued from early death are probably relatively sick and also highly vulnerable to new diseases, and their presence in the living population propels *upward* all morbidity and disability statistics for their age group. Thus individual gains (less discomfort and longer life) are not paralleled in population health statistics (which would show worsening on many dimensions) in this scenario.

Scenario 2. Assuming instead that striking (and now unknown) medical and lifestyle changes have a marvelous outcome—the prevention of fatal chronic conditions—then incidence and prevalence rates of chief killers would fall sharply. Disability/limitation rates should fall, too, but not nearly so much and mainly on severity dimensions. This is because people may be just as likely as before to acquire key *nonfatal* conditions, such as arthritis and sensory impairments, which commonly cause disability in daily life. Overall, the distribution of fatal and nonfatal chronic conditions will shift, with increasing prominence of the latter, in both health statistics and individuals' lives. Mortality gains will occur, but this will *not* rebound to push up morbidity and disability, since there is no special pool of rescued ill people.

Other scenarios can be put forth, but the above two are fundamental ones hinging on secondary and primary disease prevention, respectively. I believe the first scenario is more likely than the second in coming decades, although the second has been strongly argued to be near at hand (Fries, 1980, 1983; Fries & Crapo, 1981). Other theoretical and empirical assessments side

---

[17]This leads to intelligent discussion of alternative futures. By contrast, when assumptions are vaguely stated or unstated and a single scenario is announced as the way things will be, argument is certain. Any merits that scenario has become undermined by its presentation.

with the first, more modest view (Brody, 1986; Manton, 1982; Myers & Manton, 1984; Schneider & Brody, 1983; Verbrugge, 1984b).

Beyond the medical and lifestyle aspects, we might also ask how anticipated improvements in rehabilitation, better access to public places, higher social acceptance of disabled people, increased economic supports for ill people, and aging within the older population would influence morbidity rates of older people. The task of creating a scenario depends not only on the nature of each assumption, but also on their strength relative to one another.

Dynamic relationships among morbidity, disability, and mortality can be nicely framed in the "survival curve" perspective first presented in World Health Organization (1984) and elaborated since then by Manton and Soldo (1985). Coherent and plausible profiles are generated by careful thinking and given grist by computer modeling. An example of modeling some of the links is in Manton (1986).

Analyses of past trends can be good guides for the process and substance of forecasts. There are several analyses of recent trends in the health of the U.S. population, with suggestions about reasons for the trends (Colvez & Blanchet, 1981; Palmore, 1986; Verbrugge, 1984b) and empirical estimates of such reasons (Chirikos, 1986).

We have mainly discussed future trends in rates, or health in the *aggregate*. It is also important to consider *individual* health profiles—what a future older person's health will be like, on the average, compared to the health of an older person today. For example, with better disease control, older people will be more comfortable and functional in daily life. Improved survival may mean that they will acquire more chronic conditions over their lifetime and be more likely to have some disability, but that condition severity and pervasive disability will be less (Verbrugge, 1984c). In all forecasting efforts, the implications of trends in medicine, lifestyle, and the other factors must be thought through and modeled for *both* population and individual levels.

CONCLUSIONS

The diverse views of population health seen in health statistics are all true and all valuable. All of the series concern people's health experiences, some private and others inherently public. The origin of some series in self-reports rather than medical diagnoses does not diminish their truthfulness.

Each view is especially valuable to different parties. For example, daily symptoms are the essence of physical well-being for individuals, and they influence mental and emotional well-being, too. Incidence and prevalence rates reveal the extent of population morbidity (symptomatic or not) to epidemiologists. Limitations are important not only to the sufferers but also their family, friends, employers, and helping professionals. Physician visit and hospital stay statistics are crucial for planning primary, secondary, and tertiary health services, for production of pharmaceuticals and medical instruments, for training new physicians, and for planning reimbursement programs. Mortality rates are of interest to living individuals, giving them signals about likely endpoints that they might strive to avoid. Those rates have greatest immediate importance to health professionals and planners, who construct a fabric of services to help slow disease progress in patients, reduce limitations, and, ideally, prevent such diseases and injuries from occurring at all.

We have called these views "stages of health," and visually they constitute layers of the "iceberg of morbidity." The stage and iceberg concepts help convey the multiplicity of health experience in a population, which health professionals need to appreciate and which scientists should measure completely.

Health statistics in the United States and other industrial nations began to be collected many decades ago, with attention to mortality. Gradually, statistical series have been added for medical care, disability, and morbidity incidence and prevalence. But the bulk of the iceberg still remains underwater. We know virtually nothing about daily health experiences, self-care actions, and help-seeking from nonmedical health professionals for the U.S. or other national populations. With increasing longevity and improving control of chronic diseases, concern has shifted toward the quality of people's lives. That quality depends greatly on physical symptoms felt in daily life and the strategies individuals devise to care for them.

It is high time that we measure people's sneezes as well as their adieux.

REFERENCES

Allen, George I., Lester Breslow, Arthur Weissman, and Harold Nisselson. 1954. "Interviewing Versus Diary Keeping in Eliciting Information in a Morbidity Survey." *American Journal of Public Health* 44: 919–927.

Alonzo, Angelo A. 1979. "Everyday Illness Behavior: A Situational Approach to Health Status Deviations." *Social Science and Medicine* 13A: 397–404.

Brody, Elaine M. and Morton H. Kleban. 1983. "Day-to-Day Mental and Physical Symptoms of Older People: A Report on Health Logs." *The Gerontologist* 23: 75–85.

Brody, Jacob A. 1986. "The Best of Times/The Worst of Times: Aging and Dependency in the 21st Century." In *Philosophy and Medicine,* edited by S. R. Ingman and H. T. Engelhardt, Jr. Boston: D. Reidel Pub. Co.

Chirikos, Thomas N. 1986. "Accounting for the Historical Rise in Work-Disability Prevalence." *Milbank Memorial Fund Quarterly/Health and Society* 64: 271–301.

Christenson, William N. and Lawrence E. Hinkle, Jr. 1961. "Differences in Illness and Prognostic Signs in Two Groups of Young Men." *Journal of the American Medical Association* 177: 247–253.

Cockerham, William C., Kimberly Sharp, and Julie A. Wilcox. 1983. "Aging and Perceived Health Status." *Journal of Gerontology* 38: 349–355.

Collins, Selwyn D. 1940. "Cases and Days of Illness Among Males and Females, With Special Reference to Confinement to Bed." *Public Health Reports* 55: 47–94.

Collins, Selwyn D., Katharine S. Trantham, and Josephine L. Lehmann. 1955. *Sickness Experience in Selected Areas of the United States. Public Health Monographs.* No. 25. Washington, DC: Public Health Service.

Colvez, Alain and Madeleine Blanchet. 1981. "Disability Trends in the United States Population 1966–76: Analysis of Reported Causes." *American Journal of Public Health* 71: 464–471.

Dingle, John H. 1973. "The Ills of Man." *Scientific American* 229(September): 76–84.

Dingle, John H., George F. Badger, and William S. Jordan, Jr. 1964. *Illness in the Home.* Cleveland: The Press of Case Western Reserve University.

Dominion Bureau of Statistics and Department of National Health and Welfare. 1960. *Canadian Sickness Survey 1950–51.* Ottawa, Canada.

Dunnell, Karen and Ann Cartwright. 1972. *Medicine Takes, Prescribers and Hoarders.* London: Routledge & Kegan Paul.

Fabrega, Horacio, Jr. 1973. "Toward a Model of Illness Behavior." *Medical Care* 11: 470–484.

Ferraro, Kenneth F. 1980. "Self-Ratings of Health Among the Old and the Old-Old." *Journal of Health and Social Behavior* 21: 377–383.

Fries, James F. 1980. "Aging, Natural Death, and the Compression of Morbidity." *New England Journal of Medicine* 303: 130–135.

Fries, James F. 1983. "The Compression of Morbidity." *Milbank Memorial Fund Quarterly/Health and Society* 61: 397–419.

Fries, James F. and Lawrence M. Crapo. 1981. *Vitality and Aging.* San Francisco: W. H. Freeman.

Hammond, E. Cuyler. 1964. "Some Preliminary Findings on Physical Complaints From a Prospective Study of 1,064,004 Men and Women." *American Journal of Public Health* 54: 11–23.

Hannay, David R. 1979. *The Symptom Iceberg.* London: Routledge & Kegan Paul.

Hing, Esther, Mary Grace Kovar, and Dorothy P. Rice. 1983. *Sex Differences in Health and Use of Medical Care: United States, 1979. Vital and Health Statistics.* Series 3, No. 24. DHHS Pub. No. (PHS) 83-1408. Hyattsville, MD: National Center for Health Statistics.

Hinkle, Lawrence E., Jr, Norman Plummer, and L. Holland Whitney. 1961. "The Continuity of Patterns of Illness and the Prediction of Future Health." *Journal of Occupational Medicine* 3: 417–423.

Hinkle, Lawrence E., Jr., Ruth Redmont, Norman Plummer, and Harold G. Wolff. 1960. "An Examination of the Relation Between Symptoms, Disability, and Serious Illness, in Two Homogeneous Groups of Men and Women." *American Journal of Public Health* 50: 1327–1336.

Kasl, Stanislav V. and Sidney Cobb. 1966a. "Health and Illness Behavior." *Archives of Environmental Health* 12: 246–266.

Kasl, Stanislav V. and Sidney Cobb. 1966b. "Sick-Role Behavior." *Archives of Environmental Health* 12: 531–541.

Kohn, Robert and Kerr L. White (eds.). 1976. *Health Care: An International Study.* London: Oxford University Press.

Kovar, Mary Grace. 1977a. "Elderly People: The Population 65 Years and Over." Pp. 3–26 in *Health—United States—1976–77.* DHEW Pub. No. (HRA) 77-1232. Hyattsville, MD: National Center for Health Statistics.

Kovar, Mary Grace. 1977b. "Health of the Elderly and Use of Health Services." *Public Health Reports* 92: 9–19.

Last, John M. 1963. "The Iceberg—Completing the Clinical Picture in General Practice." *Lancet* 2: 28–31.

Linn, Bernard S. and Margaret W. Linn. 1980. "Objective and Self-Assessed Health in the Old and Very Old." *Social Science and Medicine* 14A: 311–315.

Logan, William P. D. and E. M. Brooke. 1957. *The Survey of Sickness, 1943–1952. Studies on Medical and Population Subjects.* No. 12. London: General Register Office.

Manton, Kenneth G. 1982. "Changing Concepts of Morbidity and Mortality in the Elderly Population." *Milbank Memorial Fund Quarterly/Health and Society* 60: 183–244.

Manton, Kenneth G. 1986. "Past and Future Life Expectancy Increases at Later Ages: Their Implications for the Linkage of Chronic Morbidity, Disability, and Mortality." *Journal of Gerontology* 41: 672–681.

Manton, Kenneth G. and Beth J. Soldo. 1985. "Dynamics of Health Changes in the Oldest Old: New Perspectives and Evidence." *Milbank Memorial Fund Quarterly/Health and Society* 63: 206–285.

Marcus, Alfred C., Teresa E. Seeman, and Carol W. Telesky. 1983. "Sex Differences in Reports of Illness and Disability: A Further Test of the Fixed Role Hypothesis." *Social Science and Medicine* 17: 993–1002.

McKinlay, John B. 1972. "Some Approaches and Problems in the Study of the Use of Services—An Overview." *Journal of Health and Social Behavior* 13: 115–152.

Mechanic, David. 1972. "Social Psychologic Factors Affecting the Presentation of Bodily Complaints." *New England Journal of Medicine* 286: 1132–1139.

Mechanic, David. 1978. *Medical Sociology.* Second edition. (See Chapter 9.) New York: Free Press.

Mooney, H. William. 1962. *Methodology in Two California Health Surveys. Public Health Monographs.* No. 70. PHS Pub. No. 942. Washington, DC: Public Health Service.

Myers, George C. and Kenneth G. Manton. 1984. "Compression of Mortality: Myth or Reality?" *The Gerontologist* 24: 346–353.

Nathanson, Constance A. 1977. "Sex, Illness, and Medical Care: A Review of Data, Theory, and Method." *Social Science and Medicine* 11: 13–25.

Nathanson, Constance A. and Gerda Lorenz. 1982. "Women and Health: The Social Dimensions of Biomedical Data." Pp. 37–87 in *Women in the Middle Years,* edited by J. Z. Giele. New York: Wiley.

Palmore, Erdman B. 1986. "Trends in the Health of the Aged." *The Gerontologist* 26: 298–302.

Proprietary Association, The. 1984. *Health Care Practices and Perceptions.* (Office of Public Affairs, The Proprietary Association, 1700 Pennsylvania Ave. N.W., Suite 700, Washington, DC 20006)

Ries, Peter W. 1983. *Americans Assess Their Health: United States, 1978. Vital and Health Statistics.* Series 10, No. 142. DHHS Pub. No. (PHS) 83-1570. Hyattsville, MD: National Center for Health Statistics.

Schneider, Don, Linda Appleton, and Thomas McLemore. 1979. *A Reason for Visit Classification for Ambulatory Care. Vital and Health Statistics.* Series 2, No. 78. DHEW Pub. No. (PHS) 79-1352. Hyattsville, MD: National Center for Health Statistics.

Schneider, Edward L. and Jacob A. Brody. 1983. "Aging, Natural Death, and the Compression of Morbidity: Another View." *New England Journal of Medicine* 309: 854–855.

Shanas, Ethel. 1962. *The Health of Older People.* Cambridge, MA: Harvard University Press.

Siegel, Jacob S. and Maria Davidson. 1984. *Demographic and Socioeconomic Aspects of Aging in the United States. Current Population Reports.* Series P-23, No. 138. Washington, DC: Bureau of the Census.

Stoeckle, John D., Irving K. Zola, and Gerald E. Davidson. 1963. "On Going to See the Doctor: The Contributions of the Patient to the Decision to Seek Medical Aid." *Journal of Chronic Diseases* 16: 975–989.

Stoller, Eleanor P. 1984. "Self-Assessments of Health by the Elderly: The Impact of Informal Assistance." *Journal of Health and Social Behavior* 25: 260–270.

Suchman, Edward A. 1965. "Stages of Illness and Medical Care." *Journal of Health and Human Behavior* 6: 114–128.

Sudman, Seymour and Linda B. Lannom. 1980. *Health Care Surveys Using Diaries.* NCHSR Research Report Series. DHHS Pub. No. (PHS) 80-3279. Hyattsville, MD: National Center for Health Services Research.

Sydenstricker, Edgar E. 1928. "Sex Differences in the Incidence of Certain Diseases at Different Ages." *Public Health Reports* 43: 1259–1276.

Verbrugge, Lois M. 1976a. "Females and Illness: Recent Trends in Sex Differences in the United States." *Journal of Health and Social Behavior* 17: 387–403.

Verbrugge, Lois M. 1976b. "Sex Differentials in Morbidity and Mortality in the United States." *Social Biology* 23: 275–296.

Verbrugge, Lois M. 1980. "Health Diaries." *Medical Care* 18: 73–95.

Verbrugge, Lois M. 1982. "Sex Differentials in Health." *Public Health Reports* 97: 417–437.

Verbrugge, Lois M. 1983. "Women and Men: Mortality and Health of Older People." Pp. 139–174 in *Aging in Society: Selected Reviews of Recent Research,* edited by M. W. Riley, B. B. Hess, and K. Bond. Hillsdale, NJ: Lawrence Erlbaum Associates.

Verbrugge, Lois M. 1984a. "Health Diaries—Problems and Solutions in Study Design." Pp. 171–192 in *Health Survey Research Methods,* edited by C. F. Cannell and R. M. Groves. NCHSR Research Proceedings Series. DHHS Pub. No. (PHS) 84-3346. Rockville, MD: National Center for Health Services Research.

Verbrugge, Lois M. 1984b. "Longer Life but Worsening Health? Trends in Health and Mortality of Middle-Aged and Older Persons." *Milbank Memorial Fund Quarterly/Health and Society* 62: 475–519.

Verbrugge, Lois M. 1984c. "A Health Profile of Older Women With Comparisons to Older Men." *Research on Aging* 6: 291–322.

Verbrugge, Lois M. 1985. "Gender and Health: An Update on Hypotheses and Evidence." *Journal of Health and Social Behavior* 26: 156–182.

Wadsworth, Michael E. J., W. J. H. Butterfield, and R. Blaney. 1971. *Health and Sickness—The Choice of Treatment.* London: Tavistock Publications.

Waldron, Ingrid. 1982. "An Analysis of Causes of Sex Differences in Mortality and Morbidity." Pp. 69–116 in *The Fundamental Connection Between Nature and Nurture,* edited by W. R. Gove and G. R. Carpenter. Lexington, MA: Lexington Books, D.C. Heath and Co.

Waldron, Ingrid. 1983. "Sex Differences in Illness Incidence, Prognosis, and Mortality: Issues and Evidence." *Social Science and Medicine* 17: 1107–1123.

White, Kerr L. 1973. "Life and Death and Medicine." *Scientific American* 229(September): 22–33.

White, Kerr L., T. Franklin Williams, and Bernard G. Greenberg. 1961. "The Ecology of Medical Care." *New England Journal of Medicine* 265: 885–892.

Wingard, Deborah L. 1984. "The Sex Differential in Morbidity, Mortality, and Lifestyle." Pp. 433–458 in *Annual Review of Public Health,* Volume 5, edited by L. Breslow, J. E. Fielding, and L. B. Lave. Palo Alto, CA: Annual Reviews Inc.

World Health Organization. 1984. *The Uses of Epidemiology in the Study of the Elderly.* Technical Report Series, No. 706. Geneva, Switzerland: Author.

Zola, Irving K. 1973. "Pathways to the Doctor—From Person to Patient." *Social Science and Medicine* 7: 677–689.

2

The Graying of America: Implications of Life Extension for Quality of Life

Charles F. Longino, Jr. and Beth J. Soldo

In this paper we attempt to integrate a qualitative emphasis that follows from biomedical research and service delivery experience with the quantitative insights of demography. We do so in order to broadly assess: (1) the vulnerability of the elderly, (2) the supportive quality of the social and physical environment they occupy, and (3) potential changes in the mix and distribution of markers of vulnerability over time.

Eugene Yates (1985) summed it up. Speaking at the closing session of the National Academy of Science's symposium on social and built environments in December 1985, he said we should stop thinking of young-old and old-old. Chronological age is not so important. The more important categories are independent and dependent, vigorous and frail. No matter how old people are, we want them to stay independent and vigorous for as long a time as possible, and to be dependent and frail for as short a time as possible. The problem is biological, not chronological. If we find solutions to heart disease and cancer, we will extend life chronologically, but until we find answers to many of the forms of dementia that plague the very old, lengthening life only lengthens the down time at the end.

Aging eventually brings a gradual decline in the functioning of almost all biological systems. But more than that, the declines associated with aging are also due to an accumulation of deferred maintenance problems with teeth, feet, joints, the senses, and sleep. Each alone is tolerable, but they interact. None is intolerable alone or causes a great sense of loss, but together they do. In addition to deferred maintenance problems there are the bodily abuses of smoking, drinking, overeating, and abusive lifestyles that are impoverished in the areas of exercise, stress management, and nutrition. The accumulated losses caused by biological aging, deferred maintenance, and abuse blur together in the lay mind and collectively are summed up in one word, "aging."

Progress is being made today in both the health maintenance and lifestyle areas. This progress is extending not only chronological age, but also what Yates calls biological age. In addition, more attention will be given in the future to the design and evaluation of prosthetics to compensate for losses due to normal aging. Inner-ocular lenses, hearing aids, and plastic joints are here today. Others are on their way.

There is also a cohort effect in process. There is the promise of a vigorous, independent old age for an increasing number of Americans in the decades after the turn of the century. The G.I.'s from World War II, who benefited the most from the postwar economic expansion, collectively will have a higher income in retirement, more education, and better health than any generation before them. On the whole, they may be more vigorous, for longer, than the cohort before them. That is the positive side.

The negative side is that while there is progress in life extension and the quality-of-life extension, we will also experience an increase in the number of the dependent, frail persons. This is expected to happen largely because of the rapidly increasing size of the very old segment of the population. The number of persons 85 and older in the United States is increasing at a rate equal to our total population growth during the baby-boom years of the 1950s. A majority of these persons have multiple chronic illnesses, and it is doubtful that the proportion of them with functional dependencies will decline in the near future. This trend will undoubtedly put increasing pressure on society to find better ways of delivering long-term care to the very old. This chapter will not ignore the positive features of our aging society, but it will focus deliberately on the negative ones.

THE SOCIAL CONTEXT OF VULNERABILITY

The growth of the older vulnerable population must be understood in social context. In all societies there are some persons whose needs are met in abundance and others for whom even basic needs are not well met. Vulnerability, therefore, is a variable and comparative concept.

A universal value in natural human communities, within the limits of their resources, is to care for and protect the dependent. The infant and the child receive special attention, for they are its future. The old and the incapacitated are its trust. There is even a general concern for the temporarily dependent, such as the sick and the pregnant, when resource levels are adequate.

This universal human value for the care and protection of dependent people has been implemented by national social legislation as our resources, as a nation state, have grown. When we temporarily reached the limits of the welfare state in the early 1980s, we were called to reassess our values, our resources, and our commitments.

FUNCTIONAL DEPENDENCY

We begin our inquiry by estimating the functional dependencies in the general aged population and by comparing the disabled and nondisabled elderly persons on their choices of living arrangements. Then we will document the functional dependencies of the community-based disabled population and demonstrate how increases in disability affect living arrangements. Finally, we will explore the extent to which the frail elderly of today are also vulnerable financially, socially, and environmentally.

Our point of departure for examining the dimensions of vulnerability among the aged is to consider their health status. A functional assessment of health examines the behavioral consequences of chronic disease morbidity. Deficient functional capacities are viewed as relating directly to the need for assistance, usually from another person, in such basic activities as eating, bathing, and dressing (Katz, 1983). Such functional dependency has both an objective and a subjective component. The need for help may be emphatically denied by one person, while another person with the same physical condition may eagerly assert it. For that reason it is difficult to assess. In addition, the degree or severity of functional dependency can vary substantially from one person to another.

The National Long-Term Care Survey was conducted in 1982. It was sponsored by the Health Care Financing Administration (HCFA) and the Assistant Secretary for Planning and Evaluation, and it was fielded by the Bureau of the Census. It is from this source that our basic data were obtained. Thirty-six thousand persons from HCFA's health insurance file provided the sampling universe, and it was screened for persons 65 years of age and older who were not in institutions and who had limitations in their activities of daily living (ADL) or in instrumental activities of daily living (IADL) that were expected to last for three months or longer. The screening interview qualified 6,393 persons and the personal follow-up interview confirmed the presence of such limitations in 5,580 cases. This sample represents 18.9% of approximately 4.6 million disabled (but noninstitu-tionalized) older persons in the United States.

Estimates of functional dependency, by age and gender, are shown in Table 2-1. Two aspects of functional disability are represented. Limitations in the Activities of Daily Living are broadly accepted by gerontologists as indexing incapacities for self-care. In the 1982 study, restrictions in per-formance of six activities were assessed: eating, toileting, bathing, bed transference, dressing, and inside mobility. Since these activities scale in the order in which they are lost, a simple count of the number of ADL limita-tions is a useful summary index of loss of function. The Instrumental Activities of Daily Living reference the capacity to perform basic activities that do not focus on personal care, such as managing money or making a phone call. To a large extent the IADLs summarize cognitive functioning in that those with a severe disability should still be able to use the phone or manage their own money, if they are not cognitively limited as well (Man-ton and Soldo, 1985b).

TABLE 2-1 Percentage Distribution of Persons Age 65+ Living in the Community with Functional Dependencies, by Age and Gender

| Age and gender | Only IADL limited* | ADL score** | | | Total |
		1–2	3–4	5–6	
65–74	4.5	4.2	1.8	2.1	12.6
Male	4.2	3.4	1.7	2.4	11.7
Female	4.8	4.7	1.9	1.9	13.3
75–84	7.9	9.0	3.6	4.5	25.0
Male	7.1	6.5	2.5	4.6	20.9
Female	8.5	10.3	4.3	4.4	27.6
85+	10.2	17.4	7.8	10.4	45.8
Male	9.9	15.7	7.7	7.5	40.8
Female	10.3	18.2	7.9	11.8	48.2
Total 65+	6.0	6.6	2.8	3.5	18.9
Male	5.4	5.1	2.3	3.3	16.0
Female	6.4	7.7	3.2	3.6	20.9

*Instrumental Activities of Daily Living (IADL): Need assistance with managing money, shopping, light housework, meal preparation, making a phone call, and taking medication (one or more of these).
**The ADL score is the sum of the number of activities of daily living with which respondent requires assistance. These include eating, bed transference, inside mobil-ity, dressing, bathing, and toileting.
SOURCE: The 1982 National Long-Term Care Survey.

The data shown in Table 2-1 indicate that even though rates of functional dependency increase with age and are typically higher for females than for males, functional loss is not an inevitable consequence of aging. Even at age 85 and older, over half of all those who remain in the community have no measurable loss in basic activities. Related analyses of these same data indicate that among the noninstitutionalized elderly, loss of function among those 65–74 years of age is associated with life-threatening diseases, such as malignant neoplasms, but in advanced old age, 75 or older, disability is usually related to the chronic degenerative diseases, such as senility, arteriosclerosis, or cerebrovascular accidents (Soldo & Manton, 1985c).

Current rates of functional disability among those 85 or older (coupled with unprecedented, and largely unanticipated, improvements in life expectancy at age 65 and 85) are often interpreted as implying that there will be dramatic increases in the numbers of frail elderly persons in the United States in the years ahead (National Center for Health Statistics, 1984; New York State Office for the Aging, 1983; Rice & Feldman, 1983; Soldo & Manton, 1985a, b, c). Both the existence and magnitude of morbidity–mortality linkages have been the subject of recent and intense debate. However, we believe it is reasonable to assume that those same factors that have produced increases in old-age life expectancy have also modified the disease and disability profile of the elderly (Feldman, 1982; Fries, 1980, 1983; Gruenberg, 1977; Manton, 1982; Manton & Soldo, 1985a, b; Verbrugge, 1984; Walford, 1983). This is no mere academic debate. As illustration of this point, consider Figures 2-1 and 2-2, reprinted from Manton and Soldo (1985a). The figures show, for males and females respectively, the projected growth in the absolute number of the frail elderly, aged 85 and over, under alternative assumptions.

The baseline projections assume that there will be no improvements in rates of disability while there will be modest gains in old-age life expectancy. In this analysis, current age–sex specific rates of disability, by type, were superimposed on the age–sex structure implied by Social Security Administration projections (Social Security Administration, 1981). These baseline projections can be compared with those prepared under the assumptions that age–sex-specific disability rates will be reduced proportionate to projected mortality declines. Because of the simple demographic imperative of increasingly larger cohorts of older ages, the number of frail elderly persons aged 85 and over increases under either scenario. But by allowing for the interdependence of morbidity, disability, and mortality there will be a 27% reduction for males and a 39% reduction for females in disability rates by 2040. Assuming statistical interdependence, there would be approximately 1.4 million fewer disabled persons 85 years old and older in 2040 than if rates of disability are assumed to be independent of mortality declines. These alternative scenarios probably represent best- and worst-case projections in that additional years of life expectancy are unlikely to translate

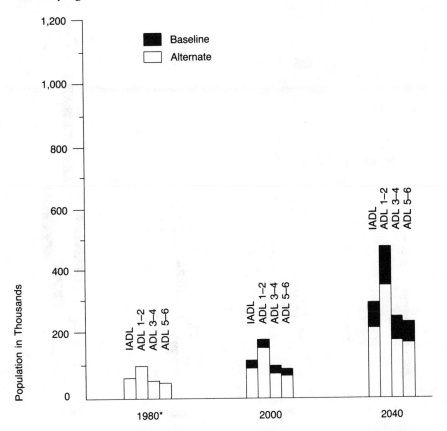

FIGURE 2-1 *Baseline and alternate projections for males aged 85+ in years 1980, 2000, 2040 (population in thousands).*

*Baseline and alternate figures for 1980 are the same.
Source: From K. Manton and B. Soldo. 1985. "Dynamics of health changes in the oldest old: new perspectives and evidence." *Milbank Memorial Fund Quarterly/Health and Society* 63: 206–285. Used by permission.

directly into additional disability-free years of life (Wilkins & Adams, 1983). Thus the two projections may be thought of as indicating the upper and lower bounds on the number of the community-based disabled elderly persons in the future. These two projections also suggest the potential role of health care policy in shaping the disability profile of the elderly in the future. Changes in the health status of the elderly are caused by, and in turn cause, major shifts in both the composition of the U.S. population as a whole and in the needs profile of the older ages. But the health care requirements of the aged population in the long run also respond to the amount of resources allocated to disease prevention and treatment (Manton & Soldo, 1985a).

In the short run, the course of disability for individuals and the aggregate

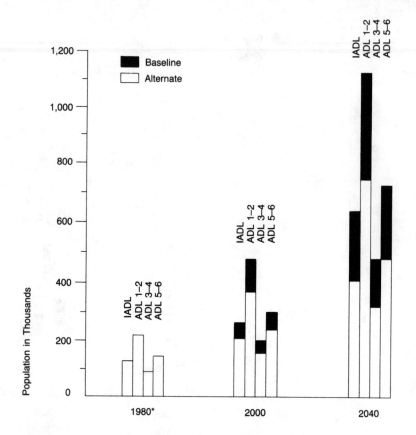

FIGURE 2-2 *Baseline and alternate projections for females aged 85+ in years 1980, 2000, 2040 (population in thousands).*

*Baseline and alternate figures for 1980 are the same.
Source: From K. Manton and B. Soldo. 1985. "Dynamics of health changes in the oldest old: new perspectives and evidence." *Milbank Memorial Fund Quarterly/Health and Society* 63: 206–285. Used by permission.

volume of demand on the public sector depends, in part, on the "natural" or informal resources available to the disabled elderly person (Litwak, 1985). These are the qualitative aspects of the aging American population.

The Andrus Foundation of the American Association of Retired Persons funded the Center for Social Research in Aging at the University of Miami to create state profiles of the population over 75 years of age (Longino, 1986a). That population was divided into two age categories, 75–84 and 85 and above. The profiles were derived from the 1980 census microdata files that contained a 1-in-20 sample of all individual census records. The microdata sample is the only data set that can provide 100% population estimates of the population characteristics of the disabled and nondisabled for the nation.

There is only one item on the 1980 census that could measure functional disability among the elderly. The item asks if the person has had a physical or mental or other health condition that has lasted for six months or longer that would prevent him or her from using buses, trains, subways, or other forms of public transportation. It is hardly an ideal question, since public transportation is not equally accessible to everyone. This item was included on the 1980 census despite the fact that an analysis of the 1976 National Content Test showed that the indexes of inconsistency for responses to the transportation disability question were in the moderate to high range. The measure of disability used here is relatively "soft" compared to other census items. It can only be taken as a surrogate measure of functional disability. Nonetheless, using this measure, a table was prepared that compares persons in the two advanced age categories who do, and who do not, have a public transportation disability.

The census data are displayed in Table 2-2. We see that 23.9% of the 75–84 age group recorded a long-standing health problem that renders them functionally disabled. As shown in Table 2-1, the National Long-Term Care (NLTC) Survey had generated a disability estimate of 25.0% in this age category for the noninstitutionalized population. Among those 85 years and older, 47.9% registered a public transportation functional disability in the 1980 census. We find in Table 2-1 that 45.8 percent of noninstitutionalized persons in this category had any serious functional disabilities. The census imposes a health condition of six months, which is double the duration of the three-month limitation used in the Long-Term Care Survey. Also, public transportation disability is a more severe condition than the Instrumental Activities of Daily Living measures that are included in Table 2-1. So, even though the census disability measure is limited to only one item, it is the more stringent of the two. The NLTC Survey screens out the more severely disabled persons from the community-based, noninstitutionalized population. The census data are for the entire population in these age categories, including those in institutions. The proportions of disabled persons in the two data sets are not as comparable in proportion as they at first seemed.

Using the census microdata, it is possible to compare marital status and living arrangements of the disabled and the nondisabled, a task that cannot be accomplished with the NLTC Survey. The proportions in Table 2-2 indicate that the disabled are more likely to be widowed, or never married, than the nondisabled in both age categories. While widowhood increases with age, that factor barely diminishes the difference. Perhaps disability is spurred by widowhood. The disabled are also less likely than the nondisabled to be living alone in both age categories, but the difference widens with advancing years. The disabled are increasingly less able to maintain the luxury of this living arrangement. Finally, while even the very old disabled

TABLE 2-2 Percentage Distribution of the 1980 Relational Characteristics of Nondisabled and Disabled Persons Age 75–84 and 85+ in the United States

| Relational characteristics | Age categories | | | |
| | Age 75–84 | | Age 85+ | |
	Nondisabled	Disabled	Nondisabled	Disabled
Total number	5,870,340	1,848,540	1,147,020	1,050,100
Disabled*		23.9		47.9
Marital status				
Married	45.0	31.1	26.0	14.9
Widowed	45.8	57.5	65.4	75.1
Never married	6.1	7.8	6.6	7.9
Living arrangements:				
Householders or spouses	86.7	59.3	71.0	36.1
Parent of house-holder	7.0	11.3	16.0	16.8
Sibling of house-holder	2.0	2.0	1.8	1.3
Other relative of householder	.9	1.4	2.2	2.0
Not related to householder	1.1	1.2	1.3	1.2
In institution	2.3	24.8	7.6	42.7
In home for the aged**	1.6	22.3	6.2	39.6
Live alone***	36.9	27.0	38.9	19.6

*A health condition for six months or longer that would prevent the person from using public transportation.
**Homes for the aged are primarily nursing homes.
***Outside of institutions.
SOURCE: A.A.R.P. Older Americans Project, based on 1980 Census Microdata Files.

persons do not live mainly in institutions, over a third of them do (43%). All but about 3% of these are in nursing homes and other health-care-related homes for the aged. Another fifth live dependently in the homes of children, siblings, and other relatives. Almost none live with nonrelatives (1.2%). Finally, over a third continue to live independently in their own residence, despite their 85+ years and their functional disabilities. The nondisabled are actually as likely to be living with a child as age advances.

As we turn back to the National Long-Term Care Survey, it is important to keep a perspective that compares the disabled elderly with age-peers who are not disabled. Three-quarters of those persons between the ages of 75 and 84 and half of those over 85 are not so disabled as to be unable to negotiate public transportation. In the younger category, a majority of both the nondisabled and the disabled are living independently in their own homes. Even in the older category, over a third of the disabled are still living independently; and a fifth still manage to live alone. Independent residence, it seems, is the lifestyle of choice. Even the great advantage of living with children for the very old and functionally disabled does not make it a more attractive alternative than living alone. Finally, the drop in independent residence (householders or spouses) in both age groups is offset almost entirely by increases in institutional residence.

DISABILITY AND OTHER MARKERS OF VULNERNABILITY

We will now focus on the social and physical environments of disabled persons living in the community and seek to determine from the NLTC Survey the extent to which environment confounds or ameliorates disability among the elderly. As disability increases, the social world of the elderly often contracts. For the most disabled, their social world may be fully defined by the housing space they occupy. Cross-sectional data offer persuasive, but not definitive, evidence of the changing usefulness the frail elderly assign to the types of living arrangements. The presence of a person who is a "caring unit" within the household, for example, often allows the functionally impaired older person to continue living in the community (Branch & Jette, 1982; Brody, Poulshock, & Masciocchi, 1978; Weissert & Scanlon, 1982).

Within the community population of the frail elderly, a natural sorting process also appears to operate, such that the disabled find themselves in living arrangements consistent with the degree of support they need from their immediate environment (Lawton, 1981). Such a gradient of need across types of living arrangements is evident in the data presented in Table 2-3. Clearly the luxury of living alone is reserved for those who can meet the physical demands of independence (Tissue & McCoy, 1981).

Very few of the severely disabled elderly (i.e., those whose functional self-care capacities are limited in five or six areas) live alone. Different types of shared living arrangements, however, vary in their supportive quality. This is indicated by the percentage distribution of unmet IADL and ADL dependencies shown in Table 2-4.

In this analysis, unmet care needs were defined as a situation in which an older person indicated that he needed, but did not receive, assistance with at least one of the IADL or ADL items. Defined in this way, the prevalence of unmet care needs is not substantial, perhaps reflecting underreporting due to the long-standing accommodations many of the frail elderly make to the gradual loss of capacity. Nonetheless, approximately 364,000 older persons in the community with long-term care needs report at least one neglected aspect of supportive or personal care.

TABLE 2-3 Percentage Distribution of Disability Among Persons Age 65+ Living in the Community with Functional Dependencies, by Type of Living Arrangements

Type of living arrangement	Only IADL limited	ADL score			Total*
		1–2	3–4	5–6	
Living alone	34.4	44.5	14.7	6.4	100.0 (1434)
Living with spouse**	32.1	30.8	15.7	21.4	100.0 (1918)
Living with other relatives***	28.5	30.6	14.1	26.7	100.0 (1175)
Living with nonrelatives	22.9	34.5	13.6	29.0	100.0 (121)
Total	31.7 (1472)	35.1 (1613)	14.9 (694)	18.3 (851)	100.0 (4648)

*The base counts in parentheses are weighted.
**Those living with a spouse include persons who live only with their spouse and also those who live with both their spouse and others.
***Those who live with children and other relatives (not with a spouse) and those who live both with relatives and nonrelatives.
SOURCE: The 1982 National Long-Term Care Survey.

While there are many unmet needs, of most interest to the present discussion are the systematic differentials in their prevalence across types of shared households. The likelihood of unmet care needs varies inversely with the closeness of the bond that relates the disabled elder to other members of his or her household. Those who live with spouses are the least likely to report areas of unmet need; those living with nonrelatives are the most likely. Related analyses also have shown that those who live with nonrelatives, and particularly those whose care needs are not fully satisfied, are the most likely to be on a waiting list for nursing home admission (Soldo & Manton, 1985c).

The evidence presented so far in our discussion suggests that the vulnerability of the frail elderly is primarily a reflection of their morbidity and disability and not of inadequate social environments. However, this conclusion leaves unanswered the more general quality-of-life question. Are persons with more severe disabilities more likely to complain about the resources that are available to them? Do they have a lower quality of life,

TABLE 2-4 Percentage Distribution of Unmet Functional Need Among Persons Age 65+ Living in the Community with Functional Dependencies, by Type of Living Arrangements

Type of living arrangement	Unmet functional dependencies			
	No unmet needs	Unmet IADL needs only*	Unmet ADL needs**	Total***
Living alone	86.8	9.8	3.4	100.0 (1434)
Living with spouse****	95.5	3.4	1.1	100.0 (1918)
Living with other relatives*****	93.4	4.1	2.5	100.0 (1175)
Living with nonrelatives	91.6	5.5	2.9	100.0 (121)
Total	92.2	5.6	2.2	100.0 (4648)

*Respondents reporting that they need but do not receive help with doing instrumental activities of daily living (see note on Table 2-2).
**Respondents reporting that they need but do not receive help with activities of daily living (see note on Table 2-2).
***The base counts in parentheses are weighted.
****Those living with a spouse include persons who live only with their spouse and also those who live with both their spouse and others.
*****Those who live with children and other relatives (not with a spouse) and those who live with both relatives and nonrelatives.
SOURCE: The 1982 National Long-Term Care Survey.

depending upon the level of their disability or the type of living arrangement they have? Apart from measurement problems, the concept of vulnerability as discussed above directs attention to additional aspects of the social and physical world of the disabled. To consider this, it is necessary to examine evidence that relates disability to evaluations of the frail older person in conjunction with multiple aspects of the environment that he or she occupies. Such data are offered in Table 2-5.

Here we see a distribution of the number of quality-of-life deficiencies by age and disability level. The quality-of-life deficiency index shown in this table was derived by summing deficiencies over five aspects of the social, economic, and housing environment. The cutting point below which each area is considered deficient is defined as:

TABLE 2-5 Percentage Distribution of Number of Quality-of-Life
Deficiencies Among Persons Age 65+ Living in the Community with
Functional Dependencies, by Age and Level of Disability

Age and disability level	Number of quality of life deficiencies*					Total
	0	1	2	3	4+	
Age 65–74						
IADL only	16.6	31.4	33.1	15.1	3.8	100.0
ADL 1–2	11.8	30.6	30.7	20.9	6.1	100.0
ADL 3–4	11.1	28.6	34.1	19.1	7.1	100.0
ADL 5–6	9.8	28.1	33.7	23.2	5.3	100.0
Total	13.1	30.2	32.6	18.9	5.3	100.0 (1948)
Age 75–84						
IADL only	19.0	28.7	34.0	15.6	2.8	100.0
ADL 1–2	12.2	31.6	32.8	18.1	5.4	100.0
ADL 3–4	11.0	27.6	38.1	16.5	6.9	100.0
ADL 5–6	9.1	30.0	32.6	20.3	5.0	100.0
Total	13.6	30.3	33.9	17.5	4.7	100.0 (1821)
Age 85+						
IADL only	11.6	32.3	38.3	14.1	3.7	100.0
ADL 1–2	11.7	34.3	30.4	17.1	6.6	100.0
ADL 3–4	11.8	30.3	31.3	23.1	3.5	100.0
ADL 5–6	10.2	30.3	31.5	24.4	3.6	100.0
Total	11.3	32.3	32.6	19.1	4.7	100.0 (879)
Age 65+						
IADL only	16.9	30.4	34.2	15.2	3.4	100.0
ADL 1–2	11.9	31.8	31.5	19.0	5.9	100.0
ADL 3–4	11.2	28.6	35.0	19.0	6.3	100.0
ADL 5–6	9.6	30.5	32.8	22.4	4.8	100.0
Total	13.0	30.6	33.1	18.4	4.9	100.0 (4649)

*Additive summary index indicating deficiencies in five areas:
Income—personal income was less than 25th percentile of all respondents.
Services—formal services are needed but not received for at least one IADL or
    ADL need.
Social—contact is less frequent than desired or nonexistent with friend or relative.
Housing—special modifications of housing, such as the installation of ramps,
    grab bars, raised toilet, hand rails, elevator, or stair lift, are needed.
Neighborhood—food/drug stores perceived as inconvenient, crime perceived as a
    serious problem, or global neighborhood dissatisfaction.
SOURCE: The 1982 National Long-Term Care Survey.

Income: Annual personal income is less than the 25th percentile.
Services: At least one IADL or ADL care need is neglected in the
                     current caregiving configuration.
Social: Contact is not maintained with family or friends
                     through personal visits or telephone calls or contact is
                     less than desired.
Housing: Perceived, but unmet, need for special housing mod-
                     ifications such as installations of ramps, grab bars,
                     raised toilets, hand rails, elevator, or stair lift.
Neighborhood: Global dissatisfaction with neighborhood or perceived
                     problems with local crime or inconvenient location of
                     food or drug stores.

Defining "vulnerability" multidimensionally, nearly 90% of the frail elderly are not simply disabled but are also socially, economically, or environmentally impoverished. That is, over a tenth of the disabled elderly have no complaints about their quality of life, as measured by the multi-dimensional deficiency index. Nearly two-thirds are deficient in at least two of the five domains, and slightly more than one-fifth have problems in three or more areas. These data suggest that for a sizable number of the frail elderly, natural or informal resources have not fused into an environment that meets all of their real and perceived needs. This is true regardless of the level of their disability or of the age of the disabled persons in the community. The number of quality-of-life deficiencies varies only slightly with either age or disability. While any across-time interpretation, particularly in the absence of a nonfrail comparison group, is problematic, the above findings are consistent with the interpretation that environmental deficiencies pre-date frailty. To the extent that such environmental problems are markers of risk for the onset of rapid progression of chronic morbidity, improving the quality of the social and economic environments in which aging occurs not only may improve quality of life for those who are already frail, but also may slow rates of transition from the healthy to the disabled state.

In an era of fiscal austerity, the targeting of limited public resources emerges as an important policy issue. The data presented in Table 2-5, however, provide little guidance for identifying the age or disability groups that would most benefit from programmatic efforts to enhance environmental quality. In contrast, the distribution of the quality-of-life deficiency index by living arrangements, shown in Table 2-6, is useful for identifying the most vulnerable segment within the older, frail population.

Actually, about the same proportion of functionally disabled older persons are found at each quality-of-life level, regardless of their living arrangements. However, there are some minor differences that may be worth

TABLE 2-6 Percentage Distribution of Number of Quality-of-Life
Deficiencies Among Persons Age 65+ Living in the Community with
Functional Dependencies, by Type of Living Arrangements

Type of living arrangements	Number of quality-of-life deficiencies*					Total**
	0	1	2	3	4+	
Living alone	12.1	29.3	34.0	18.7	5.9	100.0 (1434)
Living with spouse ***	15.4	32.5	32.3	16.3	3.5	100.0 (1918)
Living with other relatives****	10.3	28.6	33.9	21.4	5.9	100.0 (1175)
Living with nonrelatives	9.5	30.6	33.1	18.4	4.9	100.0 (121)
Total	13.0	30.6	33.1	18.4	4.9	100.0 (4648)

*See note on Table 2-5.
**Weighted base numbers shown in thousands in parentheses.
***Those living with a spouse include persons who live only with their spouse and also those who live with both their spouse and others.
****Those who live with children and other relatives (not with a spouse) and those who live with both relatives and nonrelatives.
SOURCE: The 1982 National Long-term Care Survey.

pointing out. Disabled elderly persons who live with relatives or nonrelatives (rather than independently with a spouse, or alone) have the greatest chance of indicating at least one quality-of-life deficiency. These individuals are also the most likely to have multiple deficiencies in their immediate environment. Approximately 27% of those who live with relatives and 25% of those living with nonrelatives have three or more environmental deficiencies. Since each of these arrangements has the built-in potential for social interaction, multiple deficiencies indicate economic and housing/ neighborhood inadequacies—areas of need most amenable to program intervention. Since residing with relatives and nonrelatives is a choice taken by a minority of the elderly, these data also suggest that even among the frail elderly, living with others may be, in part, motivated by economic reasons (Soldo, Sharma, & Campbell, 1984).

Additional insights into the environmental quality associated with different types of living arrangements are offered in Table 2-7. While approximately one-third of all frail elderly persons live in households with housing

TABLE 2-7 Percentage Distribution of Persons Age 65+ Living in the Community with Functional Dependencies Who Have Adapted Their Housing, by Type of Living Arrangements

Type of living arrangement	Only IADL limited	ADL score			Total**
		1–2	3–4	5–6	
Living alone	20.2	40.4	58.5	56.4	37.1 (1434)
Living with spouse***	12.1	29.3	39.2	43.1	28.3 (1918)
Living with other relatives****	10.3	26.1	37.3	32.6	24.9 (1175)
Living with nonrelatives	13.8	49.3	62.5	38.3	34.1 (121)
Total	14.4 (1472)	33.0 (1631)	45.2 (694)	40.4 (851)	30.3 (4648)

*Installation of ramps, stair lift, elevator, grab bars, handrails, raised toilet, push bars or doors, or widening of doors or hallways.
**The base counts in parentheses are weighted.
***Those living with a spouse include persons who live only with their spouse and also those who live with both their spouse and others.
****Those who live with children and other relatives (not with a spouse) and those who live both with relatives and nonrelatives.
SOURCE: The 1982 National Long-Term Care Survey.

adaptations, the incidence of such modifications is greatest for those living alone, particularly those at high levels of disability. Over half of the elderly who live alone, and are limited in three or more activities of daily living, have made housing modifications. Undoubtedly, such adaptations in the home are essential for avoiding institutionalization in the absence of a live-in care provider.

The disabled elderly who live with others may trade off personal assistance for environmental compensation. For nearly half of the extremely disabled who live with spouses, however, housing modifications would appear to supplement rather than to replace care in the home. In contrast, the very frail elderly who live with other relatives are less likely to be living in homes where environmental features reduce the demands and burdens of their care. For those living with persons other than spouses, the National Long-Term Care Survey is not sufficiently detailed to determine if this pattern reflects financial constraints operating in multigenerational house-holds or a less durable personal commitment by caregivers to home care (Hess & Soldo, 1985). Nonetheless, these data suggest that modifications to the home may be an important strategy for reducing the burdens of care, particularly in dwelling units where a relative is the primary provider of care. Further research is required to determine if such adaptive housing modifications are generally cost-effective for extending the commitment of relatives to care for the elderly and thereby to delay nursing home admissions. The effectiveness of such environmental strategies would most likely be greatest in situations where personal care needs were not complicated by cognitive impairment.

The evidence presented in our examination of disability and other markers of vulnerability has two significant implications. First, in the vast majority of cases, the needs of the elderly are not discrete; that is, they tend to cluster. Disability often is linked with multiple deficiencies in the social and economic resource base of the frail elderly. Thus, the preceding analysis provides empirical support for Lawton's (1978) argument that the number of elderly persons who are both truly independent of any help whatsoever and very frail is small indeed. If viewed longitudinally, the number of persons whose total resources across all dimensions are sufficient to sustain them over a long lifetime would be even smaller.

While this finding recommends that we adopt a multidimensional concept of vulnerability in our discussions, it also indicates that effective planning and program development must also focus on varying sets of needs. Integrated service delivery systems, however, are much more the exception than the rule. In part, this is because the federal committee system within Congress and the departmental structure within the executive branch are not organized to foster integrated program development, planning, or implementation. As a result, eligibility standards are not uniform, assessments of need are seldom coordinated, and orchestrating the necessary service bundles usually falls to the older person or her family.

Second, the preceding analysis also demonstrates the heterogeneity of the older population. While differences by age surely are of no surprise to gerontologists, diversity *within* levels of disability has only recently come to be more fully appreciated (Manton & Soldo, 1985a). Within the population who require long-term care, individuals exist at all levels of disability whose care needs are increased by inadequacies in numerous other aspects of their social and physical environments. Contrasts between these populations in the community and those in the nursing home have demonstrated significant differences between the two groups in terms of social support networks and prior living arrangements (see, for example, Weissert & Scanlon, 1982). Nonetheless, such findings cannot be allowed to overshadow the need for incorporating notions of heterogeneity into national planning efforts for the noninstitutionalized but frail elderly.

Differences within and among cohorts are important sources of such heterogeneity. Heterogeneity with respect to currently observed levels of disability reflects, in part, differences in underlying risk factors within cohorts. Such factors include genetically determined susceptibility to disease, occupational exposure, smoking history, and the effects of education and socioeconomic status accumulated over a lifetime. All of these factors may also differ between older and younger cohorts. While population data do not directly measure these factors, their effects are evident in age-specific changes in both total and cause-specific mortality (Keyfitz & Littman, 1979; Manton & Stallart, 1984; Vaupal, Manton, & Stallard, 1979). This effect is the product of the simple mechanism of selection. Failure to adjust for such factors can lead to overestimates of morbidity and mortality at advanced ages. Overestimating morbidity and mortality would produce errors in estimations of the demand for medical care and personal care services. Thus, careful attention must be paid to the effects of cohort risk heterogeneity and systematic selection by mortality in forecasting and planning for the needs of the elderly.

Differences between cohorts, and the heterogeneity to which these differences give rise, must also be factored into national planning efforts, particularly with respect to the prevalence of disease and associated health care needs. There are, for example, significant differences across cohorts in the prevalence of various chronic diseases (e.g., cardiovascular disease) (Patrick, Palesch, Feinleib, & Brody, 1982). Such differences suggest that, apart from changes in the volume of health and personal care services required in the future, there will also be significant differences in the mix of care services required by the population at any point in time. Forecasts of need based only on period data will not accurately reflect health-status changes driven by cohort differences.

RESPONSES TO DEPENDENCY

Just as there are differences in the types and clusters of the needs of the elderly at any single point in time, there is also considerable variability in the style and mix of responses made to their dependency. In this section we consider two generic strategies for accommodating dependency: service responses and environmental responses. We make this distinction for ease of discussion only. In practice, the two approaches are not mutually exclusive. Community programs, for example, may link relocation to upgraded housing units with increased access to supportive services (Lawton, 1980a). Regardless of how compensation strategies are structured, however, the implicit common denominator is the understanding of behavior within a framework of a person interacting with an environment (Lawton, 1980b; Nahemow & Lawton, 1973). In other words, the degree of a person's functional capacity is seen as being jointly determined by characteristics of the individual and of the multidimensional social and physical world that he or she occupies.

Although it would be desirable to parallel our discussion of multi-dimensional vulnerability with an examination of response clusters, existing data bases provide little opportunity for such analyses. Hence, in the following discussion we confine our attention to responses to personal care dependencies. We exclude medical care services, since these are assumed to be provided by a health care worker, usually in a health care facility.

Service Responses

Service responses to frailty can be arrayed across at least two continua. One continuum is defined in terms of the relationship of the caregiver to the frail older person. This continuum is anchored at one end by exclusive reliance on an informal support network of family and friends and on the other by receipt of formally organized services (Litwak, 1985). The second continuum is defined in terms of frequency and regularity of the service received. In general, the elderly who require only periodic assistance, such as in grocery shopping, rely on family members and friends, while those whose needs are complex and unrelenting are likely to depend on a mix of formal and informal services in the community (Longino, 1986b; Soldo, 1986).

Data on community care patterns are shown in Table 2-8. In over 90% of these cases the frail elderly receive nonmedical care service from their informal support network. In three-quarters of these cases the family is the sole provider. Only 7.5% of the frail elderly rely exclusively on formal, community services. The data shown in this table also indicate that the boundaries of the informal support network extend beyond the households of the frail elderly—nearly one-third of the frail elderly receive assistance from friends and relatives with whom they do not live. Thus the social world of the disabled often extends, albeit indirectly, outside the immediate household.

It is clear that, under current health care financing arrangements, the informal support network provides the bulk of personal care assistance. Related research testifies to the extent of family involvement (Manton & Soldo, 1985b) and the extent to which informal caregiving reduces the demand for formal care services (Soldo, 1986). Type of living arrangement is important for anticipating the formal service needs of older populations. At any level of need, the probability of formal service is lowest for the frail elderly who live either with spouses, children, or other relatives (Soldo, 1986).

**TABLE 2-8 Sources of Nonmedical Care Assistance for Persons Age 65+
Living in the Community with Functional Limitations in 1979**

Source of assistance	Percentage distributions
No assistance received	3.4
Informal care providers only:	76.5
Relatives within the same household only	(44.2)
Relatives/friends outside the household only	(19.1)
Relatives/friends in and outside the household	(13.2)
Formal care providers only	7.5
Formal and informal care providers	12.6
Total	100.0
	(53495)

SOURCE: Tabulations from the 1979 Health Interview Survey, Home Care Supplement, prepared by the Center for Population Research for DHHS, Office of the Assistant Secretary for Planning and Evaluation, Contract #HHS-100-80-0158.

These findings, in conjunction with the data presented in Table 2-6, suggest that the volume of demand for publicly financed services will be greatly influenced by the living arrangements of the disabled elderly. In anticipating service demand, a number of factors must be considered. Among these are changes in intergenerational attitudes, increasing incidence of divorce, and trends in male–female differences in old-age mortality. Allowing only for changes in the age structure, however, Glick (1979) has projected continued increases in the number of elderly persons, particularly older females, living alone. His projections indicate that the demand for community-based long-term care may far outpace the growth of even the disabled portion of the elderly population. When caregivers are in the same household with the disabled person, it is easier for them to provide assistance than when they live elsewhere. In addition, incomes are larger when combined in a larger, multigeneration household than when persons live alone. Due to these social and economic considerations, and barring changes in service delivery approaches, Glick's projections also suggest that the proportions of the elderly with unmet care needs and those with multiple social and environmental deficiencies may increase over time.

To this point in the discussion we have merely speculated on how an older age structure might combine with differing patterns of family structure and living arrangements to effect changes in aggregate service demand. To make these implications more concrete, consider the baseline projections of long-term service demand, by source of assistance, shown in Table 2-9. Assuming constant rates of nursing home use, institutional care will grow faster than any other long-term-care alternative. In fact, it will increase by 170% over the next 60 years. Increasingly, women are expected to outlive men during this period. Because of this assumed widening, the slowest-growing component will be spouse-provided services. Greater increases are projected for care services by offspring, since it is children that are the major care providers of assistance for widows. But perhaps the most dramatic implication of these data is the increase in the sheer volume of long-term care services required by our aging population. In 1985, society was called on to produce 6.9 million daily units of long-term care. By 2040, this demand may increase to 19.8 million daily units of care (Manton & Liu, 1984).

In addition to strengthening arguments for integrated long-range planning, these data also highlight the difficult policy choices involved in accommodating a rapidly growing population. Current long-term care policy directives are oriented toward reducing rates of nursing home admissions in the name of cost containment. Whether this proves to be a cost-effective strategy remains to be seen (Weissert, 1981), but this potential shift in policy is already raising questions concerning the limits of our collective and filial responsibility to the dependent elderly (Soldo, Pellegrino, & Howell, 1985). As the pace of population aging quickens, such value-based dilemmas will undoubtedly assume greater urgency.

Environmental Responses

Environmental responses to dependency are seldom independent of service responses. The two overlap nearly completely in the extreme response of institutionalization. But our concern is with the more commonplace re-

TABLE 2-9 Projections of Daily Volume of Long-Term Care Assistance by Source of Assistance (In Thousands)

	Source of long-term care assistance				
Year	Institution*	Spouse**	Offspring**	Other [relative]**	Nonrelative**
1980	1,187	1,442	1,436	1,213	655
1985	1,411	1,612	1,701	1.414	771
1990	1,623	1,801	1,950	1,610	880
1995	1,861	1,953	2,232	1,814	1,003
2000	2,081	2,049	2,484	1,989	1,110
2020	2,805	2,976	3,392	2,728	1,530
2040	4,354	3,900	5,172	4,028	2,298

*These are projections of full days of care in an institution.
**These are projections of the number of episodes of caregiving on a given day.
SOURCE: Preliminary data from the 1982 National Long-Term Care Survey, 1977 National Nursing Home Survey, and Social Security Administration Projections. Reported in K. Manton and K. Liu (1984).

sponses that occur in the community. We have already noted the tendency of the disabled elderly to alter their physical environments to accommodate their limitations. In households where care is provided for an elderly person, less dramatic and permanent changes are often made, as when the "sick" room is relocated to the dining room for the convenience of both the person providing and the person receiving care (Noelker, 1982).

But changes in structure or organization of dwelling units do not encompass the vast array of environmental responses to dependency. Often the environment of disability changes involuntarily, as when an older person continues to maintain a longstanding and familiar residence even as the neighborhood deteriorates. But in this section we focus more narrowly on the ways in which disability is accommodated by moving to a new house and neighborhood.

Our knowledge of the prosthetic effect of the immediate housing environment for the frail elderly is derived primarily from studies of special populations. These include persons who relocate to age-concentrated neighborhoods, service-saturated demonstration projects, or various kinds of age-segregated planned living environments. Such individuals are self-selected and hardly representative of the vast majority of older adults who age in place or move from one private dwelling to another. Nonetheless, prior research has demonstrated positive effects on global or subjective indicators of well-being resulting from improved living environments. For this reason we will examine the process by which supportive environments are sought out in the face of age-related changes in personal needs.

When the Social Security Administration initially funded the Comparative Study of Midwestern Retirement Communities a decade ago, its focal interest was a comparative evaluation of the costs and benefits of living in age-focused housing (Longino, 1986b; Peterson, Longino, & Phelps, 1979). Settings were chosen to represent a range of niches or localized living environments whose costs, degrees of service assistance, and natural settings differed considerably. Standardization procedures involved a system of shadow sampling (Longino, McClelland & Peterson, 1981) so that the sample from each retirement community could be compared with a matched control sample of persons from the general population. In this way, self-selection, at least on background variables, was controlled, while the issue of relative benefits was examined. It was possible to assess environmental effects with some confidence by comparing the quality of life of residents in one retirement community with people similar to themselves in the general population.

The study concluded that the factors motivating a change of housing environments are predictably related to the likely outcome of the move. The situation of most persons facing progressive disability is one of resource deficits in the face of rising support needs. This serves as a powerful triggering mechanism in the choice of housing in old age. Both subsidized public housing and nonsubsidized planned communities are service-enriched living environments designed with the needs of older residents in mind. The people who move to these places tend to be motivated by the fact that their previous housing and community environment no longer met their changing needs. In their reasons for moving they tend to emphasize those very areas of support that are the strengths of the planned community. The people who are attracted to such communities tend to have characteristics that imply greater need and vulnerability. Such persons, on the whole, are older, more often widowed, and feel less healthy than the retired people who move to unplanned, *de facto,* retirement communities like those in the Ozarks. In addition, those who move to subsidized retirement housing also tend to be much poorer. The fit between living environment and individual needs would seem, then, to be reasonably good in such settings. Persons with a greater need for support with instrumental activities of daily living tend to be attracted to communities built to meet those needs, and support indeed seems to flow from within the community to the persons who move there (Longino & Lipman, 1981, 1983).

Although most home care programs emphasize service delivery, mod-ifications of dwellings in which care is provided also may be effective in preventing or postponing institutional placements. Because housing seems to affect the style, intensity, durability, and tolerability of caregiving, it is fair to conclude that in this context, housing characteristics function as important intermediate variables. The size, condition, and location of the households involved all indirectly affect the degree of fit between the needs of older adults and the compensating social resources that are available.

FUTURE CONSIDERATIONS

In this chapter we have presented a wide array of data relating disability among the elderly to indicators of vulnerability in other areas and, finally, to a range of both service and environmental adaptations and options. Despite the data assembled here, it is clear that our current, fragmented approach to data collection is insufficient to examine all of the quantitative and qualitative dimensions of population aging. Hence, many of our com-ments have been speculative, drawing particular attention to the gaps in our knowledge concerning the functioning of different types of people in natural environments (Parr, 1980).

The sheer magnitude of change in the number of the frail elderly is impressive, even under the most optimistic scenarios. It is clear that we as a society cannot afford to dismiss out of hand any strategies of responding to this increased volume of demand that have the potential to be both cost-effective and efficient. This includes leveraging the aspects of both dwelling and social environments to enhance functional capacity.

We have seen in the past decade a widespread community awareness of the needs of handicapped persons. This awareness derives from and perhaps contributes to the parking and building regulations that help to eliminate barriers to the activities of the handicapped, thereby increasing their independence and productivity. We have seen also the adaptation of the community environment to bike riders during the national energy crisis in the 1970s. Curb cuts are now common in the business districts of most American cities. Sensitivity to the disabilities that are common in the oldest segment of the population may develop from this awareness base. Thus the possibility of adapting and thereby humanizing our physical environment for the disabled and different is no longer a novel idea.

The private sector is already vigorously exploring the marketability of planned housing for the marginally disabled elderly. This trend is likely to continue and even accelerate so long as the number of financially adequate older persons grows. There are no indications that future cohorts of the elderly will be less able than the present cohort to pay for adapted housing and planned housing. In fact, the new cohort of retirees in the late 1980s are the most advantaged in our history, having benefited most directly from the post–World War II economic expansion. Their parents are presently in the age group where decline in functional capacity is the most concentrated. As the World War II veterans themselves age into their 70s, the Veterans Administration will experience a crisis of long-term care provision. The private sector will then find that its long-term care market has reached a critical mass where competition will begin to bring down costs.

The members of this cohort who are unable to pay fully for their environmental, service, and health care needs will also expand. This is the population segment that Smeeding (1984) calls the " 'tweeners." They are neither the poor, who are caught in the government's welfare safety net, nor the affluent, who can pay for most of the solutions to their needs. It is this expansion of the " 'tweeners" that will produce the crisis that is expected to create future intergenerational competition for scarce resources. The public sector will continue to focus on the needs of the economically vulnerable. The private sector will naturally focus on the economically most able. As the political and economic climates permit, both sectors will inch gradually toward the socioeconomic middle. The future cohorts of the very old who are economically positioned in the center will continue to have the least resources available to them, as they do now.

The solution to the problem is not likely to be a carefully worked-out and integrated program from either the public or private sector. In all likelihood it will be a growing set of "building blocks" composed of adaptations to existing housing, home-delivered services, and planned living environments (with their several service packages) offered by both the private and public sectors. Much as they do now, individuals will piece together environmental, service, and medical bundles according to their resources and those of their primary relations. Public policy is far less likely to create new environments for the vulnerable elderly in this century than it is to encourage the production of these building blocks with which people whose resources permit can create their own environments.

Underlying most of the issues associated with accommodating a rapidly aging population are concerns for equity. If the state views the elderly as a totally dependent population that it somehow has to "take care of," then a rapidly aging national population would first bring on a dull trauma, followed by a frenzied total panic. Fortunately, only a small part of this population, of even the oldest old, is totally dependent on public support. However, an even smaller part is completely independent of such help when Social Security is factored into the discussion. It is the *relative* portion of the care burden that is shifted from private to public shoulders and back again that will frame the continuing public dialogue about equity. Should the state care first for those who have no families? Should it allow the very old to die from benign neglect? Or should it invest scarce resources toward the goal of extending the lives of severely disabled people for an additional year or two?

We do not claim to have the answers to these difficult questions. But when resources are finite, difficult choices must be made, and these may advantage one group at the expense of another. It is clear that no matter how objectively we attempt to construct the process of choice in formulating a national policy on aging, we must confront value questions directly in an orderly, critical, and reasonable way.

The care and protection of dependent community members, a value we share with other human societies, will continue to guide our considerations on these matters. As resources dwindle, options that encourage us to neglect those who have low functional utility may be heard in the land. Even among the Eskimos, however, it was only in times of extremely limited resources that elderly family members were voluntarily left to face the wolves alone. Our resources are obviously not so limited. The birth cohort that was 75 years of age or older in 1986 includes the parents of the cohort now approaching retirement—the cohort that gave birth to the baby-boom generation and that is often cited for its familial idealism. The very old can find at least some solace in that fact alone.

The bottom line is that Eugene Yates (1985) was right. It is not chronological age that is important here, but biological viability in advanced age. The gerontological research community and the social and health policy community in the United States should emphasize not only the extension of chronological age but the reduction of the severity of functional disability at the end of life.

REFERENCES

Branch, L. G. and A. M. Jette. 1982. "The Functional Approach to the Care of the Elderly: A Conceptual Framework." *Journal of the American Geriatrics Society* 32: 923–929.

Brody, S., S. W. Poulshock, and C. F. Masciocchi. 1978. "The Family Caring Unit: A Major Consideration in the Long-Term Care System." *The Gerontologist* 18: 556–561.

Feldman, J. J. 1982. *Work Ability of the Aged Under Conditions of Improving Mortality*. Statement before the National Commission on Social Security Reform, Washington, DC, June 21.

Fries, J. F. 1980. "Aging, Natural Death and the Compression of Morbidity." *New England Journal of Medicine* 303: 130–135.

Fries, J. F. 1983. "The Compression of Morbidity." *Milbank Memorial Fund Quarterly/Health and Society* 61: 397–419.

Glick, P. C. 1979. "The Future Marital Status and Living Arrangements of the Elderly." *The Gerontologist* 19: 301–309.

Gruenberg, E. M. 1977. "The Failure of Success." *Milbank Memorial Fund Quarterly/Health and Society* 55: 3–24.

Hess, B. B. and B. J. Soldo. 1985. "Husband and Wife Networks." Pp. 67–92 in *Social Support Networks and the Care of the Elderly: Theory, Research, Practice and Policy,* edited by W. J. Sauer and R. F. Coward. New York: Springer.

Katz, S. 1983 "Assessing Self-Maintenance: Activities of Daily Living, Mobility and Instrumental Activities of Daily Living." *Journal of the American Geriatric Society* 31: 721–727.

Keyfitz, N. and G. Littman. 1979. "Mortality in a Heterogeneous Population." *Population Studies* 33: 333–343.

Lawton, M. P. 1978. *The Housing Problems of Community Resident Elderly.* Occasional Papers in Housing and Community Affairs, No. 1. Washington, DC: Department of Housing and Urban Development.

Lawton, M. P. 1980a. *Social and Medical Services in Housing for the Aged.* Washington, DC: U.S. Government Printing Office.

Lawton, M. P. 1980b. *Environment and Aging.* Monterey, CA: Brooks/Cole.

Lawton, M. P. 1981. "An Ecological View of Living Arrangements." *The Gerontologist* 21: 59–66.

Litwak, E. 1985. *Helping the Elderly.* New York: Guilford.

Longino, C. F., Jr. 1986a. *The Oldest Americans: State Profiles for Data Based Planning.* Miami, FL: University of Miami Center for Social Research in Aging.

Longino, C. F., Jr. 1986b. "Personal Determinants and Consequences of Independent Housing Choices." In *Housing an Aging Society,* edited by R. Newcomber, M. P. Lawton, and T. O. Byerts. New York: Van Nostrand Reinhold Company.

Longino, C. F. and A. Lipman. 1981. "Married and Spouseless Men and Women in Planned Retirement Communities: Support Network Differentials." *Journal of Marriage and the Family* 43: 169–177.

Longino, C. F. and A. Lipman. 1983. "Informal Supports of Residents in Planned Retirement Communities." *Interdisciplinary Topics in Gerontology* 17: 107–118.

Longino, C. F., K. A. McClelland, and W. A. Peterson. 1981. "The Aged Subculture Hypothesis: Social Integration, Gerontophilia and Self-Conception." *Journal of Gerontology* 35: 758–767.

Manton, K. G. 1982. "Changing Concepts of Morbidity and Mortality in the Elderly Populations." *Milbank Memorial Fund Quarterly/Health and Society* 60: 183–243.

Manton, K. G. and K. Liu. 1984. *Future Growth of the Long-Term Care Population: Projections Based on the 1977 National Nursing Home Survey and the 1982 National Long-Term Care Survey.* Paper prepared for presentation at the Third Leadership Conference on Long-Term Care Issues: The Future of Long-Term Care, Washington, DC.

Manton, K. G. and B. J. Soldo. 1985a. "Dynamics of Health Changes in the Oldest Old: New Perspectives and Evidence." *Milbank Memorial Fund Quarterly/Health and Society* 63: 206–285.

Manton, K. G. and B. J. Soldo. 1985b. *Long-Range Planning for the Elderly: An Integrated Policy Perspective.* Paper prepared for the U.S. Senate Special Committee on Aging.

Manton, K. G. and E. Stallart. 1984. "Heterogeneity and its Effect on Mortality Measurement." In *Proceedings,* International Union for the Scientific Study of Population, Methodology and Data Collection in Mortality Studies Seminar, Dakar, Senegal.

Nahemow, L. and M. P. Lawton. 1973. "Toward an Ecological Theory of Adaptation and Aging." In *Environmental Design Research,* Vol. 1, edited by W. Priesen. Stroudsbury, PA: Dowden, Hutchenson and Ross.

National Center for Health Statistics. 1984. "Changes in Mortality Among the Elderly: United States, 1979–78, Supplement to 1980." *Vital and Health Statistics,* Series 3, No. 22a. Rockville, MD: Author.

New York State Office for the Aging. 1983. *Family Caregiving and the Elderly.* Albany, NY: Author.

Noelker, L. 1982. *The Impact of Environmental Problems on Caring for Impaired Elders in a Home Setting.* Paper presented at the 35th annual scientific meeting of the Gerontological Society of America, Boston, MA.

Parr, J. 1980. "The Interactions of Persons and Living Environments." In *Aging in the 1980s: Psychological Issues* edited by L. W. Poon. Washington, DC: American Psychological Association.

Patrick, C. H., Y. Y. Palesch, M. Feinleib, and J. A. Brody. 1982. "Sex Differences in Declining Cohort Death Rates from Heart Disease." *American Journal of Public Health* 72: 161–166.

Peterson, W. A., C. F. Longino, and L. W. Phelps. 1979. *A Study of Security, Health and Social Support Systems and Adjustment of Residents in Selected Congregate Living and Retirement Settings.* Washington, DC: Social Security Administration.

Rice, D. P. and J. J. Feldman. 1983. "Living Longer in the United States: Demographic Changes and Health Needs of the Elderly." *Milbank Memorial Fund Quarterly/Health and Society* 61: 393–396.

Smeeding, T. 1984. "Nonmoney Income and the Elderly: The Case of the 'Tweeners." *IRP Discussion Papers*. Madison, WI: University of Wisconsin–Madison Institute for Research on Poverty.

Social Security Administration. 1981. *Social Security Area Population Projections Actuarial Study No. 85*. SSA Publication No. 11-11532. Baltimore, MD: Social Security Administration.

Soldo, B. J. 1986. "Household Types, Housing Needs, and Disability." In *Housing an Aging Society*, edited by R. J. Newcomer, M. P. Lawton and T. O. Byerts. New York: Van Nostrand, Reinhold.

Soldo, B. J. and K. G. Manton. 1985a. "Health Status and Service Needs of the Oldest Old: Current Patterns and Future Trends." *Milbank Memorial Fund Quarterly/Health and Society* 63: 286–319.

Soldo, B. J. and K. G. Manton. 1985b. "Demographic Challenges for Socioeconomic Planning." *Journal of Socioeconomic Planning Sciences* 19: 227–247.

Soldo, B. J. and K. G. Manton. 1985c. *Heterogeneity within the Population of Functionally Limited Elderly: Differences by Medicaid Status*. Paper prepared under subcontract to Systemetrics and LaJolla Management Corporation, Contract No. 500-83-005-6, Department of Health and Human Services, Health Care Financing Administration.

Soldo, B. J., E. D. Pellegrino, and J. T. Howell. 1985. "Epilogue: Confronting the Age of Aging." *Journal of Socioeconomic Planning Sciences* 19: 289–293.

Soldo, B. J., M. Sharma, and R. T. Campbell. 1984. "Determinants of the Community Living Arrangements of Older Unmarried Women." *Journal of Gerontology* 39: 492–498.

Tissue, T. and J. L. McCoy. 1981. "Income and Living Arrangements among Poor Aged Singles." *Social Security Bulletin* 44: 3–31.

Vaupal, J. W., K. G. Manton, and E. Stallard. 1979. "The Impact of Heterogeneity in Individual Frailty on the Dynamics of Mortality." *Demography* 16: 439–454.

Verbrugge, L. M. 1984. "Longer Life but Worsening Health?: Trends in Health and Mortality of Middle-Aged and Older Persons." *Milbank Memorial Fund Quarterly/Health and Society* 62: 475–519.

Walford, R. 1983. *Testimony Before the Subcommittee on Savings, Pensions, and Investment Policy of the Committee on Finance, United States Senate*. Senate Hearing Document No. 98-359. Washington, DC: U.S. Government Printing Office.

Weissert, W. 1981. *Long-Term Care: Current Policy and Directions for the 1980s*. Paper presented at the 1981 White House Conference on Aging, Washington, DC.

Weissert, W. and W. Scanlon. 1982. *Determinants of Institutionalization of the Aged*. Working Paper No. 1466-21 (rev.). Washington, DC: The Urban Institute.

Wilkins, R. and O. Adams. 1983. *Healthfulness of Life*. Montreal, Quebec, Canada: Institutes for Research on Public Policy.

Yates, E. 1985. "Concluding Remarks." Symposium on the Social and Built Environment for an Aging Society, sponsored by the Committee on an Aging Society, National Research Council, Washington, DC, December 8–11.

3
Characteristics of Dropouts and Prediction of Mortality in a Longitudinal Study of Older Mexican-Americans and Anglos*

Kyriakos S. Markides

One advantage of longitudinal research is the opportunity it offers to sort out aging from cohort effects. However, one common problem with much longitudinal research is loss of subjects. This is particularly the case in studies of old people, many of whom can die during a given study. It might be argued that deceased subjects do not pose a particular problem to studies of aging because death is a natural outcome of the process of aging (Goudy, 1985a, b; Norris, 1985). However, it has been suggested that deceased subjects are different from survivors, and many of our conclusions about aging are based on elderly who are increasingly select, both psychologically and socially (Riegel, Riegel, & Meyer, 1967). This kind of selective survival is also a problem in cross-sectional studies that base their findings on comparisons between old and middle-aged people. One misconception might be the hypothesis that health is more likely to decline with age among whites than blacks, since very old blacks might be in better health than very old whites. A simple explanation for this difference is a crossover in racial mortality that assures that only a selected group of blacks survive to advanced years because of higher earlier mortality (Manton, Poss, & Wing, 1979; Markides & Machalek, 1984).

*This work was supported by Grant No. AG04290 from the National Institute on Aging.

Longitudinal studies do not solve these problems of cross-sectional studies unless deceased subjects and other dropouts are taken into account. We have shown in a previous analysis how misleading certain analyses can be if deceased dropouts are not taken into consideration (Markides, Timbers, & Osberg, 1984). We found that over time, when we looked at survivors only, there was evidence that women were more likely than men to show declines in their health. However, we arbitrarily decided that people who died did so because of declining health. We thus assigned to them the lowest score on our health index and included them in the analysis; the analysis then showed that men were more likely to show declines in health over time. The conclusion that aging might be kinder to men's health was reversed by the realization that aging was indeed less kind to their health by leading to early death in a greater proportion of them than it did among women.

In addition to enabling us to make more valid observations about what happens to people as they grow older, studies of deceased dropouts afford us the opportunity to study predictors of mortality, which is a recent practice in gerontology. Epidemiologists have long engaged in such work, but they typically have not included older people in their samples. This exclusion was based on the belief that traditional risk factors do not particularly apply to old people because they have already caused the deaths of those most at risk before they reached old age. The lack of interest in predicting mortality among old people is probably also related to the feeling that the payoff from such knowledge would be lower than is the case with younger people. However, the National Institute on Aging has recently funded a number of large epidemiologic studies of old people; we are therefore likely to find out in the near future to what extent traditional risk factors are predictive of the mortality of old people.

Social gerontologists have looked at predictors of mortality among old people that are different from the traditional risk factors of interest to epidemiologists. They have studied such variables as intelligence, functional and subjective health, subjective age, psychological well-being, and other social and psychological factors (Baltes, Schaie, & Nardi, 1971; Markides & Pappas, 1982; Mossey & Shapiro, 1982; Palmore & Jeffers, 1971; Powers & Bultena, 1972). And they have often been successful in their predictions. In some cases, they have found that subjective factors can be as predictive of mortality as more objective ones. Mossey and Shapiro (1982) found that self-ratings of health were predictive of subsequent mortality in the Manitoba Longitudinal Study of Aging after objective health ratings and other factors were taken into account. In an earlier analysis of our data, for example, we found that subjective age was as predictive of mortality as actual age, even after controlling for the effects of actual age, health, and such other objective factors as social class and gender (Markides & Pappas, 1982). Is there value to knowing about such relationships? We concluded that if age is an index of proximity to death, then old people know how close they are to death as well as do demographers.

This paper presents additional data from our longitudinal study of Mexican-Americans and Anglos. First, we look at differences between our dropouts and our restudied subjects, with an interest in how dropouts may influence observations about aging based strictly on survivors (restudied subjects). Subsequently, we conduct multivariate analyses to investigate how predictive a number of social and social-psychological factors are about who is likely to be a dropout, as well as of mortality over an eight-year period.

METHODS

Our analysis is based on data collected in 1976 and 1984 in San Antonio, Texas. A total of 508 persons aged 60 and over were interviewed in 1976, 70% of whom were Mexican-Americans and 30% of whom were Anglos. The original sample was drawn from a four-census tract area of southwestern San Antonio, using area probability sampling procedures involving selection of blocks and interviews with all persons aged 60 and over residing in the selected blocks (see Markides & Martin, 1983, for more details). We returned to the subjects in 1980 and were able to re-interview 338 of them, or approximately two-thirds of the original sample (see Markides, Dickson, & Pappas, 1982). A second follow-up in 1984 yielded interviews with 254 persons, or half of the original sample. Of the remainder, 119 had died during the eight-year period, accounting for 23.4% of the original sample. An additional 27 persons (5.3%) refused to be re-interviewed and 34 (6.7%) were "too ill" to be re-interviewed. Of the remainder, 12 persons were reported to have moved out of town, while no information was obtained on 62 persons (12.2%). This last group is excluded from our analyses predicting mortality below, since it could not be ascertained whether they were living or dead at the time of the restudy.

Below we compare the subjects restudied in 1984 with the various categories of dropouts on a number of demographic and socioeconomic characteristics, as well as on a number of other variables of interest to gerontologists (all measured in 1976). Variables examined include sex, ethnicity, age, marital status, income, education, occupational background, self-rated health, bed-disability days, hospital nights, subjective age, global happiness, presence of a confidant, church attendance, farthest distance traveled in the previous two weeks, times went out after dark in the previous two weeks, and life satisfaction [measured by 11 items from the 13-item version of the Life Satisfaction Index (Wood, Wylie, & Sheafors, 1969) that had demonstrated satisfactory internal consistency].

After the initial group comparisons, we present findings of regression analysis that compare restudied subjects and all dropouts, as well as analysis comparing deceased dropouts with subjects known to still be living in 1984. Of great interest in these analyses is the extent to which dropouts pose biases in longitudinal studies of older people.

RESULTS

Table 3-1 presents bivariate comparisons of restudied subjects and the various categories of dropouts. Asterisks denote statistically significant differences between the various dropout groups (columns 3–7) and re-studied subjects (column 2). There were 10 significant differences between all dropouts (column 3) and restudied subjects. Dropouts were more likely to be Anglos than Mexican-Americans, were older, were less likely to be married (and more likely to be widowed), had lower self-ratings of health, had more bed-disability days and more hospital nights, had older subjective ages, attended church less frequently, were less likely to have traveled more than 25 miles in the previous two weeks, and had lower life-satisfaction scores.

Comparisons between reinterviewed subjects and individual dropout categories yielded fewer significant differences, although these generally resulted from the fewer cases in each category taken alone. Deceased subjects were significantly older, had lower self-ratings of health, had more bed-disability days and hospital nights, reported older subjective ages, attended church less frequently, were less likely to have traveled over 25 miles, and had lower life-satisfaction scores.

The 62 people whose status was not determined at follow-up were more similar to the deceased than to the restudied subjects on a number of variables, including age, subjective health, hospital nights, subjective age, distance traveled, and life satisfaction. In addition, they were less likely to be married, had lower incomes, were more likely to be from lower occupational backgrounds, were less happy, and were less likely to have a confidant than restudied subjects.

The 27 persons who refused to be reinterviewed differed from other dropout groups in that they were generally more advantaged. For example, they were more likely to be Anglos, had more education, and were from higher occupational backgrounds than restudied subjects (or other dropouts). They were also advantaged on a number of other variables, but the small sample size prevented these differences from being statistically significant.

Finally, the 34 persons who were "too ill" to be reinterviewed were more likely to be Anglos, were older, were more likely to be widowed, had lower self-ratings of health, more hospital nights, attended church less frequently,

TABLE 3-1 Selected Characteristics of Dropouts and Restudied Persons[a]

	Original sample (N = 508) (1)	Reinterviewed (N = 254) (2)	Dropouts[b] (N = 254) (3)	Deceased (N = 119) (4)	Could not find (N = 62) (5)	Refusals (N = 27) (6)	Too ill to interview (N = 34) (7)
Sex							
Male	39.0	35.8	42.1	43.7	40.3	37.0	47.1
Female	61.0	64.2	57.9	56.3	59.7	63.0	52.9
Ethnicity							
Mexican-American	69.6	75.4	63.9*[c]	68.1	73.8	40.7**	55.9*
Anglo	30.4	24.6	36.1	31.9	26.4	59.3	44.1
Mean age	69.8	67.4	72.2**	72.8**	70.3**	69.4	75.6**
Marital status							
Married	55.4	62.5	48.2**	52.9	35.5**	65.4	44.1
Divorced/separated	7.1	6.8	7.5	5.0	8.1	11.5	5.9
Widowed	34.1	27.1	41.1	37.8	53.2	19.2	50.0
Single	3.4	3.6	3.2	4.2	3.2	3.8	
Household income							
< 200	34.0	28.0	39.9	30.5	51.7*	39.1	56.7
200–399	35.7	39.7	31.7	40.7	23.3	21.7	20.0
400+	30.3	32.2	28.4	28.8	25.0	39.1	23.3
Mean years of school	4.5	4.6	4.5	4.4	3.6	6.2	3.9
Occupational background							
White-collar	9.2	7.2	11.2	11.0	11.3*	15.4*	3.0
Blue collar-skilled	31.2	29.7	32.7	38.1	21.0	53.8	21.2
Blue collar-semi or unskilled	32.4	38.6	26.3	22.9	29.0	19.2	39.4
Service workers	15.8	14.9	16.7	15.3	21.0	11.5	21.2
Farm-owners	3.6	2.4	4.8	2.5	9.7		6.1
Farm-laborers	7.8	7.2	8.3	10.2	8.1		9.1
Self-rated health							
Excellent	7.6	9.6	5.6**	8.5*	3.2*		3.0*
Good	25.3	27.9	22.7	21.2	16.1	34.6	27.3
Fair	49.2	49.8	48.6	44.9	62.9	42.3	39.4
Poor	17.9	12.7	23.1	25.4	17.7	23.1	30.3

Characteristic							
Days in bed in previous year							
None	63.1	66.3	60.0**	58.5**	60.7	73.1	54.5
1–9	21.9	23.8	20.0	18.6	19.7	15.4	27.3
10+	14.9	9.9	20.0	22.9	19.7	11.5	18.2
Nights in hospital in previous year							
None	78.4	84.1	72.7**	67.8**	70.5*	96.0	75.8*
1–9	10.2	9.5	10.8	13.6	13.1	4.0	3.0
10+	11.4	6.3	16.5	18.6	16.4	—	21.2
Subjective age							
Young	12.2	15.5	8.9**	7.9**	8.1**	15.4	9.4
Middle-aged	46.4	51.4	41.5	38.6	38.7	50.0	46.9
Old	33.4	28.6	38.2	40.4	40.3	26.9	37.5
Very old	7.9	4.5	11.4	13.2	12.9	7.7	6.3
Happiness							
Very happy	38.6	42.5	34.8	38.7	24.2*	44.0	31.3
Somewhat happy	46.6	44.8	48.4	44.5	58.1*	44.0	43.8
Not very happy	14.7	12.7	16.8	16.8	17.7	12.0	21.9
Has confidant							
Yes	67.3	66.5	68.1	72.3	51.7*	73.1	67.6
No	32.7	33.5	31.9	27.7	48.3	26.9	32.4
Church attendance							
Once a week	42.9	45.1	40.8*	39.8*	45.9	34.6	42.4*
1–3 times per month	26.4	30.8	22.0	24.6	18.1	19.2	21.2
Less frequently	30.6	24.1	37.2	35.6	36.1	45.1	36.4
Distance traveled in previous two weeks							
< 5 miles	46.1	40.5	51.8**	53.0*	56.0**	46.1	44.1*
5–25 miles	30.2	29.8	30.7	29.9	27.4	38.5	35.3
Over 5 miles	23.7	29.8	17.5	17.1	14.5	15.4	20.6
Times went out after dark in previous two weeks							
Did not leave house	67.2	66.3	68.1	71.2	67.7	65.4	60.6
1–2 times	20.7	18.7	22.7	19.5	22.6	26.9	27.3
3+ times	12.2	15.1	9.2	9.3	9.7	3.8	12.2
Life satisfaction	13.0	13.7	12.4*	12.6*	11.8*	13.0	11.0*

a All characteristics are from 1976 survey.
b Includes columns 4, 5, 6, 7 plus 12 persons who had moved out of town.
c Asterisks denote significant difference from reinterviewed subjects (** p ≤ .01; * p ≤ .05)

and had lower life-satisfaction scores. In some ways, they appeared to have been even less advantaged than had the now-deceased subjects at the beginning of the study on a number of health indicators, a finding also obtained in a recent study by Norris (1985).

To further specify characteristics of dropouts, we performed two sets of multivariate analyses incorporating the variables shown on Table 3-1. The first set of analyses compared all dropouts with reinterviewed subjects, while the second compared deceased subjects with subjects determined to still be living at follow-up. The two dependent variables were coded as dummy variables (dropouts = 1, restudied subjects = 0; deceased subjects = 1, survivors = 0) that were subjected to a series of multiple regression analyses. Both ordinary least squares (OLS) and multiple logistic regression procedures were employed (Cleary & Angel, 1984), yielding essentially similar results. Tables 3-2 and 3-3 present results of OLS regression analyses incorporating only selected independent variables chosen on the basis of their significance in previous analyses. A few were included for theoretical reasons. Several of the independent variables were coded as dummy variables.

Because of the importance of mortality in longitudinal studies of older people, we created a control variable that measures life expectancy, to be used in the place of age. It has been suggested (see Ryder, 1975) that the projected number of years left to live is a better measure of age than chronological age in studies of old people, particularly if one of the main objectives is to study mortality. Since women live longer than men, this measure must take into account sex differences in life expectancy. We used life tables by sex for the total United States population for 1976 (National Center for Health Statistics, 1978) and assigned life expectancy values to the subjects based on their age and sex (see also Markides & Pappas, 1982). We made no distinction between Mexican-Americans and Anglos because life expectancies of the two groups have been quite similar since 1970 and virtually no differences are observed in the older years (Markides & Coreil, 1986; U.S. Bureau of the Census, 1979).

In addition to life expectancy, the following variables were included in the equations predicting dropouts and mortality: occupational background (white-collar and skilled blue-collar = 1; other = 0); years of school completed (actual years of school); distance traveled (coded 1–4); subjective health (excellent or good = 1; fair to poor = 0); subjective age (old or very old = 1; young or middle-aged =0); and life satisfaction (score on 11–item scale).

Table 3-2 shows that four of the seven independent variables are significantly related to being a dropout, the strongest of which is life expectancy. Other things being equal, dropouts are more likely to have lower life expectancy, less likely to have traveled over 25 miles in the last two weeks,

TABLE 3-2 Results of Multiple Regression Analysis Predicting All Dropouts over Eight-Year Period.

Independent variables	b	se	beta	Mean	St. dev.
Life expectancy	−.034**	.005	−.317	15.49	4.61
Occupational background	.116*	.050	.114	.41	.49
Years of school	.004	.006	.034	4.54	4.27
Distance traveled last two weeks	−.056*	.024	−.106	2.67	.95
Subjective health	−.064	.049	−.060	.33	.47
Subjective age	.094*	.047	.092	.41	.49
Life satisfaction	−.004	.004	−.042	12.97	5.61
$R^2 = .162$					

*$p \leq .05$
**$p \leq .01$

and more likely to have older subjective ages. Against expectations, drop-outs were more likely to be from higher occupational backgrounds (white-collar and skilled blue-collar). While this is partially due to the higher occupational backgrounds of refusers, even deceased dropouts (see below) appear to have been of higher occupational backgrounds. Educational attainment, subjective health, and life satisfaction do not appear to be significant predictors of who drops out of the study.

Table 3-3 presents the regression analysis results predicting mortality. The same variables that were significant in the analysis predicting dropouts are also significant here. As would be expected, the higher the life expectancy, the lower the probability of dying. The lower the distance traveled and the higher the subjective age, the higher the probability of dying. As in the previous analysis, occupational status has an effect opposite to what might have been expected: other things being equal, persons from higher occupational backgrounds were more likely to have died over the eight-year period. We can only speculate that this traditional correlate of better health and lower mortality may operate differently among older people than among younger groups. Perhaps a kind of selective survival by class, similar to that observed by race, takes place at advanced ages. It is possible that after a given age, the lower-class elderly who survive constitute a select group that can be expected to outsurvive elderly of higher classes. The fact that, in our previous analysis of mortality during the first four years of the study (Markides et al., 1982), there was no association between occupational status and mortality might lend some support to the role of the selective survival factor, which becomes more important in more advanced years. Clearly this finding deserves further thought and more research. Un-fortunately, the literature on selective survival has concentrated on race and

TABLE 3-3 Results of Multiple Regression Analysis Predicting Mortality over Eight-Year Period

Independent variables	b	se	beta	Mean	St. dev.
Life expectancy	−.022**	.004	−.232	15.58	4.68
Occupational background	.163*	.049	.181	.42	.49
Years of school	−.006	.005	−.062	4.67	4.3
Distance traveled last two weeks	−.049*	.024	−.106	2.71	.95
Subjective health	−.041	.047	−.044	.34	.48
Subjective age	.110*	.047	.121	.40	.49
Life satisfaction	.003	.004	.038	13.17	5.65
$R^2 = .116$					

*$p \leq .05$
**$p \leq .01$

has paid little attention to class (Manton et al., 1979; Markides & Machalek, 1984).

SUMMARY AND DISCUSSION

We have presented data on characteristics of dropouts in an eight-year longitudinal study of older Mexican-Americans and Anglos. These findings replicate our previous analysis (Markides et al., 1982) of characteristics of dropouts over the first four years of the study. Our eight-year findings are quite similar to our four-year findings. Dropouts as a group appear to be older, less healthy, less active, and generally less advantaged than restudied subjects, a finding that poses potential problems for longitudinal studies of older people. Deceased persons who were from a clearly disadvantaged group constitute the largest category of dropouts. Persons whose status could not be established are similar to the deceased subjects, as are persons who are "too ill" to be reinterviewed. Refusers are more advantaged but constitute only a small group (at least in this study). In general, our findings are in agreement with previous research.

With the exception of the unexpected findings with regard to occupational status discussed earlier, our multivariate analysis predicting dropouts and mortality yielded expected results. The same independent variables (life expectancy, occupational background, distance traveled, and subjective age) were significant in both equations. As in a previous analysis we conducted, subjective health lost its significance in predicting mortality when other variables were held constant, a finding not in agreement with one other study of older people (Mossey & Shapiro, 1982). Subjective age, on the other hand, remained significant after the controls were applied. However, subjective age was a considerably weaker predictor of mortality over the eight-year period than was life expectancy ("objective age"), while the two were equally as strong in their prediction of mortality over the first four-year period (Markides & Pappas, 1982). Given that subjective age tends to fluctuate over time (Markides & Boldt, 1983), it is not surprising that it would be more predictive over a shorter time interval.

The literature appears to be divided over the bias introduced by deceased dropouts in longitudinal studies of older people. While some studies have concluded that biases are definitely introduced by deceased dropouts (e.g., Markides et al., 1982; Powers & Bultena, 1972; Riegel et al., 1967), three recent papers (Goudy, 1985a, b; Norris, 1985) have suggested that they pose no threat since they represent "natural" attrition. In other words, the sample remaining after the death of certain subjects is representative of the surviving cohort of older people.

Although the above point makes sense if one is interested in describing characteristics of surviving cohorts of older people, the information obtained from such studies is little better than information obtained from cross-sectional studies of older people. The advantage of longitudinal designs is that they enable us to study change in a number of variables of interest, so that we may better understand the process of aging. As we have argued elsewhere (Markides et al., 1984), if we are interested in studying changes in health as people get older, omitting deceased dropouts from the analysis means that we exclude the extreme end of the distribution of our dependent variable. After all, people who die during our study are people who show great declines in health. Since mortality also tends to be selective of various groups, highly misleading results can be obtained.

Ignoring deceased dropouts is not a problem limited to studies of declines in health, since a number of other variables of interest might correlate with health. In a separate analysis of our data (Markides, Levin, & Ray, submitted), for example, we found that church attendance was consistently related to psychological well-being in 1976, 1980, and 1984. When only subjects available at all three points of observation were used, the effect of church attendance on well-being was only significant at the third time. Thus analysis of the data that excludes dropouts might give the impression that church attendance becomes increasingly important as people get older. Further analysis revealed that this finding results from the fact that dropouts (most of whom were deceased or "too ill" to be reinterviewed) were relatively infrequent church attenders who were in poorer health and had lower psychological well-being in earlier rounds than were persons remaining in the study.

We conclude that longitudinal studies of the health of the elderly can as ill afford to ignore deceased dropouts as can studies of variables that correlate with health and mortality. We hope that the literature continues to give attention to this issue, since more and more gerontologists are turning to longitudinal studies to obtain better insights into the process of aging.

Our results also have some implications for studies of predictors of mortality among old people. Our relatively low percentage of explained variance indicates the limitations of traditional social–gerontological variables, such as age, subjective health, subjective age, and life satisfaction, in predicting mortality. Clearly our predictions would improve if we were to take into account traditional epidemiologic risk factors, such as smoking history, alcohol consumption, diet, blood pressure, and so forth. However, it is not yet clear how predictive such risk factors are among older people. In this investigation we presented evidence of the weakening influence of social class as people get older, suggesting the possible effect of selective survival. Collaborative efforts between social gerontologists, demographers, and epidemiologists are likely to yield fruitful results in this important area of inquiry.

REFERENCES

Baltes, P. B., K. W. Schaie, and A. H. Nardi. 1971. "Age and Experimental Mortality in a Seven-Year Longitudinal Study of Cognitive Behavior." *Developmental Psychology* 5:18–26.

Cleary, P. D. and R. Angel. 1984. "The Analysis of Relationships Involving Dichotomous Variables." *Journal of Health and Social Behavior* 25:334–348.

Goudy, W. J. 1985a. "Sample Attrition and Multivariate Analysis in the Retirement History Study." *Journal of Gerontology* 40:358–367.

Goudy, W. J. 1985b. "Effects of Sample Attrition and Data Analysis in the Retirement History Study." *Experimental Aging Research* 11:161–167.

Manton, K. G., S. S. Poss, and S. Wing. 1979. "The Black/White Mortality Crossover: Investigation from the Components of Aging." *The Gerontologist* 19: 291–300.

Markides, K. S. and J. S. Boldt. 1983. "Change in Subjective Age Among the Elderly: A Longitudinal Analysis." *The Gerontologist* 23:422–427.

Markides, K. S. and M. J. Coreil. 1986. The Health of Southwestern Hispanics: An Epidemiologic Paradox?" *Public Health Reports* 101:253–265.

Markides, K. S., H. D. Dickson, and C. Pappas. 1982. "Characteristics of Dropouts in Longitudinal Research on Aging: A Study of Mexican Americans and Anglos." *Experimental Aging Research,* 8:163–167.

Markides, K. S., J. S. Levin, and L. A. Ray. Submitted. "Religion, Aging, and Well-Being: An Eight-Year Longitudinal Study."

Markides, K. S. and R. Machalek. 1984. "Selective Survival, Aging and Society." *Archives of Gerontology and Geriatrics* 3:207–222.

Markides, K. S. and H. W. Martin. 1983. *Older Mexican Americans: A Study in an Urban Barrio.* Monograph of the Center for Mexican American Studies. Austin: University of Texas Press.

Markides K. S. and C. Pappas. 1982. "Subjective Age, Health and Survivorship in Old Age." *Research on Aging* 4:87–96.

Markides, K. S., D. Timbers, and J. S. Osberg. 1984. "Aging and Health: A Longitudinal Study. *Archives of Gerontology and Geriatrics* 3:33–49.

Mossey, J. M. and E. Shapiro. 1982. "Self-Rated Health: A Predictor of Mortality in Old People." *American Journal of Public Health* 72:800–808.

National Center for Health Statistics. 1978. "Life Tables." In *Vital Statistics of the United States, 1976,* Vol II, Section 5. Washington, DC: U.S. Government Printing Office.

Norris, F. H. 1985. "Characteristics of Older Nonrespondents over Five Waves of a Panel Study." *Journal of Gerontology* 40:627–636.

Palmore, E. and F. Jeffers (eds.). 1971. *Predictors of Life Span.* Lexington, MA: D.C. Heath.

Powers, E. A. and G. L. Bultena. 1972. "Characteristics of Deceased Dropouts in Longitudinal Research." *Journal of Gerontology* 27:530–535.

Riegel, K. F., R. M. Riegel, and G. Meyer. 1967. "A Study of Dropout Rates in Longitudinal Research on Aging and the Prediction of Death." *Journal of Personality and Social Psychology* 5:342–348.

Ryder, N. B. 1985. "Notes on Stationary Populations." *Population Index* 41:3–28.

U.S. Bureau of the Census. 1979. *Coverage of the Hispanic Population of the United States in the 1970 Census.* Current Population Reports. Special Studies, Series P-23, No. 82. Washington DC: U.S. Government Printing Office.

Wood, V., M. Wylie, and B. Sheafors. 1969. "An Analysis of a Short Self-Report Measure of Life Satisfaction: Correlation with Rater Judgements." *Journal of Gerontology* 24:465–469.

PART 2
Dimensions of Informal and Formal Health Care

Introduction

These chapters encompass various approaches to understanding interactions between the elderly and their health care providers. They reflect the variety of sources and sites for health-related assistance that was noted in the Introduction to the volume. Wolinsky, Coe, and Mosely examine age-related changes in the determinants of health services utilization. George investigates the role of informal supports and formal services in caregiving. Chappell explores the interrelatedness of self-care, informal care, and formal care. Coe studies communication between physicians, elderly patients, and their families. Marshall considers the consequences of long stays in hospitals. These chapters reflect a movement from the most general or comprehensive kind of research question to the most specific. The first three chapters (Wolinsky et al., George, and Chappell) form a subset, as each addresses factors associated with the use of health services. Coe analyzes the interactions of individuals within the health care system; in this instance, among the elderly, those who bring them to their physicians, and also their physicians. Marshall, in turn, looks at how utilization (in this instance, of hospitals) affects individuals.

The factors examined for their association with the use of health services range from need, to sociodemographic and socioeconomic variables (Wolinsky et al.), to social supports (George and Chappell), to self-maintenance activities and health beliefs (Chappell). Consistent with Maddox's recommendation to use a variety of approaches and measures to tap complex behaviors, Wolinsky and associates focus on six indices of health services use; George assesses both level of support and perceived adequacy of support; and Chappell considers three types of self-maintenance activity by measuring extent of general self-maintenance, of self-care maintenance including medical checkups and immunization, and of self-care maintenance in response to symptomatology.

To be specific, Wolinsky and associates use the most general macro-approach of the five chapters, taking an innovative approach to sorting out aging, period, and cohort effects. They investigate many possible associations between the use of health services and the characteristics of individuals in six age cohorts over three four-year time periods. The need for health care services was the principal correlate of service consumption. Predicted, however, was only 25% of the variance, with other variables adding little toward explaining utilization. In turn, the correlates of utilization patterns were remarkably stable over time.

Given the heterogeneity among the elderly, perhaps 25% of predicted variance is the most that we can expect. Still, the lingering question is: What, aside from need, predicts health care utilization? Subsequent chapters in this part address factors that may supplement need in explaining utilization, particularly social supports and physician–patient interaction. Similarly, the design of the study may be responsible for the constancy of correlates of utilization patterns because of the truncated time period of four years. Other authors in this volume focus on time periods of longer duration and suggest greater fluidity in patterns of health care utilization.

George, in focusing on caregivers to memory-impaired older people, begins to clarify the role of social supports. But fine sociologist that she is, George adds further complexity to an already complex issue and then begins to solve the puzzle. That is, she first reports her finding that objective and subjective social supports are independent. Simply stated, receiving more informal assistance is unlikely to be associated with assessing assistance to be adequate. She then looks for the determinants of the two measures of supports. Although both measures are associated with caregiver well-being, the determinants of each differ indeed. George next rightly points to one important implication of her findings. Specific interventions will vary in their impact on objective and subjective outcome criteria. Because, in turn, objective and subjective measures of social support are associated with amount of formal service use, the linking rather than the substitution hypothesis is better supported. Still lacking is clarification of the processes by which higher levels of social supports induce greater use of formal health services. Helpful, according to George, may be replacement of the linking versus substitution debate with models of the complementary nature of social supports and formal service use. At another level of discourse, had Wolinsky and associates used George's social support variables, as noted earlier, they might have found a modest degree of predictive power to add to the 25% explained by need.

Chappell directs our attention to self-care maintenance. She examines the prevalence of self-care, informal care, and formal care, as well as correlations between types of care, and then compares the factors associated with each form of care. Not only are different forms of self-care associated with different amounts of informal care, and health beliefs with formal and informal care, but also, contradictory to George, informal care in her data is not associated with use of formal services. Part of the contradiction may reside in differences between U.S. and Canadian citizens in use of formal services. For example, in Chappell's data, many Canadians go for checkups and immunizations; and use of these kinds of accessible formal services is associated with the extent of self-maintenance. Chappell recognizes that part of the contradiction may also relate to differences between her sample and George's sample. Essentially, however, she interprets the lack of association between informal and formal care by arguing that the elderly tend to use informal assistance for short-term incapacity but are likely to turn to formal health providers for longer-term conditions. The obvious inference is that for longer-term conditions, informal assistance does not substitute for formal health services. Each, as does self-care, fulfills very different types of functions.

Chappell and George provide implications for practice and policy from their findings on relationships among components of the health care system, particularly between informal supports and formal services. Chappell reminds us that inappropriate and expensive use of formal services could be reduced if self-maintenance and informal supports were promoted and assisted; and George notes, and Chappell would surely agree, that more formal help is needed at earlier stages of caregiving to avoid overburdening informal support networks. The linkages among self-care, informal assistance, and formal services are certainly relevant to the issues of long-term care policy that will be addressed in the papers in Part 3.

Authors of these papers cannot be admonished by Maddox for failure to include implications for practice and policy. Issues of equity of health care and the appropriate role of informal supports, as well as self-maintenance, are precisely the kinds of issues that sociologists can illuminate through careful studies such as these. Yet because factors such as heterogeneity among the elderly and the vicissitudes of health (see Verbrugge's chapter in Part 1) add even further complexity to the already complex interactions among self-care, social supports, and formal services, it is not at all surprising that we have only begun to understand health care use in an aging society.

Coe opens up new vistas. Too little is known about communication between physicians and their elderly patients. Through the analysis of communication, variables can be identified to then investigate for their prediction of outcomes. It is not an easy task that Coe assigns himself. As he correctly notes, the conversation includes the patients' families, and thus the study of doctor–patient interaction becomes the study of coalitions among doctors, elderly patients, and patients' family members. The importance of this area of inquiry is obvious.

Marie Haug, in her comments on the Coe paper, raised issues concerning the measurement of appropriate patient outcomes. Noncompliance may be a wise choice in the case of an inappropriate treatment plan. Moreover, failure to comply may reflect a beneficial disposition of the elderly person to control his or her own fate. Good communication skills may not be the only issue: Some patients prefer not to be told everything about their illness. The key must be the success of treatment rather than compliance or satisfaction. Still, as Coe asserts, two-way communication should be a goal because doctors may then be in a better position to adapt a regimen to a patient's lifestyle. It is necessary for doctors to explain better to patients and, also, for patients to articulate why they do not wish to comply, or cannot comply, with their physicians' requests. Haug continued by observing that a neglected aspect of many studies is variability in physician characteristics that may relate to communication and to outcomes. These encompass specialty, age, and gender, as well as degree of cure-orientation and whether the physician provides dignity to the patient. Haug also noted that both patient and staff characteristics will affect the hospital "career" discussed in Marshall's subsequent chapter. Thus there is a need to combine patient, provider, and setting characteristics for a comprehensive understanding of health care and its outcomes.

Marshall turns our attention to the effects of health care use on the elderly, specifically to ways in which long stays in hospitals adversely affect elderly patients. From his report on the Canadian experience, it is apparent that our northern neighbors have not yet adopted Diagnostic Related Groups (DRGs) as a metric for reimbursing hospitals for the care they provide; thus they are not discharging the elderly "quicker and sicker." Although Canada and the United States are at different stages of resolution of the onerous cost of inpatient care, the shared experience of having large numbers of geriatric patients "backed up" in hospitals is only one kind of outcome of the organization of health care. Toronto, for example, has both large ratios of long-term care beds and of nursing home beds to its elderly population. Apparently the need for chronic care neither influences the amount of long-term care provided nor the setting in which it is given; instead, interest group behavior does. Outcomes of these behaviors help to explain not only why Wolinsky and associates found a relatively low association between need and health services use but also why there are long stays in hospitals. Because long stays appear to be destructive, earlier discharges are warranted. Consequently, a more optimal approach to the use of hospitals by the elderly must be developed that causes neither debilitation from lingering in hospital beds nor too early discharge. There are no simple answers. An ideal community health care system could allow earlier discharges with appropriate aftercare and, also, reduce rapid turnaround readmissions. Marshall illustrates a viable role for sociologists in the development of a health care system more beneficial to the elderly, as do Branch and colleagues and Wiener and colleagues in Part 3.

Alfred Gellhorn then commented on a number of issues related to health care utilization. Echoing Marshall's observations that it is not need that determines the provision of care, Gellhorn provided an illustration. Rural counties have more surgical procedures because they have more physicians and more hospital beds per capita; indeed, one rural county in New York State has eight times as many hemorrhoidectomies as any other county when corrected for age and sex. In addition to the issue of equity, this observation also indicates that we should investigate whether utilization is appropriate, too high, or too low. Of course, the greater the coverage by third-party payers, the greater the usage. But we must not only control for geographical area in studies (as Wolinsky and associates did); we must also consider how we count health services. As noted earlier, many kinds of social health services that are counted as formal health services in Canada are not counted in the United States, and some services that can be billed to Medicare in the United States cannot be billed in Canada. These differences generate quite different statistics on health utilization in the two countries. In turn, these kinds of national variations in measuring formal health care can account for different associations between, for example, use of informal supports and formal health care services. Gellhorn ended his remarks by commenting that the finding of Wolinsky and associates of less utilization of health services among the oldest old (the J curve) may be a manifestation of the wisdom of the very old, who have learned that it is in their best interest to avoid physicians and hospitals.

Mary Jo Bane, in addressing the papers by George and Chappell, observed that in her current New York State administrative job, she needs to know what she can do to conserve scarce public monies and to make life better for recipients of social services. To be sure, this set of papers helps her to understand the complexity of health care by showing how self-care, informal supports, and formal services are interrelated. Yet, as an administrator of a large public human service agency, her understanding of complexity is secondary to finding answers to questions such as: How can informal assistance be maximized so that use of formal services is reduced and public funds not exhausted? What kinds of programs help people? And what kinds of programs hinder them? Conferences such as ours, she inferred, do not provide her with sufficient direction. What then is our role? How concrete must we be in providing direction to administrators of programs and to policymakers? Is it sufficient to clarify complex phenomena without providing definitive solutions? Or should we devote more time and energy to becoming familiar with policy options and political processes? These are questions to ponder when reading the chapters in Part 2, as well as in the following section on long-term care policy.

4

The Use of Health Services by Elderly Americans: Implications from a Regression-Based Cohort Analysis*

Fredric D. Wolinsky, Rodney M. Coe, and Ray R. Mosely II

It is well known that the number and proportion of elderly persons in the United States have been and are expected to continue increasing well into the twenty-first century (Rice and Feldman, 1983). It is also well known that the elderly are disproportionately heavy users of health services (Fisher, 1980; Lubitz & Prihoda, 1983; Soldo & Manton, 1985; Waldo & Lazenby, 1984). As a result, although elderly Americans represent 12% of the population, they account for 31% of total health care expenditures. This has focused ever-increasing attention on explicit and implicit rationing schemes for providing health care to the elderly (Mechanic, 1985).

Although a great deal is presently known about the volume and the cost of health services used by the elderly, little is actually known about the reasons for that utilization (Haug, 1980; Wan, 1985). Particularly absent are sociological explanations of why the elderly use more health services

*This research was supported by a grant to Dr. Wolinsky from the National Institute on Aging (Research Career Development Award K04-AG00328). The views and opinions expressed herein are those of the authors and do not necessarily represent the official policy or position of any of the above-named institutions.

than the nonelderly (McKinlay, 1985). In an attempt to learn more about the reasons for the health and illness behavior of the elderly, we have undertaken a multiphased secondary analysis of the 1971 through 1980 Health Interview Surveys conducted by the National Center for Health Statistics. Our conceptual approach is based on Riley's (1971) age-stratification theory, which underscores the need for both within- and between-age strata analyses, as well as the use of longitudinal data for the separation of age, period, and cohort effects.

In the first phase of the study, we conducted a cohort analysis of the use of health services by six elderly cohorts (Wolinsky, Mosely, & Coe, in review). Using log-linear techniques we found statistically and substantively significant age and period effects on physician and hospital contact, with the aging effect reflecting a consistent increase in the percent of persons who saw a physician or were hospitalized in the previous year. This was as expected and is consistent with conventional sociological wisdom. The analysis of the volume of physician visits, however, quite unexpectedly revealed an inverse J-curve relationship with age; the pivotal point occurred as the cohort's members became octogenarians.

After considering nine plausible explanations for the inverse J-curve phenomenon, conceptual or empirical support was found for only three (Wolinsky et al., in review). Two of these involved substitution effects, either of hospital-based services for ambulatory-based services or social supports (especially in the form of older children as caregivers) for physicians' services. The third plausible explanation focused on the increasing risk among the octogenarians for the involuntary termination of their long-standing patient–practitioner relationships (and the concomitant decline in utilization) through either the death or retirement of their physicians.

These three explanations warrant further comment. First, all three are consistent with the age-stratification approach. They focus on both the needs of the new age stratum and its interaction with existing age strata. Second, although all three explanations are plausible, it seems unlikely that any one of them provides a sufficient explanation in itself. Rather, some admixture is probably necessary for an accurate interpretation of the inverse J-curve relationship. Finally, it is likely that the substitution of family and social supports provides the most fertile ground for a sociological explanation based on the emergence of intergenerational norms involving a new age stratum. This is not to say that the other two explanations are sociologically irrelevant; at the very least they represent the recognition of the changing demographic structure of society. However, it is in the substitution of family and social supports for physicians' services that the power of studying changes in age relationships lies.

If these (or other) substitutions are indeed occurring, then the structural relationships between various sociodemographic, socioeconomic, and health status characteristics and the use of health services probably change as elderly cohorts age. The purpose of the present chapter is to explore this possibility. To do this, we use a regression-based cohort technique that estimates the parameters of the behavioral model of health services utilization (Andersen, 1968) separately for each cell obtained in standard cohort tables. The unstandardized partial regression coefficients for each variable in the behavioral model (taken as estimates of the underlying structural relationships) then become the input data for a new set of standard cohort tables. These tables are then inspected visually and statistically to identify any aging, cohort, or period changes in the regression coefficients.

CONCEPTUAL MODEL

There are numerous models of health services utilization (Shortell, 1980). McKinlay (1972) has classified them into six categories: the economic approach; the sociodemographic approach; the geographic approach; the social–psychological approach; the sociocultural approach; and the organizational, or delivery-system, approach. The sociodemographic approach has been the most popular (McKinlay, 1985), in part because it readily lends itself to the secondary analysis of existing national data bases (Shortell, 1980). Among the sociodemographic models, Andersen's (1968) behavioral model is the best known (McKinlay, 1985) and most widely used (Wolinsky & Coe, 1984). Ward (1978, 1985) has argued that the behavioral model is particularly relevant for the elderly population, both because it identifies mutable factors that facilitate the discussion and formation of public policy and because of the significant correlation between sociodemographic factors and the use of health services among the elderly. McKinlay (1985) and Wolinsky, Coe, Miller, Prendergast, Creel, and Chavez (1983) note that the behavioral model is frequently used in studying the elderly, despite some general concern that demographic models may not be as appropriate as psychosocial models for the aged subpopulation (Rakowski & Hickey, 1980) and more specific evidence that the utility of its economic factors may have become limited since the advent of Medicaid and Medicare (Wolinsky & Coe, 1984). Nonetheless, the behavioral model of health services utilization is the dominant paradigm for studying the health and illness behavior of the elderly.

The behavioral model of health services utilization was developed by Andersen (1968) and refined with his colleagues (Aday & Andersen, 1974, 1975; Aday, Andersen, & Fleming, 1980; Aday, Fleming, & Andersen, 1984; Andersen & Newman, 1973). In the behavioral model the use of health services is defined as a function of the predisposing, enabling, and need characteristics of the individual. The predisposing characteristics reflect the fact that some individuals have a greater propensity to use services than do other individuals. These propensities can be predicted by various individual characteristics that occur prior to the incidence of episodes of specific illness. They may be classified as either demographic (e.g., age, sex, marital status, and family size), social-structural (e.g., education, occupation, social class, and race), or health beliefs (e.g., locus of control or medical knowledge). Basically, the model asserts that individuals with different demographic characteristics have different types and amounts of illness, resulting in different patterns of using health services. Individuals with different social-structural characteristics have different lifestyles, resulting in different patterns of health services utilization. Similarly, those patterns will vary with the salience of health beliefs.

The enabling characteristics in the behavioral model reflect the fact that while the individual may be predisposed to use health services, he or she will not use these services unless able to do so. An individual's ability to use health services depends on his or her family resources, including income, health insurance, and having a regular source of care, and community resources, such as physician- and hospital-bed-to-population ratios, place of residence, and geographic location. If there are sufficient family and community resources to enable the individual to use health services, then the individual will be more likely to use those services.

Finally, the behavioral model stipulates that even in the presence of the appropriate levels of the predisposing and enabling characteristics, individuals must perceive some need for using health services. In other words, need is the basic and direct stimulus for the use of health services when the appropriate levels of predisposing and enabling characteristics exist. Need is usually measured by self-reports of symptoms, functional limitations, and perceived health levels.

The behavioral model further differentiates between three basic types of health services: hospital, physician, or dental services. These also represent the nondiscretionary, mixed, and discretionary use of health services by individuals. Discretionary services are those whose use is initiated by the individual, as is usually the case with dental services. The use of nondiscretionary services, like the use of hospitals, is more likely to be initiated not only by the individual, but by the physician as well. The use of physician services is somewhat mixed because, although the initial visit may be discretionary, follow-up visits may be initiated or suggested by the physician (Wolinsky, 1980). Thus, the effects of the predisposing, enabling, and need characteristics may vary across different types of health services utilization.

Basically, then, the behavioral model of health services utilization takes the following functional form:

$$U = f(P, E, N)$$

where the use of health services *(U)* is seen as a function *(f)* of the predisposing *(P)*, enabling *(E)*, and need *(N)* characteristics. The behavioral model may also be graphically represented by the causal model shown in Figure 4-1. In Figure 4-1 the need characteristics are expressed as a function of the predisposing and enabling characteristics, and the enabling characteristics are expressed as a function of the predisposing characteristics (Wan, Odell, and Lewis, 1982, p. 90; Wolinsky, 1978, p. 385). The behavioral model has been assessed in a number of national studies of the general population (e.g., Aday et al., 1980, 1984; Wan & Soifer, 1974; Wolinsky, 1978), the results of which have been influential in shaping national health care policy (Shortell, 1984).

Recently, several studies have applied the behavioral model to the special case of the elderly's use of health services (e.g., Branch, Jette, Evashwick, Polansky, Rowe, & Diehr, 1981; Evashwick, Rowe, Diehr, & Branch, 1984; Eve, 1982, 1984; Eve & Friedsam, 1980; Haug, 1980; Russell, 1981; Wan et al., 1982; Wolinsky et al., 1983; Wolinsky & Coe, 1984). In general, these studies find that: (1) the need characteristics are the major determinants of the use of health services; (2) the amount of variance explained by the model is not large; and (3) the regression coefficients obtained for the predisposing and enabling characteristics are quite modest (if not substantively unimportant). Indeed, the behavioral model has explained less of the variance in the elderly's use of health services than it has for the general population in the United States (Wolinsky et al., 1983).

The principal explanation for the lower predictive utility of the behavioral model has been that the predisposing and enabling characteristics may no longer be important in the elderly's use of health services. Most

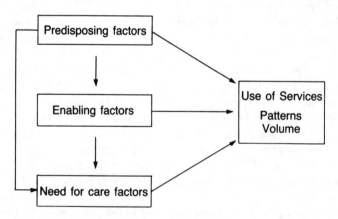

FIGURE 4-1 *The behavioral model of health services utilization.*

health services (e.g., physician and hospital services) are now commonly covered by private or public health insurance programs. Thus, the salience of the predisposing and enabling characteristics has been eroded (although cost-containment efforts begun in the late 1970s may be restoring the importance of these factors). Snider (1980a, b), however, has suggested that the behavioral model may be more successful in predicting the use of ancillary services by adults. These services typically (1) encompass more health maintenance and/or preventive health care than is the case with physicians and hospitals; (2) are more relevant to the needs of the elderly than formal acute care services; and (3) are less likely to be covered by insurance policies or included in outreach programs. Coulton and Frost (1982) provide some evidence to support Snider's interpretation.

Wolinsky and associates (Wolinsky et al., 1983; Wolinsky & Coe, 1984) have taken a different approach, arguing that the limited predictive utility of the behavioral model among the elderly stems from measurement and modeling issues. On the measurement side, they point out that most studies have not included comprehensive sets of indicators of the predisposing, enabling, and need characteristics. Particularly absent have been measures of the health care delivery system to which the elderly had access. In studies of the general population, Dutton (1979) and Kronenfeld (1980) have shown that the nature of the delivery system has marked effects on the use of health services.

Building on Mechanic's (1979) work, Wolinsky and associates (1983) also argue that restricted-activity and bed-disability days represent illness behavior more than illness. As such, they should be considered measures of health services utilization, albeit in an informal sense. This argument is based on the fact that a person's taking a restricted-activity or bed-disability day usually involves both the provisional validation of the sick role by the individual's lay referral groups (Suchman, 1965a, b) and the initiation of some form of self-treatment (such as the consumption of over-the-counter medications, especially among the elderly [see Denton, 1978]).

On the modeling side, Wolinsky and Coe (1984) have argued that the poor predictive utility of the behavioral model may also be a result of distortions introduced by the nonnormally distributed indicators of health services utilization. Specifically, it is argued that the extreme positive skew observed in most utilization data significantly attenuates the assessment of the behavioral model in parametric analyses. As a corrective technique, Wolinsky and Coe (1984) suggest truncating the positive skew at the point where the curve becomes exceedingly flat (somewhere around the 95th percentile, or about 13 visits to the doctor, or 15 nights spent in the hospital, per person per year). This has the effect of reclassifying the most excessive users of health services as merely heavy users of health services.

DATA

The data used herein are taken from the 1972, 1976, and 1980 Health Interview Surveys conducted by the National Center for Health Statistics. This is an ongoing annual survey that first began in 1956, as authorized by PL 84-652. The Health Interview Survey follows a multistage probability design that permits a continuous sampling of the noninstitutionalized civilian population of the United States. The sampling design is such that each week a representative sample of this population is interviewed, resulting in 52 weekly samples that may be pooled at the end of the year to provide a fully representative sample of all individuals from all places during all seasons. Thus it is not necessary to adjust the data for seasonal or geographic fluctuations. (For a more complete discussion of the history, design, and logistics of the Health Interview Survey, see National Center for Health Statistics [1975, 1985]; for other reports on the secondary analysis of the Health Interview Survey, see Eve [1982, 1984], Mosely & Wolinsky [1986], Wolinsky & Coe [1984], Wolinsky, Coe, Mosely, & Homan [1985], Wolinsky et al. [in review].)

The number of cases available for analysis for each cohort for each survey year is shown in Table 4-1. Using these six cohorts over this eight-year period has particular theoretical advantages for detecting age, period, and cohort effects. In terms of aging effects, these data allow each cohort to be "aged" through meaningful life-cycle stages: from preretirement to postretirement status or from young-old to very-old age strata. (See Riley [1971] and Suzman & Riley [1985] for an elaboration of the general significance of these changes.) Thus important age-strata comparisons of the use of health services over time can be made using the data on these cohorts.

The relevance of the opportunities for detecting cohort effects can be seen by comparing the life-cycle stages of the youngest and oldest cohorts at

TABLE 4-1 Number of Cases in Each Cohort for Each Health Interview Survey

Age category	Health Interview Survey		
	1972	1976	1980
56–59	5,242		
60–63	4,733	4,071	
64–67	4,115	3,554	3,467
68–71	3,232	2,998	2,965
72–75	2,659	2,332	2,214
76–79	1,866	1,696	1,518
80–83		1,097	1,019
84–87			598

three important points during the twentieth century (i.e., World War I, the Great Depression, and World War II). Members of the youngest cohort were preschoolers during World War I, adolescents during the Great Depression, and young adults during World War II. In contrast, members of the oldest cohort were young adults during World War I, adults (likely with their own families) during the Great Depression, and middle-aged (likely with their offspring serving in the armed forces) during World War II. Accordingly, although all six cohorts lived through these same important points in time, they are likely to have been differentially affected by them due to their different life-cycle stages (see Elder, 1974, 1975). This may result in different patterns of health services utilization by cohort, with earlier cohorts using fewer services (especially through governmental programs, such as Medicare) due to their aversion to accepting or relying on external supports (see Butler, 1975).

Finally, although these data cover only the period from 1972 to 1980, it was precisely during this time that cost controls for Medicare (and other health insurance programs) were implemented. As a result, some constriction of the use of health services is likely to have occurred among the elderly between 1976 and 1980 (see Aday et al., 1984). Accordingly, these data provide a legitimate opportunity for the application of cohort-based analytic techniques to the analysis of the use of health services by elderly Americans.

METHOD

The primary analytic method involves comparing and contrasting the unstandardized partial regression coefficients across the appropriate cohorts. For example, to determine whether the effect of sex on the use of health services varies from one age category to another, the unstandardized partial regression coefficients for sex obtained from each age cohort are compared and contrasted. This was done using two methods. First, the unstandardized partial regression coefficients were graphed, as were their 95% confidence intervals. Intuitively, when the regression coefficient for sex from each age group falls within the confidence interval of that for sex for each other age group, the coefficients cannot be said to be significantly different from each other. (These graphs are summarized but not presented herein.)

Even for the simple case of the six age groups, however, such comparisons are both tedious and difficult. Accordingly, a second method was also employed. This method involves using the Relative Instability Ratio (RIR) developed by Wolinsky (1977, 1981, 1983). Essentially, the RIR takes the standard deviation of the observed unstandardized partial regression coefficients and norms it to the weighted pooled estimate of their standard error, an analog to the common F-ratio of the variance between groups to the variance within groups. The value of the RIR is a metric indicating how many times the standard deviation is greater than the standard error. As such, $RIR^2 \times (N - 1)$ is distributed as chi-squared at $N - 1$ degrees of freedom, where N is the number of observed unstandardized partial regression coefficients being compared (in examining aging effects among the six age cohorts, $N = 6$). (The RIRs are summarized but not presented herein.)

MEASUREMENT

The indicators of the predisposing, enabling, and need characteristics, as well as the various measures of health services utilization, are shown in Table 4-2. Also shown are their coding algorithms, means, and standard deviations. (Due to space constraints, only aggregate data [for the six cohorts combined] for the 1980 survey are presented.) All of the indicators shown in Table 4-2 are standard measures routinely used in major multivariate studies of the use of health services (see Aday et al., 1980, 1984; Andersen, 1968; Wan et al., 1982; Wolinsky, 1978; Wolinsky & Coe, 1984).

Suffice it to say here that the indicators of the predisposing characteristics include sex, widowhood status, living arrangements, race, education, and labor-force participation. Because previous studies by Andersen (1968) and others (e.g., Wolinsky et al., 1983) failed to find health beliefs to be significantly related to the use of health services, and because there are no measures of health beliefs in these surveys, this dimension of the predisposing characteristics was not included. The indicators of the enabling characteristics include having a telephone in the house (which facilitates contact with physicians and other providers), family income, a set of dummy variables for geographic location, and a set of dummy variables for population density. The need characteristics are measured by perceived health status and the degree of limited activity. Informal health services utilization is measured by restricted activity and bed-disability days in the past two weeks. Formal health services utilization is measured by physician contact, the volume of physician visits in the past year, the number of hospital episodes, and the number of nights spent in the hospital in the past year.

Standard procedures were used to assess the assumptions inherent in the use of ordinary least squares (OLS) regression analysis with these measures, including an initial review of all univariate, bivariate, and multivariate distributions (see Hartwig & Dearing, 1979). Special consideration was given to checking for multicollinearity, following the method of Lewis-Beck

TABLE 4-2 Coding Algorithms, Means, and Standard Deviations for the Indicators of the Predisposing, Enabling, Need, and Health Services Utilization Characteristics in the 1980 Health Interview Survey, All Cohorts Combined

Indicator	Algorithm	Mean	Standard deviation
Predisposing characteristics			
Sex	1 = female	0.58	0.49
	0 = male		
Widowed	1 = yes	0.32	0.47
	0 = no		
Lives alone	1 = yes	0.28	0.45
	0 = no		
Race	1 = nonwhite	0.09	0.29
	0 = white		
Education	number of years	9.80	3.79
Labor-force participation	1 = yes	0.16	0.37
	0 = no		
Enabling characteristics			
Telephone in house	1 = yes	0.96	0.20
	0 = no		
Family income	thousands of dollars	11.24	7.33
Northeast region	1 = yes	0.24	0.42
	0 = no		
Southern region	1 = yes	0.33	0.47
	0 = no		
Western region	1 = yes	0.18	0.38
	0 = no		
Major-city residence	1 = yes	0.37	0.48
	0 = no		
Farm residence	1 = yes	0.03	0.18
	0 = no		
Need characteristics			
Perceived health status	1 = poor	2.89	0.92
	2 = fair		
	3 = good		
	4 = excellent		
Limited activity	1 = cannot perform usual activity	3.02	1.96
	2 = limited in amount and kind		
	3 = limited in outdoor activities only		
	4 = not limited		

(continued)

TABLE 4-2 (*continued*)

Indicator	Algorithm	Mean	Standard deviation
Health services utilization			
Restricted-activity days	number of days in past two weeks	1.48	3.94
Bed-disability days	number of days in past two weeks	0.51	2.29
Physician contact in last year	1 = yes 0 = no	0.79	0.41
Physician visits in past year	actual number of visits (truncated at 13 or more)	4.90 (3.98)	9.39 (4.08)
Hospital episodes in past year	actual number of episodes (truncated at 2 or more)	0.25 (0.20)	0.66 (0.42)
Hospitalized days in past year	actual number of days (truncated at 15 or more)	2.45 (1.64)	8.59 (4.08)

(1980), wherein each independent variable was regressed on all other independent variables, with no cases of harmful multicollinearity being detected (i.e., no R^2 values approached .64). To check for nonadditivity, all two- and three-way interaction terms among the independent variables were hierarchically added into the predictive equations; subsequent F-tests showed no significant improvements in the overall model. Similar procedures were used to assess linearity by hierarchically introducing root, squared, and cubed terms into the equations; subsequent F-tests showed no significant improvements in the overall model. It was, therefore, assumed that the measurement and modeling assumptions inherent in the application of OLS regression to these data had been met.

RESULTS

The results of the regression analysis (i.e., the unstandardized partial regression coefficients, intercepts, and R^2 statistics) are shown in Tables 4-3 through 4-9 for the number of restricted activity days, the number of bed disability days, physician contact, hospital contact, the number of physician visits, the number of nights spent in the hospital, and the number of hospital episodes. For the latter three measures, the analysis was restricted to those respondents who had at least one physician visit (or night spent in the hospital).

Note that the format of Tables 4-3 through 4-9 is not that of standard cohort tables (as is Table 4-1). There are two reasons for this. First, space constraints augured for a more condensed presentational format, and this method results in 7 as opposed to 15 tables. The standard cohort tables can be reconstructed from these tables, or one can make the appropriate comparisons using these tables. For example, consider Table 4-3, which contains the results from predicting the number of restricted activity days. Aging effects may be examined in Table 4-3 by comparing the impact, say of sex, for cohort 2 across the three survey years. In 1972 the members of cohort 2 were 60 to 63 years old (with a regression coefficient for sex of .38), in 1976 they were 64 to 67 years old (with a regression coefficient for sex of .32), and in 1980 they were 68 to 71 years old (with a regression coefficient for sex of .40).

Continuing with Table 4-3 as an example, period effects may be examined by comparing the impact, say of widowhood, for cohort 3 in 1972 (with a regression coefficient for widowhood of .51), with that for cohort 2 in 1976 (which does not have a statistically significant regression coefficient for widowhood), and with that for cohort 1 in 1980 (which also does not have a statistically significant regression coefficient for widowhood). Note that the members of each of these cohorts were 56 to 59 years old at the time they were interviewed. Concluding with Table 4-3 as an example, cohort effects may be examined by comparing the impact, say of living alone, for each of the six cohorts within a given survey year (such as 1976). This provides the appropriate cross-sectional comparisons, revealing regression coefficients for living alone of .40, .51, and .45 for cohorts 1, 2, and 3, but no significant regression coefficients for living alone among cohorts 4, 5, or 6.

The second reason for using this presentational format is that it simplifies the visual understanding of what is (or is not) happening overall. In particular, it allows us to see which independent variables (1) consistently affect a measure of health services utilization across all cohorts from all years (i.e., within a given table) and (2) consistently affect all measures of health services utilization across all cohorts from all years (i.e., across all tables). The data clearly show that the two measures of the need characteristics (i.e., perceived health status and the degree of limited activity) have the largest impact on health services utilization and the only consistent impact across all measures of health services utilization. The only other factor to consistently affect even one measure of health services utilization (i.e., within a given table) is family income. It has a rather consistent positive effect, but only on the measure of physician contact.

TABLE 4-3 Unstandardized, Partial Regression Coefficients Obtained for the Predisposing, Enabling, and Need Characteristics in Predicting the Number of Restricted-Activity Days, by Survey Year and Cohort*

Independent variables	1972						1976 Cohort						1980					
	1	2	3	4	5	6	1	2	3	4	5	6	1	2	3	4	5	6
Sex		.38						.32				.82	.41	.40		.70		
Widowhood			.51															
Living alone		.56	.51				.40	.51	.45					.84	.72			
Race																		−1.59
Education	−.03				.06					.07								
Labor-force participation	−.45							−.30					−.05					
Telephone in the home								.65	−.64					1.26				
Family income												−.09						
Northeastern U.S.		−.29	.30															
Southern U.S.																		
Western U.S.							.25	.64					.51	1.21	1.02			
Major-city residence																		
Farm residence																		
Perceived health status	−.69	−.65	−.72	−.74	−.68	−.95	−.73	−.71	−.82	−.95	−.79	−.95	−.81	−.94	−.91	−.83	−1.32	−.71
Degree of limited activity	−.80	−.78	−.68	−.54	−.64	−.50	−.78	−.67	−.75	−.76	−.65	−.77	−.71	−.89	−.68	−.73	−.65	−.70
Intercept	6.27	5.65	4.86	4.64	4.93	4.99	5.53	4.64	6.22	5.14	4.96	6.56	5.64	5.14	6.04	6.35	5.85	4.68
R^2	.16	.14	.14	.11	.10	.11	.15	.13	.15	.14	.12	.16	.17	.19	.14	.14	.16	.12

*Coefficients not significant at the .05 level or beyond have been omitted for clarity.

TABLE 4-4 Unstandardized, Partial Regression Coefficients Obtained for the Predisposing, Enabling, and Need Characteristics in Predicting the Number of Bed-Disability Days, by Survey Year and Cohort*

Independent variables	1972						1976 (Cohort)						1980					
	1	2	3	4	5	6	1	2	3	4	5	6	1	2	3	4	5	6
Sex														.24				
Widowhood																		
Living alone																		
Race			.37		.56													
Education										.04								
Labor-force participation	-.15																	
Telephone in the home					.34											-.90		
Family income		-.01							-.41									
Northeastern U.S.																		
Southern U.S.																		
Western U.S.																		
Major-city residence							.22	.33	.28							.28		
Farm residence	-.21																	
Perceived health status	-.26	-.24	-.32	-.33	-.36	-.54	-.29	-.43	-.38	-.61	-.40	-.67	-.24	-.34	-.39	-.28	-.73	-.64
Degree of limited activity	-.27	-.22	-.26	-.09	-.16	-.13	-.19	-.19	-.28	-.18	-.24	-.28	-.13	-.30	-.22	-.27	-.24	-.46
Intercept	2.14	2.05	1.96	1.62	1.36	2.27	1.89	1.95	2.61	2.33	2.33	3.92	1.46	1.89	2.47	2.73	2.78	3.65
R^2	.07	.06	.07	.04	.06	.06	.05	.07	.08	.08	.07	.10	.05	.08	.06	.07	.09	.13

*Coefficients not significant at the .05 level or beyond have been omitted for clarity.

TABLE 4-5 Unstandardized, Partial Regression Coefficients Obtained for the Predisposing, Enabling, and Need Characteristics in Predicting Physician Contact, by Survey Year and Cohort*

Independent variables	1972						1976 (Cohort)						1980					
	1	2	3	4	5	6	1	2	3	4	5	6	1	2	3	4	5	6
Sex	.08	.06	.07	.08		.06	.07	.09	.11	.08			.11	.08		.09		
Widowhood	.05				.06								.06					
Living alone									.06	.06	.07							
Race						-.11	.07				-.11							
Education	.01	.01		.006	.005	.01	.01	.01	.005	.005	.01					.01		
Labor-force participation	.04						.04											
Telephone in the home	.21	.12	.15	.20	.13	.17	.09	.14	.14	.14	.13	-.16	.18	.09	.14			.22
Family income	.005	.005	.01	.003	.01	.01	.01	.003	.003	.005		.01	.006	.004		.004		.01
Northeastern U.S.																	.08	
Southern U.S.					.07										.07			
Western U.S.																		.13
Major-city residence																	.06	
Farm residence												-.18						
Perceived health status	-.09	-.08	-.08	-.08	-.07	-.07	-.06	-.04	-.05	-.04	-.05	-.04	-.07	-.06	-.05	-.06	-.03	-.05
Degree of limited activity	-.07	-.07	-.06	-.05	-.05	-.05	-.08	-.07	-.06	-.06	-.06	-.05	-.07	-.06	-.04	-.05	-.03	-.08
Intercept	.83	.91	.89	.83	.83	.82	.84	.82	.83	.86	.91	.95	.83	.92	.84	.91	.89	.76
R^2	.08	.07	.08	.08	.08	.10	.09	.08	.07	.08	.09	.07	.09	.07	.05	.09	.04	.10

*Coefficients not significant at the .05 level or beyond have been omitted for clarity.

TABLE 4-6 Unstandardized, Partial Regression Coefficients Obtained for the Predisposing, Enabling, and Need Characteristics in Predicting Hospital Contact, by Survey Year and Cohort*

Independent variables	1972 1	1972 2	1972 3	1972 4	1972 5	1972 6	1976 (Cohort) 1	1976 2	1976 3	1976 4	1976 5	1976 6	1980 1	1980 2	1980 3	1980 4	1980 5	1980 6
Sex							−.04											
Widowhood			.04				.04											
Living alone														.06	−.08			
Race		.06							−.07									
Education	.004				−.06													
Labor-force participation			.005								−.09	−.24						
Telephone in the home	.04						.05	.07					.10					
Family income		.002		.08	.004	.005		.003			.12			.003	.004			
Northeastern U.S.																		
Southern U.S.		−.05					−.04		−.05									
Western U.S.	−.04										−.07		−.04					
Major-city residence	−.03						−.04											
Farm residence		−.05	−.06							−.09						−.14		
Perceived health status	−.05	−.04	−.05	−.03	−.06	−.05	−.04	−.05	−.04	−.04	−.05	−.07	−.04	−.06	−.04	−.07	−.06	−.06
Degree of limited activity	−.06	−.05	−.06	−.04	−.04	−.05	−.06	−.07	−.05	−.06	−.08	−.03	−.06	−.07	−.06	−.05	−.04	−.07
Intercept	.41	.46	.38	.28	.47	.43	.41	.38	.41	.36	.50	.50	.44	.37	.43	.48	.43	.62
R^2	.07	.06	.07	.04	.06	.08	.08	.08	.06	.07	.12	.08	.07	.09	.06	.08	.06	.12

*Coefficients not significant at the .05 level or beyond have been omitted for clarity.

TABLE 4-7 Unstandardized, Partial Regression Coefficients Obtained for the Predisposing, Enabling, and Need Characteristics in Predicting the Number of Physician Visits (Among Those Who Had at Least One), by Survey Year and Cohort*

Independent variables	1972						1976 (Cohort)						1980					
	1	2	3	4	5	6	1	2	3	4	5	6	1	2	3	4	5	6
Sex	.31		.60	.45	.46		.47	.56	.78				.59					
Widowhood																		
Living alone																		
Race	-.51									.90		1.08	.65		1.29			
Education											-.10							
Labor-force participation					-.06													
Telephone in the home	-.57	-.38	-.41				.75								.67	1.46		
Family income	.68		.03							1.47	1.18	1.51						
Northeastern U.S.																		
Southern U.S.								.51										
Western U.S.						.89						.22						
Major-city residence	.58	.51	.37				.33	.61		.54	.82		.36					.86
Farm residence													-1.05					
Perceived health status	-1.09	-1.12	-1.28	-1.19	-1.10	-1.03	-1.08	-1.06	-1.00	-.85	-.94	-.83	-1.02	-1.23	-.65	-1.09	-1.15	-.73
Degree of limited activity	-.95	-.78	-.77	-.54	-.65	-.46	-.94	-.86	-.84	-.89	-.48	-.77	-.80	-.53	-.73	-.42	-.49	-.35
Intercept	10.79	10.76	10.15	9.71	10.28	9.69	9.94	9.95	9.72	8.27	8.20	7.88	8.95	9.10	8.38	7.81	9.32	8.29
R^2	.20	.18	.19	.14	.15	.12	.21	.20	.17	.17	.12	.15	.18	.16	.13	.12	.14	.10

*Coefficients not significant at the .05 level or beyond have been omitted for clarity.

TABLE 4-8 Unstandardized, Partial Regression Coefficients Obtained for the Predisposing, Enabling, and Need Characteristics in Predicting the Number of Nights Spent in the Hospital (Among Those Who Had at Least One), by Survey Year and Cohort*

Independent variables	1972						1976 (Cohort)						1980					
	1	2	3	4	5	6	1	2	3	4	5	6	1	2	3	4	5	6
Sex	−1.21						1.07											
Widowhood					1.31													2.42
Living alone																		
Race																	.36	
Education																		
Labor-force participation				−1.66														
Telephone in the home	1.85							−2.75										
Family income					1.71													
Northeastern U.S.																		
Southern U.S.	−1.35						−1.70											
Western U.S.				−2.08	−2.16	−3.08			−1.36	−2.15			−1.95		−2.10	−3.06		−4.49
Major-city residence	1.54		1.76					−1.53		1.24								2.36
Farm residence		−2.15										2.64						
Perceived health status				−.60				−.94	−.59	−.73	−1.14				−.88			−1.26
Degree of limited activity	−1.00	−.89	−.55	−.66	−.87	−.68	−.81	−.60	−.50	−.61	−.71		−.85	−.90		−.93	−.98	
Intercept	11.66	13.65	11.64	13.10	11.34	14.37	12.94	14.18	12.57	14.90	12.18	12.29	11.83	11.50	12.72	12.52	9.40	13.50
R^2	.15	.13	.10	.11	.13	.14	.12	.12	.08	.12	.15	.16	.12	.10	.13	.12	.18	.32

*Coefficients not significant at the .05 level or beyond have been omitted for clarity.

TABLE 4-9 Unstandardized, Partial Regression Coefficients Obtained for the Predisposing, Enabling, and Need Characteristics in Predicting the Number of Hospital Espisodes (Among Those Who Had at Least One), by Survey Year and Cohort*

Independent variables	1972						1976 Cohort						1980					
	1	2	3	4	5	6	1	2	3	4	5	6	1	2	3	4	5	6
Sex																		
Widowhood													.14					
Living alone			.12															
Race								.21										
Education															−.20			
Labor-force participation				−.15							−.27				−.02			
Telephone in the home				.24		−.22												
Northeastern U.S.																		
Southern U.S.			.10													.15		
Western U.S.						−.19												
Major-city residence																		
Farm residence																		
Perceived health status	−.06	−.07	−.05	−.07	−.06			−.07			−.06		−.06			−.08		
Degree of limited activity	−.05	−.05					−.05	−.07					−.05	−.06	−.06			
Intercept	1.34	1.53	1.35	1.27	1.39	1.68	1.52	1.64	1.38	1.66	1.60	1.43	1.57	1.28	1.58	1.40	1.48	1.22
R^2	.10	.08	.07	.10	.05	.11	.05	.11	.06	.05	.09	.15	.08	.06	.10	.09	.07	.16

*Coefficients not significant at the .05 level or beyond have been omitted for clarity.

Although the primary effect of the need characteristics is not surprising (indeed, it is quite consistent with the literature reviewed above), the absence of any other factors as consistent predictors of a wide range of health services utilization (i.e., across tables) is somewhat unexpected. In particular, one might have expected sex, widowhood, living arrangements, or the various measures of socioeconomic status to have been consistent predictors of the use of health services. The dominance of the need characteristics and the absence of consistent effects from the predisposing and enabling characteristics imply the existence of an equitable health care delivery system. We shall return to this issue in greater detail below in the discussion section.

Focusing on the two measures of informal health services utilization (i.e., the number of restricted activity and bed disability days in the past two weeks) reveals that, aside from the need characteristics, virtually nothing else has a consistent effect. Indeed, only for sex and living alone were six or more (out of 18 possible) significant coefficients observed. Moreover, both of these indicators only affect the measure of restricted-activity days. Women and those who live alone were more likely to have taken restricted-activity days than were men or those who lived with others. Individuals with better-perceived health and those without activity limitations were less likely to have taken restricted-activity days. The visual inspection of these coefficients and their 95% confidence intervals (as well as the statistical application of the RIR) revealed no significant patterns of change (neither aging, nor period, nor cohort).

The results for the two measures of physician and hospital contact are somewhat the same and somewhat different from those for the two measures of informal health services utilization. For hospital contact, only the two need characteristics produced consistently significant effects. As expected, individuals in better health were less likely to have been hospitalized. The effects of perceived health status and the degree of limited activity were virtually constant across cohorts and survey years. Besides the need characteristics, only race, having a telephone, and income produced six or more significant coefficients. The sign of the coefficients for race fluctuated, suggesting that the underlying population parameter was really zero. Having a telephone in the home increased the likelihood of hospitalization from 4% to 12%. Each $10,000 increment in income increased the likelihood of hospitalization by 2–4%. No evidence of aging, period, or cohort changes was found for any of these predictors of having been hospitalized in the past year.

In addition to the consistent (if not virtually constant) effects of the need characteristics on physician contact, at least six significant coefficients were obtained for sex, education, having a telephone, and family income. Women were 6–11% more likely than men to have seen a physician. Each additional year of education increased the likelihood of having seen a physician by about 1%. Having a telephone in the house increased the likelihood of seeing a physician by 9–21%; this seemingly large effect results from the fact that in the Health Interview Survey, telephone contacts to physicians are counted as visits. Every $10,000 increment in income increased the likelihood of having seen a physician by 3–10%. No evidence of any aging, period, or cohort changes was found for any of these predictors of having seen a physician in the last year.

A somewhat similar story can be told about the predictors of the number of physician visits in the past year. Again, only the two need characteristics consistently produced significant coefficients, indicating that those in better health went to see the doctor less often. Sex, having a telephone, and living in a major city were the only other indicators that produced six or more significant coefficients. Women had between .31 and .78 more physician visits than men. Individuals with telephones in their homes had between .68 and 1.51 more physician visits than those without telephones (recall that telephone contacts with physicians are counted as visits). Living in one of the 31 largest Standard Metropolitan Statistical Areas (SMSAs) was associated with having between .33 and .86 more physician visits than living in less urbanized (or nonurbanized) areas. No evidence of any aging, period, or cohort changes was found for any of these predictors of the number of physician visits in the past year.

The coefficients obtained from the analysis of the number of nights spent in the hospital in the past year present a slightly different picture. On the one hand, it is the need characteristics, again, that have the principal and most consistent effects on this measure of hospital utilization. On the other hand, neither of the two need characteristics produces a significant coefficient across all cohorts for all survey years. Indeed, the effect of perceived health status is significant only half the time, and the effect of the degree of limited activity is insignificant in three out of 18 cases. Nonetheless, the coefficients are quite consistent, indicating that, among those who had been hospitalized at least once in the past year, individuals in better health spent fewer nights in the hospital.

The only other indicator to produce at least six significant regression coefficients here is living in the western United States. Compared to those who live elsewhere, westerners who are hospitalized spend between 1.35 and 4.49 fewer days in the hospital. This is consistent with the generally shorter length of hospital stays in the western United States. Although several of the coefficients for these three indicators (i.e., perceived health, degree of limited activity, and western residence) appear to be rather different, there are no statistically significant aging, period, or cohort changes among them. This results in part from the considerably larger confidence intervals surrounding these coefficients because of the reduced sample size (recall that only individuals with at least one hospital episode are included in the analysis).

The coefficients obtained from predicting the number of hospital episodes form an even simpler pattern. Here, only the perceived health status and degree of limited activity indicators produce six or more significant coefficients. Although neither indicator produces significant coefficients across all cohorts for all years, the significant coefficients that are produced are virtually identical. Thus there is no evidence of any aging, period, or cohort changes. As expected, even though they were hospitalized at least once, individuals who are healthier have fewer hospital episodes overall than those who are sicker.

CAVEATS

Before turning to a discussion of the findings and their implications for health care policy concerning the elderly, there are two related caveats that warrant some attention. The first concerns the sample size, especially among the oldest cohorts. Although the average number of cases per sampling cell in Table 4-1 is large (about 2,500), among the octogenarians there are only 600 to 1,100 cases. Moreover, because the analysis of the volume measures of health services utilization excludes those who had no contact with physicians or hospitals, the number of cases is further reduced. This is especially salient for the analysis of hospital utilization among the oldest cohort, where the number of available cases drops to about 110. As a result, the confidence intervals around the regression coefficients for the predisposing, enabling, and need characteristics become relatively large. Therefore, it becomes increasingly more difficult to detect either significant coefficients themselves or significant differences between significant coefficients. It is possible, then, that no aging, period, or cohort changes were detected because the sample sizes became too small.

It should be noted, however, that this caveat applies primarily to the analysis of the volume of hospital utilization. More than 80% of the respondents (at all age groups) reported some physician contact during the past 12 months. Thus, even among the oldest cohort, there are at least 400 cases available for the analysis of the volume measure of physician utilization. (For the contact and informal measures of health services utilization, the numbers of cases available for analysis are those shown in Table 4-1.)

The second and related caveat is that this study does not permit an assessment of the determinants of health services utilization among those elderly who enter their ninth decade (or become centenarians). Although desirable, such analyses are precluded by the declining sampling cell sizes that are obtained when these additional cohorts are introduced at the bottom of Table 4-1. Therefore, if aging, period, or cohort effects do exist, but are not initiated until after the eighth decade, the present design simply cannot detect them. This is somewhat troubling, especially because the pivotal point in the inverse J-curve phenomenon was observed as the oldest cohorts became octogenarians.

DISCUSSION AND POLICY IMPLICATIONS

Two principal findings emerged from the analyses reported herein. Both have important implications for health care policy concerning the elderly. First, our results show that regardless of which type or measure of health services utilization (either formal or informal) is considered, the need characteristics have the greatest impact. Moreover, only the need characteristics produced significant coefficients across all types of health services utilization. Clearly, need is the primary determinant of the use of health services among elderly Americans.

The policy implications of this finding are of considerable import. Because the primary determinant of health services utilization is need, and because no other sociocultural or socioeconomic factors were found to have much impact, one might infer that the health care delivery system is equitable. Indeed, Andersen and his colleagues (see Aday et al., 1980, 1984) have already made such inferences, based on their analysis of the general population in the United States. At first glance, such an interpretation appears reasonable enough.

There are, however, two reasons why we think it is premature to draw such inferences. First and foremost, although the need characteristics are the principal determinants of health services utilization, they are not the *sole* determinants. Other factors do have significant effects (albeit not consistently across all measures of health services utilization). Moreover, the need characteristics explain less than 25% of the variance in any measure of health services utilization. Thus, the vast majority of the variance in the use of health services remains unexplained. Although better measurement (of need, health insurance, the patient–practitioner relationship, and health beliefs) and modeling (e.g., log-linear, LISREL, and stochastic) techniques would probably enhance the explanatory power of the behavioral model, it is unlikely that these developments would account for the 75% of the variance that is presently unexplained. Because so little of the variance in the use of health services is explained by the fairly complex predictive models used herein, we believe it is premature to say that the health care delivery system is an equitable one, despite the fact that what we can explain is explained primarily by the need characteristics.

The second reason we are not willing to infer, from the results presented herein, that the health care delivery system is equitable involves the time when these data were collected. Six years have passed since these six cohorts were last interviewed. During that time the economic situation of the elderly (as well as that of the general population) has changed somewhat. Among the most important of these changes has been access to health care. Berki and his colleagues (see Berki et al., 1985) have shown that health insurance levels and other access measures declined considerably during the early 1980s for those who became unemployed. Others have discussed similar reductions in access to health care during this period for veterans (see Wolinsky et al., 1985) and for the poor and the elderly (see Mechanic, 1985). Therefore, even if the health care delivery system had been more equitable for the elderly during the 1970s, as Andersen and his colleagues suggest (see Aday et al., 1980), it is not clear that the same could be said for the 1980s.

The second principal finding to emerge from our analyses was actually a negative finding. No evidence was found to corroborate the existence of any aging, period, or cohort changes in the determinants of health services utilization among the elderly. As a result, these analyses do not inform the interpretation of the inverse J-curve relationship we identified earlier (see Wolinsky et al., in review) between the aging process and the use of physician services. Indeed, these results suggest that the determinants of the use of health services are rather stable within a cohort as it ages, as well as across cohorts and periods.

Although the absence of any aging, period, or cohort changes in the determinants of health services utilization does not inform our understanding of the inverse J-curve phenomenon, it also does not dismiss it. The reason for this is that neither social supports nor the patient–practitioner relationship are measured in the Health Interview Surveys. As a result, it was not possible to include these factors in the predictive models; thus, we cannot assess whether changes in their levels affect the use of health services. Accordingly, further research with more comprehensive data will be needed to explicate the causes of the observed inverse J-curve phenomenon.

REFERENCES

Aday, L. A. and R. Andersen. 1974. "A Framework for the Study of Access to Medical Care." *Health Services Research* 9: 208–220.

Aday, L. A. and R. Andersen. 1975. *Access to Medical Care*. Ann Arbor: Health Administration Press.

Aday, L. A., R. Andersen, and G. Fleming. 1980. *Health Care in the U.S.: Equitable for Whom?* Beverly Hills: Sage.

Aday, L. A., G. Fleming, and R. Andersen. 1984. *Access to Health Care in the U.S.: Who Has It, Who Doesn't.* Chicago: Pluribus Press.

Andersen, R. 1968. *Behavioral Model of Families' Use of Health Services.* Research
    Series No. 25. Chicago: Center for Health Administration Studies.
Andersen, R. and J. Newman. 1973. "Societal and Individual Determinants of
    Medical Care Utilization in the United States." *Milbank Memorial Fund Quar-
    terly* 51: 95–124.
Berki, S., L. Wyszewianski, R. Lichtenstein, P. Gimotty, J. Bowlyow, E. Papke, T.
    Smith, S. Crane, and J. Bromberg. 1985. "Health Insurance Coverage of the
    Unemployed." *Medical Care* 23: 847–863.
Branch, L., A. Jette, C. Evashwick, M. Polansky, G. Rowe, and P. Diehr. 1981.
    "Toward Understanding Elders' Health Services Utilization." *Journal of Com-
    munity Health* 7: 80–91.
Butler, R. 1975. *Why Survive: Growing Old in America.* New York: Basic Books.
Coulton, C. and A. K. Frost. 1982. "Use of Social and Health Services by the
    Elderly." *Journal of Health and Social Behavior* 23: 330–339.
Denton, J. 1978. *Medical Sociology.* New York: Houghton-Mifflin.
Dutton, D. 1979. "Patterns of Ambulatory Care in Five Different Delivery Systems."
    Medical Care 17: 221–243.
Elder, G. 1974. *Children of the Great Depression.* Chicago: University of Chicago
    Press.
Elder, G. 1975. "Age Differentiation and the Life Course." *American Sociological
    Review* 40: 165–190.
Evashwick, C., G. Rowe, P. Diehr, and L. Branch. 1984. "Factors Explaining the
    Use of Health Care Services by the Elderly." *Health Services Research* 19:
    357–382.
Eve, S. 1982. "Use of Health Maintenance Organizations by Older Adults." *Re-
    search on Aging* 4: 179–203.
Eve, S. 1984. "Age Strata Differences in Utilization of Health Care Services Among
    Adults in the United States." *Sociological Focus* 17: 105–120.
Eve, S. and H. Friedsam. 1980. "Multivariate Analysis of Health Care Services
    Utilization Among Older Texans." *Journal of Health and Human Resources
    Administration* 3: 169–191.
Fisher, C. 1980. "Differences by Age Groups in Health Care Spending." *Health Care
    Financing Review* 1: 65–90.
Glenn, N. 1977. *Cohort Analysis.* Beverly Hills: Sage.
Hartwig, F. and B. Dearing. 1979. *Exploratory Data Analysis.* Beverly Hills: Sage.
Haug, M. 1980. "Age and Medical Care Utilization Patterns." *Journal of Gerontol-
    ogy* 36: 103–111.
Kronenfeld, J. 1980. "Sources of Ambulatory Care and Utilization Models." *Health
    Services Research* 15: 3–20.
Lewis-Beck, M. 1980. *Applied Regression.* Beverly Hills: Sage.
Lubitz, J. and R. Prihoda. 1983. "Use and Costs of Medicare Services in the Last
    Years of Life." In *Health, United States, 1983.* DHHS Publication 84-1232.
    Washington, DC: U.S. Government Printing Office.
McKinlay, J. 1972. "Some Approaches and Problems in the Study of the Use of
    Services: An Overview." *Journal of Health and Social Behavior* 13: 115–152.
McKinlay, J. 1985. *Health Care Utilization by the Elderly: Special Considerations,*

Methodological Developments and Theoretical Issues. Discussant comments prepared for the Workshop on Aging and Health Care, jointly sponsored by the National Institute on Aging and the National Center for Health Statistics.

Mechanic, D. 1979. "Correlates of Physician Utilization: Why Do Major Multivariate Studies of Physician Utilization Find Trivial Psychosocial and Organizational Effects?" *Journal of Health and Social Behavior* 20: 387–396.

Mechanic, D. 1985. "Cost Containment and the Quality of Medical Care: Rationing Strategies in an Era of Constrained Resources." *Milbank Memorial Fund Quarterly* 63: 453–475.

Mosely, R. and F. Wolinsky. 1986. "The Use of Proxies in Health Surveys: Substantive and Policy Implications." *Medical Care* 24: 496–510.

National Center for Health Statistics. 1975. *Health Interview Survey Procedure, 1957–1974.* DHEW Publication 75-1311. Washington, DC: U.S. Government Printing Office.

National Center for Health Statistics. 1985. *The National Health Interview Survey Design, 1973–1984, and Procedures, 1975–83.* DHHS Publication 85-1320. Washington, DC: U.S. Government Printing Office.

Rakowski, W. and T. Hickey. 1980. "Late Life and Health Behavior: Integrating Health Beliefs and Temporal Perspectives." *Research on Aging* 2: 3–20.

Rice, D. and J. Feldman. 1983. "Living Longer in the United States: Demographic Changes and Health Needs of the Elderly." *Milbank Memorial Fund Quarterly* 61: 362–396.

Riley, M. 1971. "Social Gerontology and the Age Stratification of Society." *The Gerontologist* 11: 79–87.

Russell, L. 1981. "An Aging Population and the Use of Medical Care." *Medical Care* 19: 633–643.

Shortell, S. 1980. "Factors Associated with the Use of Health Services." In *Introduction to Health Services,* edited by S. Williams and P. Torrens. New York: Wiley and Sons.

Shortell, S. 1984. "Factors Associated with the Use of Health Services." In *Introduction to Health Services.* Second edition, edited by S. Williams and P. Torrens. New York: Wiley and Sons.

Snider, E. 1980a. "Awareness and Use of Health Services by the Elderly: A Canadian Study." *Medical Care* 18: 1177–1182.

Snider, E. 1980b. "Factors Influencing Health Services Knowledge Among the Elderly." *Journal of Health and Social Behavior* 21: 371–377.

Soldo, B. and K. Manton. 1985. "Changes in Health Status and Service Needs of the Oldest Old: Current Patterns and Future Trends." *Milbank Memorial Fund Quarterly* 63: 286–323.

Suchman, E. 1965a. "Social Patterns of Illness and Medical Care." *Journal of Health and Human Behavior* 6: 2–16.

Suchman, E. 1965b. "Stages of Illness and Medical Care." *Journal of Health and Human Behavior* 6: 114–128.

Suzman, R. and M. Riley. 1985. "Introducing the 'Oldest-Old.' " *Milbank Memorial Fund Quarterly* 63: 177–186.

Waldo, D. and H. Lazenby. 1984. "Demographic Characteristics and Health Care

Use and Expenditures by the Aged in the United States: 1977–1984." *Health Care Financing Review* 6: 1–49.

Wan, T. 1985. *Antecedents of Health Services Utilization by the Elderly: Some Empirical Results and Research Directions.* Discussant comments prepared for the Workshop on Aging and Health, jointly sponsored by the National Institute on Aging and the National Center for Health Statistics.

Wan, T., B. Odell, and D. Lewis. 1982. *Promoting the Well-being of the Elderly.* New York: The Haworth Press.

Wan, T. and S. Soifer. 1974. "Determinants of Physician Utilization: A Causal Analysis." *Journal of Health and Social Behavior* 15: 100–116.

Ward, R. 1978. "Services for Older People: An Integrated Framework for Research." *Journal of Health and Social Behavior* 18: 61–70.

Ward, R. 1985. *The Aging Experience,* 2nd ed. New York: Harper & Row.

Wolinsky, F. 1977. *Continuities in Health Services Utilization Research: The Longitudinal Stability of Structural Coefficients.* Unpublished doctoral dissertation. Carbondale: Southern Illinois University.

Wolinsky, F. 1978. "Assessing the Effects of Predisposing, Enabling, and Illness-Morbidity Characteristics on Health Service Utilization." *Journal of Health and Social Behavior* 19: 384–396.

Wolinsky, F. 1980. *The Sociology of Health: Principles, Professions, and Issues.* Boston: Little, Brown.

Wolinsky, F. 1981. "The Problems for Academic and Entrepreneurial Research in the Use of Health Services: The Case of Unstable Structural Relationships." *The Sociological Quarterly* 22: 207–223.

Wolinsky, F. 1983. *Physician Utilization Among Elderly Cohorts.* Washington, DC: AARP Andrus Foundation.

Wolinsky, F. and R. Coe. 1984. "Physician and Hospital Utilization Among Noninstitutionalized Elderly Adults: An Analysis of the Health Interview Survey." *Journal of Gerontology* 39: 334–341.

Wolinsky, F., R. Coe, D. Miller, J. Prendergast, M. Creel, and M. Chavez. 1983. "Health Services Utilization Among the Noninstitutionalized Elderly." *Journal of Health and Social Behavior* 24: 325–336.

Wolinsky, F., R. Coe, R. Mosely, and S. Homan. 1985. "Veterans' and Nonveterans' Use of Health Services: A Comparative Analysis." *Medical Care* 23: 1358–1371.

Wolinsky, F., R. Mosely, and R. Coe. In review. "A Cohort Analysis of the Use of Health Services by Elderly Americans." *Journal of Health and Social Behavior.*

5

Easing Caregiver Burden: The Role of Informal and Formal Supports*

Linda K. George

Concomitant to recognition of the primary caregiving role played by families of impaired older adults (cf. Brody, Poulshock, & Masciocchi, 1978; Shanas, 1979) has been heightened awareness of and concern about the risks associated with caregiving. It has now been documented that caregiving responsibilities typically have negative implications for mental health and social/recreational involvement and also may lead to financial difficulties or physical health problems (cf. Brody, 1981; Cantor, 1983; George & Gwyther, 1986). This configuration of potential problems posed by the responsibilities of caring for an impaired older adult is commonly referred to as "caregiver burden."

For both economic and social reasons, it is important to facilitate and encourage the continued involvement of families in the care and supervision of their impaired older relatives. Economically, family caregiving is cost-effective in that public funds are conserved if institutionalization of impaired older persons is delayed or prevented. Socially, the quality of life of the impaired older person is enhanced by remaining in the community and family network for as long as possible. And even after institutionalization, quality of life and quality of care are enhanced by continued involvement of the family (cf. Greene & Monahan, 1982; York & Calsyn, 1977).

Although family care of impaired older adults is desirable, its benefits must be balanced against the costs of caregiver burden. Caregivers' willing-

*The research reported in this paper was supported by grants from the AARP Andrus Foundation. Their support is gratefully acknowledged.

ness and abilities to continue to provide care for their older relatives are limited when such efforts generate substantial decrements in personal well-being. Indeed, even if the motivation for caregiving remains strong, one must be concerned about the quality of care provided by family members who have become what Fengler and Goodrich (1979) aptly described as "hidden patients." In order to encourage family caregiving without inducing disability in caregivers, there are increasing calls for community-based service programs specifically targeted toward easing caregiver burden and enhancing caregiver effectiveness (cf. Crossman, London, & Barry, 1981; Stafford, 1980). There also is growing interest in the informal supports received by caregivers and how such supports affect caregiver well-being (cf. George & Gwyther, 1986). Both formal services and informal social supports may mediate the risks to well-being posed by caregiving responsibilities and maximize the quality of family care provided to impaired older adults.

The purpose of this chapter is to examine the informal and formal services received by a heterogeneous group of family caregivers of older adults suffering from Alzheimer's disease or a related dementing disorder. More specifically, the topics examined include the amounts of formal and informal services received by these caregivers; the associations of formal and informal service receipt with caregiver well-being as measured in multiple dimensions; and the determinants of formal and informal services received by family caregivers.

CONCEPTUAL ISSUES

In this section, the conceptual underpinnings of the research are explicated. First, conceptual definitions of the major variables (i.e., social support, formal service use, caregiver well-being) are presented. Second, the theoretical significance of jointly examining services received from both formal and informal providers is addressed.

Three primary concepts are examined in this chapter: informal social support, formal service utilization, and caregiver well-being. For reasons of convenience, the term "patient" is used to refer to the memory-impaired older adult and the term "caregiver" is used to refer to a family member who cares or helps to care for a memory-impaired older adult. As noted below, the caregivers in this sample are not all primary caregivers (i.e., the person with greatest responsibility for patient care).

Social Support

Interest in the nature and impact of social support has exploded during the past decade (cf. Berkman & Breslow, 1983; Cassel, 1976; Cobb, 1976; House, 1981). In spite of this, there has been little consensus about the meaning and measurement of social support—though, fortunately, important convergences are emerging. In particular, there is now widespread recognition (1) that support networks must be distinguished from social support services (cf. Blazer & Kaplan, 1983; Cassel, 1976) and (2) that both phenomena are multidimensional (cf. Blazer & Kaplan, 1983; House, 1981). Social support refers to the tangible and intangible forms of assistance that individuals receive from informal providers, usually family and friends. The services provided by informal supporters range from financial assistance to the performance of tasks to the less concrete, but important, contributions of reassurance and validation of attitudes or perceptions. The support network refers to the configuration of people available to provide assistance to the individual.

Investigators have found that multiple dimensions of both support networks and social support are important for understanding the nature and impact of interpersonal relationships on personal well-being. Multiple proposals have been made concerning the underlying dimensions of support networks and social support services—a topic beyond the scope of this chapter. But one particularly important distinction is that between objective characteristics and subjective evaluations (cf. Blazer & Kaplan, 1983; House, 1981; Ward, Sherman, & LaGory, 1984a). Objectively, social support and support networks can be measured in terms of such characteristics as size and proximity of the network and the number and types of services provided by the network. Distinct from objective parameters are subjective perceptions of adequacy and satisfaction. Individuals receiving identical amounts of assistance may differ in their perceptions of the adequacy of that support—either because they differ in the need for assistance or because their expectations concerning adequate social support differ.

In this chapter, caregivers' objective receipt and subjective evaluations of social support are examined. Objective social support is measured in terms of the frequency with which caregivers receive 12 kinds of assistance from friends and family. The support services examined include both general services that are helpful to all of us and services particularly relevant to family care of impaired older adults. Subjective perceptions of the adequacy of social support are also examined. Because this chapter focuses on the amounts of assistance received by family caregivers, characteristics of the support network are not included in the analysis.[1]

[1]Although characteristics of the support network are not included in the analyses, they are available in the data set. All respondents reported the availability of multiple friends and relatives within an hour's proximity, although the size of the support network varied substantially across respondents. The availability of a support network is obviously a prerequisite for receipt of social support services. Nonetheless, it is not clear that larger support networks necessarily translate into increased levels of social support services. In this sample, the relationships between support network size and social support are weak and nonsignificant. More specifically, the correlation between support network size and objective social support was .06; that between network size and subjective social support was −.04.

Formal Service Use

Conceptualizing the configuration of services relevant to a particular population is a difficult task for which there are few sociological guidelines. The task is perhaps even more difficult in the case of family caregivers because relevant services include both those directly targeted at the patient and those designed to relieve the caregiver of responsibility for patient care. Indeed, for demented older adults and their caregivers, it is often difficult to identify the service recipient. Any service that impacts favorably upon patient functioning also eases caregiver burden. Conversely, services designed to relieve caregiver burden may increase caregiver effectiveness and, thus, indirectly benefit the patient.

The formal services examined in this paper consist of eight community-based health and social services targeted toward the impaired elderly. The services included were chosen on the basis of two criteria: Each service (1) is generally available in most U.S. communities and (2) has been noted as potentially relevant in the management of dementing illness (Mace & Rabins, 1981). Services specifically designed for memory-impaired older adults and their families are not included; such programs were (and largely are) unavailable in the communities surveyed. Consequently, the portrait of formal service use presented here represents the situations of caregivers without access to the innovative and targeted service programs advocated by gerontological researchers and practitioners—situations characteristic of most caregivers of memory-impaired persons.

Caregiver Well-Being

The term "caregiver burden" is now widely used to refer to the spectrum of problems experienced by family members caring for their impaired older relatives. Several instruments have been designed specifically to measure caregiver burden (e.g., the widely used Burden Interview, by Zarit, Reeves, & Bach-Peterson [1980] and the Caregiver Strain Index, by Robinson [1983]). Unfortunately, however, there are problems with these kinds of measures. For the purposes at hand, two problems are particularly relevant. First, because extant measures of caregiver burden explicitly require respondents to relate caregiving to its impact, an unwelcome kind of confounding occurs. The presumed stressor and its outcomes are intertwined such that caregiving cannot be independently related to its effects. Second, although caregiving can potentially affect multiple dimensions of well-being, extant measures of caregiver burden generate global burden scores. Reliance on summary scores masks dimension-specific patterns of caregiving impact and precludes identification of differing determinants or correlates of specific dimensions of caregiver burden. These and other problems with measures of caregiver burden are discussed in detail by George and Gwyther (1986).

Because of these problems, a different measurement strategy is employed in this chapter. The impact of caregiving is examined via measures of five dimensions of well-being: physical health, mental health, financial resources, social/recreational participation, and subjective well-being. These measures permit us to examine those outcomes that previous research and clinical reports suggest are most likely to be negatively affected by caregiving responsibilities. At the same time, the major problems posed by measures of caregiver burden are avoided.

Joint Consideration of Informal and Formal Service Use

Often—indeed, typically—services from formal and informal providers are examined separately (i.e., are not examined in the same article). Obviously, each type of service use is sufficiently important to merit individual attention; nonetheless, there are also important reasons for examining formal and informal services simultaneously. The first is simply the issue of completeness—if we are to understand the total impact of service use upon caregivers and their patients, we must examine the full range of assistance received, regardless of the source of those services.

A second reason for examining both formal and informal service use is more complex and of greater theoretical interest. A growing body of research focuses on the impact of significant others (i.e., the support network) on utilization of formal service programs. Interestingly, results concerning the impact of social support upon utilization of formal services are contradictory. Some research suggests that social support from informal providers facilitates formal service use (cf. McKinlay, 1973; Murdock & Schwartz, 1978; Salloway & Dillon, 1973); other studies report that social support decreases the likelihood of formal service use (cf. U.S. General Accounting Office, 1977)—a set of alternatives known as the linking versus the substitution hypotheses (George, 1986; Ward, Sherman, & LaGory, 1984b). Some theorists argue for the linking hypothesis; i.e., that one of the important contributions of support networks is facilitating access and entry to the formal service delivery system. Others argue for the substitution hypothesis, suggesting that individuals turn to formal providers only when and if informal sources of social support are unavailable or are unable to provide services.

Research findings based on tests of the linking versus substitution hypotheses are inconsistent. Overall, more results support the linking hypothesis than the substitution hypothesis—but the findings remain conflicting. An important research issue is identification of the conditions under which social support facilitates versus discourages use of formal health and social services (George, 1986). That goal is too ambitious for the research described here. Nonetheless, this chapter will examine both formal and informal service use among the caregivers of memory-impaired older adults. In particular, attention will be paid to (1) whether formal and informal services have similar relationships with caregiver well-being and (2) the degree to which the same independent variables predict formal and informal service use. Though these analyses cannot definitively settle the substitution versus linking controversy, insights can be brought to bear on the debate.

METHODS

Sample

The sampling frame for this research consisted of the mailing list of the Duke University Family Support Program (FSP). FSP is a statewide technical assistance program for the informal caregivers of older persons suffering Alzheimer's disease or a related disorder. Caregivers known to FSP were identified from a variety of sources, including media campaigns; contacts with community physicians, social service agencies, and nursing homes; health fairs; and other outreach activities. Survey instruments were mailed to all persons on the FSP mailing list who were currently providing some level of care to a memory-impaired older adult. The final sample includes 510 family caregivers, representing 89% of the current caregivers on the FSP mailing list—an excellent response rate by usual social science standards (cf. Dillman, 1978). The sampling frame did not generate a random sample of caregivers of memory-impaired older adults; it did, however, yield a heterogeneous sample from a geographically large area.

It should be noted that eligibility for sample inclusion required only that the caregiver be providing some level of care to a memory-impaired adult. Thus, although a majority of caregivers in the sample resided with the patients to whom they provided care (54%), some respondents reported providing care to an institutionalized older adult (28%), and other respondents indicated that the patient lived with another relative and that they provided assistance to the primary caregiver (18%) (see Table 5-1). This broad definition of who is a caregiver was helpful in understanding the circumstances under which caregiving has negative effects upon well-being (George & Gwyther, 1986).

Table 5-1 presents a statistical portrait of the caregiver sample. As expected, women comprised the majority (71%) of the sample. More than 98% of the men in the sample were spouse caregivers; the women were more evenly distributed across spouse, adult child, and other relative categories. The age range of the sample was 21–90, with an average age of 57. Compatible with the age distribution, most caregivers were the spouses (54%) or adult children (33%) of the patients. Other relatives were primari-

TABLE 5-1 Descriptive Statistics for Caregiver Sample

Personal characteristics	Descriptive statistic
Sex	
Male (%)	29
Female (%)	71
Age ($\bar{X}$ in years)	57.44
Marital status	
Married	88
Widowed	3
Divorced/separated	5
Never married	4
Race	
White	97
Black	2
Other	1
Education ($\bar{X}$ in years)	13.49
Employment status (% employed)	44
Relationship of caregiver to patient	
Spouse (%)	54
Child (%)	33
Other relative (%)	13
Living arrangements of patient	
Patient lives with caregiver (%)	54
Patient lives in institution (%)	28
Patient lives with other relative (%)	18

ly daughters-in-law and siblings. The vast majority of respondents were married (88%), with approximately equal and small proportions of widowed, divorced, and never-married caregivers. Ninety-seven percent of the caregivers were white, 2% were black, and 1% were American Indian or Asian. The modal level of educational attainment was a high school degree—and more of the caregivers had at least some college than had terminated their schooling prior to completion of high school. Almost half (44%) of the caregivers were employed. All of the employed caregivers were either adult children or "other" relatives of the patients; none of the spouse caregivers were employed.

The demographic distributions indicate that the caregiver sample is not representative of the general adult population of North Carolina. Two factors appear to account for the discrepancies. First, caregiver selection is not a random process and, compatible with other studies (cf. Brody, 1981; Cantor, 1983; Ikels, 1983), this leads to a sample that is older and more female than the general population. Second, the outreach activities of FSP evidently resulted in a sample that is somewhat higher in socioeconomic status and includes a lower proportion of nonwhites than is typical of the statewide population.

Measures

Social Support

Two measures of social support are used in these analyses: an objective measure of amount of assistance received and a subjective measure of the caregiver's perceived need for more help from family and friends. The objective social support measure is a multi-item scale. Respondents were asked to report the frequency with which family and friends provided twelve specific types of assistance, with responses to each item ranging from "never" (code = 0) to "regularly" (code = 4) (specific services included are presented in Table 5-2 below). Responses to the twelve items were summed to yield a total scale score (range = 0–48), with higher scores representing increased social support. The mean for the objective measure of social support was 18.5, reflecting relatively low levels of assistance from informal providers on average. The subjective measure of social support was measured by a single question asking caregivers whether they needed more help from family and friends. Fifty-nine percent of the sample expressed the need for more social support, and 41% indicated that they were receiving sufficient assistance from friends and relatives. We were somewhat concerned about use of a single item to assess the perceived adequacy of social support, but subsequent analyses indicated that this measure is a powerful correlate of caregiver well-being (cf. George & Gwyther, 1986).

It is interesting to note that there is virtually no association between the measures of objective and subjective social support ($r = .01$). This correlation documents the independence between objective levels of social support and perceptions of the adequacy of those social support services—a pattern also noted by previous investigators (Ward et al., 1984b).

Formal Service Utilization

Caregivers were asked whether they had used, and the frequency of use of, eight community-based service programs relevant to management of dementing illness (specific services are listed in Table 5-6 below). For these analyses, a summary measure of formal service utilization was created. Scores on this measure represent the number of services used during the year prior to the survey (range = 0–8). Sixty-three percent of the sample had used one or more services during the past year. The mean number of services used by the respondents was 1.4. It should be noted that physician services for the patient are not included in this measure. Physician services were omitted because the focus here is on the use of community-based services designed for management of the impaired older adult, rather than for diagnosis or treatment. Moreover, all the patients cared for by respondents were receiving physician services on a regular basis. Thus, though inclusion of physician services changes mean levels of formal service use, relationships between formal service use and other variables are unaltered.

Because the distinction between the linking and substitution hypotheses rests upon the size and direction of the relationships between social support and formal service utilization, correlations among those measures are of interest. Compatible with the linking hypothesis, social support and formal service use are significantly and positively related—though the magnitudes of those correlations are modest. The correlation between objective social support and formal service use is .18 ($p \leq .01$); that between perceptions of the need for more social support and formal service use is $-.15$ ($p \leq .01$).

Caregiver Well-Being

The survey included multiple indicators for five dimensions of caregiver well-being. Physical health was measured by two indicators: number of physician visits in the past six months and self-rated health (i.e., as poor, fair, good, or excellent). Financial resources were measured by two indicators: household income, a relatively objective indicator of economic status, and a multi-item scale measuring respondents' subjective assessments of their economic well-being (sample $\alpha = .85$) (Duke Center for the Study of Aging, 1978). Social/recreational participation also was measured using both objective and subjective indicators. Objective indicators included reports of the actual frequency of telephone calls and visits with family and friends, church and club attendance, and time spent in personal hobbies and relaxation. Each objective measure was accompanied by a subjective assessment of the caregiver's satisfaction with the frequency and quality of the social/recreational activity. These subjective assessments were summed to form a scale measuring satisfaction with social activities (sample $\alpha = .79$). Mental health was measured using two indicators: a checklist of psychiatric symptoms and a dichotomous measure of psychotropic drug use (0 = no use, 1 = use). The Short Psychiatric Evaluation Schedule (Pfeiffer, 1979) was used to measure psychiatric symptoms associated with stress (sample $\alpha = .85$). With regard to psychotropic medications, respondents were required to name each medication taken, and all drugs were verified as psychoactive by a physician. Over-the-counter drugs and alcohol were frequently reported but were not counted toward psychotropic drug use. The final well-being dimension, subjective well-being, was measured using four indicators. Three of these indicators were based on the Affect Balance Scale (Bradburn, 1969): amount of positive affect, amount of negative affect, and ratio of positive to negative affect (sample $\alpha = .89$). The first two indicators tap quantity of affect; affect balance indicates the predominant valence of affect. The final indicator of subjective well-being was a single-item measure of life satisfaction, also introduced by Bradburn (1969).

Levels of well-being in this sample were presented in a previous article (George & Gwyther, 1986). To recap briefly, levels of physical health and financial resources were similar among caregivers to those reported by random community samples. In contrast, subjective well-being, mental health, and social/recreational participation exhibited significant and substantial decrements among caregivers as compared to their randomly selected community peers.

Methods of Analysis

Parallel analyses were performed, and are presented below, for the measures of services received from the support network and formal service utilization. First, descriptive statistics are presented to document the extent to which specific formal and informal services are used by the sample of caregivers. Second, correlations between the measures of service use and indicators of caregiver well-being are presented. It is commonly assumed that both formal services and informal social supports significantly contribute to caregiver well-being. Though causal order remains problematic, the correlations provide evidence bearing on that assumption. Finally, the predictors of informal and formal service use are examined in a multivariate framework. Two models are estimated for each dependent variable (i.e., objective social support, subjective social support, and formal service use). In the first model, demographic variables are used to predict service use; in the second model, a broader set of independent variables is used to predict service use. Though the broader set of predictors provides better model fit, causal order is more problematic so interpretation must be more cautious.

A note is in order concerning the estimation procedures used to predict the measures of social support and formal service utilization. The measures of objective social support and formal service use are continuous variables. Consequently, ordinary least squares (OLS) regression is the technique of choice for models predicting those dependent variables. The measure of subjective social support, in contrast, is dichotomous, rendering OLS regression inappropriate. Special problems arise when the dependent variable in a regression equation is a binary response (e.g., nonnormal error terms, inconsistent error variance, constraints on the response function) (Cox, 1978). In particular, use of OLS regression may lead to inefficient regression coefficient estimates and predicted responses on the dependent variables that fall outside the constraint limits of 0 and 1. Under these circumstances, logistic regression is the preferred statistical technique.

The logistic regression procedure calculates maximum likelihood estimates for the parameters of a model that express the log of the odds of an event as a simple linear model. The logistic coefficients can be interpreted most easily by transforming them to anti-logged coefficients. The antilogged coefficient then estimates how a one-unit change in the independent variable multiplies the odds of the dependent variable (in this case, the odds of perceiving the need for more social support). The overall fit of the model is assessed by the R statistic, which is analogous to the multiple correlation coefficient in OLS regression after a correction is made for the number of parameters estimated. Individual R statistics also are produced for each independent variable in the model. R values range between −1 and +1 and provide a measure of the contribution of each variable to the fit of the model (Harrell, 1983).[2]

RESULTS

Social Support

Table 5-2 presents a descriptive portrait of the nature and amounts of social support services received by sample members, as well as the relationship of the major helper to the caregiver. The means for all 12 social support items are very low, suggesting that most caregivers receive assistance seldom, if at all. Nonetheless, for two-thirds of the support items, at least half of the caregivers report receiving assistance "rarely" or more often. Caregivers are most likely to report receiving help when ill, help with shopping, companionship, and advice on problems from members of the support network. In contrast, the types of services caregivers are least likely to receive are financial assistance, help with housework, and help grooming the patient.

Overall, in terms of the type of helpers, children and other relatives (i.e., other than spouse and children) are the major sources of help for most caregivers and for most types of services. An exception to this pattern is companionship, which, not surprisingly, is most likely to be provided by friends. The distribution of helpers must be interpreted cautiously, however. The types of helpers available are affected by the relationship between patient and caregiver. Thus family members caring for an impaired spouse obviously cannot receive support services from their marital partners; in contrast, spouses are the major sources of informal social support for adult–child caregivers. The primary conclusion here is that caregivers rely most heavily on their closest family members for tangible support services. And, with the exception of companionship, friends are major helpers only when close relatives are unavailable.

A broad body of social science literature suggests that higher levels of social support should help to ameliorate the more detrimental effects of

[2]Discriminant analysis is often used in cases where dichotomous variables, particularly group membership, are predicted. Because the logistic regression model entails fewer assumptions than the linear discriminant model (e.g., no multivariate normality assumption for covariates), logistic regression is preferable to discriminant analysis (Press & Wilson, 1978).

TABLE 5-2 Descriptive Statistics, Informal Social Supports
Received by Caregivers

| | | | Relationship of helper (in %) | | | |
Type of support[a]	Mean	% with any help	Spouse	Child	Other relative	Friend
Help when caregiver is sick	2.29	72	16	36	32	16
Help with shopping	1.91	66	17	40	27	16
Help with finances	.90	30	26	29	41	4
Help with household repairs	1.59	56	27	35	24	14
Help with housework	1.00	35	28	40	21	11
Advice on business or finances	1.25	44	25	33	27	15
Companionship	2.40	72	21	24	24	31
Advice on problems	1.85	65	20	29	26	25
Transportation	1.44	51	17	30	32	21
Help with meals	1.33	50	16	29	35	20
Help staying with patient	1.63	58	9	32	41	18
Help grooming the patient	.94	31	12	33	45	10

[a]Responses for social support items range from 0 (never) to 4 (regularly).

stressful situations. Thus we would anticipate positive relationships between levels of social support and measures of caregiver well-being. Conversely, the perceived need for more social support should be negatively related to measures of caregiver well-being. Table 5-3 reports the correlations between caregiver well-being, as measured in multiple dimensions, and both objective and subjective social support. There are no significant correlations between objective social support and either financial resources or physical health. Objective social support, however, is positively related to three of seven indicators of social/recreational activity, one of the two mental health measures, and all four measures of subjective well-being. All of the significant correlations are in the expected direction (i.e., greater amounts of assistance are associated with increased well-being), but the magnitudes of the correlations are only modest (i.e., range of significant correlations = .08–.16).

The subjective measure of social support is significantly related to all of the well-being indicators except use of physician services. All of the significant correlations are in the expected direction (i.e., the perceived need for more social support is negatively related to well-being). These correlations range in size from −.10 to −.42.[3] Some of the correlations are

[3]Pearson product moment correlations are not always the preferred method for correlations involving dichotomous variables (such as those involving the subjective social support measure). Depending upon the "split" in the dichotomous variable, Pearson product moment correlations may underestimate the size of the correlation. Point biserial correlation is more robust for estimating the relationship between a dichotomous and continuous variable. All the correlations reported in Table 5-3 are Pearson product moment correlations. Point biserial correlations were also calculated for the subjective social support measure, however. There were no meaningful differences in the sizes of the correlations generated by the two techniques.

TABLE 5-3 Zero-order and Partial Correlations of Caregiver Well-Being and Social Support

Well-being dimensions and indicators	Objective social support	Perceived need for social support	Partial correlation[a]
Physical health			
Doctor's visits in past six months	.02	−.02	−.01
Self-rated health	.01	−.18**	−.19**
Financial resources			
Household income	−.01	−.16**	−.16**
Perceived economic status	.02	−.30**	−.30**
Social activities			
Phone contacts with family/ friends	.12**	−.16**	−.14**
Visits with family/friends	.14**	−.22**	−.21**
Frequency of church attendance	.04	−.10*	−.10*
Frequency of club attendance	.10*	−.13**	−.12**
Time spent in hobbies	.00	−.20**	−.20**
Time spent relaxing	.01	−.24**	−.24**
Satisfaction with social activities	.07	−.42**	−.42**
Mental health			
Stress symptoms	−.04	.38**	.38**
Used psychotropic drugs	.08*	.16**	.17**
Subjective well-being			
Positive affect	.14**	−.25**	.16**
Negative affect	−.09*	.38**	−.10*
Affect balance scale	.16**	−.39**	−.37**
Life satisfaction	.16**	−.23**	−.22**

*$p \leq .05$
**$p \leq .01$
[a] Partial correlation is the relationship between subjective social support and the well-being indicator, controlling upon objective levels of social support.

quite strong, especially those between subjective social support and other subjective measures (i.e., perceived economic status, satisfaction with social activities, stress symptoms, and all the measures of subjective well-being).

Some theorists would argue that perceptions of social support adequacy are largely a reflection of the levels of social support actually received. As noted previously, the relationship between objective and subjective social support is nonsignificant. Nonetheless, in order to rule out the effects of intercorrelation between the social support measures, the partial correlations between subjective social support and the well-being indicators were calculated, controlling on objective levels of social support services. As shown in Table 5-3, there are minimal differences between the zero-order and partial correlations between subjective social support and caregiver well-being. Thus, the relationships between well-being and perceptions of the adequacy of social support are stronger than and virtually independent of the relationships between objective levels of social support and caregiver well-being.

The final issue examined with regard to informal social supports is their predictors. Table 5-4 presents two OLS regression equations predicting the levels of objective social support received by the family caregivers. The first model is restricted to demographic variables and characteristics of the caregiving situation (i.e., relationship between patient and caregiver, patient living arrangements). These variables explain a significant but small 6% of the variance in the measure of objective social support. Only one independent variable is statistically significant: spouse caregivers report significantly lower levels of support than "other" caregivers (i.e., the omitted category). The second model adds a series of other predictors that tap aspects of the caregivers' personal resources and functioning, as well as levels of formal service use. Again the explained variance is modest, though larger (i.e., 9%) than in Model 1. Four predictors achieve statistical significance. Younger age, lower income, perceptions of poorer health, and increased use of community services are significantly associated with higher levels of objective social support.

TABLE 5-4 Predictors of Objective Social Support

Independent variable	Model 1		Model 2	
	b	B	b	B
Sex	.47	.02	.29	.01
Age	−.05	−.06	−.12	−.13*
Education	−.08	−.02	.03	.01
Employment status	−.53	−.02	−.57	−.02
Patient lives with caregiver	−1.53	−.06	−2.05	−.08
Patient lives in institution	1.11	.04	−.65	−.02
Spouse caregiver	−3.17	−.13*	−2.26	−.09
Adult-child caregiver	1.54	.06	2.07	.08
Household income			−.70	−.14*
Self-rated health			−2.11	−.13*
Stress symptoms			−.25	−.10
Perceived economic status			.54	.10
Satisfaction with social activities			.14	.02
Use of community services			1.55	.18*
Intercept	24.61		31.09	
R^2	.06**		.09**	

*$p \le .05$
**$p \le .01$

A note of caution is merited at this point. Causal order is largely nonproblematic in Model 1—levels of social support can hardly cause one's age, sex, socioeconomic status, and so forth. Causal order in Model 2 is much less compelling. Clearly one could argue that levels of assistance from family and friends can causally impact upon perceptions of health, for example, just as one can argue that poor health elicits increased assistance from the support network. Indeed, in Table 5-3 it is assumed that social support affects well-being and in Table 5-4 the opposite assumption is made. Problems of causal order cannot be resolved using cross-sectional data; consequently, the regression results should be interpreted cautiously. Though this point will not be repeated, it is equally relevant to the models predicting subjective social support and formal service use.

Table 5-5 presents the results of two logistic regression equations predicting the perceived need for more social support. In terms of the predictors included, the two logistic models are identical to the OLS models presented in Table 5-4. In Model 1 the model fit is statistically significant, but the fit is not particularly good. Four independent variables significantly predict the odds that caregivers will perceive the need for more social support. Older age and higher education decrease the probability that more social support is desired. Caregivers who live with their patients and caregivers who provide care to institutionalized patients are more likely to desire more social support than those who are secondary caregivers (i.e., who provide assistance to a caregiver who lives with the patient). Model 2, with its expanded set of predictors, fits the data considerably better than Model 1. Five individual predictors are statistically significant. Males, older respondents, and caregivers who are satisfied with their social activities are less likely to want more social support. Caregivers who live with their patients and those with high levels of stress symptoms are significantly more likely to desire additional assistance from the support network. Comparing Tables 5-4 and 5-5, there is little overlap between the predictors of objective and subjective social support, suggesting that the two dimensions of social support have different determinants.

Formal Service Utilization

Table 5-6 presents the simple descriptive statistics concerning utilization of formal services among sample members. Overall, relatively small proportions of caregivers report using any particular type of service during the past year. By a wide margin, the most popular service among sample members is part-time paid help (used as sitters for the patients). Virtually all the service users in the sample reported purchasing these services in the private sector rather than relying upon public programs. The only public service used with some frequency was visiting nurses (who are based in North Carolina county health departments).

TABLE 5-5 Predictors of Perceived Need for More Help from
Family/Friends

Independent variable	Model 1 AC^a	R	Model 2 AC	R
Sex	.92	.00	.60*	−.05
Age	.96**	−.13	.96**	−.10
Education	.91**	−.11	.95	.00
Employment status	.86	.00	.90	.00
Patient lives with caregiver	3.51**	.13	3.12**	.10
Patient lives in institution	2.02*	.07	1.93	.04
Spouse caregiver	.96	.00	.52	−.02
Adult-child caregiver	1.54	.00	1.13	.00
Household income			.95	.00
Self-rated health			.81	.00
Stress symptoms			1.12**	.12
Perceived economic status			.90	−.03
Satisfaction with social activities			.73**	−.19
Use of community services			1.01	.00
Model Chi Square	44.28**		149.08**	
Model R	.20**		.44**	

$*p \le .05$
$**p \le .01$
$^a AC$ = antilogged logistic regression coefficient

TABLE 5-6 Utilization of Community Services by Caregivers

Type of community service	% used service in past year
Visiting nurse services	19
Adult day care services	12
Homemaker or chore services	13
Part-time paid help	43
Full-time paid help	11
Respite services in nursing home	9
Respite services in hospital	7
Mental health counseling	22

Compatible with the reasoning applied to services received from the
informal support network, use of formal services was expected to be beneficial in fostering caregiver well-being. Table 5-7 presents the correlations
between amount of formal service use and the indicators of well-being. In
general, there is little evidence that use of formal services is significantly

TABLE 5-7 Relationships between Community Service Use and Caregiver Well-Being

Well-being dimensions and indicators	r
Physical health	
Doctor's visits in past six months	.04
Self-rated health	.06
Financial resources	
Household income	.11*
Perceived economic status	−.01
Social activities	
Phone contacts with family/friends	.03
Visits with family/friends	.05
Frequency of church attendance	−.02
Frequency of club attendance	.14**
Time spent in hobbies	−.02
Time spent relaxing	−.04
Satisfaction with social activities	−.01
Mental health	
Stress symptoms	−.06
Used psychotropic drugs	.07
Subjective well-being	
Positive affect	.06
Negative affect	.01
Affect balance scale	.04
Life satisfaction	.07

*$p \leq .05$
**$p \leq .01$

related to caregiver well-being. Only two correlations achieve statistical significance, and they are quite modest in size. Formal service use is positively related to household income ($r = .11$) and frequency of attending meetings of voluntary organizations ($r = .14$).

Table 5-8 presents the results of the OLS regression equations predicting amount of formal service use. Again, two models are estimated. In Model 1, demographic variables and characteristics of the caregiving situation are used to predict formal service use. This model is poor in terms of overall fit—only 5% of the variance, which is statistically significant but small, is explained. Only one regression coefficient is statistically significant: surprisingly, caregivers whose patients were institutionalized were most likely to report having used formal services in the past year. Model 2, with an expanded set of predictors, is only slightly superior to Model 1—the explained variance increases to 8%, and two predictors are statistically significant. The effect of being a caregiver for an institutionalized patient remains statistically significant. In addition, higher levels of objective social support predict greater utilization of formal services.

TABLE 5-8 Predictors of Community Service Use by Caregivers

Independent variable	Model 1		Model 2	
	b	*B*	*b*	*B*
Sex	−.09	−.03	−.04	−.01
Age	.01	.07	.01	.14
Education	.01	.01	−.01	−.02
Employment status	.27	.09	.22	.07
Patient lives with caregiver	.12	.04	.16	.05
Patient lives in institution	.70	.22*	.72	.22*
Spouse caregiver	−.04	−.01	−.04	−.01
Adult-child caregiver	.30	.10	.21	.07
Household income			.07	.12
Self-rated health			.15	.08
Stress symptoms			.01	.04
Perceived economic status			−.05	−.09
Satisfaction with social activities			.01	.01
Objective social supports			.02	.19*
Perceived need for social support			.17	.06
Intercept	.56		−.69	
R^2	.05*		.08*	

*$p \leq .05$

DISCUSSION

This chapter has explored the levels and correlates of formal and informal services received by a sample of family members caring for memory-impaired older adults. A descriptive but important issue concerns the amounts of assistance these caregivers receive from formal and informal service providers. Overall, sample members receive very little help from either type of provider. More caregivers receive help from friends and relatives than use formal services, but levels of objective social support are low in absolute terms. Moreover, caregivers with full-time, live-in caregiving responsibilities are least likely to use formal service programs and reported the lowest levels of objective social support. Not surprisingly, more than half of the caregivers reported needing more help from family and friends—a perception most frequently reported by caregivers who live with their patients.

Although objective levels of social support are low and a majority of caregivers perceive the need for more support, the relationship between objective and subjective support measures is nonsignificant. In addition, the results suggested that objective and subjective social support may have different determinants. Nonetheless, both measures of social support are substantially related to levels of caregiver well-being, particularly the measure of subjective social support. Though the importance of distinguishing between objective and subjective dimensions of social support has been previously recognized, lack of correlation was unexpected. This pattern of findings has important implications. First, because both social support dimensions are independently related to caregiver well-being, programs or interventions to foster social support should be targeted at both dimensions. Moreover, because they may have different determinants, different programs may well be needed to bolster objective and subjective social support. These findings also have potentially important implications for the interpersonal relationships between caregivers and members of their support networks. For example, increased assistance by the support network may not increase caregivers' perceptions of social support adequacy—a situation that may be distressing to members of the support network. An important issue for future research is further exploration of the relationship between objective and subjective dimensions of social support.

Unlike the measures of social support, amount of formal service use is largely unrelated to caregiver well-being. This is not to say that caregivers who utilize such services are dissatisfied with them or perceive them to be unimportant. Caregivers using formal services were asked to rate those services in terms of helpfulness. And, indeed, all service users rated the formal services they received as "somewhat helpful" or "very helpful." It is not clear why formal service use does not contribute to caregiver well-being. One possibility is that even those caregivers using formal services are not receiving services in the amounts needed to impact positively on personal well-being. Along those lines, many caregivers commented on the need for more or different services, especially services specifically designed to provide substantial respite from their caregiving responsibilities. Alternatively, however, it may be that personal well-being is less sensitive to contributions by formal providers than those by friends and relatives. If this is the case, the contributions of formal service programs may be better observed by examining outcomes other than caregiver well-being (e.g., such as decisions to delay institutionalization of the patient or other patient outcomes).

One of the disappointing features of the results was the relative lack of success in predicting social support and formal service use—though the prediction of subjective social support was considerably more successful than that of formal service use and objective levels of support. Based upon both this research and that of others, it appears that little is known about the antecedents of active support networks and help-seeking from formal service programs. There is, of course, a large literature about the determinants of seeking medical care (see George, 1986, for a review of that literature). But the fact remains that we are unable to explain the majority of variance in the antecedents of personal help-seeking for health problems among competent adults (see, for example, Chapter 4, by Wolinsky, Coe, and Mosely, in this volume). And, clearly, we have only scratched the surface in terms of help-seeking from nonphysicians and the help-seeking strategies that caregivers use to obtain services for their impaired relatives.

A major reason for examining both informal and formal supports was the desire to test the linking versus substitution hypotheses. In this sample, the linking hypothesis was better supported. Both the objective and subjective measures of social support were significantly related to amount of formal service use. Compatible with the linking hypothesis, greater levels of assistance from the support network were positively related to formal service use, and perceptions of the need for more social support were negatively related to formal service use. Moreover, the positive relationship between objective social support and formal service use remained significant when controlling for other correlates (see Tables 5-4 and 5-8). Though our results support the linking hypothesis, more effort is needed to delineate the process by which higher levels of social support induce greater levels of formal service utilization.

Some recent research, especially the work of Litwak (1985), recommends that the issue of linking versus substitution be replaced with a view toward the complementarity of social supports and formal service use. From this perspective, support networks and formal service providers are best equipped to fill different functions. Assistance provided to impaired older adults should be shared by the two support systems, with formal and informal providers performing those tasks that each is best equipped to handle. According to this view, informal providers are best equipped to handle unpredictable, nontechnical, and specific tasks. In contrast, formal agencies are most appropriately used for predictable, technical, and specific tasks. In addition, the informal network is responsible for recognizing its own strengths and limitations—and, in the case of the latter, for seeking out appropriate formal services. Litwak demonstrates the utility of this viewpoint using national and local data sets.

In spite of the conceptual and analytic elegance of Litwak's work, the demands facing caregivers of demented older adults appear to pose a major challenge to his conclusions. The major tasks shouldered by the caregivers of Alzheimer's patients are precisely those that Litwak would consider appropriate for informal rather than formal providers. Feeding, bathing, grooming, constant supervision, meal preparation, and mobility assistance are among the most common tasks that caregivers of Alzheimer's patients must perform on a regular basis. Though these tasks are quite predictable, given the course of the disease, they are nontechnical and diffuse. The burden shouldered by the caregivers of Alzheimer's patients is not that the tasks exceed usual levels of competence or skill. Rather, it is that the time commitment and total volume of assistance required by Alzheimer's patients outstrip the resources of the social support network. Caregivers recognize the nature of the burden they shoulder—the services they desire, but seldom receive, are companions/sitters, chore workers, and respite care, all of which are nontechnical and diffuse services. It is unclear what Litwak would recommend for this target group. But it clearly seems unreasonable to agree with his conclusion that formal providers should be reserved for the provision of specific, technical tasks. That conclusion is based on an incomplete awareness of the nature of the demands placed on informal providers by older persons with severely disabling chronic conditions.

Moreover, the insights contributed by the complementary perspective on formal and informal providers do not negate the importance of further investigation of the substitution versus linking issue. Litwak's perspective is an ideal one—in his view, a rational world would divide tasks between formal and informal providers on the bases of predictability, level of technical skill required, and level of specificity. But, as most social scientists are aware, the world is not always a rational place. The linking versus substitution issue focuses upon the extent to which informal providers actually substitute for or facilitate use of formal services (rather than upon the rationality or appropriateness of service use). Thus, although it is important to devote greater effort to issues of appropriateness, it is also important to continue to explore the behaviors of social support networks and to identify the conditions under which those networks do and do not facilitate use of formal services.

A promising avenue for understanding the conditions under which social support substitutes for versus facilitates use of formal services is the distinction between strong and weak ties within the support network (Granovetter, 1973; Ward et al., 1984b). According to this perspective, strong ties, such as those found among immediate family, increase the likelihood of service provision within the network and decrease the likelihood of seeking assistance from formal providers. In contrast, weak ties, such as those found among friends and more distant kin, increase the likelihood of seeking external, formal assistance. Previous research suggests that the distinction between strong and weak ties may be useful when examining the service use and knowledge of older adults. O'Brien and Wagner (1980) and Wagner and Keast (1981) suggest that high levels of family interaction and assistance are related to lower levels of formal service use. With regard to knowledge of formal services, Ward and associates (1984b) found that contacts with friends and neighbors are associated with greater service knowledge, whereas frequent contacts (especially co-residence) with children, confidants, and instrumental helpers reduced knowledge of services among older adults.

In the case of dementing illness, the impaired older adult must rely on the caregiver both to provide informal services and to obtain formal services. This situation adds two wrinkles to the strong versus weak ties distinction. First, the caregiver's access to strong and weak ties is probably more relevant to formal service use than is the patient's access to such ties. Second, because the vast majority of caregivers are spouses and adult children of the Alzheimer's patients, caregiving itself is evidence of the presence and intensity of strong ties. Our data provide some evidence that the strong versus weak tie distinction may be relevant to formal service use among caregivers of Alzheimer's patients. Several categories of caregivers are especially likely *not* to use formal services: spouse caregivers, caregivers who live with their patients, and caregivers who spend less time in social activities and organizational participation. These relationships suggest that relatively isolated caregivers who are intensely involved in full-time caregiving are less likely to use formal services. On the other hand, those caregivers who receive more tangible assistance (i.e., objective social support) also are more likely to use formal services—a pattern that does not support the theory of strong and weak ties. Unfortunately, these data were not designed to permit a rigorous examination of the differential impact of strong and weak ties upon formal service use. Nonetheless, the caregiving arena appears to be a fruitful context for further exploration of this distinction.

This study has two major limitations, which should be explicitly noted. First, the results are based upon cross-sectional data, rendering assumptions about temporal order problematic. This issue, as noted earlier, is especially relevant to the models predicting levels of social support and formal service use. Though the data presented here were cross-sectional, this is in fact a longitudinal study. The sample of caregivers was surveyed on two occasions, a year apart. Because the follow-up data became available only recently, our longitudinal data analyses are only partially complete. Nonetheless, it is already obvious that the longitudinal data will be inadequate for resolving many questions about causal order. Thus, for example, the longitudinal correlation between caregivers' self-rated health and levels of objective social support is nearly identical to the cross-sectional correlation—and temporal order remains unclear.

Although longitudinal data cannot resolve all the questions raised by cross-sectional results, some issues can be clarified. One of the surprising findings in this study is the fact that caregivers whose patients reside in institutions reported using more formal services than either caregivers residing with their patients or secondary caregivers. Ordinarily, one would assume that caregivers providing services to institutionalized patients would have the *least* need for community-based services. The longitudinal data are helpful in explaining this apparent anomaly. During the one-year interval between surveys, 21% of the caregivers who lived with their patients at the first test date institutionalized their patients. And these caregivers also were the most likely to report a substantial increase in the use of formal services during the past year (Colerick & George, in press). It appears, then, that a period of relatively intense utilization of formal services often precedes institutionalization of the patient. There are a number of possible reasons for this pattern of service use. It may be that as patients experience rapid deterioration of functioning, increased help is sought from formal providers—first in the community and ultimately in institutional settings. Alternatively, caregivers may reach a breaking point in their willingness and/or ability to provide full-time care to their older relatives. At this time, community-based services may be sought as a stop-gap measure until relocation to an institution can be arranged. Regardless of the reason, this pattern is disturbing. The major rationale that policymakers offer for community-based geriatric services is the desire to delay or prevent institutionalization. These data suggest that such services are used primarily in the few months prior to institutionalization. Perhaps the problem facing advocates of community-based services is not merely ensuring their availability, but also inducing their use at earlier stages of the caregiving process.

A second limitation of the study concerns the nature of the sample. The data used in this chapter were obtained only from caregivers of memory-impaired older adults. It is likely that the nature and course of caregiving are substantially affected by the nature of the patient's illness. Caregiving is probably especially difficult when the older person suffers significant mental deterioration (cf. Poulshock & Diemling, 1984; Sainsbury & Grad de Alarcon, 1970). An especially striking difference between caring for mentally versus physically impaired older adults is the fact that the former cannot participate in caretaking decisions, whereas physically impaired but mentally competent older adults typically are active participants in such decisions (George, in press). Thus it is possible that the findings reported here would not generalize to caregivers coping with the demands posed by other kinds of patients.

In spite of unresolved issues and limitations in the study, this chapter has contributed to our understanding of the role of formal and informal supports in the caregiving process. The most exciting findings concern the independence between objective levels of social support and subjective perceptions of support adequacy. Of particular importance is that fact that these two dimensions of social support are significantly but independently related to caregiver well-being. It is to be hoped that these findings will both contribute to the extant knowledge base of information about formal and informal supports and provide a springboard for future efforts.

REFERENCES

Berkman, Lisa F. and Lester Breslow. 1983. *Health and Ways of Living: The Alameda County Study.* New York: Oxford University Press.

Blazer, Dan G. and Bert H. Kaplan. 1983. "The Assessment of Social Support in an Elderly Community Population." *American Journal of Psychiatry* 3: 29–36.

Bradburn, Norman M. 1969. *The Structure of Psychological Well-Being.* Chicago: Aldine.

Brody, Elaine M. 1981. " 'Women in the Middle' and Family Help to Older People." *The Gerontologist* 21: 471–480.

Brody, Stanley J., S. Walter Poulshock, and Carla F. Masciocchi. 1978. "The Family Caring Unit: A Major Consideration in the Long-Term Support System." *The Gerontologist* 18: 556–561.

Cantor, Marjorie H. 1983. "Strain Among Caregivers: A Study of Experiences in the United States." *The Gerontologist* 23: 597–604.

Cassel, John. 1976. "The Contribution of the Social Environment to Host Resistance." *American Journal of Epidemiology* 104: 107–114.

Cobb, Stanley. 1976. "Social Support as a Moderator of Life Stress." *Psychosomatic Medicine* 38: 300–314.

Colerick, Elizabeth J. and Linda K. George. In press. "Predictors of Institutionalization Among Caregivers of Alzheimer's Patients." *Journal of the American Geriatrics Society.*

Cox, David R. 1978. *Analysis of Binary Data.* London: Chapman and Hall.

Crossman, Linda, Cecilia London, and Clemmie Barry. 1981. "Older Women Caring for Disabled Spouses: A Model for Supportive Services." *The Gerontologist* 21: 464–470.

Dillman, Don A. 1978. *Mail and Telephone Surveys: The Total Design Method.* New York: Wiley.

Duke Center for the Study of Aging and Human Development. 1978. *Multidimensional Functional Assessment: The OARS Methodology.* Durham, NC: Duke University Center for the Study of Aging and Human Development.

Fengler, Alfred P. and Nancy Goodrich. 1979. "Wives of Elderly Disabled Men: The Hidden Patients." *The Gerontologist* 19: 175–183.

George, Linda K. 1986. *Psychological and Social Determinants of Help-Seeking.* Paper prepared for National Depression Awareness, Recognition, and Treatment Program, National Institute of Mental Health.

George, Linda K. Forthcoming. "Caregiver Burden: Conflict Between Norms of Reciprocity and Solidarity." In *Conflict and Abuse in Families of the Elderly: Theory, Research, and Intervention,* edited by Karl Pillemer and Rosalie Wolf. Boston: Auburn House.

George, Linda K. and Lisa P. Gwyther. 1986. "Caregiver Well-Being: A Multidimensional Examination of Family Caregivers of Demented Adults." *The Gerontologist* 26: 253–259.

Granovetter, Mark S. 1973. "The Strength of Weak Ties." *American Journal of Sociology* 78: 1360–1380.

Greene, Vernon L. and Deborah J. Monahan. 1982. "The Impact of Visitation on

Patient Well-Being in Nursing Homes." *The Gerontologist* 22: 418–423.

Harrell, Frank E. 1983. "The LOGIST Procedure." Pp. 181–202 in *SUGI: Supplemental Library User's Guide,* edited by Stephenie Joyner. Cary, NC: SAS Institute.

House, James S. 1981. *Work Stress and Social Support.* Reading, MA: Addison-Wesley.

Ikels, Charlotte. 1983. "The Process of Caretaker Selection." *Research on Aging* 5: 491–510.

Litwak, Eugene. 1985. *Helping the Elderly.* New York: Guilford Press.

Mace, Nancy L. and Peter V. Rabins. 1981. *The 36-Hour Day.* Baltimore: Johns Hopkins University Press.

McKinlay, John B. 1973. "Social Networks, Lay Consultation, and Help-Seeking Behaviors." *Social Forces* 51: 275–292.

Murdock, Steve H. and Donald F. Schwartz. 1978. "Family Structure and the Use of Agency Services: An Examination of Patterns Among Elderly Native Americans." *The Gerontologist* 18: 475–481.

O'Brien, John and Donna Wagner. 1980. "Help Seeking by the Frail Elderly: Problems in Network Analysis." *The Gerontologist* 20: 78–83.

Pfeiffer, Eric. 1979. "A Short Psychiatric Evaluation Schedule: A New 15-Item Monotonic Scale Indicative of Functional Psychiatric Disorder." Pp. 403–414 in *Proceedings of the Bayer-Symposium,* Vol. VII, *Brain Function in Old Age.* New York: Springer-Verlag.

Poulshock, S. Walter and Gary Diemling. 1984. "Families Caring for Elders in Residence: Issues in the Measurement of Burden." *Journal of Gerontology* 39: 230–239.

Press, James and Sandra Wilson. 1978. "Choosing Between Logistic Regression and Discriminant Analysis." *Journal of the American Statistical Association* 73: 699–705.

Robinson, Betsy C. 1983. "Validation of a Caregiver Strain Index." *Journal of Gerontology* 38: 344–348.

Sainsbury, Peter and Jacqueline Grad de Alarcon. 1970. "The Psychiatrist and the Geriatric Patient: The Effects of Community Care on the Family of the Geriatric Patient." *Journal of Geriatric Psychiatry* 1: 23–41.

Salloway, Jeffrey C. and Patrick B. Dillon. 1973. "A Comparison of Family Networks and Friend Networks in Health Care Utilization." *Journal of Comparative Family Studies* 4: 140–147.

Shanas, Ethel. 1979. "The Family as a Social Support System in Old Age." *The Gerontologist* 19: 169–174.

Stafford, Florence. 1980. "A Program for Families of the Mentally Impaired Elderly." *The Gerontologist* 20: 656–660.

U.S. General Accounting Office. 1977. *Report to the Congress on Home Health— The Need for a National Policy to Better Provide for the Elderly.* Washington, DC: U.S. General Accounting Office.

Wagner, Donna and Frederick Keast. 1981. "Informal Groups and the Elderly: A Preliminary Examination of the Mediation Foundation." *Research on Aging* 3: 325–332.

Ward, Russell A., Susan R. Sherman, and Mark LaGory. 1984a. "Subjective Network Assessments and Subjective Well-Being." *Journal of Gerontology* 39: 93–101.

Ward, Russell A., Susan R. Sherman, and Mark LaGory. 1984b. "Informal Networks and Knowledge of Services for Older Persons." *Journal of Gerontology* 39: 216–223.

York, Jonathan and Robert J. Calsyn. 1977. "Family Involvement in Nursing Homes." *The Gerontologist* 17: 500–505.

Zarit, Steven H., Karen E. Reeves, and Julie Bach-Peterson. 1980. "Relatives of the Impaired Elderly: Correlates of Feelings of Burden." *The Gerontologist* 20: 649–655.

6

The Interface Among Three Systems of Care: Self, Informal, and Formal*

Neena L. Chappell

Medical sociology, as indicated by its very name, has been preoccupied with the formal health care system, in particular with the profession of medicine. Less attention has been devoted to a broader concept of the sociology of health and health care, although this is changing. Over a decade ago, Pratt (1973) and Levin (1976) informed us that the majority of those experiencing illnesses take care of them without professional consultation. More recently, Helman (1978) and Blumhagen (1980) reported that between 70% and 90% of all illness episodes are managed without recourse to expert knowledge. Despite the fact that self-care is the predominant and most basic form of primary health care, it is the most neglected in basic research (Dean, 1981). This is especially true for studies of the elderly.

There is no reason to suspect that elderly individuals differ dramatically from younger ones in the predominance of self-care. If anything, an argument can be made that elderly persons engage in self-care and informal care practices more than younger individuals. The extent to which the professional system can effectively deal with deteriorations in health associated

*Data for this study were collected through a grant from the Social Sciences and Humanities Research Council of Canada (#492-83-0048) to Chappell and co-investigator, Strain (research associate, Centre on Aging). Partial support was also received through a Health Research Scholar award (#6607-1340-48) from Health and Welfare Canada to the author. The research assistance of Mark Badger is gratefully acknowledged.

with old age is questionable (Evans, 1984). The elderly have relatively few years remaining, and the professional system has been unable to alter this universal fate. Indeed, many argue that the medical care system is ill suited to treating the chronic conditions of old age, that it is focused on acute and institutional care rather than assistance in coping with chronic conditions and gradual declines while individuals remain within the community (Chappell, Strain, & Blandford, 1986; Tsalikis, 1982).

The folk health system has been reported as more active if the condition involved is one for which scientific medicine has not been able to effect a cure (Gould, 1957). Folk practices are more likely to be used when dealing with chronic, nonincapacitating dysfunctions, such as arthritis, rather than with critical, incapacitating dysfunctions, such as acute appendicitis. In this regard, it can be noted that the three most common chronic conditions of old age are heart disease, arthritis and chronic rheumatism, and hypertension (Neugarten, 1982). Furthermore, those who are elderly today grew up before the advent of universal medical care in Canada and before some of the medical advances that we know today.

Relatively little is known about self-care and informal care among the elderly. Even less is known about the interrelationships among the care systems: self, informal, and formal. Are they mutually exclusive? Does one substitute for another? Are they interdependent? Fleming, Giachello, Anderson, and Andrade (1984) report those more involved in self-care to be less likely to visit physicians as often or to spend as much time in hospital. Others talk about a continuum of care, with different types of care as supplementary to one another (Dunnell & Cartwright, 1972; Jefferys, Brotherston, & Cartwright, 1960).

In this chapter interest lies in distinguishing types of care engaged in by elderly individuals, with particular emphasis on the relationship the types of care have with one another. What is the overlap among or distinctiveness of self-care, informal care, and formal care? Data come from a pilot study of 100 individuals randomly chosen from one area of Winnipeg, Manitoba, Canada.

TYPES OF CARE

As others have noted (see, for example, Butler, Gertman, Oberlander, & Schindler, 1979–80; Green, 1985), the terms "self-care," "self-help," "self-maintenance," "self-health management," and "self-surveillance" have been used, often synonymously, to refer to various behaviors an individual engages in to remain healthy. Some definitions, such as that used by Butler and associates, refer to the individual's actions on his or her own behalf as well as on the behalf of family and neighbors. Most (Dean, 1981; Levin,

Katz, & Holst, 1976; Oren, 1971) refer only to the individual's efforts on his or her own behalf.

Frequently definition excludes professional assistance. Levin and Idler (1983) speak of self-care as those activities individuals undertake to promote their own health, prevent their own disease, limit their own illness, and restore their own health without professional assistance. Others, such as Barofsky (1978), specifically include professionals in a continuum of self-care: regulatory self-care (referring to maintenance activities such as eating and sleeping), preventive self-care (referring to self-initiated activities in the absence of illness), change in behavior to alleviate symptoms, and provider-initiated care. Further, behaviors subsumed under the term can vary. Self-care can include maintenance, prevention, promotion, diagnosis, and/or treatment.

In her review of the literature, Green (1985) notes that two common themes shared by most conceptualizations of the term are preventive behavior and response to acute illness. Less frequently studied aspects include information-seeking, use of professional services, care for chronic illness, compliance with treatment, and health education. As Dean (1981) points out, many studies are conducted within a perspective that views individuals as "responders and compliers"; that is, a perspective that assumes they are participants in a formal professional treatment system without taking into account that they may be active participants within the process and, further, that they are simultaneously involved in other care systems, notably self-care and, frequently, informal care. Even among the more recent studies of self-care, many focus on patient populations and are restricted to self-medication.

While we know self-care dominates personal health care, details about particular practices, by whom, in what circumstances, and related to what outcomes are lacking. It is an area in need of much research, both in its own right and as a component of the total care system. Nevertheless, self-care practices have been found to be associated with socioeconomic status, education, level of perceived health, race, gender, and age (Chang, 1980; Dean, 1980; Neves, 1980). Studies focusing on the elderly are harder to find.

Haug (1984) studied older respondents' reactions to five symptoms: depression, difficulty in sleeping, gas in the stomach, heavy cold, and an infected cut. A comparison of three age groups (46–59, 60–74, and 75 and older) indicates that older respondents are more likely to avoid professional care. As age increases, self-care is favored more in response to these symptoms, with the exception of heavy cold symptoms, where no relationship emerges between age and type of care. Haug argues that one of the appeals of self-care is that it is a source of feelings of independence and self-esteem. Haug and Lavin (1982) report people in better overall health and with less convenient access to formal services are more likely to engage in self-care. Dean (1980), however, finds older people more likely than younger people to rely on the medical sector.

Self-care, however, is part of a complex network involving various degrees of assistance from family and friends. Within gerontology, more is known about assistance from informal sources than about self-care. The prevalence of assistance from family and friends is now fairly well established. Estimates suggest that 80% of all care (not including socioemotional interaction) provided to the elderly comes from informal sources (Biaggi, 1980; Horowitz, Dono, & Brill, 1983). Among the community-dwelling elderly, that is, those not in long-term institutional care, over half are known to receive assistance from informal sources, that is, from family and friends. Assistance in this instance refers to help with activities ranging from household chores to nursing care. A small proportion, approximately 15% of the community-dwelling elderly, receive care from the formal health care system in Manitoba at any one time (Chappell & Havens, 1985).

Much of this literature focuses on the sources of support, specifically sources within the family. Studies of intergenerational exchanges inform us that while the social class of the old person is related to the magnitude and direction of parent–child help, old persons in every social class help their children and their children help them (Shanas, 1979a,b). Marshall, Rosenthal, and Synge (1981) report that long-term care, consisting mainly of help with chores and errands, followed by help with personal care, letter writing, and medications, is provided in about half the cases by a spouse or child. Cantor (1975) notes that elderly people express feelings about the appropriateness of assistance within kin structures and the desirability of interdependency between parents and children. In her study two-thirds receive help from children when ill, and two-thirds receive help in chores of daily living. The amount of help from children is positively related to age and to paucity of income.

The role of daughters is well documented as different from that of sons. Treas (1977) informs us that, devoted though sons may be, the major responsibility for the psychological sustenance and physical maintenance of the elderly falls traditionally to women. Daughters provide direct service, while sons play a more substantial role in decisionmaking and financial assistance. This has been confirmed more recently by Horowitz (1981). The spouse has also been identified as important as physical health deteriorates. Older couples can maintain considerable independence by nursing one another and reallocating housekeeping chores. Because women tend to marry men older than themselves and to have a greater life expectancy, the caregiver role tends to fall to the wife (Fengler & Goodrich, 1979).

The formal care system refers to governmental and nongovernmental service agencies, as well as health and other service professionals and paraprofessionals who work on their behalf. This definition includes both traditional medical services and community and social services (Branch & Jette, 1981). The definition is intended to include formally organized programs. Admittedly, there are gray areas, such as self-help and volunteer groups.

The formal health care system in Canada is centered around physician services and short-term institutional care. The major role played by physicians has been demonstrated by Evans (1976) in cost figures. This author estimates that physicians control about 80% of health care costs. Even though only about 19% of total insured Canadian health care expenditures goes directly to physicians, this group largely controls hospital utilization, prescribing of drugs, and so forth (Bennett & Krasny, 1981; Detsky, 1978). Most telling are the proportions of total expenditures within the system. For the period 1970–1979, 50% of total health care expenditures went to hospitals and nursing homes (institutional care), 25% to salaries for professional services (including but not exclusively to physician services), 10% went to drugs and appliances, and 15% to all other costs (Statistics Canada, 1983, p. 9).

For the purposes of this chapter it is important to recognize that the medical emphasis within the formal health care system means that many of the tasks of self-care and informal care of elderly people would not be expected to overlap with the formal care system. Indeed, many of the types of assistance required by elderly people (frequently assistance with activities of daily living on a long-term basis) do not receive government support because they are viewed both as cost add-ons to the current system and as activities that families should provide (Chappell, forthcoming). However, it has long been noted that utilization of formal services is not necessarily determined by need, with differential use related to gender, knowledge of the system, ethnicity, income, and so forth.

Even less is known about the interplay between the types of care. Gourash (1978) reviewed the literature on help-seeking generally and concluded that people turn initially to their informal network, that is, to family and friends; they turn to relief agencies or professional service organizations only as a last resort. Evans and Northwood (1979) and Schmidt (1981) confirm this finding among elderly individuals. The sole use of formal services is found much less frequently than either exclusive reliance on the informal network or help-seeking from both sources.

This chapter directs attention to the relations between types of care. Correlations among the three types of care, as well as comparisons of the factors associated with each type of care, assist in this task. The potential correlates of each type of care include a variety of sociodemographic factors, social support indicators, and health belief measures.

The importance of the informal network in the person's decision to engage in formal care has been recognized for some time, although details on its nature are few. Freidson (1961) coined the phrase "lay referral system" for the network of consultations, ranging from intimate and information exchanges within the nuclear family to more select and distant authoritative laymen to professionals. Those studying social networks suggest that various characteristics are related to different roles played by that network for the individual. Size of the network, household composition or living arrangements, and interactional context have all received attention in this regard (Pilisuk, Heller, Kelly, & Turner, 1982; Soldo & Lauriat, 1976).

The concept of health beliefs has also emerged as potentially important for the type of care an individual uses. It has long been recognized that one of the reasons people with heart disease or cancer delay seeking medical advice is because they believe the disease is incurable and the physician can do nothing for them. Beliefs in the efficacy of medical treatment and in the efficacy of other forms of treatment influence whether one visits a physician or engages in other types of care. For example, Pill and Stott (1982) report extensive belief in the germ theory as the cause of disease, and the concomitant belief that there was little they could do to prevent it, among a sample of working-class women.

There seems to be general consensus that the folk or lay health belief system is related to both the types of symptoms experienced and the social characteristics of the individual. Severity of the symptom and the effectiveness of medical treatment are positively related to the use of professional care (Gould, 1957; McKinlay, 1980). However, folk beliefs and practices have tended not to be studied in their own right as part of an organized system, but to be treated as part of the individual's subjective experience as a noncompliant patient (Dean, 1981). Individuals, however, could be complying with an alternative belief system.

Social factors include social class, ethnicity, and sex, among others (Burke & Goudy, 1981; Kahana & Kiyak, 1980). There is sufficient evidence documenting sex differences in health utilization behavior, and in particular the greater use of the health care system among women (Cleary, Mechanic, & Greenley, 1982), as not to require repetition here. Suffice it to say that these differences hold true among the elderly (Chappell & Havens, 1980). Similarly, knowledge of the formal health care system has been found to be related to use (Snider, 1982).

One specific attempt to measure the relevance of beliefs for health-related behaviors is in the area of locus of control. It is of interest here because it can be applied to self-care as well as professional care. Locus of control is defined as the expectancy that reinforcement is controlled by the individual (internal) or by outside forces (external) and is referred to as internal–external locus of control (Rotter, 1954, 1975). Wallston, Wallston, and DeVellis (1978) developed health locus of control scales with three dimensions (internal health locus of control, external control by powerful others such as doctors, and external control by chance or luck). Lau (1982) similarly proposed three such dimensions: self-control over health or belief in the efficacy of self-care (internal control), provider control over health or belief in the efficacy of doctors (external control by powerful others), and chance health outcomes (external control by chance). A fourth dimension, general health threat, correlated so highly with chance health outcomes that it appears as if the same construct was being measured.

As Lau has noted, internal locus of control has been found to be related to knowledge of disease, ability to stop smoking, ability to lose weight, compliance with medical regimens, effective use of birth control, getting preventive inoculations, wearing seatbelts, and getting regular checkups; that is, there is some evidence that locus of control is related to health behavior. However, as Pill and Stott (1981) argue, belief in internal control implies an acceptance of personal responsibility for health without giving any clear indication of the types of behavior likely to result, whether they be prevention, maintenance, or specific responses to illness.

This chapter examines the association of both social networks and health beliefs with the three types of care, while controlling for several sociodemographic factors.

DATA AND METHODOLOGY

Data come from a pilot study of 100 individuals interviewed face to face for approximately an hour and a half in one postal code area of Winnipeg, Manitoba (the area was restricted to hold distance from services more or less constant). This study was designed specifically to devise and field test questions to elicit information on the elderly's decisionmaking process to use or not use formal care services when various symptoms were identified. The study proper, following from this pilot, consists of a random sample of 743 individuals citywide. The data reported here come from the pilot study.

Data were collected in the fall of 1984. Names for the sample were randomly generated by the Manitoba Health Services Commission, which processes all provincial health claims. The sample was stratified by age and sex to obtain similar cell sizes. Half of those interviewed were male, half female. All interviews were conducted in English. An additional eight individuals were excluded because of language barriers. The refusal rate was 27%. Almost half (48)[1] of those interviewed were born in Manitoba, with just under a third (31) born outside of Canada. Almost three-quarters (72) had lived in Winnipeg for 20 years or more. The same proportion went no

[1] N and percentages are equal because the sample totals 100.

further than grade 12 in their formal education. Most (69) named Pro-
testant as their religious affiliation. Just under a third (31) had worked in a
professional or semiprofessional occupation, another 30 in the technical or
farming category, 21 in semiskilled occupations, and 18 as housewives. Half
were married, with a third (32) widowed.

The dependent variables are the types of care. As noted earlier, self-care
has been conceptualized and operationalized differently, depending on the
study. Here, two indicators were used. First, a self-maintenance question
was asked: "Which of these do you do to stay healthy (i.e., maintain your
health)?: eat a balanced diet, exercise regularly, avoid smoking, use car
seatbelts, avoid stress, get enough sleep, get routine medical checkups, do
self-examination, immunization, and other." Both routine checkups and
immunization were deleted because they involve health care professionals
and therefore contact with the formal health care system. An unrotated
principal components factor analysis was performed with the remaining
items, resulting in a health maintenance factor in which all but two of the
items (eating a balanced diet and "other") had factor scores of .30 or above.
The items were combined with appropriate weights to form the self-care
maintenance variable.

Second, individuals were asked their responses to 10 symptomatologies.
Specifically, the following question was used: "I am now going to read a
series of health conditions that people sometimes experience. What I would
like to know is your first response if these conditions happen to you. For
example, would you do nothing, treat yourself, or contact a health professional immediately?" Interviews probed for elaborated responses. Data
were coded in terms of whether the condition had happened in the past;
what their initial reaction had been (or would be, if the situation was
hypothetical); whether they would discuss it with anyone (layperson) and, if
so, who; if they engaged in self-treatment and what that would be; and if
they sought expert advice and who it was from. The 10 conditions were:
feeling of dizziness, bowel irregularity, constant tiredness, frequent
headaches, rash or itch, shortness of breath, difficulty sleeping, stomach
cramps, pulled muscle, and depression.

All symptomatologies to which a person's initial response was any form
of self-care (taking it easy, altering diet, applying heat or ointment, etc.)
were summed. It should be pointed out that the individual had to indicate a
change in behavior for it to be classified as self-care. If they indicated they
did nothing, it was not coded as self-care; but if they indicated they took it
easy as a response to the condition, it was coded as self-care. Cronbach's
alpha equals .71. This measure is referred to as self-care responses to
symptomatology. The higher the score, the more symptoms to which the
person initially responded with some form of self-care.

The self-maintenance measure is not significantly correlated with self-care responses to symptomatologies ($r = -.10$, gamma $= -.11$). Not only are they uncorrelated with one another, but the direction is negative. Those engaging in more self-maintenance activities are less likely to choose a self-care response to various symptomatologies, thereby confirming the two types of self-care (maintenance and response to illness) as very different from one another. The two should not be categorized together. Health behavior and illness behavior are very different forms of behavior.

Informal care was measured in terms of assistance received from others when the individual is unable to perform an activity of daily living; that is, it is tied to functional disability. This is reflected in the correlation between the two ($r = .66$). A person could be coded as receiving assistance only if he or she indicated some disability in the following activities of daily living: using the telephone, shopping for groceries or clothing, preparing meals, doing household tasks, handling own money, dressing and undressing, eating, bathing or showering, walking, and using the toilet. For example, if a man reported he was able to prepare his own meals but did not, his wife prepared them for him, this is considered a division of labor, not assistance. All areas in which the individual receives assistance were summed, so that a higher score indicates more assistance (Cronbach's alpha $= .70$). Analyses examining the correlates of informal care were therefore conducted, forcing in functional ability and removing its effects to examine which factors are more highly correlated with informal assistance after the effects are removed.

Formal care was measured in terms of the respondent's use of the following services in the last six months: general practitioner, medical specialist, emergency clinic, other hospital services, day hospitals, medical laboratories, dentist, psychiatrist, chiropractor, occupational/physical therapist, chiropodist/podiatrist, pharmacist, optometrist/optician, nutritionist, audiologist, public health nurse, social worker, minister, psychologist, senior center, home care, fitness program, community health clinic, and lawyer. When combined into a summative index of services used, Cronbach's alpha $= .66$. It will be noticed that community and social services are included, in addition to traditional medical services.

Two measures of health beliefs were used. One asked respondents how important they believed the following were to their overall health: regular exercise, taking vitamins, prayer or faith, having close friends, avoiding stress, diet and nutrition, positive thinking, avoiding germs, avoiding smoking, using car seatbelts, and getting routine medical checkups. This measure combined self-maintenance and preventive use of the formal care system (i.e., medical checkups and immunizations), because they are so highly correlated. The items are summed. The higher the score, the more important the person thinks the behaviors are (Cronbach's alpha $= .90$). This measure refers to the perceived importance of health behaviors. It will be noted that the Cronbach's alpha is much higher on this measure than for the reporting of actual behaviors; that is, respondents are more consistent in reporting their beliefs than their behaviors. This could well reflect greater consistency in beliefs than in behaviors.

A second measure of health beliefs refers to health locus of control. In total, 22 questions were asked, six referring to external control by chance, five to external control by powerful others, specifically doctors, five to internal control in terms of the efficacy of self-care, and six to internal control in terms of self-reliance. When unrotated principal component factor analyses were performed, one major (usable) factor emerges, consisting of 10 of the items. The following items were combined into a scale:

1. I have my doubts about some things doctors say they can do for you;
2. I believe in trying out different doctors to find out which one I think will give me the best care;
3. If you wait long enough, you can get over most sicknesses without going to the doctor;
4. Some home remedies are still better than prescribed drugs for curing sickness;
5. A person understands his/her own state of health better than most doctors;
6. Doctors often tell you there's nothing wrong with you, when you know there is;
7. Whenever I get sick it is because of something I've done or not done;
8. When I think I am getting sick, I find it difficult to talk to others about it;
9. When I feel ill, I know it is because I have not been getting the proper exercise or eating right;
10. The trouble with being ill is that you have to depend on other people.

The majority of these items refer to external locus of control by doctors, some refer to internal locus of control in terms of the efficacy of self-care, and a few refer to internal locus of control in terms of self-reliance internal control. Within these data, internal and external loci of control are negatively correlated; they co-exist. The higher the score, the more likely the person believes in the efficacy of self-care and simultaneously reveals skepticism about medical doctors. The two health belief measures, importance of health behaviors and locus of control, are correlated with one another (r = .50), in the expected direction.

Information was also collected on size, contact with, and normative context of the informal network. The total number of individuals in the network (size) was computed to include the number of other people in the household and all persons outside the household: parents, brothers, sisters, sons, daughters, other relatives, nonkin friends, neighbors, and other contacts. Only one person said he or she was totally isolated, that is, named no one in their network. Most had large networks; fully half the sample named over 30 people. Size of household was also examined separately.

Interaction with members of the network was also measured. When at least weekly contact was examined and the normative contexts (contact with parents, siblings, children, other relatives, friends, and neighbors) analyzed separately, the results were that 27% had at least weekly contact with siblings; 48% with children; 24% with other relatives; 50% with friends; and 61% with neighbors.

Several control variables were included. Health is necessarily introduced as a control when studying correlates of care. Chronic conditions were measured by asking respondents which of a list of health problems they had had within the last year or otherwise still had effects from, having had them earlier. The conditions included: heart and circulation problems, stroke, arthritis or rheumatism, palsy, eye trouble not relieved by glasses, ear trouble, dental problems, chest problems, stomach trouble, kidney trouble, diabetes, foot trouble, nerve trouble, skin problems, and "other," including cancer. The items were summed, with the higher number indicating more chronic conditions.

Respondents were also asked what special equipment they use (never, sometimes, always): cane, crutches, walker, wheelchair, leg brace, back brace, artificial arm, artificial leg, hearing aid, telephone volume control, colostomy equipment, catheter, kidney dialysis machine, other special equipment. The items were summed to obtain an indication of the use of special equipment. Perceived health, number of days spent in the hospital during the past 12 months, and number of days spent sick in bed at home during the past 12 months were also measured.

Functional ability was measured as the ability, irrespective of assistance received, to use the telephone, shop for groceries or clothing, prepare meals, do household tasks, handle own money, dress and undress, eat, bathe or shower, walk, and use the toilet. The items were scored such that a higher number indicates more disability (Cronbach's alpha = .86).

The Life Satisfaction Index—Z was used to measure overall well-being. It consists of 13 questions to which the respondents are asked whether they agree. Examples of questions include: "As I grow older, things seem better than I thought they would be" and "This is the dreariest time of my life." The items were summed (Cronbach's alpha = .71), with a higher score depicting higher satisfaction with life.

Other control variables included age, sex, ethnicity, education, marital status, and income.

Data analyses utilized multiple regression to examine the correlates of the types of care.

FINDINGS

We look first at the use of the different types of care. All individuals engage in some types of health maintenance behaviors. The proportion varies for specific items, from a low of 39% who do self-examinations to a high of 87% who report eating a balanced diet in order to stay healthy. In terms of self-care responses to symptomatologies, all except one individual report an initial response for at least one of the 10 symptoms listed. In terms of the individual items, those reporting an initial response of self-care range from a low of 40% for a pulled muscle to a high of 69% for bowel irregularity.

The situation changes dramatically when looking at informal care. Fully 75% are currently receiving no assistance from family or friends. This is considerably lower than the 50% reported in citywide studies from the same area (Chappell & Havens, 1985). However, only four used no formal services in the last six months. The high proportion using formal services presumably reflects the breadth of services asked about.

The correlations among the different types of care are shown in Table 6-1. Informal care is not correlated with self-care, either maintenance activities or responses to symptomatologies; nor is it correlated with formal care in the last six months. Whether one receives assistance from family or friends in activities of daily living is unrelated to self-care practices or utilization of formal services. The extent to which the availability of network members is the major factor here is explored below.

Self-care responses to symptomatologies are not related to formal care. This could be due to the fact that the latter refers to an initial response and we know, from previous research and as these data confirm, that most

TABLE 6-1 Sources of Care: Correlation Matrix

	Self-care maintenance	Self-care responses	Informal care	Formal care (6 mo.)
Self-care maintenance	1			
Self-care responses	$r = -.10$ $g = -.11$	1		
Informal care	$r = -.07$ $g = -.07$	$r = .15$ $g = .28$	1	
Formal care (6 months)	$r = .20^*$ $g = .34$	$r = .05$ $g = .07$	$r = .10$ $g = .23$	1

$^*p < .05$

individuals, even those using formal services, engage in self-care initially. Perhaps a more interesting question would be how those who end up using only self-care for specific symptomatologies differ from those who do not, but these data do not permit pursuing such a direction (although this can be explored further in the study proper).

The self-maintenance measure is correlated with formal care. Self-maintenance is significantly correlated with formal care in the last six months. The more a person engages in self-maintenance behavior, the more likely he or she is to utilize formal services. The two types of care, in other words, are not mutually exclusive. Rather, the use of the formal care system (as it exists in Canada; it would also be true of the United States) is, to a substantial degree, a type of self-care. It necessitates the active involvement of the individual; at minimum, it usually means leaving the residence to go to the appropriate site. This is confirmed in a further examination of the items asking whether an individual uses medical checkups and immunizations to stay healthy. Those engaging in other health maintenance behaviors are more likely to engage in these two as well. In addition, respondents state that many of their visits to the formal care system (especially to general practitioners) are for checkups; these visits are less often for immunization.

While the data do not directly address the link between self-maintenance behavior and formal care, those available do allow for speculation. Of all the formal services utilized, only a few were used by 25% or more of the sample in the past six months: general practitioner, medical specialist, medical laboratory, dentist, pharmacist, and minister. That is, those formal services that respondents tend to use, except perhaps a minister, require active involvement by the individual. At minimum he or she must keep an appointment and leave the home to do so. If the individual did not initiate the contact or make the appointment him- or herself, he or she must at minimum comply.

We turn next to the correlates of care, using multiple regression analyses. The results for self-care are shown in Table 6-2. Age and gender emerge as significant correlates of self-maintenance. At least weekly contact with children approaches significance. Younger respondents, women, and those with more contact with children are more likely to engage in self-maintenance activities. The correlation with age suggests that older individuals may perceive the benefits of such behavior as less likely as they grow nearer to death. The data, however, do not allow us to pursue this. The relationship with gender confirms women's greater concern with health matters. The relationship with children is not immediately obvious but suggests the importance of contact with others for self-maintenance activities. Of course, to disentangle cohort effects, longitudinal data with cross-sectional designs is required. While each of these three variables explains 5% or more of the variance, the total variance explained is not high (19%).

TABLE 6-2 Correlates of Self-Care*

Self-care maintenance					
Independent variables	B	Beta	r^2	t	p
Age	−.03	−.27	−.07	−2.65	<.01
Gender	.51	.26	.07	2.51	<.01
At least weekly contact with child	.44	.22	.05	−2.15	ns
F = 5.40; df = 3 and 79; p < .01					
R^2 = .19					

Self-care responses to symptomatology					
Independent variables	B	Beta	r^2	t	p
Gender	.11	.23	.05	2.31	<.05
Income	−.02	−.25	.06	−2.40	<.05
Life satisfaction	.02	.31	.10	2.92	<.01
Chronic conditions	.03	.23	.05	2.15	<.05
Daily contact with others	−.11	−.20	.04	−2.04	<.05
F = 6.25; df = 5 and 73; p < .000					
R^2 = .30					

*Variables not shown in the table are not statistically significant.

Looking at self-care responses to symptomatology, five variables together account for 30% of the variance. Life satisfaction accounts for the most (10%), followed by income (6%), gender and chronic conditions (5% each), and daily contact with others (4%). Those with higher life satisfaction, women rather than men, those with less income, those with more chronic conditions, and those with less daily contact with others are more likely to respond initially to more symptomatologies in terms of self-care. The relatively strong correlation with life satisfaction suggests the importance of subjective well-being for engaging in self-care as a response to illness. The correlation with gender suggests that women not only use the formal care system more, but also are more likely to begin with self-care. The correlation with income is contrary to Dean's (1981) review of the self-care literature, suggesting that those with more money are more likely to engage in such behavior (her review deals mainly with medication-taking). Again, a social network variable, but not a health belief variable, emerges as important.

As already mentioned, the informal care variable is tied to functional ability. The regression therefore forced disability in first, and the extent of remaining variation explained by the significant factors was then computed. The results are shown in Table 6-3. It is the adjusted r^2 that is of interest

TABLE 6-3 Correlates of Informal and Formal Care*

Informal care (with Effects of Functional Disability removed)

Independent variables	B	Beta	r^2	Adjusted r^2	t	p
Functional disability**	1.33	.56	.31	—	6.39	<.000
Days sick in bed	.01	.26	.07	.35	3.20	<.01
Weekly contact with child	.51	.22	.05	.26	2.82	<.01
Widowhood	−.40	−.17	.03	.14	−2.08	<.05
Special aids used	.23	.17	.03	.14	1.99	<.05

F = 19.28; df = 5 and 68;
  p < .000
R^2 = .49
Adjusted R^2 = .89

Formal care (last 6 months)

Independent variables	B	Beta	r^2	t	p
At least weekly contact with siblings	.22	.21	.04	2.03	<.05
Locus of control	−.13	−.23	.05	−2.24	<.05
(Gender)***	(.18)	(.19)	(.04)	(1.99)	(<.05)
Health beliefs	.12	.21	.04	2.11	<.05
Chronic conditions	.05	.20	.04	2.03	<.05

F = 5.62; df = 4 and 82; p < .000
R^2 = .17

*Only variables that are statistically significant are shown.
**Functional Disability was forced into the analysis first. Adjusted r^2 refers to variance explained by the additional variables after the effects of functional disability had been removed.
***Variables appearing in brackets were multicollinear with those immediately preceding them and were run in separate regressions.

here. Days sick in bed, use of special aids, at least weekly contact with a child, and widowhood emerge in the analysis. Specifically, those using more special aids, having more sick days in bed or in hospital, those not widowed, and those having more contact with at least one child are likely to be receiving more informal assistance.

When the effects of functional disability are removed, and the percent of remaining variation explained by the other variables computed, fully 89% of the variation is explained. Most of this variation is explained by days spent sick in bed and contact with a child. If one has an illness that confines one to bed and has a child who will help out, one is more likely to receive informal care. Once again, like the self-care regressions, social network variables emerge as more important than health beliefs.

Turning to formal care, the results are shown in the second part of Table 6-3. Chronic conditions, health beliefs, and locus of control are correlated with formal care in the last six months. Those with more chronic conditions, with a greater belief in self-maintenance activities, and with an external locus of control (belief in doctors) are more likely to have used more formal care services. The relationship with health beliefs confirms the earlier suggestion that utilization of formal services can be viewed as a type of health maintenance behavior. In addition, more contact with siblings and being female are also associated with using more health services. The relationship with gender confirms that women use the formal system more than men. The greater contact with siblings suggests they may provide networking to the formal system, perhaps as individuals sharing information on similar problems. However, little variation is explained (17%). In terms of the use of services, the health belief variables tend to be better correlates than the social network variables, a clear difference from self- or informal care.

A comparison of the variables emerging for each type of care is of greater interest here than the amount of variance explained. The social network variables are important correlates of self-care and informal care, but not of formal care. Of particular importance for self-care (either as maintenance or as a response to illness) is frequent contact with others. With frequent contact, one is more likely to engage in such behavior. Informal care is related to frequent contact with children and marital status, due in part to the fact that children and spouses are frequently the providers of such assistance.

Health beliefs, on the other hand, emerge as important for the use of formal services. Indeed, both beliefs in self-care maintenance activities and locus of control are related to formal care. The fact that social network variables, not health beliefs, are more important for self- and informal care, while health beliefs and not social networks tend to be important for formal care, points to the relative separateness of the three care systems.

It is also informative to look more closely at the role of health in the use of the three care systems, since each is presumably there to assist with this aspect of our lives. Chronic conditions are related to all types of care, including self-care responses to illness, informal care, and formal care, although not to the self-care maintenance activities. It is most strongly related to use of formal services; not unexpectedly, given the focus of such services on medicine and the list of chronic conditions that are tied mainly to diseases. Functioning is tied to informal care, but also to self-maintenance. When one's normal daily role performance is impaired, one becomes more involved with self-maintenance activities. Use of special aids and equipment and days in bed are also related to informal care. In other words, the data reveal most of the major health variables related to informal care, pointing to the critical role of interference with daily routines in the receipt of informal care.

This chapter has examined three systems of care among the elderly but has not looked at the circumstances in which the different types of care are appropriate or inappropriate. Nor has it examined ways to encourage or discourage different types of care. It has, however, revealed the heterogeneity among the elderly, especially differences between men and women, those younger and older, the healthy and the less healthy, those with more social contacts and those with less, and those who believe in doctors and those who do not. Class differences, as measured by education and income, do not appear important for the three types of care examined here among this sample.

IMPLICATIONS FOR POLICY

While these data come from a pilot study and await confirmation in the study proper, they nevertheless point to the relative separation between the three types of care engaged in by many elderly individuals.

The data confirm existing sociological literature, documenting that utilization of the formal care system (and indeed the self- and informal care systems) is not based only on "need" and that "need" is a complex phenomenon. Of particular interest here are the facts that social network variables are significantly correlated with self- and informal care and that health belief variables are significantly correlated with utilization of the formal care system. Given the self-initiated nature of contact with formal services, it is not surprising that locus of control emerges as important, with those highly skeptical of medical doctors less likely to engage in formal care.

Further, informal care co-exists with, but is unrelated to, self-care activities and utilization of formal services. It seems quite clear from the correlates of informal care that individuals within the social network do help elderly individuals in times of short-term incapacity, provided they are available. However, for longer-term conditions the elderly tend to turn to the formal health care system. (This is revealed when examining use of formal services for 12 months, not shown here.)

Most utilization of the formal care system appears to be a type of self-care, at least for individuals, like those studied here, who live independently in the community. The self-initiated nature of contact generally required to receive formal care accounts for a relationship between self- and formal care. However, the two systems are in other ways very distinct from one another. This is most evident in the fact that different variables are significant correlates of each. The relative distinctiveness of the three care systems is not particularly surprising, given that the Canadian medical care system is primarily oriented around acute and institutional services (Chappell et al., 1986). Given that type of system, one would not expect it to overlap extensively with self-care and informal care.

It is worthy of note that one does not find a "substitutability" between the care systems (i.e., a negative correlation). In this case one would expect a greater involvement in self-care or informal care to be related to the receipt of less formal care. This is not the case. Rather, the systems appear to be complementary, co-existing with one another. In fact, they appear to be fulfilling relatively different functions. The extent to which these functions are consistent with their structures (Litwak, 1985) has not been pursued here.

This becomes problematic if, as in an aging society, the major problems are chronic and the ability of both individuals and their informal networks to provide self- and informal care for optimal functioning becomes overstrained. Then the existing formal care system is open to criticism because of an emphasis that is unable to help individuals and their informal care systems to maximize their health or at least minimize deterioration (Chappell et al., 1986; forthcoming). This can become especially costly if individuals and families have no recourse but to access the existing expensive system when their own resources become overtaxed; but since there is no alternative, it means additional inappropriate use of that system.

REFERENCES

Barofsky, I. 1978. "Compliance, Adherence, and the Therapeutic Alliance: Steps in the Development of Self-Care." *Social Science and Medicine* 12: 369–372.

Bennett, J. E. and J. Krasny. 1981. "Health Care in Canada." Pp. 40–66 in *Health and Canadian Society: Sociological Perspectives,* edited by D. Coburn, C. D'Arcy, P. New, and G. Torrance. Don Mills, Ontario: Fitzhenry and Whiteside Ltd.

Biaggi, M. 1980. *Testimony before the Select Committee on Aging, House of Representatives, 96th Congress.* Washington, DC.

Blumhagen, D. 1980. "Hyper-Tension: A Folk Illness with a Medical Name." *Culture, Medicine and Psychiatry* 1: 197–227.

Branch, L. G. and A. M. Jette. 1981. *Elders' Use of Informal Long-Term Care Assistance.* Paper presented at the annual meeting of the Gerontological Society of America, Toronto, Ontario. 1981.

Burke, S. C. and W. J. Goudy. 1981. *Older Men and Their Kinship Networks.* Paper presented at the annual meeting of the Midwest Sociological Society, Minneapolis, MN.

Butler, R. N., J. S. Gertman, D. L. Oberlander, and L. Schindler. 1979–80. "Self-

Care, Self-Help and the Elderly." *International Journal of Aging and Human Development* 10: 95–117.

Cantor, M. H. 1975. "Life Space and the Social Support System of the Inner City Elderly of New York." *The Gerontologist* 15: 23–27.

Chang, B. L. 1980. "Evaluation of Health Care Professionals in Facilitating Self-Care: Review of the Literature and a Conceptual Model." *Advances in Nursing Sciences* 3: 43–58.

Chappell, N. L. Forthcoming. "Long-Term Care in Canada." In *North American Elders: United States and Canadian Comparisons,* edited by E. Rathbone-McCuan and B. Havens. Westport, CT: Greenwood Press.

Chappell, N. L. and B. Havens. 1980. "Old and Female: Testing the Double Jeopardy Hypothesis." *The Sociological Quarterly* 21: 157–171.

Chappell, N. L. and B. Havens. 1985. "Who Helps the Elderly Person: A Discussion of Informal and Formal Care." Pp. 211–227 in *Social Bonds in Later Life,* edited by W. Peterson and J. Quadagno. Beverly Hills, CA: Sage Publications.

Chappell, N. L., L. A. Strain, and A. A. Blandford. 1986. *Aging and Health Care: A Social Perspective.* Toronto, Ontario: Holt, Rinehart and Winston of Canada, Ltd.

Cleary, P. O., D. Mechanic, and J. R. Greenley. 1982. "Sex Differences in Medical Care Utilization: An Empirical Investigation." *Journal of Health and Social Behavior* 23: 106–119.

Dean, K. 1980. *Analysis of the Relationships Between Social and Demographic Factors and Self-Care Patterns in the Danish Population.* Unpublished doctoral dissertation, University of Minnesota, Minneapolis.

Dean, K. 1981. "Self-Care Responses to Illness: A Selected Review." *Social Science and Medicine* 15A: 673–687.

Detsky, A. S. 1978. *The Economic Foundations of National Health Policy.* Cambridge, MA: Ballinger Publishing Co.

Dunnell, K. and A. Cartwright. 1972. *Medicine Takers, Prescribers and Hoarders.* London, England: Routledge & Kegan Paul.

Evans, R. G. 1976. "Does Canada Have Too Many Doctors? Why Nobody Loves an Immigrant Physician." *Canadian Public Policy* II: 147–160.

Evans, R. G. 1984. *Strained Mercy: The Economics of Canadian Health Care.* Toronto, Ontario: Butterworth and Company (Canada) Ltd.

Evans, R. L. and L. K. Northwood. 1979. "The Utility of Natural Help Relationships." *Social Science and Medicine* 13A: 789–795.

Fengler, A. and N. Goodrich. 1979. "Wives of Elderly Disabled Men: The Hidden Patients." *The Gerontologist* 19: 175–184.

Fleming, G. V., A. L. Giachello, R. M. Anderson, and P. Andrade. 1984. "Self-Care: Substitute, Supplement or Stimulus for Formal Medical Care Services?" *Medical Care* 22: 950–966.

Freidson, E. 1961. *Patients' Views of Medical Practice.* New York: Russell Sage Foundation.

Gould, H. A. 1957. "The Implications of Technological Change for Folk and Scientific Medicine." *American Anthropologist* 59: 507–516.

Gourash, N. 1978. "Help-Seeking: A Review of the Literature." *American Journal of Community Psychology* 6: 413–423.

Green, K. E. 1985. "Identification of the Facets of Self-Health Management." *Evaluation and the Health Professions* 8: 323–338.

Haug, M. R. 1984. *Doctor–Patient Relationships and Their Impact on Elderly Self-Care.* Paper presented at the annual meeting of the Gerontological Society of America, San Antonio, TX.

Haug, M. R. and B. Lavin. 1982. *Self-Care and the Elderly: An Empirical Assessment.* Paper presented at the tenth world congress of the International Sociological Association, Mexico City, Mexico.

Helman, C. 1978. "Feed a Cold, Starve a Fever." *Culture, Medicine and Psychiatry* 2: 107.

Horowitz, A. 1981. *Sons and Daughters as Caregivers to Older Parents: Differences in Role Performance and Consequences.* Paper presented at the annual meeting of the Gerontological Society of America, Toronto, Ontario.

Horowitz, A., J. E. Dono, and R. Brill. 1983. *Continuity or Changes in Informal Support? The Impact of an Expanded Home Care Program.* Paper presented at the annual meeting of the Gerontological Society of America, San Francisco, CA.

Jefferys, M., J. Brotherston, and A. Cartwright. 1960. "Consumption of Medicines on a Working-Class Housing Estate." *British Journal of Preventive Social Medicine* 14: 64.

Kahana, E. F. and H. A. Kiyak. 1980. "The Older Woman: Impact of Widowhood and Living Arrangements on Service Needs." *Journal of Gerontological Social Work* 3: 17–29.

Lau, R. R. 1982. "Origins of Health Locus of Control Beliefs." *Journal of Personality and Social Psychology* 42: 322–334.

Levin, L. 1976. "The Layperson as the Primary Health Care Practitioner." *Public Health Report* 91: 206–120.

Levin, L. and E. Idler. 1983. "Self-Care in Health." *Annual Review of Public Health* 4: 181–201.

Levin, L., A. H. Katz, and E. Holst. 1976. *Self-Care: Lay Initiatives in Health.* New York: Prodist.

Litwak, E. *Helping the Elderly.* 1985. New York: Guilford Press.

Marshall, V. W., C. J. Rosenthal, and J. Synge. 1981. *The Family as a Health Organization for the Elderly.* Paper presented at the annual meeting of the Society for the Study of Social Problems, Toronto, Ontario.

McKinlay, J. B. 1980. "Social Network Influences on Morbid Episodes and the Career of Help Seeking." Pp. 77–107 in *The Relevance of Social Science for Medicine,* edited by L. Eisenberg and A. Kleinman. D. Reidel Publishing Co.

Neugarten, B. L. (ed.) 1982. "Older People: A Profile." Pp. 33–54 In *Age or Need? Public Policies for Older People.* Beverly Hills, CA: Sage Publications.

Neves, E. P. 1980. "The Relationship of Hospitalized Individuals' Cognitive Structure Regarding Health to Their Health Self-Care Behaviors." *Dissertation Abstracts International* 41: 522.

Oren, D. E. 1971. *Nursing: Concepts of Practice.* New York: McGraw-Hill.

Pilisuk, M., S. Heller, J. Kelly, and E. Turner. 1982. "The Helping Network Approach: Community Promotion of Mental Health." *Journal of Primary Prevention* 3: 116–132.

Pill, R. and N. C. Stott. 1981. "Relationships Between Health Locus of Control and Belief in the Relevance of Lifestyle to Health." *Patient Counseling and Health Education* 3: 95–99.

Pill, R. and N. C. Stott. 1982. "Concepts of Illness Causation and Responsibility: Some Preliminary Data from a Sample of Working Class Mothers." *Social Science and Medicine* 16: 43–52.

Pratt, L. 1973. "The Significance of the Family in Medication." *Journal of Comparative Family Studies* 4: 13–35.

Rotter, J. B. 1954. *Social Learning and Clinical Psychology.* Englewood Cliffs, NJ: Prentice-Hall.

Rotter, J. B. 1975. "Some Problems and Misconceptions Related to the Construct of Internal Versus External Control of Reinforcement." *Journal of Consulting and Clinical Psychology* 43: 56–67.

Schmidt, M. G. 1981. "Personal Networks: Assessment, Care and Repair." *Journal of Gerontological Social Work* 3: 65–76.

Shanas, E. 1979a. "The Family as a Support System in Old Age." *The Gerontologist* 19: 169–174.

Shanas, E. 1979b. "Social Myth as Hypothesis: The Case of the Family Retirement of Old People." *The Gerontologist* 19: 3–9.

Snider, E. L. 1982. "The Needs of Health and Related Community Agencies Serving Elderly Families." *Canadian Journal of Public Health* 73: 119–122.

Soldo, B. and P. Lauriat. 1976. "Living Arrangements Among the Elderly in the United States: A Loglinear Approach." *Journal of Comparative Family Studies* VII: 351–366.

Statistics Canada. 1983. *Fact Book on Aging in Canada.* Ottawa, Ontario: Minister of Supply and Services.

Treas, J. 1977. "Family Support Systems for the Aged: Some Social and Demographic Considerations." *The Gerontologist* 17: 486–491.

Tsalikis, G. 1982. "Canada." Pp. 125–162 in *Linking Health Care and Social Services,* edited by M. C. Hokenstad and R. A. Ritvo. Beverly Hills, CA: Sage Publications.

Wallston, K. A., B. S. Wallston, and R. DeVellis. 1978. "Development of the Multidimensional Health Locus of Control (MHLC) Scales." *Health Education Monograph* 6: 160–170.

7
Communication and Medical Care Outcomes: Analysis of Conversations Between Doctors and Elderly Patients

Rodney M. Coe

This chapter reports on the results of a pilot study of communication between physicians and elderly patients. Specifically, the conversation between doctor and patient is examined in detail to gain more insight into the nature of the doctor–patient relationship. In addition, selected research linking communication with outcomes of the encounter is reviewed.

Few examples of a social relationship have received more examination and discussion than the medical encounter between doctor and patient. This is both natural and important because of the (1) frequency of occurrence—there were 850 million physician visits in the United States reported for 1977 (NCHS, 1983) and the frequency of visits rises with age of patient; (2) the salience of health (and health behavior) in American culture; and (3) the fascination with what goes on in a privileged relationship, shrouded in secrecy, in which the differences in status and power are often great.

Despite the focus of attention on the doctor–patient relationship, until recently there has been little empirical research on the behavior of the parties to the encounter (Fisher & Todd, 1983; Inui & Carter, 1985). As a consequence, much of our understanding of the structure and processes of the relationship remains anecdotal and conjectural. Some of these recent empirical research efforts have revealed the importance of patterns of communication between doctor and patient and the outcomes of the encounter (Carter, Inui, Kukull, & Haigh, 1982; Inui, Carter, Kukull, & Haigh, 1982; Putnam, Stiles, Jacob, & James, 1985; Wooley, Kane, Hughes, & Wright, 1978). For example, the physician's ability to communicate affects the degree to which he or she has a "placebo effect" on the patient (Reiser & Rosen, 1984). Lack of communication skills is related to iatrogenic effects (Steel, German, & Crescenzic, 1981). Many studies have examined the relationship between communication and patient "compliance," especially with respect to medications (Becker, 1985; Davis, 1968; Davis & Eichhorn, 1963; Eraker, Kirscht, and Becker, 1984; Stewart, 1984). Finally, but not exhaustively, communication patterns, such as the use of jargon, have been used to mask lack of knowledge of "physician uncertainty" (Katz, 1984). Communication skill, then, is seen as a key element in effecting desired therapeutic outcomes. Cousins (1984) has stated the case succinctly:

"In health care the words a physician uses have a profound effect on the well being of the patient. . . . The right words can potentiate a patient, mobilize the will to live, and set the stage for heroic response. The wrong words can produce despair and defeat or impair the usefulness of whatever treatment is prescribed."

APPROACHES TO THE STUDY OF COMMUNICATION

How does one go about investigating communication in a doctor–patient encounter? We are all familiar with early reports of interviews with physicians or with patients that describe recollection of what was said in relation to record audits of outcomes of encounters. These studies have obvious methodological weaknesses, and they seldom provide data in sufficient detail to permit examination of communication styles. A relatively new approach to establishing a link between communication process and outcome is the detailed analysis of recorded conversation of doctor and patient in an actual encounter. In a general review, Waitzkin and Stoeckle (1972) concluded that the direct recording of doctor–patient interaction provides the greatest potential for drawing valid conclusions about the flow of information in an encounter. They also suggest that improved communication leads to better outcomes, such as increased compliance and greater patient satisfaction.

In a later review, Wasserman and Inui (1983) provided a detailed review of various approaches to analysis of recorded conversation. The critique focused on Bales's (1950) Interaction Process Analysis (IPA) or variations of the IPA (Roter, 1977) and other classifications such as "verbal response modes" (Stiles, Putnam, Wolf, & James, 1979). Wasserman and Inui (1983) concluded that doctor–patient interaction contains information at multiple levels and in multiple modes. Thus it is necessary to develop multifaceted analytic approaches that include the clinical goal as well as measures of the sequence, form, and content of the interaction. The validity of these conclusions has been demonstrated in a refinement (Buijs, Sluijs, & Verhaak, 1984) of a procedure first developed by Byrne and Long (1976). This process permits identification (and labeling) of a physician's "interview style" in the diagnostic phase and the therapeutic phase of the encounter. Some of these studies have produced interesting information, but all have obvious methodological problems. In addition, Tuckett and Williams (1984) and Levanthal (1985) have also noted that these studies require a better conceptual framework on information exchange to enhance understanding of the process of the encounter and its relationship to outcomes.

A general theoretical perspective derives from the microanalysis and interpretation of everyday interaction made popular by the works of Goffman (1959, 1961, 1967) and formalized by Garfinkel (1970), Schenkein (1978), and Psathas (1979). It is an approach to the study of social organization and the "orderliness" of social activity through examination of the form, sequence, and content of conversational exchanges. Goffman (1974) also reminds readers that all social interaction is bounded by rules of interaction, both formal and informal, that involve some degree of ritual and ceremony, the close examination of which should lead to better understanding of the social organization of a particular relationship.

The sociological conceptualization of what takes place in the doctor–patient encounter specifically has been expressed from a *functionalist* perspective by Parsons (1951), with a focus on social role expectations in an inherently asymmetrical relationship; this was later modified by Szasz and Hollender (1956) to describe three types of doctor–patient relationships. It has also been expressed from an *exchange* perspective (Bloom, 1963), which incorporates the notion of transactions and gives recognition to the influence of reference groups and broad sociocultural values, and from a *conflict* perspective (Freidson, 1970), which emphasizes the dissimilar interests and resources of doctor and patient and the need to negotiate outcomes of an encounter.

Variations of these themes are seen in the writings of clinicians who are just as interested in outcomes as they are in the interaction process itself. Three relevant examples will suffice. Engel (1977) has proposed a "biopsychosocial" model as an alternative to the biomedical model that currently dominates medical thinking and practice. The bio-psychosocial model stresses the art of communication as the key to a more holistic perspective on the patient's problems, as well as improving accuracy in diagnosis and gaining cooperation in therapy. A second clinical concept is the "cultural construction of clinical reality" of Kleinman, Eisenberg, and Good (1978).

The main thrust of their argument is that the physician's biomedical or disease perspective may not represent reality to the patient, and the patient's generalized illness perspective may not represent reality to the physician. Effective outcomes, however, require a shared perspective on clinical reality and therapeutic approaches to the problem; thus the importance of communication skills in developing a shared "construction."

A more recent approach by Mishler (1984) accepts the notion that illness is "constructed" (not discovered) and that patient and doctor may have very different perspectives and approaches to the problem that he calls the "voice of the lifeworld" and the "voice of medicine." Specifically, he writes

> . . . the voice of the lifeworld refers to the patient's contextually-grounded experiences of events and problems in [her] life . . . the timing of events and their significance are dependent on the patient's biographical situation and position in the social world. In contrast, the voice of medicine reflects a "technical" interest and expresses a "scientific attitude." The meaning of events is provided through abstract rules that serve to detextualize events, to remove them from particular personal and social contexts. (Mishler, 1984, p. 104)

However, Mishler's analytic approach is very different from others. He rejects the assumption that the discourse ought to be "doctor-driven." Thus, the model of "doctor asks, patient answers, doctor acknowledges" is not necessarily the appropriate one for achieving good therapeutic outcomes. Doctor-driven or "doctor-centered" interviews in Byrne and Long's (1976) terms would be effective and acceptable only if you also accept the assumptions underlying the biomedical model of treatment. Rather, Mishler focuses his analytic attention on what story the patient is trying to tell—it is, after all, the patient's problem and the patient's anxiety. For the vast majority of patients, the description will be in the contextual terms of the voice of lifeworld, sometimes vague and diffuse, but always integrated with other elements of the patient's life experiences and environments. One can then examine how and to what degree the physician, who is fluent in the language of the voice of medicine as well as the voice of the lifeworld, is able to help the patient tell his or her story. At one extreme, the physician may "interrupt" the patient's narrative by trying to force it into the language of the voice of medicine and ignoring the clues relevant to the voice of the lifeworld (West, 1984). At the other extreme, the physician may respond to lifeworld clues, encourage elaboration, and incorporate them into the voice of medicine. To the degree the latter can be achieved, one would expect better outcomes of "humane treatment" in Mishler's terms. He says

> . . . the physician's effort to impose a technocratic consciousness, to dominate the voice of the lifeworld by the voice of medicine, seriously impairs and distorts

essential requirements for mutual dialogue and humane interaction. To the extent that clinical practice is realized through this type of discourse, the possibility of more humane treatment in medicine is severely limited. (Mishler, 1984, p. 127)

There seems to be a convergence of concepts in the doctor–patient relationship that are presumed to be associated with better outcomes. The cultural construction of clinical reality (Kleinman et al., 1978) would seem to require negotiated exchanges (Freidson, 1970; Bloom, 1963) and mutual participation (Szasz & Hollender, 1956) in a holistic approach to therapy (Engel, 1977; Mishler, 1984). However, this does not tell us how conversational exchanges are to accomplish this; nor is there a clear link between conversation with improved outcomes.

COMMUNICATION AND MEDICAL CARE OUTCOMES

A major emphasis in analysis of conversation in doctor–patient interaction has been on developing reliable and valid procedures for determining the process and meaning in the exchanges. Most of the analysts assume that a particular style—more patient-centered (Byrne & Long, 1976) or more in the "voice of the lifeworld" (Mishler, 1984)—will lead to better outcomes. Thus the association between conversational styles and outcomes of the encounter remains a testable hypothesis.

There were some early efforts to do this, based largely on coding observed or taped conversations according to Bales's IPA categories (Davis and Eichhorn, 1963; Korsch & Negrete, 1972). These studies did show, in general, that the amount of clear instructions provided by the doctor, as well as the physician's showing emotional support and meeting the patient's perceived needs for information, were associated with better compliance with treatment regimens and greater expressed satisfaction with the encounter. However, many of these studies also showed considerable inconsistency in these relationships.

More recent reports, which employ somewhat different approaches, reveal more consistent results. Svarstad (1976), for example, analyzed conversations between staff physicians and 131 patients in a neighborhood health center. Her analysis revealed several styles of communication employed by physicians to gain patient compliance with medication regimens: (1) friendliness and seeking social approval; (2) justification or appealing to reason; (3) use of medical authority, or "you must do this." Svarstad developed a composite index called Physician's Total Effort, which was then correlated with information from interviews concerning patient satisfaction with the treatment plan and compliance with it. She reported a modest relationship between the index and patient satisfaction and a strong relationship between the index and degree of compliance.

Another approach to analysis of conversations, called the Verbal Response Mode (VRM), was developed and used by Stiles and associates (1979). The VRM is a set of eight mutually exclusive categories of response, such as Disclosure, Question, Acknowledgment, and so on. Tape-recorded conversations can be reliably coded with this procedure. This study reports a strong association between patient satisfaction and use of the modes of Question, Acknowledgment, Interpretation, and Reflection. More importantly, this study and its recent replication (Putnam et al., 1985) demonstrate that the relationship between communication and outcomes can vary from one stage or segment of the encounter to another. Specifically, they report that affective satisfaction was associated with the early part of the encounter when the patient is encouraged to describe the problem in his or her own words, called the "patient exposition" stage. Cognitive satisfaction was associated with the latter part of the encounter when the physician gave instruction, or the "physician explanation" stage. The replication study also examined VRM and patient compliance with health promoting behaviors such as nonsmoking, exercise, and proper diet, but correlations were not statistically significant (Putnam et al., 1985).

Similar results for cognitive and clinical outcomes were obtained in a study that employed a different coding scheme to classify conversation (Heszen-Klemens & Kapinska, 1984). This study identified conversational segments according to "spheres of intended influence," that is, cognition, emotion, behavior, and combinations of these three basic categories. Outcome data were obtained by follow-up interviews and physical examination. The relevant findings were that patients learned instructions better (cognitive outcomes) when the physician was "more friendly" and allowed patients to act as partners, and when patients asked more questions. In addition, positive clinical outcomes (both subjective and objective improvements in health status) were significantly associated with the physician's positive emotional attitude toward the patient, the proportion of physician questions on the first visit, and efforts to improve the patient's emotional state on follow-up visits.

These three examples give support to the hypothesis that positive outcomes are associated with particular communication styles, especially those that reduce status differences between doctor and patient and incorporate the patient's perceptions into joint decisions on diagnosis and management of the problem. Some other studies of doctor–patient conversation give indirect support by identifying factors that inhibit communication between doctor and patient. Some factors that have been noted are the use of jargon (Korsch & Negrete, 1972), exploitation of superior physician status (Fisher, 1984; Waitzkin, 1984, 1985), use of cultural stereotypes (Fisher & Groce,

1985), "ageist" bias (Greene, Adelman, Charon, & Hoffman, 1986), and use of closed-ended questions by physicians (Beckman & Frankel, 1984); even such factors as physician gender (Weisman & Teitelbaum, 1985) and nonverbal gestures (Heath, 1984) have been used by physicians to control the conversation and, thus, the outcomes of the encounter.

SPECIAL CONSIDERATIONS WITH THE ELDERLY

Up to this point, little has been said about communication with elderly patients, and there are some considerations that should be taken into account. In the first place, there may be a *cohort* effect. It has been found, for example, that the present generation of elderly patients tends to accept doctors' decisions and advice with little challenge to their authority. Nor do elderly patients press their physicians for detailed information about their conditions. This tendency toward dependence is expected to decline in future cohorts of the elderly (Haug, 1979; Nuttbrock & Kosberg, 1980).

Second, there may be an *age* effect in the decline in auditory and visual acuity, memory, and certain psychomotor reflexes (Botwinick, 1973). These factors have obvious implications for the ability of the elderly patient to receive, process, and respond to information. There are implications as well for the special efforts necessary on the part of the physician to insure that the elderly patient understands.

Third, there may be a problem of *unmet expectations*. This refers to the orientation of American medical care (in both organizational and biomedical ideology) to dealing with acute disorders when, in fact, the major health problems of the elderly are chronic in nature. The expectation of the physician and patient may be "cure," while the more realistic goal is "care." It is not uncommon for both doctor and patient to be dissatisfied with the outcomes of these encounters (Coe & Wessen, 1965).

None of these generalizations have been derived from studies of conversational exchanges in the doctor–elderly patient relationship. In fact, there are no studies of conversation and outcomes that focus on elderly patients that can be reviewed here. However, some preliminary but encouraging results of a pilot investigation can be described. Data were collected from tape-recorded encounters of two staff physicians trained in geriatrics and elderly patients and an accompanying relative seen in a university's ambulatory care center. For purposes of the pilot study, two sessions were taped with each of seven patients, once with the physician only and once with the physician and the relative. The tapes were transcribed and analyzed by means of Bales's IPA and variations (Roter, 1977) as well as a computerized format (National Board of Medical Examiners,

1981). Unfortunately, we did not collect information on outcomes of the encounter, so our analysis is limited to the form, content, and sequence of conversational exchanges.

Even so, the analysis of these conversations resulted in two reportable findings. The first was identification of educational strategies employed by physicians to promote compliance with medication regimens (Coe, Prendergast, & Psathas, 1984). We learned, for example, how physicians engage the relative of the elderly patient as "supervisor" or "manager" of the medication regimen at home, as a partner in the therapeutic enterprise. One can also see how physicians adapt the level of their language to the perceived level of understanding of the patient and relative. The use of reminders or aids, such as charts and egg cartons, to separate pills was also noted. For example, the following exchange took place between a doctor, an elderly patient, and the patient's daughter:

DAU: Doctor, would you write down on here what she's supposed to be taking, in laymen's terms?
DR: Sure. ⎡She's⎤. . .
⎣So I ⎦ know what I'm talking about.
DR: . . . supposed to be taking Timolol.
DAU: M'm h'm.
DR: It's a heart medicine. One tablet, twice a day.
DAU: OK.
DR: She's supposed to be taking Isordil, which is another heart medicine.
DAU: M'm h'm.
DR: Both of these, one slows the heart down, Timolol slows it down and the other, Isordil, is supposed to get more blood to the heart.

Finally, these physicians seemed sensitive to the patient's input—or voice of the lifeworld—in adapting the medication schedule to the patient's activities at home or at work. One encounter involved the physician, an elderly male patient, and the patient's wife, who had been keeping the patient in strict compliance with a literal interpretation of a medication regimen, about which the patient complained.

PT: Seems like I'm takin' an awful lot of pills.
WIFE: (laugh)
PT: Every time I turn⎡around⎤. . .
DR: ⎣Yeah ⎦. . .
WIFE: Yeah, but I can't, uh, there's not much else I can do, honey, 'cause there's some that you're on four hours, some that you're on six hours and some of 'em, eight hours.

Later in the exchange, the patient said he often stayed up until midnight to take medicine, then said:

PT: But lots of times I wanna go to bed at 11:00, ⎡10:30⎤ . . .
WIFE: ⎣Yeah ⎦ . . .
          . . . and you gotta sit up.
DR: Just to take the⎡medicine?   ⎤
PT: ⎢then I have to take the damn medicine. ⎥
WIFE: ⎣to take the medicine.   ⎦
DR: No, no, let's take them at 11:00, that's OK. You, you, if it doesn't work, if
          it doesn't work you let me know and we'll have to change it back. But I
          think that'll be OK.
WIFE: 'Cause he starts out at 6:00 in the morning. We set an alarm and he
          sits—he gets up at six and takes his ⎡first.   ⎤
PT: ⎢Yeah, that's . . .   ⎥
WIFE: ⎣his first medication ⎦ . . .

The other focus of analysis was the impact of the third person, the
relative, on the interaction between the traditional doctor and patient dyad.
That was the reason for taping two encounters of the doctor and elderly
patient, once alone and once with the relative. We found, first, that the
addition of the third person meant that much of the doctor's conversation
was directed at that person rather than the patient. Second, the role of the
third person in this kind of triad was very much like that which had been
predicted by Rosow (1981). That is, the relative acted as an *interpreter;* not
as a literal translator from one language to another, but more in terms
of upgrading and elaborating the patient's complaint and even correct-
ing the patient's original report. For example, after an elderly male
patient had reported having muscle cramps, the following exchange
took place:

DR: Are they gettin' worse, these cramps?
PT: No, they ain't gotten no worse.
DAU: Dad, they gettin' worse. That's why you mention it. Everyday you complain
          that your hand, that it's just like pins, like it stings
DR: So, everyday he complains to you⎡about it.⎤
DAU: ⎣Right.   ⎦

Relatives also acted to explain how the physician's orders—for example, for
exercises—could be carried out in the home setting.
    In addition, there was evidence that the third person acted as a *negotiator*
with the physician, especially in terms of altering the frequency of appoint-
ments when travel was inconvenient or substituting less costly medications
for more expensive brands. One example appears in the following exchange
between a doctor, an elderly male patient, and the patient's daughter.
The doctor had just suggested that he would put the patient back on po-
tassium.

DAU: Since he was on that before, we got a big bottle at the house, would that be too old for⌈ him to take? ⌉
DR: ⌊ No, you can use that.⌋ Give him a couple of tablespoons each day with some, uh, orange juice . . . and we'll see you in about a month and we'll see how it's goin' . . .OK?
PT: Yeah.
DAU: Doctor, that's another question I wanted to ask you about. You know, with him comin' every month, is it necessary for him to come every month?
DR: No, only, the only . . .
DAU: He . . .
DR: . . . time we need to do it is when he's having some problems. So what we can do is have him come in two or three months—if his leg pain goes away. OK?
DAU: Don't you want to see him back in a month to see⌈how . . .⌉
DR: ⌊How   ⌋ about it?
        Well, no. We can bring him back in three months, 'cause I know it's difficult on you to bring him in. You have to take time off and stuff.

This example also illustrates a third role task, in which the family member is encouraged by the physician to become a *caretaker* in monitoring the patient's health status, supervising the taking of medications, and providing psychological support. Other obvious role tasks include being a companion and a source of transportation.

Finally, we used this opportunity to examine the formation of coalitions in triads, in this case Rosow's (1981) "geriatric triad." A coalition was defined as an interaction between two members of a triad who adopt a common strategy in contention with the third. We found that in any given encounter, more than one coalition could form and, as Rosow had suggested, the alignment of members could vary. Sometimes it was the doctor and relative versus the patient; sometimes the patient and relative versus the doctor; and sometimes even the doctor and patient versus the relative. We also found that coalitions in encounters varied in duration (number of utterances) and that some coalitions failed to achieve their goals (Coe & Prendergast, 1985).

One kind of coalition was illustrated in the interaction described above, in which the patient attempted to get the physician to modify his medication regimen despite the objections of his wife. A later part of that transcript revealed a possible reason for the wife's resistance, namely, she had memorized the present, complicated schedule and did not want to learn a new schedule. In this case, the patient–physician coalition prevailed and the schedule was altered to interfere less with the patient's regular activities.

An example of a relative–physician coalition that did not succeed involved an elderly female patient (Coe & Prendergast, 1985). Analysis of the transcript showed some prior tension between the patient and her daughter. The physician wanted the patient to exercise by walking every day, which the patient was able to do with her daughter's help. The daughter wanted her mother to use a cane so the patient could get out alone. The patient rejected the idea of a cane and other suggestions of both the doctor and daughter throughout the conversation. Finally, the physician understood that the patient's resistance was not to the exercise or the cane but to doing it alone and that needing her daughter's help ensured that she would have some company. The doctor suggested that arrangements be made for a friend or neighbor to give the daughter some respite from daily walking with her mother.

A FINAL NOTE

These brief examples of conversation in doctor–patient–relative interaction are encouraging. Clearly there is much developmental work to do. The methodology for data collection has been tested and approaches to analysis are feasible, if somewhat labor-intensive. Questions remain about sampling designs to obtain representativeness and to be able to generalize findings. These kinds of data offer great opportunities for extending our understanding of how what transpires in a doctor–patient encounter affects desired cognitive, affective, behavioral, and clinical outcomes. This should also provide insight useful in developing more effective programs of training in communication skills. Finally, detailed study of the "geriatric triad" provides an opportunity to test hypotheses and extend a theory of coalitions, a venerable sociological tradition.

REFERENCES

Bales, R. F. 1950. *Interaction Process Analysis.* Cambridge, MA: Addison-Wesley.

Becker, M. H. 1985. "Patient Adherence to Prescribed Therapies." *Medical Care* 23: 539–555.

Beckman, H. B. and R. M. Frankel. 1984. "The Effect of Physician Behavior on the Collection of Data." *Annals of Internal Medicine* 101: 692–696.

Bloom, S. W. 1963. *The Doctor and His Patient.* New York: Russell Sage.

Botwinick, J. 1973. *Aging and Behavior.* New York: Springer Publishing Co.

Buijs, R., E. M. Sluijs, and P. F. M. Verhaak. 1984. "Byrne and Long: A Classification for Rating the Interview Style of Doctors." *Social Science and Medicine* 19: 683–690.

Byrne, P. S. and B. E. L. Long. 1976. *Doctors Talking to Patients.* London: HMSO.

Carter, W. B., T. S. Inui, W. A. Kukull, and V. H. Haigh. 1982. "Outcome-Based Doctor–Patient Interaction Analysis. II. Identifying Effective Provider and Patient Behavior." *Medical Care* 20: 550–566.

Coe, R. M. and C. G. Prendergast. 1985. "The Formation of Coalitions: Interaction Strategies in Triads." *Sociology of Health and Illness* 7: 236–247.

Coe, R. M., C. G. Prendergast, and G. Psathas. 1984. "Strategies for Obtaining Compliance with Medication Regimens." *Journal of the American Geriatrics Society* 32: 589–593.

Coe, R. M. and A. F. Wessen. 1965. "Social-Psychological Factors Affecting the Use of Community Health Resources." *American Journal of Public Health* 55: 1024–1031.

Cousins, N. 1984. "Foreword." In *Medicine as a Human Experience*, by D. E. Reiser and D. H. Rosen. Baltimore: University Park Press.

Davis, M. S. 1968. "Variations in Patients' Compliance with Doctors' Advice: An Empirical Analysis of Patterns of Communication." *American Journal of Public Health* 58: 274–288.

Davis, M. S. and R. L. Eichhorn. 1963. "Compliance with Medical Regimens: A Panel Study." *Journal of Health and Human Behavior,* 4: 240–249.

Engel, G. 1977. "The Need for a New Medical Model: A Challenge for Biomedicine." *Science* 196: 129–136.

Eraker, S. A., J. P. Kirscht, and M. H. Becker. 1984. "Understanding and Improving Patient Compliance." *Annals of Internal Medicine* 100: 258.

Fisher, S. 1984. "Doctor–Patient Communication: A Social and Micro-Political Performance." *Sociology of Health and Illness* 6: 1–29.

Fisher, S. and S. B. Groce. 1985. "Doctor–Patient Negotiations of Cultural Assumptions." *Sociology of Health and Illness* 6: 1–29.

Fisher, S. and A. D. Todd (eds.). 1983. *The Social Organization of Doctor–Patient Communication.* Washington, DC: Center for Applied Linguistics.

Freidson, E. 1970. *The Profession of Medicine.* New York: Dodd Mead.

Garfinkel, H. 1970. *Studies in Ethnomethodology.* Engelwood Cliffs, NJ: Prentice-Hall.

Goffman, E. 1959. *Presentation of Self in Everyday Life.* New York: Anchor Books.

Goffman, E. 1961. *Encounters.* Indianapolis: Bobbs-Merrill.

Goffman, E. 1967. *Interaction Ritual.* Chicago: Aldine.

Goffman, E. 1974. *Frame-Analysis.* Cambridge, MA: Harvard University Press.

Greene, M. G., R. Adelman, R. Charon, and S. Hoffman. 1986. "Ageism in the Medical Encounter: An Exploratory Study of the Doctor–Elderly Patient Relationship." *Language and Communication* 6: 113–124.

Haug, M. 1979. "Doctor–Patient Relationships and the Older Patient." *Journal of Gerontology* 35: 852–860.

Heath, C. 1984. "Participation in the Medical Consultation: The Coordination of Verbal and Non-Verbal Behavior Between the Doctor and the Patient." *Sociology of Health and Illness* 6: 311–338.

Heszen-Klemens, J. and E. Kapinska. 1984. "Doctor–Patient Interaction, Patients' Health Behavior and Effects of Treatment." *Social Science and Medicine* 19: 9–18.

Inui, T. S. and W. B. Carter. 1985. "Problems and Prospects for Health Services Research on Provider–Patient Communication." *Medical Care* 23: 521–538.

Inui, T. S., W. B. Carter, W. A. Kukull, and V. H. Haigh. 1982. "Outcome-Based Doctor–Patient Interaction Analysis. I. Comparison of Techniques." *Medical Care* 20: 535–549.

Katz, J. 1984. "Why Doctors Don't Disclose Uncertainty." *Hastings Center Report* 14: 35.

Kleinman, A., L. Eisenberg, and B. Good. 1978. "Culture, Illness and Care." *Annals of Internal Medicine* 88: 251–258.

Korsch, B. M. and V. F. Negrete. 1972. "Doctor–Patient Communication." *Scientific American* 227: 66–74.

Leventhal, H. 1985. "The Role of Theory in the Study of Adherence to Treatment and Doctor–Patient Interactions." *Medical Care* 33: 556–563.

Mishler, E. G. (1984). *The Discourse of Medicine: Dialectics of Medical Interviews.* Norwood, NJ: Ablex.

National Board of Medical Examiners. 1981. *ISIE-81: Interpersonal Skills Assessment Technique.* Philadelphia: Author (mimeo).

National Center for Health Statistics. 1983. *Contacts with Physicians in Ambulatory Settings.* Data Preview 16, National Health Care Expenditure Study. Washington, DC: U.S. Department of Health and Human Services.

Nuttbrock, L. and J. I. Kosberg. 1980. "Images of the Physician and Help-Seeking Behavior of the Elderly: A Multivariate Analysis." *Journal of Gerontology* 35: 241–248.

Parsons, T. 1951. *The Social System.* Glencoe, IL: Free Press

Psathas, G. 1979. *Everyday Language: Studies in Ethnomethodology.* New York: Halstead.

Putnam, S. M., W. B. Stiles, M. C. Jacob, and S. A. James. 1985. "Patient Exposition and Physician Explanation in Initial Medical Interviews and Outcomes of Clinic Visits." *Medical Care* 23: 74–83.

Reiser, D. E. and D. H. Rosen. 1984. *Medicine as Human Experience.* Baltimore: University Park Press.

Rosow, I. 1981. "Coalitions in Geriatric Medicine." In *Elderly Patients and Their Doctors,* edited by M. Haug. New York: Springer Publishing Co.

Roter, D. L. 1977. "Patient Participation in the Patient–Provider Interaction: The Effects of Patient Questioning on the Quality of Interaction, Satisfaction and Compliance." *Health Education Monograph* 5: 281–315.

Schenkein, J. 1978. *Studies in the Organization of Conversational Interaction.* New York: Academic Press.

Steel, K., R. M. Gertman, and C. Crescenzic. 1981. "Iatrogenic Illness on a General Medical Service at a University Hospital." *New England Journal of Medicine* 304: 638.

Stewart, M. A. 1984. "What Is a Successful Doctor–Patient Interview? A Study of Interactions and Outcomes." *Social Science and Medicine* 19: 167.

Stiles, W. B., S. M. Putnam, M. H. Wolf, and S. A. James. 1979. "Interaction Exchange Structure and Patient Satisfaction with Medical Interviews and Outcomes of Clinic Visits." *Medical Care* 23: 74–83.

Svarstad, B. L. 1976. "Physician–Patient Communication and Patient Conformity with Medical Advice." In *Growth of Bureaucratic Medicine,* edited by D. Mechanic. New York: Wiley.

Szasz, T. S. and M. H. Hollender. 1956. "A Contribution to the Philosophy of Medicine: The Basic Models of the Doctor–Patient Relationship." *Archives of Internal Medicine* 97: 585–592.

Tuckett, D. and A. Williams. 1984. "Approaches to the Measurement of Explanation and Information-Giving in Medical Consultations: A Review of Empirical Studies." *Social Science and Medicine* 18: 571–580.
Waitzkin, H. 1984. "The Micropolitics of Medicine: A Contextual Analysis." *International Journal of Health Services* 14: 339–378.
Waitzkin, H. 1985. "Information Giving in Medical Care." *Journal of Health and Social Behavior* 26: 81–101.
Waitzkin, H. and J. D. Stoeckle. 1972. "The Communication of Information About Illness: Clinical, Sociological and Methodological Considerations." *Advanced Psychosomatic Medicine* 8: 180–215.
Wasserman, R. C. and T. S. Inui. 1983. "Systematic Analysis of Clinician–Patient Interactions: A Critique of Recent Approaches with Suggestions for Future Research." *Medical Care* 21: 279–293.
Weisman, C. S. and M. A. Teitelbaum. 1985. "Physician Gender and the Physician–Patient Relationship: Recent Evidence and Relevant Questions." *Social Science and Medicine* 20: 1119–1127.
West, C. 1984. *Routine Complications: Troubles with Talk Between Doctors and Patients.* Bloomington, Indiana: Indiana University Press.
Woolley, F. R., R. L. Kane, C. C. Hughes, and D. D. Wright. 1978. "The Effects of Doctor–Patient Communication on Satisfaction and Outcome of Care." *Social Science and Medicine* 12: 123–128.

8

Older Patients in the Acute-Care Hospital Setting*

Victor W. Marshall

Most older people have little or no experience with acute-care hospitals. The same may be said of younger people. However, with increasing age, the likelihood that a person will spend some time in an acute-care hospital increases dramatically. This is, of course, especially true in the period immediately preceding death. Nonetheless, the research literature of social gerontology has little to say about the experience of the older patient in the hospital.

If attention turns from the individual to the health care setting, it may also be said that the acute-care hospital is increasingly coming to be populated by older patients; yet the research literature in the sociology of health and health care is largely devoid of references to the experience of the older patient in the acute-care hospital environment or to the impact on the acute-care hospital environment of the "population aging" of its clientele.

The dearth of research literature on this topic stands in strong contrast to the wealth of research reports on the aged in nursing homes and other

*This chapter draws on previous and current work. Early research on acute care wards was supported by grants from the Ontario Ministry of Health (DM196 and PR402) to A. S. Macpherson, S. French, and V. Marshall. C. Rosenthal was actively involved in the analyses and interpretation of some of these data. Current research on patients awaiting discharge is supported by Health and Welfare Canada's National Health Research and Development Program through a Health Scientist Award, and by a Laidlaw Foundation Award. I am particularly grateful to J. Aronson and J. Sulman, with whom I co-authored a paper drawn on extensively here.

long-term care institutions. We might be able to extrapolate from studies of older patients in long-term care institutions to arrive at some idea of what it is like to be an older acute-care patient, but it is unlikely that such extrapolation would prove to be highly reliable. At most, it might apply in selected areas of interest. However, it is particularly unlikely to prove satisfactory for research on the consequences of *inappropriate* patienthood of the older person in an acute-care hospital; that is, a length of stay in an acute-care hospital whose duration is medically unjustified but caused by inability to discharge the patient to a less intensive level of care. Further research is needed on the experiences of *all* older patients in the acute-care hospital; but this chapter is concerned with that particular subset of geriatric patients in the acute-care hospital who have been living there for a very long time.

This chapter begins by describing the situation of the geriatric patient inappropriately placed in an acute-care hospital, briefly addresses the possible causes of this predicament, then proceeds to concentrate on the likely consequences of inappropriate placement of the geriatric patient in an acute-care hospital.

My research on the consequences of protracted length of stay of geriatric patients in an acute-care hospital has just begun; consequently, where data are introduced they are either drawn from my previous research in related areas or from the published research literature. There is, in fact, little focused research specifically on the long-stay geriatric patient (although expressions of concern by clinicians are often found in medical journals). As a result, this chapter is somewhat speculative.

In addition to this caution, it should be emphasized that this chapter reflects the Canadian social and health care contexts, which are quite different from those in the United States (Kane & Kane, 1985, pp. 18–21).

The phenomenon of protracted, inappropriate stays by geriatric patients in acute-care hospitals is quite likely more severe in Canada than in the United States, especially since the introduction of diagnostically related groupings (DRGs) as a means to contain length of stay in the United States (such a system does not exist in Canada). However, such patients are not completely absent from U.S. hospitals. Moreover, the situation of the so-called bed-blocking patient in Canada and Britain (where the phenomenon is of great concern) may bring into sharper focus some of the general issues of the older patient in the acute-care hospital.

Comparative analysis is, in any case, the very stuff of the sociological approach. A few general comments about similarities and differences between health care in the United States and Canada are offered to provide a rough comparative perspective.

THE NATURE OF ACUTE-CARE HOSPITAL USE BY GERIATRIC PATIENTS

Available Canadian data suggest that, while age is associated with increasing utilization of acute-care hospitals, the majority of older Canadians nonetheless do not spend time in them. Chappell, Strain, and Blandford (1986, p. 106) cite data concerning short-term hospitalization showing that Canadians over age 64 consume 5,186 bed days per thousand, compared to Canadians aged 64 or less, who consume 1,161 bed days per thousand.[1] The older group accounts for 280 discharges per thousand, more than twice the 119 per thousand recorded by persons aged 64 or less. Average length of stay is 18.0 days for those age 65 or greater, but only 9.7 days for those 64 or younger. In other words, older Canadians spend more days in hospital, are less likely to be discharged, and therefore spend more days per visit than younger Canadians.

Here a comparison with the United States is insightful. The comparable U.S. figures show a bed utilization rate for younger people greater than that for Canada, but older people consume 1,061 fewer bed days per thousand population (i.e., about a day less in hospital, on average) than in Canada. The U.S. discharge rate for young and old is higher than that for Canada and is 1.38 times the Canadian rate for persons aged 65 and older. Finally, while average length of stay for younger people in the United States is three-quarters that in Canada (7.3 vs. 9.7 days), that for persons aged 65 or older was just 59.4% of the Canadian average length of stay. These data are for Canada in 1978–1979 and for the United States in 1980 (before the effects of DRGs); but they no doubt reflect the comparative situation today with reasonable accuracy.

Equally important to the crude relationship between age and likelihood of hospitalization is the differentiation among the older population. Overall Canadian data for 1977 report that 9% of Canadians aged 65 and over accounted for fully 43% of all acute-care hospital days. U.S. data for 1978 are similar: 11% of those aged 65 and over accounted for 43% of all short-stay hospital days (cited in Roos, Shapiro, & Roos, 1984, p. 31). With data from the Manitoba Longitudinal Study on Aging (MLSA), Roos, Shapiro, and Roos (1984) established that, over a five-year period beginning

---

[1]Using a broader definition of bed days in acute-care and allied specialty hospitals (which includes chronic-care hospitals as well as maternity hospitals), a recent report prepared for the Canadian Medical Association (Woods Gordon, 1984, Append. 5) shows utilization rates as follows:

65–74	male	5676.24
	female	4896.13
75+	male	14576.22
	female	15051.32
all ages	male	1552.01
	female	2004.48
all ages	both sexes	1780.13

in 1972, 42% of elderly Manitobans spent no days at all in hospital and a mere 2% of the elderly consumed 20% of all acute-care days consumed by the elderly (days are counted only if the stay lasted no longer than 30 days, but the general pattern of differentiation is similar when acute-care and chronic-care hospital stays are combined).

Shapiro, Roos, and Kavanaugh (1980) have also argued that average length of stay is an unduly crude measure. Focusing on lengths of stay less than and greater than 90 days, they found that over the time period 1972–1976, the former dropped while the latter increased from 117 days to 218 days for patients aged 75 and older. This latter group is the primary focus in this paper: a small group of patients, usually very old, whose length of stay in hospital becomes protracted. These are not typical old people, who do not spend much time in hospital at all; nor are they typical older hospital patients, whose average length of stay is, as noted above, only 18 days. They are probably less frequently found in the United States than in the United Kingdom and in Canada—but they are nonetheless found.

EMERGENCE OF THE BED-BLOCKING PROBLEM

It is widely recognized that there is a serious problem of delay in discharge and placement of geriatric patients from acute-care hospitals to more appropriate and less costly long-term facilities. Terms such as "delayed placement," "placement problems" (Sloan, Redding, & Wittlin, 1981), "geriatric bed-blocking" (Grant, 1985; Hall & Blytheway, 1982; McAlpine, 1979; Rubin & Davies, 1975; Seymour & Pringle, 1982), and "administratively necessary days" (Markson, Steel & Kane, 1983) have been employed to describe this phenomenon.

Some investigators have deplored the use of the term "bed-blocking" as pejorative (Fisher & Zorzitto, 1983; Robertson, 1985); yet the pejorative nature of the term is a major aspect of sociological interest because, as we shall later see, of its implications for the patient trajectory.

Regardless of terminology, protracted hospital stays for geriatric patients are not just a Canadian problem. British studies have documented the growth of the problem (Arie, 1981; Hall & Blytheway, 1982; McAlpine, 1979; McCardle, Wylie, & Alexander, 1975; Murphy, 1977; Rubin & Davies, 1975; Seymour & Pringle, 1982). In the United States, Markson, Steel, and Kane (1983) studied 49 acute-care hospitals and found considerable variation in length of stay of elderly patients on "administratively necessary days." Patients who were most difficult to place were most often Medicaid patients with no extra financial resources or insurance, followed by those with incontinence and inability to perform activities of daily living, that is, those requiring more intensive nursing care.

That the problem exists in Canada was argued by Paget (1983), who suggested that between 10% and 20% of acute-care hospital beds are occupied by patients waiting for long-term placement. Gross and Schwenger (1981) estimated the figure for Ontario at 12.7%, while a recent Toronto study put the Toronto figure at 13.9% (Metropolitan Toronto District Health Council, 1984).

FACTORS AFFECTING THE RECALCITRANCE OF DELAYED DISCHARGE

The cause of protracted length of stay, with its consequent blockage of hospital beds, is often attributed to population aging: The hospital system has just not grown fast enough to keep up with the greater demand caused by increased numbers of older people. Another cause is held to be the unwillingness of families to provide adequate care and take back older persons upon discharge. These alleged causes are not, in fact, real. There appears not to be a direct relationship between the number of long-term care beds available and the ability to discharge acute-care hospital patients to them. For example, Toronto, which has a severe problem of protracted stays, also has one of the highest per capita long-term bed stocks of any jurisdiction in the world. A Toronto newspaper story, headlined, "Bed-Blockers Blamed for Emergency Ward Crunch" (Grant, 1985), quoted a source who suggested that "The problem . . . is how to take care of these long-term care patients who seem to be 'imposing' on the system. Nobody wants them. The hospitals don't. The families don't and certainly the government doesn't."

While availability of chronic-care beds seems to be unrelated to length of stay, the availability of acute-care beds does have an impact. In Manitoba, Shapiro and Roos (1986) found that hospital bed availability accounted both for 40% of the variance in physician hospitalization styles (that is, whether they were likely to hospitalize few or many of their patients) and for the proportion of repeated high use by physicians of hospital beds for their patients. The greater the availability of beds in a region, the more likely were doctors in that region to keep patients in them for longer periods of time.

As to the allegation that families do not want to take care of their elderly members, there is little evidence to suggest that families in Toronto specifically or in Canada generally are abandoning their elderly members (see Rosenthal, 1987, for a review). Canadian family members are probably little different from American family members.

In terms of interests, however, it may be that governments and hospitals, while not necessarily wanting long-stay patients, are willing to tolerate them in large numbers, for reasons outlined below; and it may also be the case that family members, and even the patients themselves, are by and large tolerant of protracted lengths of stay in many instances (see Aronson, Marshall, & Sulman, 1987).

The causes of the problem may be suggested by the characteristics of those patients for whom the problem is most serious. Those geriatric patients who have the greatest difficulty getting out of acute-care hospitals are disproportionately female, over age 75, possessed of a high incidence of dementia, awaiting transfer to heavy-care facilities as opposed to alternative destinations, and suffering from a variety of debilitating conditions and functional impairments (Fisher & Zorzitto, 1983; Markson, Steel, & Kane, 1983; McCardle, Wylie, & Alexander, 1975; Robertson, 1985; Rubin & Davies, 1975). They are, in short, patients who are likely to require more than a minimal level of care in the nursing home context and even in the chronic-care hospital or extended care setting. However, in the acute-care hospital setting, by contrast with acutely ill patients, they do require minimal amounts of care.

In the Canadian reimbursement system, nursing homes, chronic-care hospitals, and acute-care hospitals are typically reimbursed on set schedules that do not take account of severity or level of care. The hospital will be reimbursed for an acute-care bed day even if that bed is filled by a nonacute-care patient. The nursing home will be reimbursed for a patient whether that patient requires a minimum 1.5 hours per day of nursing care or a much more intensive regimen of care. In the acute-care hospital, the long-stay patient awaiting discharge is a low-cost patient consuming few health care resources. In the nursing home, as well as in the chronic-care hospital or extended-care setting, the same patient is likely to be a high-cost patient requiring much more than the level of care that would earn that governmentally set per diem reimbursement. The incontinent or severely demented patient is therefore not wanted in the nursing home or chronic hospital.

Patients and their families may not be highly motivated to press for discharge to a nursing home. Nursing homes in Canada, as in the United States, are not generally highly regarded; hospitals are preferred alternatives, especially in a society in which hospital care is financed by "free" (i.e., taxpayer provided) medical and hospital insurance.

Continuing to regard this problem in the Canadian context, we see that government has been politically frustrated in attempts to put a cap on acute-care hospitalizations, which are the most expensive drain on the medical care budget. Beds filled by nonacute-care patients constitute a limited form of cap on the number of acute-care beds, since such patients create fewer demands for surgery and other expensive applications of medical technology. It is therefore not in the interests of government to pressure hospitals into discharging such patients; nor is it in the interests of nursing homes to accept them.

However, this situation is not without its strains and contradictions. Some physicians, perhaps especially surgeons, may be expected to be highly frustrated by their inability to admit patients whose needs for care constitute the demand for their services. This frustration need not be seen as purely monetary. A system based on cure rather than care, in which physicians are socialized to an activist, high-technology approach to medical care, can be expected to produce physicians who will not consider the long-stay patient their most rewarding type of patient (Marshall, 1981). Besides some physicians, other hospital personnel, such as social workers and discharge planners, are professionally motivated to assist in discharge. That is their job, and one can assume that most of them wish to do it well.

At this point in time, the interests against solving the protracted-stay situation seem to outweigh those which would call for a solution. In the Canadian health care context, the long-stay situation appears to have become worse in recent years.

The current state of research is such that the magnitude of the long-stay problem is now well recognized and documented. The causes of the problem are much argued but still open to considerable debate, if for no other reason than that the several interest groups implicated in the problem each have their own interests in attributing responsibility for it to other groups. In this situation, the patients and their families are the least powerful interest groups. Not surprisingly, as noted earlier, they are frequently blamed for the long-stay problem. They are labeled bed-blockers, in a classic example of blaming the victim.

When research interest shifts from the causes to the consequences of long-stay acute-care hospitalization of the geriatric patient, it is necessary to be much more speculative because the research base is very small.

CONSEQUENCES OF PROTRACTED LENGTH OF STAY

We are currently studying the experiences of geriatric acute-care patients and their families over time, using a longitudinal design. The sociological concept of "career" (Hughes, 1971), which has been extended to the hospital setting under the rubric of "status passage" (see Glaser & Strauss, 1968, 1971; Strauss, Fagerhaugh, Suczek, & Wiener, 1985; Strauss & Glaser, 1975), is ideal for this purpose. Hughes (1971) distinguished between "objective career" as a series of social statuses and clearly defined offices, and "subjective career" as "the moving perspective in which the person sees his life as a whole and interprets the meaning of his various attributes, actions, and the things which happen to him."

Objectively, the patient career within the acute-care hospital is defined by formal diagnoses and prognoses, assignments to wards and treatment regimens, and the objective passage of time (see Strauss et al., 1985). A track of this career is found in patient charts, but only partly so. Other structural properties of the patient's career are not recorded in the individual patient's chart but are nonetheless discernible from aggregate data. The number of similarly situated patients is such a structural feature and may determine whether or not the career is experienced in the company of others (see Glaser & Strauss, 1971; Marshall, 1980). For our research interests, whether a patient is thought by caregiving staff as appropriately situated on a given ward constitutes an objective feature of his or her career; and this, as will be described below, can be affected by how many such patients there are in a ward.

Subjective career refers to the patient's interpretation of the objective career. We are interested in the patient's time perspective. In tuberculosis wards, Roth (1963a,b) has shown that information about the timing of hospital careers is hard for the patient to get but that patients establish their own benchmarks concerning prognosis. Do similar benchmarks occur for the patient awaiting discharge? Does the patient form an anticipation of the time when discharge will occur? How is this anticipation grounded?

Do patients awaiting discharge have a sense that they are out of place, not fitting in with the goals for care in an acute-care hospital ward? Do they sense that staff members are less interested than before in their well-being? Is there a sense of being in transition between one set of caregivers in the hospital and another set in an as yet unselected nursing home? How do patients evaluate the lack of movement in their careers? Does their evaluation lead to depression, fatalism, changes in locus of control, and so forth? How does lack of movement in the career affect adherence to recommended medical regimens?

Objective and subjective aspects of the career of the long-stay geriatric patient intertwine. Strauss and associates (1985, p. 8) employ the concept of "trajectory" to capture this. This term refers "not only to the physiological unfolding of a patient's disease but to the total *organization of work* done over that course, plus the *impact* on those involved with that work and its organization."

Looking for insight about this particular type of patient trajectory, in which there is little unfolding of the course of the disease, we look for analogous situations. It may be, for example, that patients awaiting discharge can be likened to airline passengers who are in the departure lounge waiting for an international flight. All preliminaries of ticketing, customs, and security clearances have been taken care of, but the plane is delayed. In such cases, airline and airport personnel have little interest in the waiting passengers, because their jobs have been done. If the aircraft continues to be delayed, however, the passengers start posing problems for airline and airport personnel, who must resume a concern for their comfort or who may wish that these waiting passengers were not there, since the departure lounge is needed for passengers awaiting subsequent flights.

What is the psychological state of passengers waiting for a delayed airline departure? Is it similar to that of long-stay geriatric patients, who are also "on hold" without any fixed departure date and aware that their major point of interest to hospital staff lies in the latter's desire to be rid of them? (This shows how the analogy is somewhat overdrawn, since airline personnel may wish the passengers to continue flying that airline.)

What little evidence we have suggests that long-stay geriatric patients are viewed with some disdain by at least some hospital personnel, with potential spinoff effects. The simple fact of inappropriately being in the hospital can engender resentment even, Mizrahai (1985, p. 229) pointed out, when the situational appropriateness is no fault of the patient's. Mizrahai described participant-observation data about interns and residents in a southern U.S. major medical center. Among them, a widely shared perspective referred to as GROP—get rid of patients—developed. GROP holds that the ideal patient is one who can be got rid of, either by cure or redirection to other hospital resources. The perspective is the same as that described novelistically by Shem (1978) in his book *House of God,* which is widely read by house staff. The long-stay geriatric patient is precisely a nonideal patient in these terms.

As distinct from perceived or genuine inappropriateness, older patients come to be viewed derisively when they are characterized by neurological problems and declining mental status as well as protracted hospital stays. Liederman and Grisso (1985) investigated the characteristics of patients labeled "gomers" (get out of *my* emergency *r*oom) by internal medicine residents in a U.S. university hospital and found that these three characteristics discriminated "gomers" from controls. These patients had an average length of stay of 69.8 days, compared to 9.4 days for controls. Over this period, they were the subjects of a great many more consultations than control patients (4.5 vs. 1.8), but the reverse was true if consultations are calculated in relation to length of stay. "Gomers" had .064 consultations per day, compared to .191 consultations per day for controls; put another way, a "gomer" was getting a consultation about every fifteen days, while a patient in the control group was getting one every five days. This may well have created an impression of lack of activity for the "gomers." Liederman and Grisso (1985, p. 226–227) noted that, "Because of delays in obtaining nursing home beds, gomer patients frequently were hospitalized long after the resolution of their acute problems. Housestaff progress notes became less frequent and less descriptive, eventually consisting of such perfunctory comments as, 'Stable. Awaiting nursing home placement.' "

The long-stay patients are an overlapping set with "gomers." Not all long-stay geriatric patients are "gomers," and not all "gomers" are characterized by protracted length of stay. For example, the average length of stay of the "gomer" patients subsequently placed in nursing homes in the Liederman and Grisso study was 132 days, compared to 27 days for the other "gomer" patients.

Liederman and Grisso also pointed to another distinction between "gomers" and non-"gomer" patients that merits further investigation. They note that:

> The hospitalizations of the control patients appear as organized sequences of events, which provided definitive diagnoses, and a predictable, if not always happy, outcome. In contrast, the admitting problems of the gomers were much harder to define, the course of treatment much less predictable, and the outcome much less satisfactory. (Liederman & Grisso, 1985, p. 226)

Liederman and Grisso may have confused the characterization of the "gomer" by failing to calculate consultations on a per-bed-day basis, as was done above. This may have led them to overestimate the extent to which the "gomer" label is attributed to patients because they are diagnostically puzzling or troublesome. That feature was given some importance in their analysis but does not pertain to long-stay geriatric patients awaiting discharge.

The long-stay geriatric patient awaiting discharge is, from the acute-care hospital's perspective, in a status at the end of an organized sequence of events. Diagnosis is likely no longer an issue. There is no longer an active course of treatment. The outcome has perhaps not been fully satisfactory, since discharge is most often planned to a nursing home setting. These characteristics only partly, then, match those described for "gomers."

Another source of insight may be found in Glaser and Strauss' analysis of terminally ill patients for whom there is "nothing more to do" (1965, Ch. 12). This is a stage in the dying status passage at which a decision is made that nothing more can be done to help the patient recover. Attention shifts to "comfort care" (Glaser & Strauss, 1965, p. 205).[2] The basis of similarity lies in the judgment that there is nothing more to be done except to ensure comfort. The difference is that in terminal illness this judgment is rooted in the belief that active intervention will not be efficacious, while in the case of patients awaiting discharge, the judgment is based on everything having been done to meet the goals of acute-care hospitalization.

---

[2]Comfort care is not the same as "comfort work," which has a place in all phases of most illness trajectories and is not restricted to that phase when recovery is ruled out (see Strauss et al., 1985, Ch. 5).

In either case, however, it is likely that active treatment will decrease, that nurses will take over more of the care while doctors decrease their involvement, and that there will also be a decrease in the level of nursing care (Glaser & Strauss, 1965, p. 205). In research on four acute-care hospital wards in a Canadian hospital (Rosenthal, Marshall, Macpherson, & French, 1980), nurses were found vulnerable to becoming emotionally involved with long-stay patients, but the dominant reaction to them was one of resentment or anger. Several categories of "problem patients" were identified through field research focusing on caring staff. While the minority of patients deemed to be problem patients were less likely to have management plans formulated than were nonproblematic cases,

> The category of problem patients for which a plan was least often arrived at was the career group. This was especially true for the patients for whom there was no longer any reason for continued hospitalization or whose hospitalization is seen as a result of the doctor's weakness or inability to refuse the patient's or family's wishes. (Rosenthal, Marshall, Macpherson, & French, 1980, p. 77)

In the "nothing is to be done" stage, Glaser and Strauss (1965, p. 206) note that a division of labor often arises in which some nurses with special interest or talent in providing comfort care are assigned to such patients, or simply end up giving special attention to them, while others may withdraw from such caregiving. In the Canadian research referred to above, we found that family members may also, in such circumstances, be allowed to join the health care team in the provision of comfort care. However, the incorporation of new members into the health care team caused a number of problems for the nursing staff's ability to retain control over their own work situation (Rosenthal, Marshall, Macpherson, & French, 1980, pp. 101–104).

A focused analysis of one ward from this Canadian study sheds additional light on the potential impact of protracted length of stay on the caregiving staff. One of the four wards in this study stood out from all the others, on a number of measures, as having lower staff morale. This was also the ward where the placement problem for long-stay patients was most serious. Many of the staff came to think of their ward as a geriatric ward and became preoccupied with placement issues. Patients discussed at team conference rounds came to typify staff notions of ward patients, and those discussed were disproportionately older, long-stay patients. Over a six-month period, field notes of conference rounds showed that 59.5% of patients discussed were age 70 or older, while the actual percentage of patients in that age category was less that 20% and the mean age was less than 55—not significantly different from that on other acute-care wards. Half the patients discussed were over 80 years of age. In one instance, a social worker accustomed to arranging placement automatically asked, during discussion of a patient, "Will the family take him back?" Amidst laughter, the head nurse said, "But . . . he's only 18!" The presence of a small number of patients who had been on the ward for a very long time had an inordinate effect in focusing staff attention on discharge problems and away from other aspects of patient management. Our analysis suggests that this "discharge mentality" led to declines in staff morale (Rosenthal & Marshall, 1978; Rosenthal, Marshall, Macpherson, & French, 1980, p. 37).

In summary, available research literature provides little direct data concerning the experience of protracted length of stay of geriatric patients or the ways in which this experience impacts on and interweaves with the experiences of caregiving staff. Drawing on literature that is focused on acute-care hospitals but that recognizes the increasing prevalence of older, chronic patients on acute-care wards, I have suggested some possible dimensions of the subjective and objective careers of patients in this particular, "departure-lounge" phase of the acute-care hospital patient trajectory. The moral career of the geriatric patient awaiting discharge is probably highly conditioned by the continuing emphasis in acute-care hospitals on high-technology intervention and cure. Patients for whom the hospital has fulfilled its mandate, in bringing them to the point where they are ready for discharge, are now "out of place." They are considered inappropriate by the health care staff. They may see themselves as inappropriately housed (I am unaware of any research evidence on this point); and they may suffer benign neglect or active avoidance by health care staff. At the least, they are likely to be underserviced with continuing active rehabilitation because the acute-care hospital has not institutionally adapted to the continuing presence of large numbers of patients awaiting discharge.

CONCLUSIONS

To understand the social situation of the geriatric long-stay acute-care hospital patient requires a sifting and comparison of the objective and subjective career properties of old patients from those of young patients, of acutely from chronically ill patients, of patients undergoing active treatment from those whose active treatment is essentially at an end. This chapter has reviewed some of the hospital literature in search of conceptual stimulation and has identified a number of issues in the care of acutely and chronically ill patients that might also be of interest for the particular case of the long-stay patient awaiting discharge.

Other equally important issues will no doubt become evident in the course of the planned research, among them a concern with the legitimation of protracted stay. How do staff explain to each other and to the patients their inability to secure discharges? How do patients (who, it will be recalled, are usually happy to remain in the hospital rather than take the "final step" to the nursing home) and their families account for prolonged stays? How is increasing length of stay related to the relationship among the patient, family, and broader social network of the patient? How does the changing patient pool in the acute-care hospital affect the morale of physicians, nurses, and others who have, perhaps, chosen a working context on the basis of their own interests in acute-oriented, curative medicine and health care? How do the perception and treatment of the long-stay geriatric patient in an acute-care hospital vary by professional group, by individual-level characteristics of the various health care professionals (such as their own age and gender), or by organizational properties on the wards?

This search for information about the experiences of older patients awaiting discharge has disclosed how little general information we have about the experiences of older patients in hospital, whether they are awaiting discharge or under active or rehabilitative treatment. While large numbers of older people are not hospitalized in acute-care hospitals, large proportions of patients in these hospitals are elderly; yet the research emphases of social gerontologists appear to be on long-term care facilities or on the community-dwelling elderly.

The little we know about the impact of older patients on the health care staff in acute-care hospitals comes largely from the work of Anselm Strauss and associates. In a recent book, Strauss et al. (1985, p. ix) argue that "the work of physicians, nurses, and associated technicians has been radically and irrevocably altered by today's prevalence of chronic illness—the illnesses that bring patients into contemporary hospitals—and by the technologies developed to manage them." Their research gives us some purchase on the problem, but their focus on the care of chronic patients is only partially applicable to older patients. Moreover, they do not write at all about the geriatric patient whose presence on the acute-care ward is no longer required.

Acute-care hospitals are important way stations for many people moving from the community to long-term care. They are themselves undergoing considerable changes, due in part to changing demands associated with population aging. We need to know more about the place of the acute-care hospital in the continuum of care and about the placement, or misplacement, of older patients in them.

REFERENCES

Arie, Tom. 1981. "The Demented Patient: Making Services Work." Pp. 27–31 in *Appropriate Care for the Elderly: Some Problems*, edited by J. M. G. Wilson. Edinburgh: Royal College of Physicians.

Aronson, Jane, Victor W. Marshall, and Joanne Sulman. 1987. "Patients Awaiting Discharge from Hospital." In *Aging in Canada: Social Perspectives,* second edition, edited by V. W. Marshall. Don Mills, Ontario: Fitzhenry and Whiteside.

Chappell, Neena L., Laurel A. Strain, and B. Audrey Blandford. 1986. *Aging and Health Care: A Social Perspective.* Toronto: Holt, Rinehart & Winston of Canada.

Fisher, Rory H. and Mariza L. Zorzitto. 1983. "Placement Problem: Diagnosis, Disease or Term of Denigration?" *Canadian Medical Association Journal* 129: 331–334.

Glaser, Barney G. and Anselm L. Strauss. 1965. *Awareness of Dying.* Chicago: Aldine.

Glaser, Barney G. and Anselm L. Strauss. 1968. *Time for Dying.* Chicago: Aldine.

Glaser, Barney G. and Anselm L. Strauss. 1971. *Status Passage.* Chicago: Aldine Atherton.

Grant, Donald. 1985. "Bed-Blockers Blamed for Emergency Ward Crunch." Toronto: The Globe and Mail (February 18).

Gross, M. John and Cope W. Schwenger. 1981. *Health Care Costs for the Elderly in Ontario: 1976–2026.* Occasional Paper 11. Toronto: Ontario Economic Council.

Hall, David and William Blytheway. 1982. "The Blocked Bed: Definition of a Problem." *Social Sciences and Medicine* 16: 1985–1991.

Hughes, Everett C. 1971. "Cycles, Turning Points and Careers." Pp. 1214–1231 in *The Sociological Eye,* edited by E. C. Hughes. Chicago: Aldine Atherton.

Kane, Robert L. and Rosalie A. Kane. 1985. *A Will and a Way: What the United States Can Learn from Canada about Caring for the Elderly.* New York: Columbia University Press.

Liederman, Deborah B. and Jean-Anne Grisso. 1985. "The Gomer Phenomenon." *Journal of Health and Social Behavior* 26: 222–232.

Markson, Elizabeth W., Knight Steel, and Ellen Kane. 1983. "Administratively Necessary Days: More than an Administrative Problem." *The Gerontologist* 23: 486–492.

Marshall, Victor W. 1980. "No Exit: An Interpretive Perspective on Aging." Pp. 51–60 in *Aging in Canada: Social Perspectives,* edited by V. W. Marshall. Don Mills, Ontario: Fitzhenry and Whiteside.

Marshall, Victor W. 1981. "Physician Characteristics and Relationships with Older Patients." Pp. 94–118 in *Elderly Patients and Their Doctors,* edited by M. Haug. New York: Springer.

McAlpine, C. Joan. 1979. "Unblocking Beds: A Geriatric Unit's Experience with Transferred Patients." *British Medical Journal* 2: 646–648.

McCardle, Christine, J. C. Wylie, and W. D. Alexander. 1975. "Geriatric Patients in an Acute Medical Ward." *British Medical Journal* 4:568–569.

Metropolitan Toronto District Health Council. 1984. "Long Term Care Bed Needs in Metropolitan Toronto." Toronto: Author.

Mizrahai, Terry. 1985. "Getting Rid of Patients: Contradictions in the Socialization of Internists to the Doctor–Patient Relationship." *Sociology of Health and Illness* 7: 214–235.

Murphy, F. W. 1977. "Blocked Beds." *British Medical Journal* 1: 1395–1396.

Paget, A. Gwyneth. 1983. "Acute Care Hospitals: Their Role in Long-Term Care." *Dimensions of Health Service* 60: 28–29.

Robertson, Duncan. 1985. *Long Term Care Patients in Acute Care Beds: Implications for Action.* Report to the Capital Regional Hospital District Hospital and Health Planning Planning Commission. Victoria, British Columbia.

Roos, Noralou P., Evelyn Shapiro, and Leslie L. Roos. 1984. "Aging and the Demand for Health Services: Which Aged and Whose Demand?" *The Gerontologist* 24: 31–36.

Rosenthal, Carolyn J. 1987. "Aging and Intergenerational Relations in Canada." In V. W. Marshall (Ed.), *Aging in Canada: Social Perspectives* (2nd ed.). Toronto: Fitzhenry and Whiteside.

Rosenthal, Carolyn J. and Victor W. Marshall. 1978. *Perceived Age of Patient: Consequences for Organizational Goals in an Acute Care Hospital.* Paper presented at the annual meeting of the Canadian Sociology and Anthropology Association, London, Ontario.

Rosenthal, Carolyn J., Victor W. Marshall, A. S. Macpherson, and Susan E. French. 1980. *Nurses, Patients and Families: Care and Control in the Hospital.* New York: Springer.

Roth, Julius. 1963a. "Information and the Control of Treatment in Tuberculosis Hospitals." Pp. 298–318 in *The Hospital in Modern Society,* edited by E. Freidson. New York: Free Press.

Roth, Julius. 1963b. *Timetables.* Indianapolis: Bobbs-Merrill.

Rubin, S. G. and G. H. Davies. 1975. "Bed-Blocking by Elderly Patients in General Hospital Wards." *Age and Ageing* 4:142–147.

Seymour, David G. and Robert Pringle. 1982. "Elderly Patients in a General Surgical Unit: Do They Block Beds?" *British Medical Journal* 284: 1921–1923.

Shapiro, Evelyn and Noralou P. Roos. 1986. "High Users of Hospital Days." *Canadian Journal on Aging* 5:165–174.

Shapiro, Evelyn, Noralou P. Roos, and Steve Kavanaugh. 1980. "Long-Term Patients in Acute Care Beds: Is There a Cure?" *The Gerontologist* 20: 342–349.

Shem, Samuel. 1978. *The House of God.* New York: Dell.

Sloan, Philip D., Ralph Redding, and Lori Wittlin. 1981. "Long-Term Placement Problems in an Acute Care Hospital." *Journal of Chronic Disease* 34: 285–290.

Strauss, Anselm, Shizuko Fagerhaugh, Barbara Suczek, and Carolyn Wiener. 1985. *Social Organization of Medical Work.* Chicago: The University of Chicago Press.

Strauss, Anselm, and Barney Glaser. 1975. *Chronic Illness and the Quality of Life.* St. Louis: C. V. Mosby.

Woods Gordon Management Consultants. 1984. *Investigation of the Impact of Demographic Change on the Health Care System in Canada.* Report for the Task Force on the Allocation of Health Care Resources, Canadian Medical Association. Toronto: Author.

PART 3
Issues in Long-Term Care

Introduction

The titles of the two chapters in this part consist of rather catchy phrases. "A Study in Trench Warfare" is the subtitle of the Branch, Sager, and Meyers chapter; "Money, Money, Who's Got the Money?" is the title of the Wiener, Hanley, Spense, and Coupard chapter. These phrases indeed capture the battle, as well as the frustration, over the future of long-term care services and their financing. Both sets of authors provide ample background to the field of combat. It is to be hoped that there will soon be some resolution to the present conflict, so that we can begin to concern ourselves with the needs of, and resources for, the future aging (which Bengtson and Dannefer speculate about in Part 4).

Branch and associates begin with desirable outcomes of long-term care services. They follow with a discussion of current issues and trends and the forces behind them, such as the demography of aging, the economy, and the congressional paralysis resulting from fear about expanding public funding for long-term care. Finally, recent and contemplated innovations are discussed, including financing, organizing services using case management, and integrating long-term care through, for example, continuing-care retirement communities (CCRCs). They end with an argument for experimentation at the state level, the New Deal's "laboratories of democracy," as a prelude to implementation of new national initiatives, should the battle subside. Their comprehensive chapter on a complex societal issue nicely integrates sociological insights and policy perspectives.

The chapter by Wiener and associates, although more narrowly focused on financing options, also reflects the sociologist at work on the future directions for long-term care. Maddox's observations about the unwillingness of sociologists to interpret the policy implications of their findings are not relevant to either of the chapters in this part. Yet these authors caution that dissemination of knowledge is insufficient for social change because, in part, of benefits from the status quo to some special interest groups. Marshall, in his chapter in the previous part, also noted this source of resistance to change when discussing the extended lingering of the elderly in hospitals.

Both chapters in this part show how collaboration with members of other disciplines can be synthesized into excellent contributions. Fortunately, the paper by Wiener and associates is not narrowly focused on financing options, nor is it replete with the algebraic formulas beloved by economists. Rather it is a readable and sensible discussion of the pros and cons of financing options.

Wiener and associates examine both private- and public-sector options. Private-sector initiatives for reform encompass private long-term care insurance, CCRGs, home equity conversions, and individual retirement accounts for long-term care. Public-sector approaches to long-term care reforms, in turn, encompass block grants, modification of Medicare and Medicaid, public long-term care insurance, and tax credits for care of the disabled elderly. The authors conclude that private financing mechanisms cannot solve financing problems but can make a larger contribution, that insurance and CCRCs need to be less expensive if they are to impact on public expenditures, that making public programs more stringent could create incentives for private approaches but only at the expense of the poorer and more disabled elderly, and that public expenditures must increase to meet the needs of the increasing numbers of frail elderly.

In responding to the two papers, James Callahan applauded the speakers for presenting the policy alternatives in a manner that cost-conscious legislators can readily understand. He cautioned, however, that we can neither foresee the outcome of the battle, nor a resolution acceptable to us, because we cannot forecast the direction of the push toward privatization and the ongoing realignment of political forces. Singled out by him as an omission in both papers was the inattention to the special issues of women, particularly since strong sentiments currently exist to address concerns and problems of women, such as including the contributions of women to their families as part of the GNP.

Mildred Shapiro portrayed how the elderly consume Medicaid funds through reimbursements to nursing homes for their care. Shortly after entering a nursing home in New York State, where reimbursements to nursing homes are indeed generous, finances are depleted ("spent down") and the reimbursement for the elderly person's care is paid by Medicaid. Because half of these monies are contributed by the state, there must be some reasonable ceiling on expenditures. New York State's Medicaid budget currently is $9 billion or so. Because one-third of these dollars go for long-term care and are mounting, the health care of the chronically poor can become underfunded. Unless there is a partnership between the public and the private sectors, the Medicaid bill can become even more onerous for states. Thus New York State is actively examining the pros and cons of long-term care insurance. Still, the heterogeneity among the elderly, particularly social-class differences, necessitates a variety of approaches to financing long-term care. There is no simple panacea that will reduce the burdens of costs to the public and to individuals while at the same time maximizing freedom of choice for consumers. Yet solutions must be sought. Societal resources are not unlimited, and there are obvious conflicting demands by different age and need groups. This issue, of the allocation of societal resources, we will leave for a future conference that should include, at the very least, presentations by economists and political scientists.

9

Long-Term Care in the United States: A Study in Trench Warfare

Laurence G. Branch, Alan Sager, and Allan R. Meyers

The Great War (World War I), as it was called, killed millions because politicians insisted on victory and their technical experts promised it through attrition. It ended only when new devices such as the tank and new resources from the United States were introduced. Long-term care policy, like the Great War in its early years, is now mired in trench warfare.

Although the need for adequate and decent long-term care is widely acknowledged, neither the public nor the political and administrative leadership has faith that acceptable solutions will be found soon. To some extent, this consensus manifests today's broad pessimism concerning effective public action in the United States. But, more important, it is rooted in the difficult problems inherent in long-term care in this nation. Our purpose is to illustrate the current issues and trends in long-term care, explore some reasons for them, and examine a group of recent innovations.

Some of these innovations may help break our current stalemate and move us toward a long-term care system we can age with and respect. Desirable long-term care services would have several aims: (1) to optimize personal independence and autonomy of elders; (2) to serve people where they wish to be cared for, in a decent and dignified manner, with elder/ family participation in care planning; (3) to employ well-trained, well-paid, and satisfied workers; (4) to offer competent professional care planning able to identify and assemble needed/wanted packages of paid services without displacing appropriate levels of family aid; and (5) to provide adequate public funding for these services.

If all these are not possible or if, like clear victory during the Great War, we can achieve them only at an unacceptable price, what is the shape of an *acceptable* publicly funded long-term care system? What is the floor below which we will allow no one in need of long-term care to fall? Is it less than what is desirable, across-the-board, or is it something different? Given the knotty problems inherent in long-term care—and the impossibility of disentangling long-term care from income maintenance issues—we will not lack for work as we seek to answer these questions.

CURRENT ISSUES AND TRENDS

Four sets of longstanding issues and unfolding trends manifest the current stalemates in long-term care policy and programs. These concern (1) eligibility for publicly funded care, (2) organization and delivery of services, (3) their financing, and (4) their technical quality and effectiveness (influence on recipient well-being).

Eligibility

It is useful to distinguish among the concepts of need, want, demand, eligibility, and receipt of publicly financed long-term care services. Need is usually the largest category; it registers the number who, by some objective standard (perhaps set, in part, by professional experts), might benefit from the services in question.

Want is an expression of desire for service from a potential recipient or member of his/her family. Some of those in need might not want a service, and some who do not really need might want.

Demand is want with a willingness to pay stapled to its lapel. It is seldom appropriate to use this concept in the realm of publicly funded services because individuals pay little or nothing out-of-pocket. They are buffered from the financial consequences of their care-seeking decisions. And to a great extent we probably want them to be buffered. Publicly funded long-term care services therefore cannot be rationed by willingness to pay. Consequently, administrative mechanisms must be designed to decide which of those potential recipients who need and want care shall be served, and to what extent.

Eligibility is determined by the legislation and regulations that structure programs. Typically, only a subset of those who need and want a service are declared eligible for it. Only some of these citizens actually seek care. In turn, only a subset of these actually get it, along with some who are not eligible.

Related to individual eligibility is the matter of which services are covered. Medicare has refused to cover appreciable amounts of long-term care, either in nursing homes or at home. Most states offer only weak public coverage of any long-term in-home services under their Medicaid and social services programs. During the 1960s and especially the 1970s, a series of efforts was made to expand public funding for in-home services. Medicare's prior hospitalization requirement and the 100-visit limit were eliminated for Part A home care services. But efforts to strip away the much more constricting homebound or skilled nursing requirements failed. This meant that the great majority of those needing long-term in-home care have remained ineligible for Medicare's home health benefit. (More ambitious Medicare reform initiatives are discussed in the final section of this chapter.)

In the 1970s long-term care reformers had sought to expand long-term care services to aid those otherwise unserved on the continuum of need, mainly those unable to be independent but not so dependent as to require the total care of institutions. More recent trends in long-term care eligibility are marked by efforts to employ home care services to delay or prevent institutional placement. The federal waivers for noninstitutional alternatives financed by Medicaid under section 2176 of the 1981 Omnibus Budget Reconciliation Act illustrate this. They have expanded the range of noninstitutional services financed by Medicaid but have narrowed the target group to those who—but for the home care services—might enter nursing homes. Congressional intent seems to have been somewhat broader here, but administration of the program has been constricted. States have been required to design and run their waivered programs to avoid any increase in total Medicaid spending.

Those who advocate devoting existing noninstitutional services to a restricted target group claim that many not-especially-needful citizens have been receiving small and ineffective amounts of in-home care. They assert that scarce funds for noninstitutional care should be focused on those in danger of serious harm or at risk for institutionalization. It appears that existing home care programs may be employed increasingly as substitutes for nursing home care. Some hope this will slow the costly nursing home construction that would otherwise be needed to maintain a constant age-specific rate of nursing home use as our population grows older.

This substitutional goal is at the heart of the 2176 waiver program as it has been administered. The aims of its original advocates—more flexible use of Medicaid funds to sustain greater numbers of disabled elders at home—have been largely subordinated to the goal of containing total federal spending on long-term care. Advocates won greater flexibility, but only if no increase in total long-term care Medicaid spending resulted. Thus, the waivers that seem to point in different directions—one toward narrowing the focus on a smaller group, and the other toward loosening regulatory restrictions—are actually aligned toward the common aim of employing noninstitutional services as a lower-cost or equal-cost substitute for the nursing home. These waivers can be defended as reducing pressure on elders to enter nursing homes as the price of receiving care, but they fail to expand meaningfully the number of disabled older citizens eligible for publicly funded home care. To a great extent, they signal a substitution of rhetoric about freedom of choice of site of long-term care for the reality of expanding noninstitutional alternatives.

Organization and Delivery

Two enduring issues in long-term care have been the supply and turnover of direct service workers and the quality of labor–management relations. Emerging trends have involved integration and corporatization, signaled by vertical and horizontal integration of caregivers, and by the rise of proprietary interests in home health care.

Both quality of care and quality of life for the dependent, frail, and often confused older citizens who receive long-term care in institutions or in their own homes depend intimately on the dedication, compassion, patience, and skill of front-line direct-service workers. About one million citizens—the great majority of them women—work as nurses' aides, diet aides, homemakers, and home health aides. They typically receive low wages, few fringe benefits, little training, and little opportunity for advancement. There is seldom a real career ladder in long-term care.

Their jobs are tough. Those for whom they care often resent their own dependence and therefore sometimes fail to display gratitude. Some recipients of care employ passivity as their only weapon, angering uncomprehending workers. Many recipients have problems that are objectively unpleasant to cope with—bed sores, incontinence, and others. Many recipients are uncommunicative and most are not going to recover and cease needing long-term care.

The combination of low pay and a tough job make for frequent turnover, further reducing organizational efficiency and effectiveness. Worker efforts to organize in unions in order to improve working conditions and pay often meet strenuous resistance from employers—both proprietary and nonprofit. Management fears loss of both power and income. A unionized nursing home or home health agency fears that it will be at a price disadvantage when competing against one that is not unionized. And many caregivers dependent on unresponsive or miserly publicly regulated rates worry that union-won wage increases will be reflected in higher payments only slowly and inadequately.

Difficult working conditions, low wages, and poor labor–management relations are all associated with low public payments for long-term care services. We seem to witness a cycle of recrimination, under which public payors blame a few individual nursing homes for poor care and refuse to pay more until visible abuses are cleaned up. Caregivers claim that they do not get enough money to pay workers enough or to deliver better services. These longstanding issues are not moving closer to resolution and are likely to be exacerbated if the level of needfulness of the average long-term care recipient rises faster than public payments. States with tight labor markets (low unemployment levels) and relatively high rates of provision of long-term care, such as Massachusetts, may indicate what the future holds. It is increasingly difficult in high-employment states to recruit and retain aides at wages close to the minimum legal level. Higher reimbursement will be necessary to allow nursing homes and home care agencies to pay more money. If this is not forthcoming, staffing levels will suffer or turnover will increase. If payment levels do rise, greater numbers of competent and dedicated workers may be attracted to the difficult jobs in long-term care. But will public payors suffering fiscal stress compensate for higher wages by reducing the number of disabled citizens served? While low unemployment usually runs with solid state finances, will the political decisions to make funds available for long-term care be forthcoming?

An important related issue concerns how to deliver good long-term care services. Some nursing homes and home care agencies deliver superbly effective and compassionate care, with fine worker–management relations and low turnover, though they are paid no more than other caregivers. How do they do it? Are rare owners, managers, or clinicians involved? If so, can their skills be analyzed and diffused? This bears careful study; it has received little.

A decade ago, some observers of long-term care delivery lamented the small and apparently inefficient, uncoordinated, and poorly managed agencies common in the field. Today, some of the same observers (and others) decry the trend toward corporatization. We have seen horizontal integration through the merging of smaller home health agencies serving individual cities or towns into larger regional organizations. Also, nursing home chains have resumed the growth they first manifested during the late 1960s.

Horizontal integration among home health agencies has been spurred by desires for improved managerial efficiency through reducing duplication, and by a chance for larger organizations to offer a wider range of needed services. It is not clear to what extent these hopes have been realized, nor to what degree gains in these areas may have been offset by losses of local control and the responsiveness to individual communities possible in smaller agencies. Horizontal integration among nursing homes has been driven by the desire of successful managers to acquire additional facilities. Has this resulted in upgraded care? We know little about this, but it is likely that chain ownership compresses both extremes of the quality distribution.

Superb care may be unaffordable, and horrible care is an unacceptable embarrassment.

Recently, vertical integration of health care has been visible. Hospitals have taken the lead in establishing or acquiring institutional long-term care capacity. Some have sought to use emptying acute-care beds as swing beds (licensed and reimbursed for either acute-care or long-term use, as need warrants); others have bought or built nursing homes. Still others have established, expanded, or merged with Medicare-certified home health agencies. This vertical integration between acute- and long-term care is mirrored by a parallel attempt to align acute care and physician services. It is hoped that the consolidated caregiving organizations that result from both facets of vertical integration will be able to better manage care, revenues, and costs—and to retain the loyalty of patients. In particular, integrated hospitals paid for acute care prospectively by Medicare through diagnosis-related groups (DRGs) (or most other prospective methods) can promptly discharge patients requiring either recuperation at home or short- or long-term institutional placement. Acute-care costs are contained and long-term care revenues generated.

The proprietary shares of nursing homes and beds have increased gradually in recent years. The for-profit percentage of Medicare-certified home health agencies has risen dramatically. This results in large part from a DHHS initiative undertaken during the Ford administration. Observing that many parts of the nation were underserved by existing Medicare-certified home health agencies, and that legislation in many states prohibited certification of for-profit agencies, DHHS secured passage of legislation requiring states to certify all appropriate home health agencies for Medicare, regardless of ownership status. In part as a result, the number of for-profit Medicare-certified home health agencies rose from 166 (5.8%) in 1979 to 1,571 (30.0%) in 1984 (Levit, Lazenby, Waldo, & Davidoff, 1985, p. 5). During this time, Medicare spending on home health care rose by 20 to 25% annually. The degree to which the growth of the for-profits has engendered higher spending is unclear. Even less certain is the degree to which they have expanded access to basic in-home health care. At least some proprietary firms have been attracted to provide Medicare-funded home health care by the opportunity to deliver profitable and costly high-technology in-home services, such as total parenteral nutrition and respiratory therapy. Considerable amounts of durable medical equipment have been rented.

When needed, and when unpaid family members are available to help, the total public cost per recipient of providing these costly services at home is probably lower than their cost in an institution. But the appropriateness of provision may be questioned. Some observers have accused some for-profits of pricing basic RN, LPN, or home health aide services below cost, in order to obtain patients who might subsequently be provided profitable esoteric care. If frequently employed, this "loss leader" strategy suggests that patterns of service provision by for-profits bears investigation. One possible response would be to work to restore a balance in home care by improving coverage for less costly routine services.

Also meriting scrutiny are the activities of proprietary home health agencies that serve only Medicare-sponsored clients. Favorable bottom lines may reflect cream-skimming, if more difficult cases are left to the voluntary or public sectors. This increases average cost of care for the latter, while reducing their abilities to cross-subsidize non-Medicare clients with surplus income earned through Medicare. In this way, the growth of for-profits may undermine the broader community service activities of other home health agencies.

More important, if for-profits have engaged in inappropriate behavior, they may help undermine opportunities for improved public funding for home care generally. Even the perception of abuses in renting durable medical equipment, or the explosive growth in Medicare home health spending, can have this effect. Legislators, endemically ambivalent about for-profits, can seize on their abuses. A few bad actors may suffice to harm a program. Witness Medicare's absurd and destructive decision to pay for only one physician visit per month to a nursing home patient because a very few individuals billed for many superfluous visits during the early days of the program.

Finances

The most important trend in this area has been the gradual decline in real public spending per person in need of long-term care. A consequence has been the growth of interest in private long-term care insurance.

We believe that real public spending per person in need has declined recently (and we anticipate continued drops), although we realize that the data required to demonstrate this are not ideal. While data on current spending are adequate, choice of the appropriate price deflator is not obvious and evidence of need is even less firm. We point to the decline in the public share of total nursing home spending from 57.0% in 1980 to 49.0% in 1984 (Gibson & Waldo, 1981; Levit et al., 1985). Similarly, by our calculations, real public spending (constant dollars) on nursing homes per elder in need of nursing home care (using 1973 age-adjusted rates of use as a standard) fell from $7510 in 1980 to $7397 in 1984.

Private long-term care insurance is today enjoying one of its periodic resurgences. Realizing Medicare's failure to cover long-term care, and fearing impoverishment, individuals hope to protect themselves. Insurance companies anxious to explore potentially profitable lines of business have sought to design benefit packages and identify customers they could sell to profitably. This has been difficult.

All the hazards of adverse selection and moral hazard that plague acute-care health insurance are visibly worse for long-term care. Group sales to guard against adverse selection are difficult. Fears of moral hazard are heightened by the imagined attractiveness of benefits. A homemaker's services are appreciably less painful than a surgeon's. A nursing home admission may boost one's objective standard of living through improved nutrition, housing, safety, and personal care. Insurance companies therefore include high barriers to use: waiting periods, deductibles, co-insurance, only short-term coverage. Even so, premiums often look high in relation to benefits. This is owing to a combination of insurance company uncertainty, fears of high use, and high marketing costs. High cost and low benefits reduce the value of private long-term care insurance to potential buyers.

Government intervention seems indicated. While we suspect that ill-conceived public action might be unbearably costly, we hope that well-designed public mandatory long-term care coverage would both reduce administrative costs and guard against adverse selection. The remaining issue of controlling service use depends on careful assessment and care planning, and on mobilization of informal supports.

We do not favor the various forms of tax spending that have been proposed to subsidize family care. Tax deductions visibly favor the well-to-do, who least need public aid. Tax credits are somewhat more equitable. But neither form of tax benefit will be felt by families until the end of the tax year, unless withholding or estimated tax payments are adjusted in expectation of the benefit. We believe that few families will do this. Therefore, only little influence on families' behavior can be expected. For this reason, tax benefits are likely to reward those families able to provide care without them.

Tax spending has the advantage of administrative simplicity, but it is enormously inefficient, owing to its inability to target benefits where they will do the most good—either for disabled older citizens or for their families. All tax spending is relatively invisible, difficult to evaluate, and (once legislated) difficult to repeal even if shown to be unwise. It should not be a first choice.

Quality/Effectiveness

Goals and desire are two enduring issues in both the assessment of the technical quality of long-term care and its outcomes (effectiveness). By goals we mean the specification of what one hopes to accomplish through long-term care services. By desire, we raise the question of how ardently society and caregivers wish to pursue good services.

We seek technically competent, proficient services that promote desired outcomes. Over time, the outcomes emphasized by long-term care professionals have evolved. Professionals have moved gradually and incompletely from emphasizing delaying death, to slowing the decline in functional ability, to promoting cognitive/emotional well-being, to compensating for those functional deficits to which informal supports are not able to respond.

Disagreement or uncertainty about desired outcomes makes it difficult to allocate resources, evaluate their accomplishments, or even monitor adherence to standards. If most long-term care services are devoted to compensating for functional deficits, it is foolish to focus evaluation on bolstering functional ability. The more sensitive measures are those that would address the success of the compensatory activities on their own terms: Is the disabled person well-fed, clothed, allowed to travel with a measure of self-determination, and the like?

If there is disagreement about what is sought from long-term care services, clear-cut administrative enforcement is difficult. And such enforcement is not easy under the best of circumstances. All regulatory agencies find it hard to establish standards to monitor what is most important without opening the door to being challenged as "arbitrary and capricious." Thus, we find nursing home regulations that focus on the cleanliness of the facility and the nutritional value of the foods bought, not on whether the care is compassionate, whether the food is appetizing, or whether one would be willing to live out one's days there. Most of us could evaluate the last three things, but probably too subjectively (with insufficient interrater reliability) to allow them to be used to regulate individual nursing homes.

Notwithstanding that any efforts to improve quality would likely be flawed, we probably have given insufficient attention to improving techniques for using state regulation to upgrade technical quality, effectiveness, and compassion of care. We might not achieve perfection, but we can do better.

Perhaps one reason for this insufficient attention is an underlying ambivalence about the level of decency we seek from publicly funded long-term care services. We fear that better nursing home care, for example, will cost more per patient-day than worse care. Even more important, we may fear that if we improve nursing homes in the absence of a more generous home care benefit, we will persuade much larger numbers of eligible older citizens to line up for publicly funded nursing home services. Another view is that a combination of inertia and uncertainty about how to improve nursing homes has slowed reform.

This ambivalence is an enduring manifestation of the poorhouse principle on which public benefits for long-term care have been founded in this nation. Make the benefit unattractive, and oblige an individual to enter an institution as the price of public support. Given the large numbers of low-income and disabled older Americans residing in the community, it is reasonable to expect that many would seek admission to improved nursing homes. This would probably mean a substantial improvement in their objective standards of living. A good nursing home provides good food, warm shelter, and physical security in addition to long-term care services. Impoverished older Americans have good reason to value these things. And good nursing homes, other things being equal, would allow some families to lay down in better conscience the very heavy burdens of caring for disabled parents in their own homes. Clearly, then, systematic improvement in the nation's nursing homes needs to be part of a broader effort to upgrade both living standards for low-income older citizens and long-term care services in all settings.

FORCES BEHIND THESE ISSUES AND TRENDS

Three longstanding issues and an equal number of developing trends help explain the problems and other phenomena just described. The issues are (1) the demographic time bomb, (2) legislative paralysis concerning long-term care, and (3) the more general public policy dilemmas stemming from a weak economy. The more recent trends, to which we only allude, are (1) the use of prospective payment through DRGs to slow the rate of increase in Medicare spending on hospital care, (2) the growing preference for competitive, nonregulatory attacks on public problems, and (3) heightened privatization.

Demographic Time Bomb

From some perspectives, improved longevity can be a mixed blessing. More Americans are living long enough to require long-term care, and increasing numbers are doing so without the financial and family resources that avoid or reduce need for publicly funded services. The HCFA white paper on long-term care calculated that the age- and gender-adjusted rates of use of nursing home beds, taking 1977 as a standard, would rise from 1.3 million in that year, to almost 2.0 million in 2000, and to almost 3.0 million in 2030 (Health Care Financing Administration, 1981, p. 13). In light of likely economic and political trends, it is very hard to imagine that current or future certificate-of-need programs will permit construction of this many additional beds, that state Medicaid programs will entitle this many citizens to care, or that state rate setters will authorize payments adequate to permit decent care in this many beds. The hope that Americans will age with less disability, expressed most notably by Fries (1980), has been questioned by Manton and Soldo (1985) and by others. The evidence, although scant, seems to favor the latter position.

Legislative Paralysis

Congress has not been anxious to expand public funding for long-term care. Particularly, it has been unwilling to establish a home care program even approaching the current institutional effort. It fears that the cost of any public initiative will far exceed advocates' estimates. This happened under both Medicare and Medicaid, and Congress has little reason to expect better performance from any new entitlement program. Careful design under a fixed budget is probably warranted.

The current $200 billion deficit and the doubling of the national debt during the past five years of supply-side fantasies do not encourage federal initiatives. States expect that they will be called on to plug gaps in existing programs left by looming federal budget cuts; few are oriented toward new initiatives.

The Economy

We believe that, barring technological breakthroughs, the United States will face declining average real standards of living and increasingly maldistributed incomes. While lower energy prices have given the Reagan administration a respite, long-term trends point to a declining international competitiveness of the economy, caused in part by a failure by industry to undertake needed capital investments. Our competitors in Western Europe have slowly adapted to more austere times during the years since 1973. We have not. Today, efforts to ameliorate unprecedented federal budget deficits, unemployment rates, and trade deficits will tend to exacerbate the others. Absent creative innovation, the scope for public attacks on social problems seems inevitably to have narrowed.

INNOVATIONS: RECENT AND CONTEMPLATED

Over the past decade or so, several types of reforms in the financing or organization of long-term care have been proposed. They rely on varying combinations of public funds (old and new), private financial and nonfinancial resources, and changes in structure and thinking about service delivery in long-term care. Some are being tested. Each has promising aspects but raises serious questions as well. When they require a shift of individual or societal resources to long-term care, they remind us that there is no free lunch.

Financing

Innovations that have been principally financial include various proposals for federal legislation to establish a long-term care Title XXI of the Social Security Act or a new long-term care benefit under Medicare. Some would create a new trust fund; others a consolidated bloc grant. Each would cover a wider range of noninstitutional services without a means test. While there are some differences in covered services, administration, and financing (some call for voluntary enrollment and monthly premium payments; others do not), the proposals generally would relax Medicare's current skilled nursing and homebound requirements, add nontechnical services, such as those of homemakers, provide for more flexible shifting of funds between nursing home and home care, and envisage a prominent role for case management to control both eligibility and use of services.

Such proposals have little chance of passage today. Legislative support of programs that would require increased federal spending is hard to assemble. Even broad social welfare programs such as these, which are not means tested and therefore entitle the entire population in need, require some income transfers, and these seem about as unpopular as new taxes.

But circumstances change. Should the economy be restored to health over the next few decades, rising pressure from dozens of millions of aging baby-boomers (one born in 1945 turns 65 in 2010) for both adequate incomes in old age and protection against the chance of needing long-term care could lead to passage of a Title XXI or a new Medicare benefit. Older citizens might agree to defer retirement benefits somewhat longer in exchange for federal long-term care insurance.

These numbers are only crude approximations to illustrate a concept, but if 2 million individuals or couples become eligible for full Social Security retirement benefits each year (regardless of the age at which benefits are taken), and if the average benefit is $8,000, then the payment to new retirees in their first year is $16 billion. A three-month delay in initiating benefits would therefore finance a $4 billion long-term care program. We do not assert that this sum is necessarily the correct one; it is offered only illustratively.

The political feasibility of such a proposal is uncertain at best. Delays in retirement age have already been legislated in order to bolster the retirement fund. Would enough retirees be willing to vote to forgo income in exchange for long-term care insurance? This depends on their concerns about future needs for long-term care and on their ability to obtain that care through other channels. For example, those able to afford private long-term care insurance could calculate whether its price to them would be less than that of a public benefit that included subsidies to lower-income workers. Additionally, would employers be willing to pay older workers for an additional three months? This depends on future demographics and labor market conditions.

Organization

Two innovations here involve case management and mobilizing informal supports. Each hopes to do more for older citizens without spending additional public funds.

Case management has several meanings. It can involve more careful screening of prospective nursing home admissions, especially for individuals covered by Medicaid or thought likely to become a burden to the program. Related to this, case management can mean more careful coordination of noninstitutional resources, thereby helping older citizens remain outside nursing homes for as long as possible.

Case management responds to two related perceptions—that elders have been institutionalized "inappropriately" and that a rich mix of fragmented community services exists and needs only be coordinated in order to help many more older Americans live out their lives at home. There are two problems here. The first is that "inappropriate institutionalization" has a horde of meanings, ranging from (1) persons obliged to enter nursing homes who do not wish to be there, to (2) those who need to be there but have been placed at the wrong level, to (3) those whose conditions do not seem to warrant nursing home residence and who *could* be cared for in the community at some undetermined cost, to (4) those who would be less costly to serve outside the nursing home. Given the wide range of meaning, it is not surprising to find estimates of inappropriate institutionalization ranging from 7% to 76% of nursing home residents.

When state governments paying costly Medicaid bills for nursing home care learn about assertions of inappropriate institutionalization, they could become anxious to control purportedly unnecessary use of nursing homes. They sometimes fail to realize that individuals slated for nursing home admission typically do need considerable amounts of help and that additional public funds might be required to pay for such help outside the nursing home if admission is denied.

The coordinating function of case management has clear attractions in this regard. It promises improved efficiency as a way out of the dilemmas surrounding the delivery of noninstitutional care. It is hard for very dependent citizens to remain at home, especially when alone or confused. An enormous number of aids need to be mobilized and coordinated. In-home services are certainly fragmented today. Physicians are typically uninvolved clinically, doing little more than formally certifying eligibility for service. Medicare-certified home health agencies seldom coordinate their efforts with the important services provided in some areas by social service agencies' homemakers.

The second problem is that while improved coordination is necessary, it is certainly not enough. Noninstitutional services are probably inadequate in most of the nation. Further, it is not even clear that case management is the best vehicle for accomplishing coordination. Although larger organizations can be unwieldy, a merger of long-term care functions into single units might be preferable. Internal control and communication could then be substituted for a case manager's possibly more limited powers to negotiate and cajole.

An alternative approach to case management might be to provide the manager with a budget with which to serve all eligible persons in an entire community. As a purchaser of services, the manager might choose in some instances to pay a relative, in others to bring in a homemaker/home health aide, and in others to finance nursing home care. The manager might offer a family a part-time homemaker on the condition that it sustain its own level of effort. In this way, a major concern impeding financing of more adequate public long-term care services—displacing family aid without raising the level of well-being of elders commensurate with increased spending—would be assuaged. Any such approach would be open to abuse. Relying on individual discretion and latitude to negotiate violates the national conception of administrative due process. It invites discrimination, bribery, and favoritism. We may wish to experiment with this approach carefully, perhaps with the aim of discovering devices for promoting a good mix of flexibility and fairness.

Mobilizing informal supports on behalf of disabled older citizens is another attractive idea that carries with it a number of problems. If there are idle resources of time and energy in American society, and if these could be mobilized voluntarily on behalf of disabled citizens, aggregate social welfare (in the sense of overall well-being) could be improved without raising taxes or establishing a costly administrative apparatus (Sager, 1983).

By way of background, it is important to reflect on the nature of the enormous efforts expended by family members—usually daughters or spouses—on behalf of those in need. An older citizen's need for help can be massive and unpredictable. It is hard to schedule. It may arise when potential caregivers have competing obligations or desires, such as childrearing or earning needed income outside the home. Some who would be willing to help are never called upon; others are crushed by the burden; most fear it.

What makes sense, then, is to spread risk through insurance, allowing premium payment over time, when convenient. Since long-term care requires most or all the time of a caregiver, it is appropriate that time be the medium of exchange. Good deeds could be banked in units of time. Individuals willing to help and older citizens in need would be identified and matched. Time contributed would be recorded. Tokens might be paid out in lieu of a passbook. These could be used to purchase time insurance. If the chances are one in ten that a given person will need long-term care, any helper need contribute only one-tenth of the expected amount of aid.

Organizations that endure over time could be pilot coordinating vehicles. Religious congregations, service-starved congregate housing for the elderly, union locals, and fraternal or neighborhood organizations might qualify.

Suppressed altruistic instincts might be liberated and allowed expression through such a mechanism. Altruism could be aligned with long-run self-interest.

A host of questions require answers. Would all tasks be valued equally, or would relative value units need to be employed to distinguish the hard from the easy, the pleasant from the unpleasant? Would citizens be willing to trust the value of the tokens? Could tokens be transferred outside the family? What backing (as paper money was once backed by specie) might be required? What about the jobs that volunteers could not and should not be expected to undertake? How much public money would be required to pay RNs, LPNs, or home health aides for the jobs too difficult or highly skilled for volunteers? Who would manage and organize the enterprise? Would it corrupt ordinary, decent human exchange with the taint of market thinking? These questions call for the answers that carefully designed demonstrations might provide. Several current pilot efforts to employ time tokens to encourage and bank voluntary aid may provide some of the answers.

Integrating

The continuing-care retirement community (CCRC), or life care community, and the social/health maintenance organization (S/HMO) integrate financing and organizational innovations. Each employs a type of prepayment to marshal funds, and each promises flexibility to provide a broader range of noninstitutional services to supplement nursing home care.

In some respects, the CCRC is intended as a device for converting accumulated savings, including home equity, into a retirement more free of worries about involuntary nursing home admission or about impoverishment owing to need for long-term care services (Branch, 1987). In most current models, the high costs of new construction must be borne, but alternatives call for employing cheaper existing housing. The individual pays an endowment and monthly service fees. Together, these contractually entitle the resident to lifetime use of a residence, amenities, and services. The latter includes meals, care of the home and grounds, and, in the event of disability, personal and other care at home or in a nursing home.

The housing and the new community become vehicles for mobilizing resources adequate for financing long-term care, for spreading risk, and for providing services efficiently in a spatially concentrated site. Except when nursing home admission is required, individuals are not obliged to relocate to obtain needed care. Even then, many CCRCs maintain on-site nursing homes for residents. In these ways, CCRCs respond to many Americans' powerful desires for community, stability, and security.

There are two important questions about CCRCs. The first concerns the proportion of the population for which they are affordable. Can one-tenth, one-quarter, one-half of older Americans manage the admission and monthly fees? Is there a risk that CCRCs, like equity conversion and other housing-based long-term care financing vehicles (and like private long-term care insurance itself), may in part serve to satisfy the upper-middle class's desires for a more secure old age and thereby reduce effective public pressure for adequate long-term care services for all disabled citizens?

Second, how robust are CCRCs' actuarial calculations? Can CCRCs (or other housing-based mechanisms) withstand an inflation like that of the 1970s? How about a strong recession? Is there danger in a failure to diversify the implicit portfolio of assets (the CCRCs physical plant itself), leaving the CCRC overinvested in real estate of a very particular kind? In other words, is the CCRCs' very strength of using pooled housing assets as a vehicle for funding future residential and long-term care services and as a mechanism for defining the risk-sharing group also potentially dangerous, should the market price of its housing units fall? In another area, how accurate are assumptions about need for care? Will CCRCs be able to deliver the long-term care they promise if their residents live a bit longer than projected, with lower average lifetime levels of functional ability? Some CCRCs do better jobs of addressing these questions. Adequate prefunding of future long-term care obligations, with these funds invested in a diversified portfolio, minimizes some of these potential problems.

As originally conceived by Morris (1971) and Caro (1973), the S/HMO would combine funding for physician, hospital, and a wide range of institutional and noninstitutional long-term care services in one prepaid program (Diamond, Gruenberg, & Morris, 1983). This program would be controlled by a single organization, which would have both the incentive and the ability to spend money as flexibly and wisely as possible for an enrolled population. The S/HMO is modeled after the health maintenance organization, which has demonstrated an ability to control costs of certain services for certain populations. However, the health maintenance organization for a healthy working population does not save money by making members healthy. They already are. It may keep members healthy by removing the financial barrier to seeking early care, thereby encouraging quicker diagnosis and treatment.

But for a disabled and chronically ill older population, health maintenance of various kinds makes enormous medical and social sense. Continuous primary medical care from physicians, nurse practitioners, physician assistants, and registered nurses could mean regular monitoring of chronic problems, promoting continuity of care, and raising the chances of early detection of destabilization or exacerbation. If a problem does occur, it could be treated in the least costly setting. This makes it possible to pay for in-home or nursing home visits, reducing the number of emergency room trips by ambulance or hospital admissions. Savings on acute care could finance the extra primary care. Similarly, provision of adequate meals and personal care through homemaker or home health aide services could reduce the frequency of preventable problems that can be costly to treat. Long-term care becomes more affordable because it becomes in part an investment by the organization. The CCRC and the S/HMO share this important orientation. Several of the most important aspects of this design have been pioneered and successfully tested by members of the Urban Medical Group in Boston (Master et al., 1980).

Importantly, these changes typically could mean an improved quality of life. The citizen would have more secure access to steady physician care and better circumstances at home—both in place of disproportionately high spending on hospital services during the last weeks of life. Money becomes easier to spend on the living, possibly harder to spend on the dying. All societies ration health care services to almost all citizens. The S/HMO might become a way to ration through cooperative care planning between trusted primary care physician and citizen.

An important component for integrated programs like the S/HMO or the CCRC is financial neutrality for decisionmakers. Funds saved through more careful service delivery must be recycled through enriched services. Any incentive payments to caregivers ("if you provide or authorize less care, you earn more money") or returns to holders of equity would subvert the trust that must sustain rationing through the S/HMO.

Four federally waivered S/HMO experiments (Portland, Oregon; Brooklyn; Minneapolis; and Long Beach, California) are in their early phases. Coverage of only some services and restriction on duration of care limit the organization's exposure to risk. An important early decision was to enroll relatively few of the very ill or disabled. Risk-spreading was the aim. This has meant that expertise in managing the very costly cases may be acquired only slowly. An alternative model would be to enroll only very needful citizens. A critical mass of need may spur development of innovative methods of care.

CONCLUSIONS

In conclusion, we have reviewed a number of longstanding issues and emerging trends, suggested several reasons why problems associated with these may be hard to resolve, and examined the state of financial and organizational innovation in long-term care.

Opportunities to develop and test new ideas seem lacking today. Political and economic barriers are high on the horizon. But national administrations and economic circumstances do change, often for the better. When change occurs, it would be good to have available well-tested ideas, ready for national distribution. Our concern should be long-term. The most enduring of the New Deal's reforms—unemployment insurance, old age insurance, and the like—had been tested in the states (the "laboratories of democracy") during the four decades preceding Roosevelt's election. We have time. Many states have the necessary fiscal and administrative resources. Given the need for long-term care reform, at least we won't be accused of trying to fix something that's not broken.

REFERENCES

Branch, Laurence G. 1987. "Continuing Care Retirement Communities: Insuring for Long-term Care." *The Gerontologist* 27:4–8.

Caro, Francis G. 1973. "The Personal Care Organization: An Approach to the Maintenance of the Disabled in the Community." Waltham, MA: Levinson Gerontological Policy Institute.

Diamond, Larry M., Leonard Gruenberg, and Robert L. Morris. 1983. "Elder Care for the 1980s: Health and Social Service in One Prepaid Health Maintenance System." *The Gerontologist* 23:148–154.

Fries, J. F. 1980. "Aging, Natural Death, and the Compression of Mortality." *New England Journal of Medicine* 303: 130–135.

Gibson, Robert M. and Daniel R. Waldo. 1981. "National Health Expenditures, 1980." *Health Care Financing Review* 3:1–54.

Health Care Financing Administration. 1981. *Long Term Care: Background and Future Directions*. Washington, DC: U.S. Government Printing Office.

Levit, Katharine R., Helen Lazenby, Daniel R. Waldo, and Lawrence M. Davidoff. 1985. "National Health Expenditures, 1984." *Health Care Financing Review* 7:1–35.

Manton, Kenneth G. and Beth J. Soldo. 1985. "Dynamics of Health Changes in the Oldest Old: New Perspectives and Evidence." *Milbank Memorial Fund Quarterly* 63:206–285.

Master, Robert J., Marie Feltin, John Jainchill, Roger Mark, William N. Kavesh, Mitchell T. Rabkin, Barbara Turner, Sarah Bachrach, and Sara Lennox. 1980. "A Continuum of Care for the Inner City: Assessment of Its Benefits for

Boston's Elderly and High-Risk Populations." *New England Journal of Medicine* 302: 1434–1440.

Morris, Robert. 1971. *Alternatives to Nursing Home Care: A Proposal.* Committee Print, United States Senate Special Committee on Aging. Washington, DC: U.S. Government Printing Office. Stock No. 5270-1248.

Sager, Alan. 1983. "A Proposal for Promoting More Adequate Long-Term Care for the Elderly." *The Gerontologist* 23: 13–17.

10
Money, Money, Who's Got The Money?: Financing Options For Long-Term Care*

*Joshua M. Wiener, Ray Hanley,
Denise Spence, and Diana Coupard*

Perhaps no other part of the health care system generates as much dissatisfaction as the organization and financing of long-term care (LTC) for the elderly. Long-term care is the system we love to hate. The disabled elderly and their families confront a fragmented delivery and financing system, a relative lack of noninstitutional services, long waiting lists for institutional placement, mediocre-quality care, and financial hardship (Vladeck, 1980). Paradoxically, public financing, primarily through Medicaid, is perceived as overexpensive yet resulting in an inadequate system.

The long-range demographics of the elderly will place increasing strain on this imperfect system. The aging of the baby-boom population combined with falling mortality rates for the aged suggest a sharply increasing demand for long-term care that will require substantially greater public and private expenditures. Projections of current age–sex-specific nursing home utilization rates suggest that there may be four times as many persons in nursing homes in 2040 as there were in 1980 (Manton & Liu, 1984; Rice & Feldman, 1983; Russell, 1981).

*These opinions are those of the authors and should not be attributed to other staff members, officers, or trustees of the Brookings Institution.

This large increase in demand clashes with the large federal budget deficit and generally tight fiscal constraints at all levels of government. As Lawlor and Pollak (1985) have noted, this clash has dramatically changed the terms of the long-term care debate. Only a short time ago, the federal debate centered on service delivery options, on the sparsity of noninstitutional services, and quality-of-care deficiencies. Financing received attention almost entirely on the expenditure side. What benefits should be financed and on what terms they should be covered were the major questions. The other side of financing—raising the revenue—was not seriously discussed. The budget deficit and current era of fiscal constraint have shifted the long-term care debate. Where we are going to obtain the money to pay for long-term care is now the overwhelmingly dominant issue.

The projected large increase in the need for long-term care presents both a problem and an opportunity for reform. Fundamental policy questions must be addressed if we are to do better in the future than we are doing now. Is there a better way to organize the delivery system than merely making the current system a lot larger? Will society be willing to pay for the current system multiplied by three or four? Is there a better way to finance care?

This chapter will examine some options that have been proposed to address these issues. Although organizational dimensions will be analyzed, the emphasis will be on financing issues. First, the reasons why long-term care is so hard to reform will be discussed. Second, private-sector initiatives for reform, such as private long-term care insurance, continuing-care retirement communities, home equity conversion, and individual retirement accounts for long-term care, will be examined. Third, public-sector approaches to long-term care reform, such as block grants, modifications in Medicare and Medicaid, public long-term care insurance, and tax credits for care of the disabled elderly, will be analyzed. Finally, some conclusions will be suggested.

WHY IS LONG-TERM CARE SO HARD TO REFORM?

During the last ten years there have been numerous proposals for major reform of the long-term care system. None of them have been adopted. Why has there been so little basic reform? There are several reasons. First, the much maligned status quo is not all bad. The status quo meets the needs, albeit crudely, of many of the participants in the current system. For example, the entitlement character of Medicaid means that expenditures more or less increase with need and are not arbitrarily limited by the appropriation process. While Medicaid is targeted to the poor, it also provides a safety net for the middle class. Moreover, the Medicaid spend-down requirement means that Medicaid finances only the care that the income and the assets of the elderly cannot, thus keeping public expenditures down. While the elderly may wish to leave a substantial estate to their children rather than spend it on long-term care, one may at least ask whether promotion of intergenerational transfers of wealth is a desirable social policy. The institutional bias assures that those persons receiving publicly financed care are predominantly the severely disabled and those without family supports. And, finally, noninstitutional services, while not as widespread as many would like, are moderately available. Again, the point here is not to defend the status quo but to explain why it has been so hard to change; the point is also to note that it is simply not true that nothing could be worse than the current system.

A second reason why there has been so little basic reform is that the vast system of informal care has made policymakers very cautious about expanding noninstitutional services. There are one to two times as many disabled elderly persons in the community as in nursing homes, and 77% receive no formal long-term care services (National Long-Term Care Survey, 1982). Thus there is the potential for a large demand for noninstitutional services and substantially increased public costs. Advocates of home-based care, which we are, have argued the cost-savings potential of home-based care, but the cost-effectiveness of noninstitutional services depends largely on targeting services to individuals who would be institutionalized without them. This is the essence of the Medicaid home- and community-based waivers. The fact of the matter, however, is that we do not know how to do that type of targeting very well (Doty, 1984).

A third obstacle to reform is that there is substantial excess demand for nursing home care, reflected in part by the large number of noninstitutionalized disabled elderly (Scanlon, 1980, 1982). Most nursing homes operate at 90% or higher occupancy rates (National Center for Health Statistics, 1979). Thus policymakers fear that expansion of the nursing home supply, especially at the margin, will only lead to more Medicaid patients and higher public expenditures.

In addition, some of the options commonly suggested for reforming acute care either are not applicable (or traditionally have not been considered applicable) to long-term care or are already part of the current system. Increased cost sharing is not applicable because patients already face virtually 100% cost sharing. Introducing prospective payment is not possible because 37 states already have prospective payment systems for nursing homes (HCFA, 1985). Utilization review (at least after admission) is thought to be ineffective because of the reluctance of states to force discharge of patients who have nowhere else to go.

Pooled-risk approaches, such as insurance and health maintenance organizations, have been hampered by a lack of the data needed to estimate expenditures. More fundamentally, they have also been hampered by a belief that long-term care is not an insurable risk. That is, because of the large number of disabled persons who medically qualify for but are receiving no services, the insuree would have substantial control over the insured-against event (i.e., admission to a nursing home or use of noninstitutional services).

A final obstacle is that, historically, the elderly have been poor. Thus private-sector approaches that required substantial personal expenditures were out of the question.

OPTIONS FOR REFORM: PRIVATE-SECTOR APPROACHES TO LTC

The financial position of the elderly has improved markedly in the last 15 years. For example, the poverty rate among the elderly fell by 50%, from 28.5% in 1966 to 14.1% in 1983 (U.S. Bureau of Census, various years). Danzinger, van der Gaag, Smolensky, and Taussig (1984) found that after adjusting for the lower tax rates, availability of asset income, and living arrangements, the elderly on average have about 90% of the income of nonelderly. Hurd and Shoven (1982) found that between 1970 and 1980 the real incomes of the elderly increased faster than the income of the rest of the population. Most projections of income of the elderly show an improved income position due to increased pensions and individual retirement accounts (Zedlewski, 1984). In addition, many elderly also have substantial assets, most often in the form of home equity. Even among the poor, about two-thirds of low-income elderly are homeowners (Jacobs, 1985). While few elderly are rich, there is clearly a significant group that is relatively well-off financially. This changing financial picture has increased the potential of private-sector approaches for financing long-term care.

The interest in private-sector initiatives currently far outstrips the reality. Despite considerable media and academic interest, private-sector approaches so far constitute only a tiny part of the long-term care market. Interest in private-sector approaches to long-term care comes from some very diverse groups, each with different goals and expectations. There are ideological conservatives, for whom it is axiomatic that the private sector does things better than the public sector. There are disillusioned liberals, who hope that by getting the middle class off the rolls of programs for poor people (e.g., Medicaid) and allowing them to focus on the truly needy, public support for those programs will increase. The disillusioned liberals also despair of the current unwillingness of people to pay taxes to fund public programs and hope that private funds can be used to develop an improved delivery system. There are social insurance advocates, trying to protect the dignity (and assets) of the middle class from pauperization.

There are government officials, desperately looking for a way out of large-scale increases in expenditures for long-term care. There are providers, anxious about the willingness of government to finance a large growth in long-term care utilization and looking for a way to increase their revenues. And, finally, there are businessmen, who hope to make money offering these new financing instruments, although to date there have not been very many of this last group, especially in the insurance and banking industries.

Four of the most commonly mentioned private-sector approaches are private long-term care insurance, continuing-care retirement communities, home equity conversion, and individual retirement accounts for long-term care. Private long-term care insurance and continuing-care retirement communities depend on the concept of pooled risk to control costs. Conversely, home equity conversion and individual retirement accounts for long-term care seek to provide funds to individuals (without any pooling of risk) to allow them to meet their own long-term care needs.

Private LTC Insurance

Proponents of private long-term care insurance begin with the assumption that commercial insurance can be developed that will provide a reasonable amount of financial protection at premium levels that Americans can afford. Premiums would be collected from a large group of people and benefits provided to the relatively few who need care. At present, at least 16 insurance companies already provide some form of private long-term care insurance (Meiners, 1984). In addition, the American Association of Retired Persons (AARP) and the Prudential Insurance Company are test-marketing a policy to be offered to AARP members.

Advocates of private insurance argue that this approach has many advantages. First, it builds on the well-known willingness of the elderly to purchase Medigap insurance. Approximately two-thirds of all elderly own a Medigap policy, and high levels of coverage persist even at relatively low income levels (Cafferata, 1984). Second, since it does not require the development of a major new service delivery structure, it can be expanded relatively quickly into a major financing source. Third, by spreading the risk of long-term care costs across a broad population, the burden placed on any one individual to finance the costs of catastrophic care would be reduced. Fourth, private insurance is a noncompulsory alternative that allows the individual to maximize utility and provides him greater flexibility in meeting his needs.

There are several potential difficulties with private long-term care insurance. First, there is the danger of adverse selection; that is, only people who need the insurance will buy it, driving up utilization and the price of the policies. Insurers typically try to protect themselves against this by screening for health conditions, prohibiting coverage for preexisting conditions, excluding coverage of mental illnesses (treatment of Alzheimer's disease under existing policies is unclear), requiring care to be in skilled nursing facilities, providing reimbursement only if there is a prior hospitalization, and marketing only to the well-to-do. The fact that policies have been marketed on an individual basis makes these screenings relatively easy to implement, since the insurance broker typically deals directly with the purchaser. Unfortunately, to the extent that insurers succeed in screening out high-risk individuals, they may exclude the people who most need the coverage. While insurance companies have treated their utilization data as proprietary information, the limited information available suggests that current policies have some favorable selection.

A second problem is that insurance coverage will induce increased demand and utilization ("moral hazard"). One of the consequences of insurance is to lower the effective price of services. Conventional economic theory tells us that people buy more of a good or service when the price is lower. Increased demand could be a particular problem if the insurance covered home care, which is an attractive addition to the informal care provided by the family. Insurers try to protect themselves against moral hazard by using high deductibles and by limiting coverage to nursing home care. Unfortunately, the high deductibles limit the degree of financial protection this proposed reform would offer, and the exclusion of home care may exacerbate the already strong institutional bias that exists in the current financing system.

A third potential problem is that there is uncertain market interest in private long-term care policies. First, most elderly and virtually all nonelderly substantially underestimate their chance of long-term disability. In addition, there is a widespread misunderstanding of what Medicare covers and the availability of Medicaid; in a survey of its membership, the AARP found that among respondents who believed that they would at some point have an extended stay in a nursing home, nearly four-fifths believed that Medicare would pay for all or part of their stay (AARP, 1982). This is manifestly untrue; Medicare accounts for only about 2% of nursing home revenues, and the average length of covered stay is only 30 days (HCFA, 1985). Yet many discover this only when they need care. Moreover, many in the insurance industry believe that the elderly will not buy long-term care insurance because of the availability of and willingness to use Medicaid as a safety net to pay for nursing home care (HIAA, 1984).

Fourth, it is widely believed that third-party payment for acute care has been partially responsible for rapidly rising hospital and physician costs. It is possible that long-term care insurance may have a similar inflationary effect.

Finally, premiums are high, thus limiting the market. For example, the

Fireman's Fund long-term care policy costs $450 a year for those aged 60–64 and rises to $1,200 for those aged 79–81. Assuming that people would be willing to purchase insurance if they had $3,000 in liquid assets and if the policy was 5% or less of their income, ICF, Inc. (1985) estimated that only 21% of the elderly could afford the Fireman's Fund policy. Even at these levels, long-term care insurance would represent a substantial increase in out-of-pocket health care expenditures for most elderly and a virtual doubling or more of their Medigap premiums. Reducing costs by spreading the risk over the working population seems unlikely, since many companies are reducing their health benefits and may be unwilling to make long-term care insurance a fringe benefit.

Continuing-Care Retirement Communities

Continuing-care retirement communities (CCRCs) are financially self-sufficient settings for the elderly that combine residential units with the availability of medical, nursing, and social services in specialized facilities on the premises. The underlying concept is one of pooled risk to provide a lifetime continuum of care. These communities typically require a large up-front payment of $60,000–$100,000 and then monthly fees of $1,000 or more. Although the industry has historically been dominated by nonprofit providers, the for-profit sector (e.g., Beverly Enterprises, Marriott Corporation) is becoming increasingly involved.

Proponents of CCRCs note that these organizations combine an organized system of care with financial incentives for cost-effectiveness in an insurance-like setting of pooled risk. Using an insurance-like mechanism of pooled risk, the burden on the individual of paying for his care is reduced. She "knows" that she will receive the care she needs. In addition, by having a relatively large number of elderly in one place, CCRCs may be able to provide in-home services less expensively and forestall or prevent the need for more intensive services. CCRCs have a strong financial incentive to provide care in a cost-effective manner.

Proponents also note that quality of life may be enhanced with CCRCs. Noninstitutional services are more available in CCRCs. In addition, the communal-living environment and focus on independence could have a positive effect on the elderly. A support system of peers might help buffer the stresses of aging. Moreover, when an elderly resident needs to be institutionalized, the usual stresses associated with relocation may be minimized because she is only moving to another part of the community.

On the other hand, there are many obstacles to CCRCs. First, CCRCs are expensive, thus restricting the potential market. ICF, Inc. (1985) estimated that only 10–20% of the elderly could afford to join a continuing-care retirement community. Second, not only do CCRCs select higher-income people, but they mostly restrict entry to only the healthy elderly, thus excluding those most in need of long-term care services. Third, in some relatively rare but highly publicized cases, CCRCs have been financially unsound and have gone bankrupt. Residents who have spent their life savings to join these CCRCs have been left stranded. As CCRCs become increasingly attractive to real estate speculators, this could become a more frequent occurrence (Topolnicki, 1985). Fourth, with increasing frequency, CCRCs have been charging additional fees for intensive services and therefore do not fully protect against catastrophic expenses faced by some elderly. Finally, CCRCs necessitate that people move out of their homes and into a more organized setting. Most elderly do not want to give up their homes or live in that type of setting.

Home Equity Conversion

Home equity conversion is built on the observation that the most important asset of most elderly (i.e., their homes) is not at all liquid. As a result, the elderly "live too poor and die too rich." This approach changes assets invested in home ownership into a stream of income that could be used to meet long-term care (or other) needs. In essence, the bank gives the homeowner a loan that is paid to the homeowner in monthly installments. At some time in the future, preferably after his death, the homeowner repays the loan with interest, using the proceeds from the sale of the home.

Advocates of home equity conversion note that this method is a relatively painless method to increase the income of the elderly and to provide funds for them to purchase long-term care insurance or services. Home ownership is extremely widespread. About 70% of all elderly households own their own home, including about 65% of low-income aged households (Jacobs, 1985). Thus this is one private-sector option that could include a substantial number of low-income individuals. Moreover, the amount of money that could be generated is significant. Jacobs and Weissert (1984) estimated that about one-third of all elderly could generate over $2,000 per year by converting their home equity to cash. Finally, home equity conversion appears to be especially financially attractive for single individuals at very old ages—precisely the group that faces the greatest risk of entering a nursing home.

Although technically very promising, there are several potential problems with this approach. First, the elderly are generally unwilling to let go of their home asset. A large research literature suggests that the elderly do not use up their assets at anywhere near the rates predicted by the "life-cycle hypothesis" (Bernheim, 1984; Mirer, 1979). In addition, since the home is already largely a protected asset under Medicaid, a policy that uses up the principal asset of the elderly in order to prevent Medicaid from using less important assets would seem to be contradictory.

From the perspective of the financial institutions, there are also significant problems to overcome. Since the elderly are essentially losing their home ownership, they are not encouraged to keep up their home. In addition, their ability to maintain the home diminishes with age. From the bank's perspective, potential reduction in the home's value represents a financial risk; from the aged person's perspective, lack of maintenance represents a potential safety hazard. Furthermore, lending institutions have been very reluctant to enter into nontraditional relationships with the elderly under circumstances where the elderly might outlive their actuarial expectancy, which would force the financial institution either to foreclose or to postpone claiming the asset. Banks do not like waiting to be repaid, and foreclosing on elderly widows conjures up the worst image of bankers. Neither option is very attractive to the financial community. The evolving consensus is that there is a need for some public mortgage insurance, a proposal that has scared away the Reagan administration (Beirne, 1985).

Finally, home equity conversion is an option that places the financial burden of long-term care costs on the individual and does not attempt to spread the risks across a larger population. Although it might generate enough income to purchase insurance (if it were more widely available and a better product), the income from the home equity conversion would not be enough to cover catastrophic long-term care costs. Moreover, an analysis by ICF, Inc. (1985) suggests that converting the home into equity would have only a negligible impact on the number of persons who could afford long-term care insurance at 5% or 10% of their income.

Individual Retirement Accounts (IRAs) for Long-Term Care

The idea of individual retirement accounts for long-term care builds on the popularity of general IRAs by expanding the concept to long-term care. This option, which does not currently exist, would encourage individuals to save for their own long-term care by deferring the taxes on money placed into those accounts. After age 65, these funds would become available to purchase medical and social long-term care services.

Advocates of this approach present several arguments. First, the private savings generated from IRAs could reduce the financial risk individuals face. This might enable individuals to prevent pauperization as a result of catastrophic nursing home costs. Second, individuals would have the flexibility to purchase the best service package most appropriate for their own long-term care needs. Relatedly, since service or insurance payments would be out-of-pocket, IRAs for long-term care would also provide incentives to reduce unnecessary service use and to seek cost-effective alternatives. Finally, IRAs could stimulate the long-term care industry to develop a wider range and better quality of long-term care services for the elderly. Since funds could be used for any service, the institutional bias of some other options could be avoided.

Again, there are obstacles to this approach. First, it is not clear that people are willing to save for such a single purpose, especially starting at early ages, when enough assets could be accumulated so that the IRA might be useful. Few people expect to have an extended period of disability during their old age. In addition, most people have very little knowledge of long-term care and assume that Medicare or Medigap insurance will pay for it. Second, even at fairly substantial incomes, only a minority of taxpayers currently claim IRA deductions. For example, even at incomes between $30,000 and $40,000, only 27% of tax-paying households claimed IRA deductions in tax year 1982 (IRS, 1984). Moreover, one does not have to move very far down the income distribution to find that people did not fully use their full allowable deduction for their general purpose IRA. Presumably, most people would be more likely to use a general purpose IRA than a substantially restricted one. Third, compared to many other societies, the United States has a rather low savings rate. Over the years, a variety of efforts to increase the savings rate have failed. Most economists seem to think that IRAs did not increase the savings rate much, if at all. Taxpayers merely moved money into tax-deductible accounts at a substantial loss to the Treasury. At a time of substantial federal deficits, additional revenue losses should be avoided. Finally, tax incentives are inevitably an inefficient way to achieve social goals, since they subsidize a certain number of people who were already going to do what the tax incentives sought to have them do.

Will Private-Sector Approaches Work?

The answer to this question depends on the goal chosen. From a public policy perspective, the key question is whether private-sector approaches can reach far enough down the income distribution to include those people who would otherwise spend-down to Medicaid and, therefore, materially affect public expenditures. While attention has been focused on middle-class nursing home patients who spend-down to Medicaid levels, Health Care Financing Administration actuaries estimate that only one-third of Medicaid patients were admitted as private-pay patients and spent down to Medicaid. Highly flawed U.S. census data suggests that about two-thirds of nursing home residents had incomes of less than $2,000 in 1979 (U.S. Bureau of Census, 1984). Conventional wisdom is that no more than half of all Medicaid nursing home patients were admitted as private-pay patients. Moreover, the spend-down requirements mean that Medicaid only pays for that part of care that the income and the assets of the individual cannot cover. Thus, some middle-class individuals may be eligible for Medicaid, but their Medicaid expenditures are relatively low.

To date, the only available estimates of the impact of private long-term care insurance on Medicaid expenditures have been done by ICF, Inc. (1985). Assuming that all persons for whom long-term care insurance was 5% or less of their income and who had $3,000 in liquid assets bought policies, ICF Inc. (1985) estimated that private insurance would reduce Medicaid expenditures by 8%. These purchase assumptions are quite optimistic; fewer people would probably purchase policies. Fundamentally, while 8% savings for Medicaid would be useful and positive additions to the cost-savings arsenal, these savings would not change the basic long-range story of dramatically increased demand for publicly funded services.

OPTIONS FOR REFORM:
PUBLIC-SECTOR APPROACHES

If private-sector approaches are not a panacea, what are the prospects for the public sector? The increased demand for long-term care will mean inevitable increases in public expenditures. Since the number of working persons relative to the number of elderly will decline, there will be increased financial pressure. This pressure will, however, be mitigated somewhat by the increased income and assets of the elderly that will be available to be spent-down.

It is easy, however, to work oneself into an undue level of hysteria. Even with a substantial increase, long-term care will not be a major part of gross national product (GNP). Long-term care is currently only about 1% of GNP, and even if long-term care expenses are multiplied by four, it should not result in an extraordinarily large expenditure.

The real question is whether society is willing to bear that burden. While it is an unpopular notion, the fact remains that tax effort in the United States is low compared to Western Europe. Among the European countries, Canada, and the United States, the only country that spends less total public dollars on the elderly as a percent of GNP than the U.S. is Canada (5.9% and 5.4%, respectively) (Senate Special Committee on Aging, 1984). The other countries range from 7.7% in the United Kingdom to 14.5% in Sweden.

What, then, are some of the public-sector options? The public-sector options for reform fall into three categories. Some options, such as the Medicaid cap and block grants, seek to limit federal financial responsibility while giving more flexibility to the states. Other options seek to elaborate on insurance concepts by adding long-term care to Medicare and to health maintenance organizations. Finally, other options, such as most proposals to make modifications in the current system and allow tax credits for care of the elderly, attempt to expand formal and informal noninstitutional services.

Medicaid Cap

On three occasions, the Reagan administration has proposed capping federal Medicaid expenditures and allowing them to increase only at the medical consumer price index (CPI). States would be given increased flexibility to allow them to keep expenditures within the cap.

Proponents of this approach essentially argue that at a time of $200 billion deficits the federal government can no longer afford Medicaid as an open-ended entitlement program. Moreover, the current open-ended financing system encourages states to be inefficient and to allow expenditures to increase too quickly. The discipline of a cap combined with the increased flexibility would allow states to run their programs more efficiently.

Opponents argue that a Medicaid cap is not reform, but merely a way for the federal government to shift the problem to the states. Since there is no adjustment for demographic changes, there could be serious problems in the long run. Moreover, almost all of the new flexibilities that the administration proposes are simply ways to cut people off the rolls, to eliminate services, or to be as arbitrary in reimbursement as they propose to be with Medicare. In addition, transfer programs are best financed at the federal level, which has the greatest access to the fullest range of income sources. Income redistribution within Mississippi, for example, is of limited utility because Mississippi is so poor. Finally, recent work by Holahan (1985) analyzing the effect of the Omnibus Budget Reconciliation Act of 1981 (OBRA) suggests that children and AFDC adults, groups already hard hit by earlier budget cuts, are likely to bear the brunt of the cutbacks. More broadly, it is grossly unfair to balance the budget at the expense of the lower-income population.

Variations on Block Grants

Closely related to the Medicaid cap, a block grant for long-term care would consolidate the major financing sources into a single formula-based, indexed block grant. Federal requirements would be reduced and state officials would be given considerable flexibility and discretion in organizing programs and establishing priorities. This option would eliminate the Medicaid entitlement to long-term care services.

Advocates of block grants suggest that this approach could combine budget savings with a reorganized delivery system. The federal budget would be directly controllable through the appropriations process. Potentially large future federal cost increases inherent in Medicaid could be avoided. Second, given the freedom to adapt their long-term care programs to local conditions and preferences, states would be better able than the federal government to structure programs to meet needs within the budget constraints. This approach would also provide increased state flexibility to design long-term care services by eliminating the distinctions between health and social services and by drastically reducing the financial risk that states encounter in providing noninstitutional services in entitlement programs. As a result, states could more easily substitute cost-effective noninstitutional services for nursing home care.

There are several potential difficulties with this approach. First, there is a major risk that funding would not increase with need. An indexed block grant becomes abstract and easier to cut because Congress does not have to think through how the cuts would actually be made. Freezing appropriated accounts was the first point of agreement in the current debate on deficit reduction. Second, unless states are given substantially increased funds, it is unlikely that there would be the major reorganization of the delivery system that proponents desire. Current expenditures are already committed to meeting the needs of nursing home patients. Moreover, there is little that a block grant could add in this regard to a liberally administered Medicaid home- and community-based waiver. Third, it is unlikely that more than very modest cost savings could be achieved by reallocating money to noninstitutional services. Although expansion of noninstitutional services can be justified on other grounds, there is little evidence to show that noninstitutional services are cheaper than nursing homes. Fourth, and perhaps less obvious, a block grant could undermine federal quality-assurance mechanisms by breaking the link between eligibility for Medicare and Medicaid funding and adherence to the quality standards. Few people really want to turn nursing home quality assurance entirely back to the states.

Public Long-Term Care Insurance

This approach would create a Medicare-like insurance program for long-term care as Title XXI of the Social Security Act or Part C of Medicare. Most plans would be financed through a combination of tax dollars and premiums. The universal entitlement approach has the clear advantage of avoiding many of the technical problems of private insurance, principally adverse selection. Spreading the cost over the entire population is bound to reduce the financial burden on any one individual. Moreover, in theory, it offers the opportunity to develop substantial financial reserves that can be used latter when the baby-boom population needs long-term care, a strategy being used very successfully in Social Security.

On the other hand, the program is bound to be very expensive because of the large potential demand, the entitlement mentality, and pressures to have tax revenues rather than premiums pay for an ever-increasing portion of the costs (as has happened with Medicare Part B). In 1977 the Congressional Budget Office estimated that the 1984 costs of a comprehensive public long-term care insurance program would be about $50 billion (U.S. Congressional Budget Office, 1977). Few policymakers in Washington are willing to risk expenditures of that magnitude, especially in the face of $200 billion deficits.

Social/Health Maintenance Organizations (S/HMO)

This approach extends the HMO concept of prepaid, capitated financing to include a variety of long-term care services. The principal premises are that a case-managed continuum of care will be cost-effective and that there can be enough savings on the acute care side (along with modestly increased premiums) to help finance expanded long-term care services. This approach is especially interesting because it consciously links the acute and long-term care sectors, taking from acute care to give to long-term care. Despite strong opposition from the Executive Office of Management and Budget (EOMB), Congress included a provision in the Deficit Reduction Act of 1984 directing the Department of Health and Human Services to grant waivers for a four-site demonstration of this concept.

There are several potential problems with this approach. First (and EOMB's principal concern), under conditions of excess demand, any expansion in noninstitutional benefits may result in increased costs because there cannot be any "real" savings in institutional utilization. Any nursing home bed emptied by diverting people from nursing homes may be filled by someone else waiting in the queue.

Second, an empirical question to be answered by the demonstration is whether there can be enough cost-effective substitution of long-term care for acute care, and noninstitutional services for institutional services, to make S/HMOs work. As the demonstrations are ongoing, there have not been, as yet, any systematic studies of S/HMO utilization, costs, quality of care, enrollee satisfaction, or marketing success.

Third, the comparative advantage of HMOs has always been that they had lower acute-care expenditures. To the extent that Medicare hospital prospective payment reduces length of stay, that comparative advantage in acute-care expenditures may decline somewhat, giving the S/HMOs less flexibility to design their service package. And, finally, although this is changing, the elderly have generally been reluctant to join HMOs. This is especially true of those with chronic illnesses.

Modifications of Existing Programs

This option covers a wide range of proposals, but most are geared toward increasing funding for noninstitutional services. These options include, but are not limited to, increasing funding for the Social Services Block Grant, easing the restrictions on Medicare home health and skilled nursing facility benefits, liberalizing the Medicaid home- and community-based service (Section 2176) waiver program, and varying the Medicaid matching rates to provide incentives for the provision of noninstitutional services.

Proponents argue that the current system is too biased toward institutional services. There are a large number of people in need of noninstitutional services. In addition, the pressures of the Medicare hospital prospective payment system to reduce lengths of stay cannot be adequately accommodated within the existing Medicare/Medicaid long-term care system. Many patients need services that are not covered. The result is that some patients are inappropriately discharged from the hospital into a setting where they do not receive adequate care.

On the other hand, while many of the proposals may have merit, they would increase rather than decrease public expenditures. There is no shortage of worthwhile ways to spend more money. The political environment, however, is that of retrenchment, not expansion. In addition, if we are going to have trouble sustaining the existing level of services in the future, should we really be expanding them now? Finally, all of these options are subject to the criticism that they merely tinker with the current highly defective system when more radical change is needed.

Tax Credits for Care of the Elderly and Disabled

These proposals would provide relatively modest tax credits (e.g., $500) for families who provide informal care to the elderly and disabled. Advocates of this approach, including Senator John Heinz and Congressman Mario Biaggi, hope to provide financial incentives for families to care for their relatives rather than place them in a nursing home.

This approach epitomizes the classic conflict between equity and efficiency (Okun, 1975). From an efficiency perspective, tax credits would not improve matters much. There is virtually no evidence that children dump their relatives into nursing homes and would be willing to keep them at home for a relatively small tax credit (Doty, 1985). Surveys of informal caregivers consistently find that they want services, not cash. Thus the tax credit would be unlikely to change behavior but would be very costly to the Treasury because government would end up paying for the informal care it already gets for free.

On the other hand, this type of proposal is very appealing from an equity perspective. Certainly, taxpayers should not be made worse off financially because they care for their elderly relatives. Moreover, from a symbolic point of view, it would be good to provide some tangible reward to those caregivers.

CONCLUSIONS

What will be the future of long-term care? There is no doubt that there will be a large increase in demand. While estimates differ over the exact magnitude, the policy implications of long-term care needs increasing by a factor of two are not much different from their increasing by a factor of four. There will be increasing strains on both public and private financing mechanisms.

Can private financing mechanisms painlessly solve the financing problems? Probably not, although they can make a larger contribution than they do now. Indeed, there is no place to go but up. There are only 100,000 people with LTC insurance, perhaps 150,000 in CCRCs, and there have only been a few hundred home equity conversions.

Especially for the insurance and CCRC options, market penetration depends on producing a less expensive product. Even with the improved financial position of the elderly, these mechanisms are currently beyond the financial reach of most of them. This is especially important if we want to have an impact on public expenditures. Current high costs of these products allow the inclusion of only the relatively few people who would actually spend-down to Medicaid levels.

Also from a public policy perspective, it is not clear how government could encourage these private mechanisms even if it decided that it wanted to do so. The public policy discussion to date has focused exclusively on the feasibility and desirability of private-sector mechanisms and not on how to expand their availability and use. Clearly, making the public programs meaner, more degrading, and less well-funded would create incentives for private approaches, but is that really what we, as a society, want to do to 90-year-old widows in wheelchairs?

What, then, of the public sector? Public-sector expenditures must increase if we as a society are to meet the needs of the disabled elderly. None of the possible public options offer the possibility of achieving dramatic efficiency savings. The burden will increase but it will also be manageable, if we have the will to make it so.

REFERENCES

American Association of Retired Persons. 1982. *Survey of Members Regarding Needs and Preferences for Long Term Care Insurance.* Washington, DC: Author.

Beirne, Kenneth. 1985. *Testimony on Home Equity Conversion Instruments to the Special Committee on Aging.* Washington, DC: Department of Housing and Urban Development.

Bernheim, B. Douglas. 1984. *Dissavings After Retirement: Testing the Pure Life Cycle Hypothesis.* NBER Working Paper No. 1511. Cambridge, MA: National Bureau of Economic Research.

Cafferata, Gail L. 1984. *Private Health Insurance Coverage of the Medicare Population.* Data Preview 18. National Health Cash Expenditures Study. National Center for Health Services Research. Rockville, MD: U.S. Department of Health and Human Services.

Danziger, Sheldon, Jacques van der Gaag, Eugene Smolensky, and Michael K. Taussig. 1984. "Implications of the Relative Economic Status of the Elderly for Transfer Policy." In *Retirement and Economic Behavior,* edited by Henry Aaron and Gary Burtless. Washington, DC: The Brookings Institution.

Doty, Pamela. 1984. *Can Home and Community-Based Services Provide Lower Cost Alternatives to Nursing Homes?* Working Paper. Washington, DC: Health Care Financing Administration.

Doty, Pamela. 1985. *Family Care of the Elderly: Is It Declining? Can Public Policy Promote It?* Working Paper. Washington, DC: U.S. Health Care Financing Administration.

Health Care Financing Administration. 1985. *Study of the Skilled Nursing Facility Benefit Under Medicare.* Washington, DC: U.S. Department of Health and Human Services.

Health Insurance Association of America. 1984. *Long Term Care: The Challenge to Society.* Washington, DC: Health Insurance Association of America.

Holahan, John. 1985. *The Effects of the 1981 Omnibus Budget Reconciliation Act on Medicaid.* Working Paper 3339-03. Washington, DC: The Urban Institute.

Hurd, Michael and John B. Shoven. 1982. "Real Income and Wealth of the Elderly." *AEA Papers and Proceedings* 72: 314–318.

ICF, Inc. 1985. *Private Financing of Long Term Care: Current Methods and Resources.* Final Report submitted to Office of the Assistant Secretary for Planning and Evaluation, U.S. Department of Health and Human Services. Washington, DC: Author.

Internal Revenue Service. 1984. *1982 Survey of Income, Individual Returns.* Washington, DC: Department of Treasury (Pub. 79).

Jacobs, Bruce. 1985. *The National Potential of Home Equity Conversion.* Prepared for the U.S. Senate Special Committee on Aging and the U.S. House Select Committee on Aging. Rochester, NY: University of Rochester.

Jacobs, Bruce and William Weissert. 1984. "Home Equity Financing of Long-Term Care for the Elderly." In *Long Term Financing and Delivery Systems: Exploring Some Alternatives,* edited by P. H. Feinstein, M. Gornick, and J. N. Greenberg. Baltimore, MD: U.S. Health Care Financing Administration. Conference Proceedings. HCFA Pub. No. 03174.

Lawlor, Edward F. and William Pollak. 1985. *Financing Long-Term Care: Problems and Prospects.* Paper presented at Association for Public Policy Analysis and Management, Washington, DC.

Manton, Kenneth and Korbin Liu. 1984. *Future Growth of Long Term Care Population: Projections Based on 1977 National Nursing Home Survey and*

1982 National Long Term Care Survey. Paper presented at Third National Leadership Conference on Long Term Care, Washington, DC.

Meiners, Mark R. 1984. *The State of the Art in Long-Term Care Insurance.* Washington, DC: National Center for Health Services Research.

Mirer, Thad W. 1979. "The Wealth-Age Relation Among the Aged." *American Economic Review* 69:435–443.

National Center for Health Statistics. 1979. *The National Nursing Home Survey: 1977 Summary for the United States.* Washington, DC: Department of Health, Education and Welfare. (Vital and Health Statistics, Series 13, No. 43.).

National Long-Term Care Survey. 1982. Unpublished data from the 1982 National Long Term Care Survey. Washington, DC: U.S. Department of Health and Human Services.

Okun, Arthur M. 1975. *Equality and Efficiency: The Big Tradeoff.* Washington, DC: The Brookings Institution.

Rice, Dorothy P. and Jacob J. Feldman. 1983. "Living Longer in the United States: Demographic Changes and Health Needs of the Elderly." *Milbank Memorial Fund Quarterly* 61:362–396.

Russell, Louise B. 1981. "An Aging Population and the Use of Medical Care." *Medical Care* 19: 633–643.

Scanlon, William J. 1980. "A Theory of the Nursing Home Market." *Inquiry* 17:25–41.

Scanlon, William J. 1982. "Choosing Medicaid Nursing Home Patients." In *Project to Analyze Existing Long Term Care Data, Volume V, Long-Term Care Service Supply: Levels and Behavior.* Washington, DC: The Urban Institute.

Senate Special Committee on Aging. 1984. *Long-Term Care In Western Europe and Canada: Implications For The United States.* Washington, D.C.: U.S. Government Printing Office.

Topolnicki, Denise M. 1985. "The Broken Promise of Life-Care Communities." *Money* 14: 150–158.

U.S. Bureau of Census. Various years. *Series P-60.* Washington, DC: Department of Commerce.

U.S. Bureau of Census. 1984. *Persons in Institutions and Other Groups Quarters. 1980 Census of Population.* PC80-2-4D, U.S. Department of Commerce. Washington, DC: U.S. Government Printing Office.

U.S. Congressional Budget Office. 1977. *Long Term Care for the Elderly and Disabled.* Washington, DC: U.S. Government Printing Office.

Vladek, Bruce C. 1980. *Unloving Care.* New York: Basic Books.

Zedlewski, Sheila R. 1984. "The Private Pension System to the Year 2020." In *Retirement and Economic Behavior,* edited by Henry Aaron and Gary Burtless. Washington, DC: The Brookings Institution.

PART 4
Implications for the Future

Introduction

This chapter, by Bengtson and Dannefer, returns to many of the issues addressed in previous ones—demographic stresses and fiscal constraints, the benefits and strains of informal caregiving, the impact of environmental resources on functional capacities, the heterogeneity and variability of aging. Many of the previous papers have also attended to prospects for the future. They have done so in delimited fashion, however, focusing on population aging and alterations in patterns of morbidity and mortality. Bengtson and Dannefer view the future in more comprehensive fashion. In doing so, they again remind us of the multidimensional nature of health in aging.

Bengtson and Dannefer address the implications of the graying of society and of the disordered cohort flow associated with the postwar baby boom. They take us, moreover, beyond the more obvious reality of growth in the older population to a consideration of quality-of-life issues associated with structural changes in work and family. As we noted in the Introduction to this volume, cohort succession and social change are interdependent dynamics that are synchronized to greater or lesser degrees. This is precisely the focus of Bengtson and Dannefer's chapter. They also take a life-course perspective on the intersection of aging, period, and cohort effects. In particular, changes in work experiences, family structure, and lifestyles that reduce psychological and social resources have implications throughout the life cycle. As an example, they suggest that "deskilling" of work and less prosperous economic careers experienced by members of the baby-boom cohort will reduce their ability to assist their aging parents, as well as hindering adaptation to their own aging. Thus, health-related issues of caregiving and assistance needs are related in important ways to other social processes at the individual (micro) and societal (macro) levels.

Bengtson and Dannefer also recognize the variability of aging and the heterogeneity of the older population. Indeed, they foresee an "amplification of heterogeneity," with increasing social inequality in the older population. Rose Gibson's comments at the conference focused on the need to disaggregate data to investigate the intricacies of heterogeneity, recognizing subcultural differences in resources and the harm associated with erosion of the capabilities of resource units. In particular, she noted that the social ills confronting blacks will place the black family of the twenty-first century in jeopardy by undermining the capacities of its resource generations. The problems of black teenaged women, for example, include pregnancy and out-of-wedlock births; those of black teenaged men include incarceration, homicide, and high unemployment. The result is increasing numbers of black families without men. This is an economic issue, since female-headed households make up the largest segment of the black poor. Gibson further noted that inferior education and health care of today's black children will ill equip them to become the resource generation in black families of tomorrow. These problems facing various age groups of blacks may be slow in resolution due to competition for limited resources in an aging society. Thus, problems encountered by blacks may combine with the implications of an aging society to yield a black family of the future that is top-heavy with dependents and shorthanded on resources. Gibson also observed, however, that elderly black females often serve as wellsprings of support and nurturance. Thus, the heterogeneity of the older population is further complicated by the diverse patterns found within subcultures.

The previous chapters in this volume generally represent focused analyses of relatively clearcut issues. Bengtson and Dannefer adopt a more sweeping view, and as a consequence their chapter has a more uncertain and speculative tone. It can more clearly be characterized as "work in progress," as the authors grapple with complex trends having multidimensional implications. The chapter highlights the important role of the sociologist as social analyst (and, to an extent, as social critic). Such work, of course, often yields more questions than answers, thereby contributing to the agenda for further thinking and research.

Bengtson and Dannefer present several possible futures, both in the general scenarios at the beginning of the chapter and more specifically in their consideration of family patterns. The paper also combines pessimism and optimism, as illustrated in their discussion of family patterns. On one hand, they describe possibilities of strained resources, increased intergenerational tensions, and a "cycle of induced incompetence." In contrast, they also indicate the possibility of heightened family cohesion and emphasize the resilience of family ties in the face of social and cultural change.

Bengtson and Dannefer have outlined some of the complex, interacting forces that will shape the context for aging and health in the future, but they have stopped short of providing us with a detailed map of what that future will look like. George Maddox, in his comments at the conference, suggested a number of questions that remain to be answered. Which scenario for the future is most likely to hold true? How do images of the future arise among policymakers, and how are such visions used? How can we mobilize and implement an appropriate political consensus to achieve beneficial social policies?

These questions go beyond the more narrowly defined dimensions of policy analysis described in the book's Introduction. Bengtson and Dannefer have outlined the broad parameters within which the future will take shape. Clearly there is a need to recognize and plan for new realities, and Bengtson and Dannefer provide a broad view of some of the possible temporal and structural interventions that might be undertaken.

11

Families, Work, and Aging: Implications of Disordered Cohort Flow for the Twenty-First Century*

Vern L. Bengtson and Dale Dannefer

This chapter addresses sociological issues regarding work, families, and aging in the near future. Using the concept of "disordered cohort flow" (Waring, 1975)—a term used to describe substantial differences in adjacent birth cohorts—we will explore some of the changes that are likely to affect the well-being of individuals and families early in the twenty-first century. Our general thesis is that, given a continuation of present conditions, projected changes in the labor market and in family structure may result in increased stress for both families and individuals. A second thesis is that, by combining such projections with findings and principles drawn from recent sociological research and economic projections, we can anticipate more specifically what some of these stress-producing social processes are likely to be and how other social mechanisms might help mitigate them.

* Our names are listed in alphabetical order; we share equal responsibility for the ideas reflected in this chapter. We are grateful to Clement Bezold, Margaret Campbell, Richard Campbell, Elaine Dannefer, Rose Gibson, Barbara Lawrence, George Maddox, Patricia Passuth, and Peter Uhlenberg for their comments on earlier drafts. Preparation of this chapter was supported in part by grants from the National Institute of Aging (R01-AG-04092 and T01-AG-5T32A00101) and the National Institutes of Health (R01-MH-38244).

THE TWENTY-FIRST CENTURY: ALTERNATIVE SCENARIOS OF SOCIAL CHANGE

As Halley's Comet fades into the distance, the twenty-first century looms nearer on the horizon. Especially for those of us interested in aging, the next decades promise to bring many changes. Aging in the future, even the near future, promises to be different from aging in the past. What changes can we anticipate? How radical will the changes be? How will they affect the quality of human life? What will the differential effects be for persons of different ages?

Our thinking about these questions has been stimulated by the combined efforts of a group of health care planners and the Institute for Alternative Futures, a Washington-based group who have devoted much thoughtful attention to the construction of alternative scenarios for the twenty-first century (Bezold, 1984; Bezold, Carlson, & Peck, 1986). These alternative scenarios have had considerable impact in influencing discussions among policymakers and planners. They have been employed in strategic consultation with a number of constituencies: state legislatures, agencies, professional organizations, and health care planners. They have developed 40 different alternative scenarios as constituting potential alternative futures for the United States in the twenty-first century. These scenarios are provocative in their suggestions of future possibilities. Elsewhere (Bengtson, 1986; Bengtson & Campbell, 1985) we have discussed trends in the demography of family life, with implications for these scenarios.

We begin by sharing in brief outline the four most prominent of these scenarios, and then go on to lay out some demographic and theoretical considerations drawn from the sociology of work and family and social psychology, which they largely omit. These factors—largely neglected in the present scenarios—are crucial for any attempt to apprehend fully the nature of aging individuals and families in the United States in the early twenty-first century. Let us begin by briefly presenting four quite different possible futures as they have been depicted by the Institute for Alternative Futures (this material is adapted from Bezold, 1984).

The Continued-Growth Scenario

This view of the year 2020 is predicated upon a continued positive cycle of affluence, consumer spending, high production, and technological progress, resembling Herbert Kahn's (1981) depiction of the future set forth in his book, *The Coming Boom*. The story of continued growth is one of competent management, consensus, and technological ingenuity. In this scenario, the electronic revolution has spread throughout the world and is being put to positive use in the service of humanity and further economic and technical progress. Health care expenditures continue to grow. Therapies are more complex and more effective. Vaccines are developed to prevent many diseases, and definitive cures are found for many that cannot be prevented. This includes most forms of heart disease and most cancers, although chronic diseases other than cancer and heart disease, particularly those that are stress-related, are still common because there has been little significant change in lifestyle. Life extension is made possible by organ and tissue transplants, which become common for many North Americans. The "hospital-on-the-wrist" performs many of the diagnostic and therapeutic functions of the physician and hospital of the 1980s.

The Decline-and-Stagnation Scenario

This scenario is predicated upon adverse ecological developments, perhaps combined with climatic changes, such as the greenhouse effect. Serious pollution and weather changes affecting food production are essential ingredients of this scenario, which reflects the views of the skeptics (Meadows, Meadows, Randers, & Behrens, 1972) who wrote *The Limits to Growth*. Under such conditions, a two-tier health care system evolves, reflecting more generally a two-tier society, presumably with a growing underclass, with those at the bottom subject to triage.

The Disciplined-Society Scenario

This scenario depicts a situation of explicit and legitimated social regulation and control by the federal government, benignly described as the assertive stewardship of the state. As the reader may anticipate, the disciplined-society scenario is presented as a mild version of George Orwell's *1984* (1949). In this scenario, the societal response to economic distress in the 1980s and 1990s is the abandonment of some traditional individual freedoms in the interest of security, comfort, and material success. Behavioral control, systems engineering, and centralized management techniques are put to maximum use with the aid of effective communications and information-processing techniques. And the trains run on time.

Care of the aged, like health care generally, is rationally managed for the entire society, with clearly defined standards for diagnosis and treatment and with an eye toward cost-effectiveness. People are kept comfortable but are not encouraged to pursue the expensive, high-risk procedures or death-delaying strategies that extended life for months or years in the 1980s without apparent benefit to anyone.

The Transformed-Society Scenario

Finally, the transformed-society scenario describes the kind of decentralization and "relocalization" of society that Toffler (1983) and Naisbitt (1982) envisioned. The values of voluntary simplicity and ecological balance have ended the overproduction that once drove industrial North America. Spiritual values are considered more important than material ones. Technology has continued to develop and remain important, but it is governed by different values, subject to more systematic rational reflection, and subordinate to psychological growth. Society is globally oriented, yet locally based. Alternative social arrangements and therapeutic modalities for health care, and for care of the elderly, have flourished, exemplified by parallel emergence of self-care and "body wisdom" alongside their hi-tech equivalents, the "hospital on the wrist."

Major Future Trends

These scenarios, only briefly summarized here, have utility in organizing our thinking about some possibilities in a future that is, barring catastrophes such as nuclear destruction, certain to come. They have perhaps even greater utility in stimulating thought about the kinds of conditions and events that are likely to occur in one or the other of these scenarios; conversely, they also stimulate thought about the consequences of certain kinds of events. Although they provide a useful starting point, these scenarios are also revealing in what they omit. Despite major impending changes in the age structure, they give little attention to age-related factors and the complex interplay of the demographies of age with the dominant social institutions of work and family. This chapter offers a consideration of some of the consequences of this interplay for thinking about health in the future.

We wish to draw attention to three interrelated future trends that must necessarily be added to the set of considerations used to construct such scenarios. These trends promise to offer profound challenges to the overall functioning of society over the next generation. They include (1) the graying of society; (2) the changing character of the labor market; and (3) coming changes in the character of family structure.

These three trends have not, of course, been entirely ignored, and some of them are recognized in lengthier discussions of the scenarios (Bezold, 1984; Bezold et al., 1986). Given their relative certainty and their clear importance, however, a consideration of their combined impact is worthy of central and systematic attention. Since the most fundamental of these trends is the changing demography of age, resulting from the uneven size of succeeding cohorts as they move through the collective life course, we shall begin by using this as a framework within which to analyze the anticipated changes in work and family. As will become clear, our reading of the evidence suggests that, other things being equal, the consequences of these forces are very likely to include an increase in strain, both for individuals who are members of the baby-boom cohorts and for their intergenerational family relations.

THE GRAYING OF THE BABY BOOM: CONSEQUENCES OF DISORDERED COHORT FLOW IN THE TWENTY-FIRST CENTURY

We are all aware of the dramatic shift in the age dependency ratio that will occur between the years 2010 and 2025. These are the years when baby-boomers will begin their mass exodus from the labor force and their entrance into retirement, after which they may reasonably hope to continue to enjoy decades of good health and good times. In a society where the inexorable march of persons through the life course is constrained by a strong normative system of age grading, the swollen cohorts pose a particular challenge to the smooth operation of what Norman Ryder (1965) has called the "social metabolism" of the flow of cohorts through the society. The demographic strain produced by the aging of the population is likely to influence, and in some cases obviate, other issues and trends related to aging, as we shall see.

When viewed from the perspective of cohort analysis, the coming change in the dependency ratio will be just one of the more visible consequences of the general phenomenon of "disordered cohort flow" (Waring, 1975), a term used to describe the situation that occurs when the characteristics of succeeding cohorts vary dramatically, leading to shifts in the age distribution that place stresses and strains on the existing social structure.

Our society is, in many respects, regimented by age (Cain, 1964, 1976; Hagestad & Neugarten, 1985; Riley et al., 1972). Laws, social policies, and norms direct people in synchrony through an expected and age-graded course of schooling, work, and retirement. In such a society, shifts in the societal age structure become especially crucial in any effort to understand the past and assess the present, and certainly in developing projections for the future. Over the next several decades, the changes in age structure will take an unusual course: The smaller birth cohorts following the larger baby boom will move into their middle years, transforming the traditional age structure of the labor force. It is our view that the implications of shifts in age structure for shaping the life conditions of individuals and for setting parameters on the ability of society to meet the needs of its members have not received sufficient attention.

The phenomenon of disordered cohort flow has been noted by some theorists and policymakers. The anticipated retirement of the large baby-boom cohorts, which will occur at a time when a relatively smaller population of persons will be between the ages of 20 and 65 than is presently the case, has been the focus of much debate over the viability of the Social Security system. More recently, Robert Binstock (1985a) has noted that, at the level of national fiscal planning, the attention that has been given to the Social Security problem may have been misplaced. That is, the discussion has centered on income transfers alone and has not included the much larger and growing problem of how to deal with the costs of medical and nursing care involved for the infirm aged and those who can be kept alive through initially dazzling but extraordinarily expensive technologies, often of questionable value in terms of facilitating a quality life.

The implications of disordered cohort flow are not limited to problems of retirement and caregiving in later life. Other strains arising from the lack of fit between existing social structures and the large aging cohorts are likely to have consequences that are considerably subtler but no less pervasive. Although these forces will have complex and sometimes counterbalancing effects, there is a strong likelihood of strains on family life and intergenerational relations for members of the baby-boom cohorts, as members of those swollen cohorts move through the culminating years of their work lives and enter retirement in the opening decades of the twenty-first century.

What are these forces that have implications for potential future strains? Some are economic, anchored in the age structure of work and large-scale occupational changes; others are rooted in changes in the family itself. We will discuss each of these in turn.

DISORDERED COHORT FLOW AND THE LABOR MARKET

The structural fact of disordered cohort flow, through its interaction with the labor market, is already having effects on the work and family lives of members of the baby-boom cohorts and their families. These effects can be expected to reverberate into retirement if things continue as they are at present. Moreover, largely independent changes occurring in the economy, and especially in the labor market, involving new technologies, foreign competition, and organizational innovations, are amplifying these cohort tendencies, and any additional changes in the economic climate will aggravate them still further. While attempts to come to terms with these changes may generate positive reactions, it would appear that one overall net effect will be an increase in the strains upon individuals and their families.

Among the factors affecting members of the baby-boom cohorts that are likely to be created or exacerbated by disordered cohort flow, we focus on three that appear especially salient: (1) the structural incompatibility between a top-heavy age structure and the labor market; (2) the likelihood of continued declines in job growth in the primary sectors of the labor market; and (3) the adverse implications of such realities for personal development and well-being throughout adulthood and after retirement. Although these will have differential impacts upon individuals and families based on their social location (a topic we will return to below), they may be expected to have adverse consequences for many individuals.

Age Structure and Labor Market Structure

In the domain of work life, one major problem derives from the widespread assumption that seniority brings increasing rewards, that whether one is a steelworker or a manager, one can safely expect to gain some level of intrinsic reward as well as income from work as tenure in the labor force increases. Anne Foner (1974) has noted that this assumption has traditionally acted as a "safety valve," neutralizing potential conflict between younger and older workers. Because of the inevitability of aging, there is the expectation that by playing the game, younger workers can help to ensure later gratification in the form of more prestigious and more desirable jobs. When organizations are pyramidal in shape, an integral assumption is that either the organizations will keep expanding through fairly constant and continued population growth, or else through unusually rapid economic growth, in order to continue to accommodate and support the aging workers as they move into high-prestige positions.

Research on the subjective perceptions of white-collar corporate employees, where continued upward mobility is normal, has clearly documented the existence of strong norms of mobility, which employees precisely calibrate to chronological age (Halaby & Sobel, 1979; Lawrence 1984, 1985). These are so coercive that those who do not continue the upward trek are often labeled and stigmatized (Kanter, 1977). In some organizations, getting stuck in a lateral move or dead-end job is regarded as a warning sign that one's worth to the company is in doubt—that it may be a step toward termination or that one will be the first to go in case of personnel cuts. In the context of such mobility-related assumptions, the inherent incompatibility between a job structure that gets *narrower* near the top and a top-heavy age structure is, without radical change in either age structure or organizational structure, a mathematical reality.

As noted elsewhere (Dannefer, 1983), the baby-boom cohorts confront this structural squeeze in the labor market with more education and formal training, and with greater expectations for the intrinsic and extrinsic rewards of work, than any previous generation. Raised in the boom years of the 1950s and 1960s, the majority of these individuals grew to adulthood, even through the social turmoil of the 1960s, bathed in prosperity, expecting the good life of economic security and rising affluence that their parents modeled for them (Easterlin, 1980). This combination of being socialized to prosperity and to an expectation of good jobs and continually increasing abundance has ill prepared the members of baby-boom cohorts to confront a labor market where there are "too many chiefs and not enough braves" (Jones, 1980). For example, according to a recent estimate, middle- and upper-level managerial positions in the United States will grow by 21% over the next several years, while the pool of employees expecting to move into such positions will grow by 42% (Dannefer, 1983). In addition, the very fact of being a member of a large cohort tends to depress life chances further, since it means one has many more peers, and possibly competitors, in the labor market than is the case for members of small cohorts (Easterlin, 1980).

Job Erosion and Reduced Earnings

A rapidly expanding economy with significant growth in good jobs might help significantly to absorb the surplus of highly qualified workers hoping to move into such jobs. Indeed, throughout most of the past century, increasingly large successive cohorts were, on the whole, largely accommodated into work life through this process. Although the U.S. economy in the 1980s has experienced some degree of growth, an analysis of where this growth has occurred leaves one much less sanguine about the overall state of affairs for the soon-to-be burgeoning ranks of middle-aged workers.

It is true that there has been an increase in the absolute numbers of jobs in the past two decades. But it is also true that the lion's share of job growth since 1984 has been in low-paying, high-rotation, or dead-end jobs, such as restaurant workers or hospital aides. Even when doctors, lawyers, and executives in such fields as medical service delivery and advertising are included, service workers make about 16% less per hour than manufacturing workers, and work 20% fewer hours (Judis, 1986). Retail trade workers, the fastest-growing category of service occupation, make only 73% of the average hourly wage paid to service workers as a whole, and they work almost four hours less per week. We term this "job erosion."

Lest it be assumed that such statistics represent an anomaly, a Bureau of Labor Statistics projection from 1978 to 1990 (Carey, 1981, p. 48) identified the following occupations as those in which the largest numbers of new jobs would be created, in rank order: (1) janitors; (2) nurses' aides and orderlies, (3) sales clerks, (4) cashiers, (5) waiters and waitresses, (6) general office clerks, (7) professional nurses, and (8) fast-food workers. Together, these occupations were projected to account for nearly 4.5 million new jobs over the 12-year period. It is true that the meteoric expansion in microelectronics has created some rapid job growth in high-technology areas. Computer systems analysts, operators, and programmers are among the occupations with the fastest growth *rates*. But these three occupations together are projected to create fewer than 500,000 jobs over the same 12-year period.

In sum, both the desirable career-line jobs in white-collar occupations and the high-paying seniority jobs in blue-collar occupations have been eroding as a share of the total labor market. This erosion has resulted not only from a stagnant industrial base, but also from technological advances resulting in automation of factory and office, from organizational policies and practices involving job consolidation and fragmentation, and from the exporting of jobs and entire industries to Third-World countries where labor costs are lower.

The disconcerting implications of these trends have been gaining increased popular attention recently. Most of the discussion, appropriately, has centered on the baby-boom cohorts. A recent analysis conducted for commercial marketing purposes revealed, for example, that only slightly over 5% of the members of the baby-boom cohort qualify as "yuppies" (making at least $39,000 per year), while 72% of them work for an average of about $10,000 per year at the kinds of low-paying service jobs described above (Kim, in press). These trends have been the basis for warnings that members of the baby-boom generation "collectively face a disastrous retirement" (Hewitt, 1986) and the root of the debate on "generational equity" (Longman, 1985). An additional current reflection of baby-boomers' hard times is the gradually increasing trend, which has jumped rapidly in the 1980s, for young people to continue living in their parents' households because of their inability to afford rents (Grigsby, 1986). These trends give support to claims advanced by many sociologists of work and organizations that the labor market is being "de-skilled" (Braverman, 1974) and "de-professionalized." Both of these terms refer to the decline in the complexity of work and the on-the-job autonomy of workers. It appears likely that these changes, impacting the baby-boom cohorts most directly, will result in a reduction of lifetime earnings—even though workers may be taxed more heavily for pension and Social Security plans. In particular, many fewer cohort members will experience the kind of peak in earnings in their forties to sixties that most male labor-force participants in the cohorts preceding them enjoyed.

Reduction in earnings will also mean less opportunity to accumulate private savings or other forms of resources, including home ownership. Buying a home has turned out to be a much more expensive enterprise for baby-boomers than for their predecessors. As a proportion of the paycheck, the size of mortgage payments more than doubled from 1973 to 1983, at which time it was 44% (Levy & Michel, 1985). All the same, the baby-boom cohorts have—at least so far through their collective life course—been much more effectively schooled in consumption than in saving. Again, this contrasts with the situation of currently old individuals, many of whom—having endured the Great Depression and without affluent retired parents of their own to serve as models—have been less sanguine about the ability of Social Security to contribute to their well-being in later life. Many of these individuals concentrated considerable energy upon saving for old age. Moreover, these persons were doubly advantaged in doing so, since the value of real estate and many other forms of investment continued to grow through most of their adult lives. Health care protection—whether in the form of Medicare and Medicaid or private coverage—will traverse a correspondingly conflicted path of increasing cost and reduced benefit. Currently, the elderly comprise 11% of the population and account for 33% of the health care bill. The government currently pays about two-thirds of this bill, but as the numbers of the elderly and their contributions to the health care budget continue to grow, the proportion the government is willing to pay is likely to be eroded (Binstock, 1985a, pp. 4–7).

In short, the old of the early twenty-first century will be the largest, and perhaps initially the healthiest, older population in the nation's history. However, they may also be markedly less well off than, say, persons entering old age today. This is likely to have implications, not only for the health and well-being of the baby-boomers themselves, but also for their families: for relationships with their offspring (if any) and, for some, with their still-surviving parents—those cohorts who gave birth to the baby-boomers and who will themselves be living into their eighties and beyond in unprecedented numbers in the early decades of the twenty-first century. Before turning to a discussion of these implications, let us consider some additional, but less obvious, consequences for later life of being a worker who belongs to a large cohort.

Job Fragmentation and Deskilling

Other consequences for personal life of the career-cycle squeeze that the aging baby-boomers will experience concern the psychological and health-related effects of work. The importance of physical work conditions and of the psychic demands of work—including factors such as job security—have been extensively documented (see, e.g., Kahn, 1981). Apart from issues of salary or other extrinsic rewards of work, job content—what one does while on the job—has effects of its own that are likely to shape an aging population. Some industries have been accurately described as suffering a "decline of craft" that sociologists of work have called "deskilling" (Braverman, 1974).

To the extent that craft work is fragmented, mechanized, or automated, and to the extent that white-collar and professional work is bureaucratized and regimented, workers lose not only some measure of control over how the work is done; they also lose the opportunity to exercise complex skills and activity routines.

Findings from numerous studies, including some longitudinal ones, have suggested that the *content of work* has numerous effects on the individual, influencing not only values and lifestyle preferences, but also intellectual functioning and personality characteristics. The longitudinal research of Melvin Kohn and associates (Kohn & Schooler, 1983) has shown that less complex work leads to some long-term reduction in intellectual flexibility. Suppose that an increasing proportion of a cohort's members are tracked into simpler kinds of work, due to (1) the mathematical impossibility of fitting them into a pyramidal promotion system and (2) a general decline in the richness and complexity of available jobs in society. One likely result is that these cohorts will, as a whole, enter retirement not only with fewer material resources, but also with fewer psychological resources. In other words, the baby-boom cohorts may differ from those preceding them as they enter retirement in that their work experience from their forties onward is likely, on the whole, to provide less of a basis for intellectual stimulation.

The precise significance for overall well-being of such a gradual, long-term decline in intellectual facility has not been documented. However, it seems reasonable to hypothesize that such psychological change may be associated with a loss of such adaptive characteristics as resourcefulness and creativity—characteristics that could generally influence ability to cope, remain independent, and find meaningful modes of activity in later life. Other research has shown that spouses become more like each other on measures such as IQ as time passes, which suggests that such work characteristics are likely to be transmitted to one's partner through family interaction patterns (Clausen, 1986; Eichorn, Hunt, & Honzik, 1981). Some evidence suggests that such work-life differences may remain potent in retirement (Guillemard, 1982).

In sum, then, both intrinsic and extrinsic rewards of work will be enjoyed at reduced levels by members of these cohorts, both because of their large size, creating a buyer's market for labor—which will be considerably amplified by the pyramidal age-graded norms and expectations that both workers and employers hold—and because of technological and economic pressures occurring in the economy that are largely independent of the lack of fit between age-structure and labor-market structure. It is reasonable to hypothesize that these changes in the character of cohorts may lead to reduced levels of resources, of coping and adaptive strategies for later life, and of physical and mental activity.

The Baby-Boom Cohorts and the Amplification of Aged Heterogeneity

The effects of the factors we have been describing are widespread, but they clearly will not impact all cohort members equally. What we term "aged heterogeneity" reflects the increasing diversity among aging cohorts in socioeconomic and personal characteristics in the twenty-first century. A sizable, perhaps even unprecedented, number of baby-boom individuals are economically successful—enjoying high-earnings careers, sometimes in the context of two-career marriages. For such individuals, who will enjoy the fruits of generous benefit packages and perhaps judicious financial planners, retirement may offer generous options. However, while there will be many such people, it appears that they will be proportionally fewer than those who will not enjoy such a bountiful and resource-rich retirement and old age.

The phenomenon of aged heterogeneity appears to hold, not only for medical and psychological characteristics, but for social characteristics as well (Bengtson, Kassachau, & Ragan, 1977; Dannefer, 1987; Dannefer & Sell, 1986). As a cohort ages, inequality among its members in income, wealth, and other resources appears to increase (David & Menchik, 1984; Treas, 1986). Recently, social inequality within the older age strata has been increasing, partly as a function of an increasingly large subpopulation of affluent elders, partly as a function of relatively generous pension plans (Hedderson & Harris, 1985). Nevertheless, the proportion of elderly who are poor, or just above the poverty line, has also increased substantially over the past five years (Crystal, 1986).

The current and projected future realities of the labor market described above, combined with the dramatic change in the dependency ratio that will be amplified in the early twenty-first century, suggest that the elderly age strata will be more heterogeneous with regard to income, wealth, and other resources in the twenty-first century than they were in the twentieth. Given a continuation of present trends, the aged will thus become an even more increasingly differentiated subpopulation, with some elderly continuing to fare very well and with those who for whom secure and rewarding work was never made available continuing to receive minimal rewards in retirement. Since these differences in retirement economic status are likely to be correlated with activity and health status, the differentiation of this subpopulation can be expected to be psychological as well as economic (Dannefer, 1987), a reality that may make additional types of demands on families.

Despite the gains of the late twentieth century in nutrition and health care, the forces described above may threaten the well-being and independence of many cohort members as they move through early retirement and into the later years of old age. In so doing, the effects of these trends will impact the well-being of the spouses and extended families of the individuals in question; it is our view that this impact will be in the form of an increased level of strain in comparison to that characterizing the family relations of those who are now old. Before considering these in detail, let us turn to a consideration of the expected changes in families themselves that may be salient for the lives and health of older people in the early twenty-first century.

DISORDERED COHORT FLOW AND THE FAMILY

With regard to the effects of disordered cohort flow on family relations, three interrelated considerations appear salient; unlike the work-related factors discussed above, not all would appear to contribute to increased family stress. They are (1) the reduction in family size; (2) the "verticalization" of family relations; and (3) the likelihood of increasingly intense family relations, in terms of both psychosocial support and possible conflict. Let us discuss each of these in turn, and then examine their implications for the health and well-being of family members in the early twenty-first century.

Reduction in Nuclear Family Size

The continuing decrease in fertility, which is part of the overall "disorder" of cohort flow, has numerous implications that need to be considered. The overall reduction in fertility and in mean family size suggest that the baby-boomers, as aging parents and grandparents, will have fewer children and grandchildren to whom to relate and upon whom to depend, compared to previous cohorts. Family relations have generally been regarded as a buffer against complete disengagement. In Cumming and Henry's (1960) study, one interesting, and probably durable, finding was that disengagement from family roles did not occur with the same magnitude or abruptness as did disengagement from work roles. What will happen, then, when more and more aging couples or widowed spouses have no families with whom to interact when the other activity modes that have formed the structure of their adult lives crumble around them?

Parallel to the decrease in family size has been the continuing rise in divorce and remarriage. It has been suggested that the resultant reconstituted family configurations, which multiply the numbers of parents, children, and in-laws, may help to offset the smaller absolute number of children by increasing the size of the intergenerational network (Cherlin & Furstenberg, 1986; Furstenberg, 1979; Furstenberg & Spanier, 1984). This hope has been advanced in connection with the parenting needs of children currently young, and it could be extended to the needs of the parents themselves in their old age. Research to date on this question provides little support for such a hope. According to Cherlin and Furstenberg (1986), divorce results in a marked increase in intensity of relations with the mother's extended family, but a corresponding decline in the significance of the child–father relation. Relations with stepparents and step-in-laws are very diverse in form but tend to be relatively weak. In sum, reconstituted families tend to be asymmetrical. Their intrafamilial relationships involve a greater amount of intensity in those relations that are most significant (see also Stinson, 1985). In any case, however, such relationships would necessarily increase strain in the upward flow of support because the number of elders and step-elders per child would be doubled, placing greater temporal and other demands upon middle-aged offspring.

The contemporary increase in diversity of adult lifestyles—more singles and gay couples, more divorce and family reconstitution (occurring at increasing rates even in later life)—points to a future of increasingly varied lifestyles and increasingly complex family roles as these individuals move into later life (Sussman, 1985). Thus the old age of the baby-boomers may consist of configurations of personal and familial relationships that are more diverse, less institutionalized, and perhaps less predictable than at any time since the opening years the twentieth century. Lack of predictability and institutionalization sometimes can, of course, be a plus, even when it requires more energy and perhaps more creativity to "arrange one's life course ad lib" (Modell, Furstenberg, & Hershberg, 1978). When it is a condition accompanied by reduced material and social resources, however, it is less clear that it will have emancipating qualities. It is quite plausible to imagine the 80-year-old woman, second husband now deceased, who wishes her stepdaughter felt more social pressure to provide care or support for her.

Over the past 15 years, numerous analysts have emphasized a postwar trend toward increasing *conformity* in life-course patterns, both in the timing of transitions (Modell et al., 1978) and in the individual's family role configurations over the life course. Analyses by Peter Uhlenberg (1974, 1978) have shown a long-term trend, through the first third of this century, toward the growth of a "standard life course" of childrearing and survival of both spouses in an intact marriage beyond the emptying of the nest. The "rise" of the standard life course was due, above all, to the lengthening of the life course, which reduced the proportion of marriages truncated by widowhood.

Recent analyses, however, reveal a different pattern for the future. The baby-boom cohorts are characterized by trends of increasing divorce, singlehood, and childlessness. The proportion of women who do not bear children has increased steadily since its low of 7.6% for white women in the 1933 birth cohort. For the 1945 birth cohort, for example, which is seeing the completion of its childbearing years, it appears that the percent of white women who are childless will be at least 13%. (Nonwhite women in the 1945 cohort are slightly less likely to be childless than those from the 1933 cohort.) Divorce trends have also shown a dramatic increase, from 18% of the marriages begun in 1920 to a projected 48% of those begun in 1970 (Cherlin, 1981). Although these cohorts are still relatively young, it is thus already assured that the uniformity characterizing the preceding cohorts will not describe them. It appears that uniformity in life-course patterns reached a peak for the 1930–1934 cohorts; that is, among individuals who are now about 50 to 55 (Uhlenberg, 1986). In interpreting these trends, Uhlenberg has written of the "rise and fall of the standard life course," as divorce appears to be replacing widowhood as a source of "nonstandard" life-course patterns. For better or worse, this increasing heterogeneity will mean a reduction in both the power and the clarity of the norms prescribing how family members are to relate to one another.

The heterogeneity of life-course patterns that these cohorts will experience will thus be manifested not only in economic inequality, but also in diversity of relationship networks and hence in inequalities in social and emotional support. Increasing numbers of aged individuals will be potentially deprived of social resources, or else confronting stressful situations as the boundaries of family relationships are less defined by norms and require more ad hoc negotiation.

Increase in Multigenerational Families and the Verticalization of Family Relations

The decrease in nuclear family size described above may to some extent be offset by increases of another sort: the increase in the number of generations represented in family groups at any one time. The combination of an increasing number of co-existing generations with a decreasing number of offspring in each has been described as a "verticalization" of family relations (Knipscheer 1982; forthcoming). For some aging baby-boomers, continued engagement will take the form of caring for *their* aging parents. Four or five simultaneously living generations will cease to be remarkable (Burton & Bengtson, 1985). But verticalization entails an increase not only in the numbers, but also in the *complexity* of intergenerational relations within families. Consider the consequences of the proliferation of the sibling grouping in each generation, which will result in new orders of problems in defining aunts, uncles, and cousins—all of whom will be fewer in number within each generation but lightly sprinkled out across generations and age strata.

Again, an even greater set of complicating factors arises from family breakup and reconstitution. This can bring new sets of step–great-grandparents, for example, and other inlaws for whom even a terminology does not currently exist. While in some way this trend may provide a "rehorizontalization" of relations by increasing the number of others with whom one can relate in each generation, we think it unlikely that this will have any real effect on the quality of intergenerational relations for the reasons discussed above.

While the major results of these alterations in the configuration of family ties cannot be predicted with certainty, some consequences can be identified as probable. In terms of the actual content of relationships, one possibility is that verticalization will mean an overall decrease in the closeness and predictability of relationships, because relationships beyond the immediate nuclear family of origin tend to be less close and more variable in nature. Both spatial and normative constraints contribute to this tendency.

However, another possibility is that the verticalization of family relations in the twenty-first century may create a greater sense of intergenerational solidarity (Bengtson, 1986). First, longer-lived grandparents and even great-grandparents will have more shared years with new generations of children. Second, this may lead to closer emotional bonds with their descendants. Third, to say that such verticalized intergenerational relationships are likely to be less predictable than those, say, among siblings or between children and parents means that they may be more spontaneously negotiable. Few norms exist to dictate the character of intimate interdependency between grandparents and grandchildren, especially when there is great variance in terms of geographic proximity, or between great-grandparents and great-grandchildren. As noted earlier, such negotiability may be both a source of stress and an opportunity for creativity.

To a great extent, what verticalization really entails is an increase in the number of postretirement generations represented within the family. In a sense, then, verticalization epitomizes a societal change in the dependency ratio manifest in the concrete reality of everyday life in average families. A greater proportion of extended family members will be elderly and retired—some young-old and some old-old; and the principle of aged heterogeneity suggests that some will be robust and active while others will be in need of care.

But other potential consequences should be noted. For many families, the verticalization of the family will mean sustained periods of caretaking responsibility, with its attendant demands, both emotional and economic. Although healthy members of the retired generations may themselves serve as primary caretakers, as has already been observed, the economic costs may not be so easily accommodated by families. Proportionally fewer family members will be active labor-force participants, and many of those who are may feel the press between providing materially for their own children and helping to meet the potentially overwhelming expense of medical and health care for aging parents or grandparents. If the public fear of the cost of caring for the swollen cohorts of aging baby-boomers (Longman, 1985) continues to be translated into reduced levels of retirement benefits, reduced coverage of Medicare and Medicaid, and increasing insurance costs, these burdens will be amplified for individuals at the same time that they have more older adults within their multigenerational family for whom to care.

Increased Intensity of Intergenerational Relations

One likely consequence of these changes may be an increase in socioemotional intensity in intergenerational relations, in terms of both greater tension and greater cohesion. A structural fact of family life is that the fewer the children, the more intense the relations between parents and children (Parsons, 1955). For example, the loss of an only child may be much more traumatic for parents than is the loss of a child with six siblings (Toman, 1961).

Conventional wisdom dictates that children remain emotionally important, and perhaps even increase in importance, as parents move into the postretirement years. Longitudinal data on multigenerational family relationships (Bengtson, 1986) suggest that this is true but that it is not a one-way street. Consistent with other findings reported by Shanas (1979), Furstenberg (1983), and others, this research is showing that elderly parents have regular, at least weekly, contact with one offspring (Bengtson, Mangen, & Landry, 1984; Shanas 1979) and that grandchildren have regular contact with their grandparents. Moreover, it appears that both elders and their offspring who are now parents themselves evaluate their reciprocal relations positively and as improving with time (Bengtson, 1986).

These findings contrast markedly with predictions of the erosion of family ties, and the demise of the family itself, as a result of geographic mobility and the generation gap (Bellah, Madsen, Sullivan, Swidler, & Tipton, 1985). What the empirical findings from these numerous studies suggest is the resilience of intergenerational ties in the face of social and cultural change. Nevertheless, it is probable that they will take on a somewhat different character with the change in the ratio of members of generations under discussion here. From its high of 3.69 at the peak of the baby boom (1955–1959), the fertility rate had dropped to less than half this figure, 1.7, just 20 years later (1975–1979) (Easterlin, 1980). The same trend is also reflected in cohort data, which show a drop in mean number of children per woman from 3.2 for the 1933 cohort to 1.9 for the 1950 cohort (Cherlin, 1981). These trends mean that the average elderly parents will have fewer children among whom the opportunity and responsibility to interact with parents will be spread; as elderly parents, baby-boomers will continue to live longer, creating a greater number of "contact years" with elderly parents for their adult children. Thus relations between elders and adult children may not only be more intense, but also of longer duration.

One particular issue that may amplify such tensions concerns the intergenerational issues of economic equity and the reality of intergenerational dependency. The needs of the baby-boomers for caretaking in old age will devolve upon a smaller number of adult children per aging parent than is presently the case, as the age-dependency ratio increases from .194 in 1979 to a projected .370 by 2050 (Foner & Schwab, 1981). Such middle-aged children of small families of origin will be confronted with enormously painful dilemmas by the opportunities for costly but promising medical treatment and special care arrangements, and with these dilemmas will come an increase in tension in their relationship with their aging parents.

Intergenerational relations among the current generation and their children are characterized by a substantial degree of assistance "downward"— either in direct economic assistance or in other forms such as child care (Furstenberg, 1983; Hill, Foote, Aldous, Carlson, & Macdonald, 1970)— from securely situated grandparents to parents experiencing the crunch of childrearing in a consumer-oriented society and the relatively depressed earnings caused by the flooded job market, as discussed earlier. Because of their less prosperous economic careers and because of the societal emphasis on consumption through much of their adulthood, baby-boomers may be less able to assist their own children than were their parents, who were born in the first half of the twentieth century and made more fiscally cautious by the experiences of depression and war.

Nevertheless, the fact that these aging parents have smaller numbers of adult children and grandchildren may enable them to assist in childcare or other direct labor-saving ways. Since parents are shared by fewer siblings, such forms of assistance will also be shared between fewer individuals and hence will be more significant for each. To the extent that adult children come to rely on their parents for such assistance, this will also increase the intensity and potential tension of parent–child relations.

Clearly, the intensity of intergenerational relations has potential for both negative and positive consequences. Depending on one's values, or upon the nature of a particular relationship, one may say that relational intensity means that the family members in question "care" about each other, or are "hung up" on each other. The point we wish to make is simply that relational intensity, which would appear to accompany verticalization, means that the dynamics of relationships will have a somewhat different cast; that it is likely to influence the affective quality of relationships as well as interactional patterns and objective indicators of social support. As any therapist knows, such alterations in the affective quality of relationships inevitably influence the mental health of the family members in question.

Intergenerational Strain as Consequences of Work and Family Trends

Our examination of trends in work and the family has suggested three major sources of strains for future cohorts—each having the potential for placing increased strains upon family relationships and intergenerational relations. First is the overall reduction in family prosperity, requiring more intergenerational material interdependency. Second is the mathematical fact that the reduced number of offspring of the baby-boom cohorts will make the relationships with each of these children more important for aging parents, with implications for emotional and economic health. Third, if the trend continues toward simplification of the content of work experiences over the entire life course (which will have the consequence of reducing the psychological rewards and intellectual stimulation offered by work), then workers' coping abilities may be adversely affected. It is important to note that these sources of strain are entirely distinct from those having to do with reductions in transfer payments or other forms of public resources allocated to the aged. Reduction in transfer payments can accentuate any of these strains considerably, but the sources of strain are independent of such allocations. For better or worse, they have a solid structural foundation in these trends in work and family life.

It is certainly possible that extrafamilial ties, based on religious, neighborhood, or other forms of association, may to some extent serve as family surrogates and thus could reduce the intrafamilial intensity. We think this is fairly unlikely to be a major factor, especially given the enduring consistency reported by Bengtson and associates (1984, 1986). Their findings indicate that neither geographic mobility nor lifestyle diversity keeps family members from remaining quite important to each other, and quite involved in each others' lives.

The durability of intergenerational solidarity is also evidenced by its resilience to a high incidence of change in family composition and structure. Despite mobility, despite divorce and remarriage, family members continue to interact across generations and to evaluate those relationships as stable or even improving over time, as the multiple generations move through the life course (Bengtson, 1986).

What does the likelihood of increased intergenerational strain mean for the health and well-being of family members? These strains reflect, in part, the reduction in resources that may be available to aging individuals in the twenty-first century with less saving and less pension income—a situation that may have implications for lifestyle as well as more the obvious connections to health care and nutrition. In addition to providing a narrower basis for maintaining independence and providing for oneself in terms of health care and good nutrition, reduced resources may mean fewer luxuries—less travel and fewer good times—encouraging premature social and psychological disengagement. Such withdrawal, as has elsewhere been noted by one of the authors, can sometimes be translated with alarming rapidity into a "cycle of induced incompetence" (Bengtson & Kuypers, 1986).

The analysis presented here pertains primarily to the middle-class mainstream of American families. The kinds of family and intergenerational stress we have been describing are predicated on wide-scale changes of (1) reduced resources being brought into the family from outside and (2) an unfamiliar, "nonnormative" degree of intergenerational interdependency within. For families who have been systematically excluded from the mainstream economy, these strains may not be experienced in the same way or, in some cases, at all. Analyses of family life among minorities reveal that economic deprivation and intergenerational interdependency are familiar realities around which family life has been organized for decades (Burton & Bengtson, 1985; Jackson, 1986; Stack, 1975). To the extent that such members of such families are affected by the trends we have been describing, through such factors as cutbacks in public assistance or further deterioration of living conditions, they may cope more effectively with some aspects of the attendant adversity than those encountering it for the first time.

In their analysis of life-course patterns of women's coping, Elder and Liker (1982) showed that middle-class women who had experienced deprivation during the Great Depression—during which time they were young adults—actually fared better in coping with the adversities of age than did those who had not been so deprived. It may be, as Elder and Liker suggested, that the Depression experience provided a kind of anticipatory socialization or an opportunity to develop psychological resilience or life skills that could be mobilized again to deal with the difficulties of age. However, deprived lower-middle-class respondents did not follow the same pattern of improvement.

Is it nevertheless possible that the families accustomed to surviving in poverty and adapting to factors beyond their control may in some ways become models for newly stressed members of the middle class? Certainly, accounts of such families are rich with evidence of their resourcefulness and resilience in responding to deprivation. Perhaps some enterprising citizens with firsthand experience in an ethnic subculture accustomed to economic deprivation will devise a series of workshops with some title like "Poverty: Creative Family Responses"—to be marketed through churches, community groups, or schools.

DISORDERED COHORT FLOW AND
SCENARIOS OF THE FUTURE

We began this chapter with four speculative visions of the early twenty-first century. We then reviewed evidence concerning trends in societal age structure and dependency ratios, the intercohort transformation of work experiences and opportunities for resource accumulation, and possible transformations of family intergenerational experience. In view of their relative certainty and likely magnitude, consequences of these trends must be considered in any serious effort at projecting the future. These forces have implications for the likelihood of the emergence of at least some of the scenarios, as well as for the character of life under each of them. Let us briefly return to the scenarios, reassessing them in the light of the considerations raised in this paper.

Continued Growth Revisited

The trends we have discussed, especially the increasing dependency ratios, suggest the importance of distinguishing growth *per se*—presumably measured by productivity—from the issues of what is produced and how it is distributed. The trends reviewed suggest that the key issues under a scenario of growth are not production, but rather distribution and consumption.

The gradual increase in the dependency ratio means that a smaller number of workers must support a larger number of dependents than is the case at present (Binstock, 1985a; Foner & Schwab, 1981). For support of dependents to continue at present levels would therefore require some combination of (1) a huge jump in national economic productivity, (2) pushing back the age of retirement eligibility to reduce the number of dependent adults, and (3) reallocating societal resources more heavily toward human services—presumably at the cost of the defense and foreign aid budgets. With advances in medical technology leading to greater longevity and burgeoning numbers of aged persons as potential consumers, a huge increase in productivity would be necessary to sustain the well-being of the aged without a reallocation of public resources. The issue of growth in the aggregate thus does not address the life conditions of individuals. Our analysis suggests that even if there is real economic growth, it cannot be translated into an improved, or even current, standard of living without some significant technological and/or policy innovations. Probably the simplest, most direct way of doing this would be to increase mandatory retirement age to 70 or beyond. If continued growth means that unemployment remains controlled, this will be a more viable option under this scenario than under some others.

However, another possibility is that the fruits of continued growth will not be allocated to the elderly on the same per capita basis as they are presently, because of the desire to benefit younger cohorts of the population (Longman, 1985). Those attempting to advocate or justify such an eventuality may be justifiably defensive as they present policy options reflecting various alternatives: low-budget warehousing of the aged, human euthanasia, or some other mechanism of triage devised to deal with the "aged question." Short of rescinding the voting rights of the aged and their children, such outcomes seem highly unlikely. The fact that they may be seriously discussed, however, will represent the desire of some to protect the idea of growth as a cultural image.

In sum, economic growth will not automatically translate into increases in personal health and well-being, either for the dependent—both old and young—or for those whose wages and taxes must support them.

Decline and Stagnation Revisited

One novel feature of this scenario is its reflection of naturalistic, exogenous stimuli. While the other scenarios are primarily consequences of economic and demographic conditions, including those related to age, under decline and stagnation the economy's final dependence on nature itself is revealed (although in the long run, the natural catastrophes described here have a social source). Of course, any changes in climatic and hygiene conditions that disrupt the food supply will be interpreted as a national, if not worldwide, crisis. But more than that, it will be likely to challenge the basic, taken-for-granted assumptions of the prevailing twentieth century world view, including our values and perceptions. Under such conditions, therefore, prevailing notions about the sanctity of life, and perhaps especially the dignity of age, will come under attack. Under such conditions, scapegoats will be sought; and as Robert Binstock (1985b) has argued, the aged already qualify for such scapegoating. Thus, this scenario presents the most age-polarized future of any of those examined.

The burden of such events can be expected to fall especially heavily upon old individuals, since their large numbers will constitute a large, growing, and publicly acknowledged burden for the rest of society (Longman, 1985; Preston, 1984). Ideas like "he's earned the right to a comfortable retirement" may be replaced by others: "She's had her life—are we gonna have a turn?" Euthanasia may, under these circumstances, cease to be a topic of esoteric debate and become legalized and legitimated. Moreover, altruistic suicide—especially among the infirm and advanced elderly—may come to be seen as a kind of subcultural norm, even a religious value. Cultures living in extraordinarily harsh natural settings—Eskimos and other northwestern Native Americans—developed traditions of voluntary death for aged members, which formerly were regarded as cruel or bizarre. Under this scenario, such practices may come to be regarded as positive models of social order, reflecting noble and altruistic ends. Fundamentalist and other apocalyptic denominations may find it particularly appealing to incorporate such notions into dogma, since many resonant themes—the more desirable hereafter, self-sacrifice, and submission to a divine order—are already implied in their dogma.

The two-tier system of health care, as seen emerging in this scenario, will reflect an increasingly two-tier system of industrialized society. Those who deserve to survive will be those who have the means to do so. They will also be the ones who can best forestall their own aging, through processes as diverse as good health care and cosmetic surgery. Our analysis of trends in the labor market suggests that such a situation may not require a natural catastrophe as a stimulus.

Euthanasia may become widely acceptable in such a socioeconomic order. But there is another possibility. In a society facing chronic uncertainty, with technological innovation no longer providing the sure hope it did in the twentieth century, the "wisdom" of elders representing a brighter past may be more highly valued than today.

The Disciplined Society Revisited

This societal consequence, extended to civil liberties as well as economic control, is said to be a potential result of failure to recover from economic problems. It would be difficult to seriously truncate civil liberties unless prompted by a prolonged wave of fear. Whatever economic and other decrements they may have experienced along the way, baby-boomers will be accustomed to a lifetime of considerable civil liberty and could be expected to resist encroachments in this domain. Given their experience, and the context of political movements in the western world since 1945, this scenario is perhaps unlikely.

Nevertheless, other developments might make a disciplined society a more appealing outcome. Fixed prices are advantageous for individuals on fixed incomes, especially in periods of economic instability; policies such as price controls can be expected to have considerable appeal for the politically numerous group of retired elderly if deficit economies trigger rising inflation. Centralized practices such as full employment and job training can be expected to have considerable appeal to middle-aged and older workers through the closing years of this century and the opening years of the next. If these represent aspects of a disciplined society, as is suggested by the experience of Germany and Italy in the 1920s, the trends we have described are likely to be particularly popular with a population caught in the continual erosion of economic circumstance.

In addition, this scenario reflects the consequences of a growing sense of collective hopelessness. There may be both psychological and material reductions in the ability to cope, leading to increases in social pathology evidenced by increases in chemical dependency, mental breakdown, and crime. Such problems, which may appear with greater prevalence in the lives of baby-boomers, are likely to increase the probability of attempts to collectively create some greater degree of social order, with a disciplined society one possible consequence.

If such a society were to develop, it could have significant implications for the relative position of the aged. Some are similar to those described in the decline and stagnation scenario; others may be more positive. Social regimentation has not necessarily been bad news for older people. Machiavelli observed that the collective contributions of the aged have often been affirmed under an enlightened despotism. Social regimentation has often been accompanied by rigid rules of seniority and succession to power. Such a development (leading to partial gerontocracy) might be plausible following the "failure" of a younger cohort of leadership, as occurred in Russia following the abortive 1871 revolution. Nevertheless, such advantage only accrues to a select group of elders.

The Transformed Society Revisited

This scenario, while in many ways appealing, if rather implausible, in the present, may be rendered even more implausible by some of the trends highlighted in our analysis. First, many of its elements appear as luxuries that are made possible by a strong sense of growing affluence. This includes the shift away from the values of economic productivity and conspicuous consumption to those of contemplation and social bondedness. Second, neither the general population nor its leaders have a sense of the mechanisms required to implement such a major transformation; nor is there a real commitment to those alternative images. After lifetimes of regimented and unimaginative jobs, aging baby-boomers may be likely to lack broad vision, analytical power, and any interest beyond self-interest. Thus they will contribute nothing in the direction of such social transformation.

On the other hand, it should be acknowledged that both the technological developments of the late nineteenth century and the social movements of the 1960s, which impacted the baby-boomers' cohort (Bengtson, 1986), suggest considerable capacity for massive value change. The pace of technological change has invaded middle-class households on a day-to-day basis, seen in home computer and telecommunication developments that will reach fruition in the next decades. The search for alternate values and lifestyles, most apparent in America during the youthful unrest of the 1960s, may yet see collective consummation (Toffler, 1983).

The transformed-society future suggests two extremes in terms of the elderly and their families. On the one hand, a society that values personal worth in terms of contemplation and social bondedness (instead of defining personal worth as economic productivity and conspicuous consumption) would probably accord higher status to elderly or noneconomically productive members than does contemporary society. On the other hand, in a society that has experienced a phenomenal shift in values from production/consumption to contemplation/simplicity, the elderly may be captive to their own cohort history, unable or unwilling to adapt; in such a case, they would appear superannuated, thoroughly old-fashioned, and irrelevant.

Any discussion of future scenarios must address questions of social organization, life-course experience, and social policy that are indicated by the kinds of issues we have raised; the need to expand the availability of good jobs, to make lifelong education an accessible and perhaps normative experience, integrated into the mainstream of both educational institutions and individual life course patterns (Moody, 1986; Pederson, 1984); and the need for social policies that support family life. In the final section of this chapter, we turn to a consideration of some implications for social policy and planning that may be salutary, whichever scenario eventuates.

SOME IMPLICATIONS FOR POLICY

The roots of the prospective strains described earlier are anchored in several kinds of social forces: in demographic change reflected in the dependency ratio; in the erosion of desirable and adequately remunerative jobs; in the continuing reduction in family size and the growing instability of marital relationships; and in the interactions of all these factors with each other.

We conclude by calling attention to several avenues of intervention (Dannefer, 1983) that could help ameliorate some of the problems we have outlined for individuals and families.

Policies to Promote Development Incentives

The foregoing analysis suggests that the baby-boom cohorts face a challenging future, with difficulties cutting across both work and family experiences. Following this difficult adulthood, they will enter their later years in record numbers, needing unprecedented material support and medical care. The ability to anticipate these conditions suggests the importance of devising ways of ameliorating the adverse aspects of the anticipated future. Some past social policies may have had the consequence of foreclosing options or reducing developmental possibilities for individuals, even when such options might be valuable in helping to prepare individuals financially for retirement, while sustaining mental and physical health.

To suggest how policy might be used as a vehicle of prevention and preparation, three areas of policy intervention will be mentioned briefly. First, some individual tax incentives discourage job exploration. Those preparing for a new line of work are not permitted an educational deduction by the IRS, while those improving their skills within a current occupation are (Moody, 1986). Such laws tend to keep people locked into their positions—in many cases inhibiting their psychological development and constricting their occupational options.

Second, regarding the domain of family, one can envision a set of pro-family or other pro-active policies for caregiving that do not currently exist. These might include direct subsidies to parents, perhaps especially to single parents—in effect, recognizing children as a form of capital and the subsidy as a public contribution to the nurturance and support of that capital. Less radically, tax incentives might be given to employers for a variety of pro-family employment practices, such as flexible work hours for working parents or working children of indigent parents.

Third, at the community level, incentives can also be implemented in the form of targeted grants. Programs that creatively combine the needs of children and the social resources (and indeed, social needs) of elders can be encouraged. An example is the outstandingly successful one in Brookline, Massachusetts (Moody, 1986).

Rearranging Work Life

Such incentives can also be used to promote some of the kind of workplace initiatives that are already being undertaken by employers interested in enhancing employee morale and commitment. Some of these initiatives have been the subject of wide discussion and experimentation in the corporate and managerial worlds and will not be news to those conversant with these efforts. Their relevance for aging and human development have been much less well developed, and hence we will review them briefly in this context.

Some research (e.g., Best, 1980, pp. 153–158) has shown a strong preference among respondents for rearranging the existing life-course patterns of educational and work experiences. Potential alterations might include, for example, a redistribution of retirement leisure to the middle years, of work life to the later years, and of education throughout the life course, including the postretirement years. Such findings give credence to the cautions offered by others (e.g., Sarason, 1977) of the human toll of the "one-life, one-career imperative." Numerous specific proposals for implementing such life-course flexibility have been advanced. Some, such as worker sabbaticals, have been successfully negotiated and implemented by some European unions and companies.

In relation to the strains produced by disordered cohort flow, the advantages of this kind of increased work-life flexibility would be several. First, there would be some reduction in the ratio of potential workers to good jobs at any one time (since some workers would be on sabbatical or in school). A second advantage would be some reduction in the number of financially dependent elderly, since more of them would be continuing to work. Third, there would be a reduction in the correlation of age and job, which would alleviate many of the strains caused by an age-graded labor market. Fourth, following such changes, there would be a change in the attendant normative expectations (Lawrence, 1984). Finally, we envision a reduction in strains related to their age upon members of any one *cohort* in a particular job role. In principle, such an arrangement could be implemented without any shortening of the work week, although shortening the work week would offer another way to increase the number of jobs.

Despite the attractiveness of such proposals, changes of this sort may be perceived as costly and inconvenient, if affordable at all, for employers. However, the fact that some firms have implemented such policies attests to their feasibility under certain conditions (Zwerdling, 1982). It would be possible to create government incentives for such work in the form of "human development" or "human capital" tax credits, which would be extended to employers based on the proportion or number of permanent employees granted or partially subsidized for sabbaticals, which could in part be paid for through pension funds.

Restructuring Organizations and Jobs

The bestseller *In Search of Excellence* (Stern & Cohn, 1985) brought to public awareness some appreciation of the rich diversity of existing organizational alternatives and the continued role of creative imagination in fostering new, humanly enriching organizational forms in the workplace. Significant themes in a number of the firms used as exemplars included decentralization and worker participation.

Age is correlated with a normative expectation of prestige and power on the job. Even though many older workers in fact have little sense of engagement or efficacy in terms of influencing the nature of their work or the product to which it contributes, the strong normative expectation is that increasing time on the job should result in increasing decisionmaking power. Ironically, the large cohorts are moving toward their middle years just as we are witnessing strong growth in relative low-status, low-power jobs, as noted above. Reconfiguring the content of jobs so that more individuals have a meaningful degree of control over their work and participation in the work process would reduce to some extent the overall uneven distribution of intrinsic rewards across all jobs. Worker participation experiments and initiatives (Zwerdling, 1982) have shown that such innovations can be sustained over the working life course. Thus, it could reduce inequalities in intrinsic rewards across jobs within and between age categories.

SUMMARY AND CONCLUSIONS

This chapter has focused on the future—specifically, the possible futures awaiting the baby-boomers as they grow old. We have suggested that the baby-boomers represent a striking example of *disordered cohort flow:* an unusually large birth cohort following a smaller one, creating strains in existing social institutions. We have examined some current trends in the workplace and family that have relevance to the aging of the baby-boomers and suggested some policy options that might assist in easing the strain these trends suggest.

We began with a preview of four quite different future scenarios—each of which reflects an extension of some current socioeconomic and political-technological trends. Second, we examined the concept of disordered cohort flow (a term used to reflect substantial differences in the size of adjacent birth cohorts, as it characterizes the baby-boomers who will be growing old in the early twenty-first century) and touched briefly on its implications for retirement and caregiving in later life.

Next we focused on four work-life implications of disordered cohort flow for aging baby-boomers and their families, factors that would seem to contribute to greater levels of stress:

1. There is a growing incompatibility between the increasingly top-heavy age structure and the numbers of top-level positions in the labor market, leading to a squeeze between ambition and reality.
2. There is a likelihood of job erosion—the rapid expansion of low-paying, high-rotation jobs—and a reduction in earnings as well.
3. The trends toward job fragmentation and deskilling may lead to reduced levels of resources, both economic and psychological, for baby-boomers as they enter old age.
4. The phenomenon of "aged heterogeneity" (the tendency for within-cohort inequalities to become greater as the cohort ages) suggests that, because of these trends, the aged will represent an extremely differentiated population, some quite well off, but many struggling to maintain well-being.

Fourth, we turned from the workplace to the family, examining trends that may be related to enhanced or decreased levels of stress:

1. Reduction in nuclear family size, which, along with the rising incidence of divorce, suggests a potential threat to social resources of the baby-boom elderly;
2. The "verticalization" of the family (an increase in numbers of coexisting generations, with a decrease in the number of offspring in each) and the increase in the number of multigenerational families;

3. Prospects for the increased intensity of intergenerational relations—
   seen in both greater cohesion and greater tension—resulting from the
   verticalization of family structure.

Finally, we discussed some arenas of policy intervention that might alleviate some of the strains in work and family life reviewed earlier. Promising
areas examined were policies to provide human development incentives,
rearrange work life, and restructure organizations related to jobs.

Richard Easterlin (1980) argues that American society is characterized by
a more or less continuous cycling of cohort and generation size, from boom
to bust, that will ensure an alteration between small, spacious generations
and large, crowded ones. He further suggests that such swings will have
greater impact in the future than they have had in the past, because other
forces that have previously had great impact—volatile economic swings,
immigration, and epidemics—now appear to be much better regulated. To
the extent that he is correct, the kinds of changes we are suggesting here
could have a positive social impact, not just for the impending crises of the
twenty-first century, but for the longer-term future of the United States. By
relaxing age-role rigidities characteristic of our present situation, the problems created by uneven cohort flow for social metabolism would also be
reduced.

REFERENCES

Aldous, Joan. 1985. "Parent–Adult Child Relations as Affected by the Grandparent
    Status." Pp. 117–132 in *Grandparenthood*, edited by Vern L. Bengtson and
    Joan Robertson. Beverly Hills: Sage Publications.
Bain, Mary J. 1976. *The Family: Here to Stay*. Durham, NC: Duke University
    Press.
Bellah, Robert N., Richard Madsen, William Sullivan, Ann Swidler, and Steven M.
    Tipton. 1985. *Habits of the Heart*. Berkeley: University of California Press.
Bengtson, Vern L. 1984. "Loss and the Social Psychology of Aging." Pp. 62–73 in
    Aging 2000: Psychosocial and Policy Issues, edited by C. M. Gaitz, G.
    Niederehe, and N. Wilson. New York: Springer-Verlag.
Bengtson, Vern L. 1986. "Aging, the Family, and the Future." Pp. 237–263 in
    Perspectives on Aging: The 1986 Sandoz Lectures in Gerontology, edited by M.
    Bergener. New York and London: Academic Press.
Bengtson, Vern L. 1987. "Parenting, Grandparenting, and Intergenerational Con-
    tinuity." Pp. 435–456 in *Parenting Across the Life Span: Biosocial Dimensions,*
    edited by A. Rossi, J. Lancaster, J. Altman, and L. Sherrod. Hawthorne, New
    York: Aldine.
Bengtson, Vern L. and Margaret L. Campbell. 1985. "Aging within the Family:
    Current Trends, Future Scenarios." Paper presented at the Annual Meeting of
    the Canadian Gerontological Society, Hamilton, Ontario, Canada, October.

Bengtson, Vern L., Patricia L. Kassachau, and Pauline K. Ragan. 1977. "The Impact of Social Structure on Aging Individuals." Pp. 327–354 in *Handbook of the Psychology of Aging,* edited by James E. Birren and K. Warner Schaie. New York: Van Nostrand Reinhold.

Bengtson, Vern L. and Joseph A. Kuypers. 1986. "The Family Support Cycle: Psychosocial Issues in the Aging Family." Pp. 61–77 in *Life Span and Change in a Gerontological Perspective,* edited by J. M. A. Munnichs, P. Mussen, and E. Olbrich. New York: Academic Press.

Bengtson, Vern L., David J. Mangen, and Pierre H. Landry. 1984. "The Multi-generation Family: Concepts and Findings." Pp. 63–79 in *Intergenerational Relationships,* edited by V. Garms-Homolova, E. M. Hoerning, and D. Schaeffer. New York: Hogrefe.

Bengtson, Vern L. and Joan Robertson. 1985. *Grandparenthood.* Beverly Hills: Sage Publications.

Best, Fred H. 1980. *Flexible Life Scheduling: Breaking the Education–Work–Retirement Lockstep.* New York: Praeger.

Bezold, Clement. 1984. *Pharmacy in the 21st Century: Planning for an Uncertain Future.* Alexandria, VA: Institute for Alternative Futures.

Bezold, Clement, Richard J. Carlson, and Jonathan C. Peck. 1986. *The Future of Work and Health.* Dover, MA: Auburn House.

Binstock, Robert. 1985a. "Health Care of the Aging: Trends, Dilemmas and Prospects for the Year 2000." Pp. 3–15 in *Aging 2000: Our Health Care Destiny. Vol. I: Biomedical Issues,* edited by Charles M. Gaitz and T. Samorajski. New York: Springer-Verlag.

Binstock, Robert. 1985b. "The Oldest Old: A Fresh Perspective or Compassionate Ageism Revisited?" *Milbank Memorial Fund Quarterly* 63:420–451.

Black, K. D. and Vern L. Bengtson. 1977. "Implications of Telecommunications Technology for Old People, Families, and Bureaucracies." Pp. 174–195 in *Family, Bureaucracy, and the Elderly,* edited by Ethel Shanas and Marvin B. Sussman. Durham, NC: Duke University Press.

Braverman, Harry. 1974. *Labor and Monopoly Capital: The Degradation of Work in the Twentieth Century.* New York: Monthly Review Press.

Brody, Elaine M. 1982. "Health and Its Social Implications." Pp. 189–201 in *Aging: A Challenge to Science and Social Policy,* Vol. II, *Medicine and Social Sciences,* edited by A. J. J. Bilmore, A. Svanberg, M. Marois, W. M. Beattie, and J. Piotrowski. London: Oxford University Press.

Burton, Linda M. and Vern L. Bengtson. 1985. "Black Grandmothers: Issues of Timing and Continuity in Roles." Pp. 304–338 in *Grandparenthood,* edited by Vern L. Bengtson and Joan Robertson. Beverly Hills: Sage Publications.

Cain, Leonard. 1964. "Life Course and Social Structure." Pp. 272–309 in *Handbook of Modern Sociology,* edited by Robert E. L. Faris. Chicago: Rand McNally.

Cain, Leonard. 1976. "Aging and the Law." Pp. 342–368 in *Handbook of Aging and the Social Sciences,* edited by Robert H. Binstock and Ethel Shanas. New York: Van Nostrand Reinhold.

Carey, Max L. 1981. "Occupational Employment Growth through 1990." *Monthly*

Labor Review, U.S. Department of Labor, Bureau of Labor Statistics 104(8). Washington, DC: U.S. Government Printing Office.

Cherlin, Andrew J. 1981. *Marriage, Divorce, Remarriage.* Cambridge, MA: Harvard University Press.

Cherlin, Andrew J. and Frank F. Furstenberg. 1986. *The New American Grandparent.* New York: Basic Books.

Clausen, John A. 1986. *The Life Course: A Sociological Perspective.* Englewood Cliffs, NJ: Prentice-Hall.

Crystal, Stephen. 1986. "Measuring Income and Inequality among the Elderly." *The Gerontologist* 26:56–59.

Cumming, Elaine and William E. Henry. 1960. *Growing Old: The Process of Disengagement.* New York: Basic Books.

Dannefer, Dale. 1983. "Age Structure, Values, and the Organization of Work: Some Implications for Research and Policy." *Futurics* 7:8–13.

Dannefer, Dale. 1987. "Aging as Intracohort Differentiation: Accentuation, the Matthew Effect and the Life Course." *Sociological Forum,* Vol. 2.

Dannefer, Dale and R. Sell. 1986. "Age Structure, Aged Heterogeneity and the Life Course: Prospects for Research and Theory." Paper presented at the Annual Meeting of the American Sociological Association, New York, August.

David, Martin and Paul L. Menchik. 1984. "Nonearned Income, Income Instability and Inequality: A Life-cycle Interpretation." Pp. 53–73 in *The Collection and Analysis of Economic and Consumer Behavior Data: In Memory of Robert Ferber,* edited by S. Sudman and M. Spaeth. Urbana, IL: University of Illinois Press.

Easterlin, Richard. 1980. *Birth and Fortune.* New York: Basic Books.

Eichorn, Dorothy, Jane Hunt, and Marjorie Honzik. 1981. "Experience, Personality and IQ: Adolescence to Middle Life." Pp. 89–116 in *Present and Past in Middle Life,* edited by Dorothy Eichorn et al. New York: Academic Press.

Elder, Glen H. and Jeffrey K. Liker. 1982. "Hard Times in Women's Lives: Historical Influences Across 40 Years." *American Journal of Sociology* 88:241–269.

Foner, Anne. 1974. "Age Stratification and Age Conflict in Political Life." *American Sociological Review* 39: 187–196.

Foner, Anne and Karen Schwab. 1981. *Aging and Retirement.* Monterey, CA: Brooks/Cole.

Furstenberg, Frank F. 1979. "Remarriage and Intergeneration Relations." Paper presented at the Workshop in Stability and Change in the Family, National Academy of Sciences, Annapolis, MD, March.

Furstenberg, Frank F. 1983. "Some Implications of Divorce for Kinship Relations." Paper presented at the Eastern Sociological Society Annual Meetings, Baltimore, MD, March.

Furstenberg, Frank F. and Graham B. Spanier. 1984. *Recycling the Family: Remarriages after Divorce.* Beverly Hills, CA: Sage Publications.

Grigsby, Jill S. 1986. "Adult Child Dependents: Why Don't They Leave Home?" Paper presented at the Annual Meeting of the American Sociological Association, New York, August.

Guillemard, Anne-Marie. 1982. "Old Age, Retirement, and the Social Class Structure: Toward an Analysis of the Structural Dynamics of the Latter Stage of

Life." Pp. 221–243 in *Aging and Life-Course Transitions: An Interdisciplinary Perspective*, edited by T. K. Hareven and K. J. Adams. New York: Guilford.

Hagestad, Gunhild O. 1985. "Older Women in Intergenerational Relations." Pp. 137–151 in *The Physical and Mental Health of Aged Women*, edited by Marie R. Haug et al. New York: Springer Publishing Co., Inc.

Hagestad, Gunhild and Bernice Neugarten. 1985. "Age and the Life Course." Pp. 35–61 in *Handbook of Aging and the Social Sciences*, edited by R. Binstock and E. Shanas. New York: Van Nostrand Reinhold.

Halaby, Charles N. and Michael E. Sobel. 1979. "Mobility Effects in the Workplace." *American Journal of Sociology* 85:385–417.

Hedderson, John H. and Richard J. Harris. 1985. "Rising Income in Equality: Some Influences of Life Course and Population Change." Pp. 302–319 in *Life Course Dynamics: Trajectories and Transitions 1968–1980*, edited by Glen H. Elder, Jr. Ithaca, NY: Cornell University Press.

Hewitt, Paul. 1986. "Case Statement of Americans for Generational Equity." Washington, DC: Americans for Generational Equity.

Hill, Reuben, Nelson Foote, Joan Aldous, Robert Carlson, and Robert Macdonald. 1970. *Family Development in Three Generations*. Cambridge, MA: Schenkman.

Jackson, Jacqueline. 1971. "Black Grandparents in the South." *Phylon* 32:260–271.

Johnson, C. L. 1985. "Grandparenting Options in Divorcing Families: An Anthropological Perspective." Pp. 81–97 in *Grandparenthood*, edited by Vern L. Bengtson and Joan Robertson. Beverly Hills: Sage Publications.

Jones, Landon Y. 1980. *Great Expectations: America and the Baby-Boom Generation*. New York: Ballantine.

Judis, John B. 1986. "The Good News is the Bad News." *In These Times*, January 29–February 4, 1986, p. 2.

Kahn, Herbert. 1981. *The Coming Boom*. New York: Putnam.

Kanter, Rosabeth. 1977. *Men and Women of the Corporation*. New York: Basic.

Kim, Peter. Forthcoming. *The New American Consumer*. New York: J. Walter Thompson Advertising Agency.

Knipscheer, C. P. M. 1982. "Het Familie Vetband Als Kontekst Van De Levensloop." *Tydscht. V. Gerontologie and Gerialtie* 13:232–242.

Knipscheer, C. P. M. Forthcoming. "Temporal Embeddedness and Aging within the Multigenerational Family: The Case of the Grandparenting." In *Handbook of the Theories of Aging*, edited by James E. Birren and Vern L. Bengtson. New York: Springer Publishing Co.

Kohn, Melvin L. and Carmi Schooler. 1983. *Work and Personality: An Inquiry into the Impact of Social Stratification*. Norwood, NJ: Ablex Publishing Corporation.

Lawrence, Barbara S. 1984. "Age-grading: The Implicitly Organizational Turntables." *Journal of Occupational Behavior* 5:23–35.

Lawrence, Barbara S. 1985. "New Wrinkles in the Theory of Age: Demography, Names and Employee Preferences." Working paper, UCLA School of Management, Los Angeles.

Levy, Frank S. and Richard C. Michel. 1985. "The Economic Future of Baby Boom." Washington, DC: The Urban Institute.

Longman, Phillip. 1985. "Justice Between Generations." *The Atlantic Monthly,* June.

Meadows, D. H., D. L. Meadows, J. Randers, and W. Behrens III. 1972. *The Limits to Growth.* New York: Signet.

Modell, J., Frank Furstenberg, and T. Hershberg. 1978. "The Timing of Marriage in the Transition to Adulthood: Continuity and Change." *American Journal of Sociology* 84:120–50.

Moody, H. R. 1986. *The Abundance of Life: Human Development Policies for an Aging Society.* New York: Columbia University Press.

Naisbitt, John. 1982. *Megatrends: Ten New Directions Transforming Our Lives.* New York: Warner.

Orwell, George. 1949. *Brave New World.* New York: Bantam.

Parsons, Talcott. 1955. "The American Family: Its Relations to Personality and to Social Structure." Pp. 13–33 in *Family: Socialization and Interaction Process,* edited by T. Parsons and R. F. Bales. Glencoe, IL: Free Press.

Pederson, W. 1984. "New Report Flags a Revolution in Demographics." *Public Relations Journal* 19 (October): 19–23.

Piotrkowski, Chaya. 1979. *Work and the Family System.* New York: Free Press.

Preston, Samuel. 1984. "Children and the Elderly in the U.S." *Scientific American* 251(6, December): 44–49.

Riley, Matilda W., Anne Foner, and Joan Waring. Forthcoming. "A Sociology of Age." In *Handbook,* edited by Neil J. Smelser and Ronald S. Burt. Beverly Hills: Sage Publications.

Riley, Matilda W., Marilyn Johnson, and Anne Foner (Eds.). 1972. *Aging and Society. Volume 3: A Sociology of Age Stratification.* New York: Russell Sage Foundation.

Rubin, Lillian. 1976. *Worlds of Pain.* New York: Harper.

Ryder, Norman B. 1965. "The Cohort as a Concept in the Study of Social Change." *American Sociological Review* 30:843–861.

Sarason, Seymour. 1977. *Work, Aging, and Social Change.* New York: Free Press.

Shanas, Ethel. 1979. "Social Myth as Hypothesis: The Case of the Family Relations of Old People." *The Gerontologist* 19 (1): 3–9.

Stack, Carol B. 1975. *All Our Kin: Strategies for Survival in a Black Community.* New York: Harper and Row.

Stern, Richard and Harvey Cohn. 1985. *In Search of Excellence.* New York: Dell.

Stinson, Candi. 1985. *Adolescent Support Networks.* Unpublished doctoral dissertation, University of North Carolina.

Sussman, Marvin B. 1985. "The Family Life of Old People." Pp. 415–449 in *Handbook of Aging and the Social Sciences,* edited by R. Binstock and E. Shanas. New York: Van Nostrand Reinhold.

Toffler, Alvin. 1983. *Future Shock.* New York: Bantam.

Toman, Walter. 1961. *Family Constellation.* New York: Springer Publishing Co.

Treas, Judith. 1986. "Postwar Perspectives on Age and Inequality." Paper presented at the annual meeting of the Population Association of America, San Francisco.

Uhlenberg, Peter. 1974. "Cohort Variation in Family Life Cycle Experience of United States Females." *Journal of Marriage and the Family* 36:284–292.

Uhlenberg, Peter. 1978. "Changing Configuration of the Life Course." Pp. 65–97 in *Transitions,* edited by Tamara Hareven. New York: Academic Press.

Uhlenberg, Peter. 1986. "Work–family Connection Across Cohorts." Paper presented at "Lysebu Seminar on Life Course, Family and Work," Oslo, Norway, February.

U.S. Bureau of Labor Statistics. 1985. Monthly Report, December. Washington, DC: U.S. Government Printing Office.

Waring, Joan. 1975. "Social Replenishment and Social Change: The Problem of Disordered Cohort Flow." *American Behavioral Scientist* 19:237–256.

Zwerdling, Daniel. 1982. *Workplace Democracy.* New York: Harper and Row.

Epilogue

The aging of individuals and populations poses many health-related issues and challenges for modern societies. This book seeks to clarify those issues, focusing on sociological dimensions of health and aging and their policy implications. The chapters included in this collection reflect the breadth and depth of current sociological thinking and research, serving both to assess our current levels of understanding and to establish research and policy agendas for the future.

The book is divided into four sections. Part 1 provides portraits of health in the various stages of the life cycle, underscoring the multidimensionality and heterogeneity of health patterns related to aging. Part 2 addresses the variety of sources and sites for health care, investigating the factors that shape assistance patterns and the interrelationships among the various forms of health care. Part 3 looks more explicitly at policy issues, assessing goals and options for long-term care of an aging population. Finally, Part 4 turns our attention to the future, considering the implications of cohort succession and social change.

We cannot claim to have achieved closure in any of these areas. Indeed, these chapters perhaps provide more questions than answers, as the heterogeneity and variability of aging are continually highlighted. Several major issues are raised that need further clarification. How can we best capture the processes that shape health care utilization? What is the relationship between informal and formal assistance? Will disability at the end of life increase or decrease in the future?

These chapters point the way for future research efforts. Answers to the questions they raise will depend on appropriate information and research designs. This is partly a matter of more and better data. The chapter by Verbrugge, for example, points to inadequacies of currently available information for capturing the "iceberg of morbidity" over the life cycle, while Longino and Soldo's chapter reflects the need for more comprehensive quality-of-life indicators. Simply increasing the amount of data will not suffice, however. Appropriate research designs are needed to capture the dynamic processes of aging at both individual and societal levels. A longitudinal perspective is required to comprehend health patterns and their consequences for individuals as they age and to clarify the interactions and synchronization of cohort flow and social change within societies.

The need for longitudinal research design is emphasized throughout this book. This has been understood by gerontologists for some time. A major contribution of these chapters, however, is in helping to clarify the questions to be put to such data. That is, longitudinal data are of little help if we do not know what to ask in such research. These chapters provide valuable guidance in this regard. Verbrugge points to the need to better understand the stages of health associated with individual aging. Longino and Soldo highlight the role of the environment in determining the qualitative consequences of changing physical functioning. These issues are relevant to the dynamic relationship between informal and formal health care discussed by George and Chappell and to the unfolding patient/provider interaction described by Coe. These are but a few of the guidelines for longitudinal research that can be gleaned from these chapters.

Although greater attention is paid to research issues, the chapters in this collection also address the policy implications of the social dimensions of health and aging. These policy issues must also be viewed in their complexity. Projections into the future represent perhaps the area of greatest uncertainty in these chapters. Different assumptions yield different scenarios, and the views of the future presented here yield both optimism and pessimism. Moreover, policymaking occurs in a turbulent environment where various interest groups contend within a context of limited resources. Still, the forms of policy analysis embodied in these chapters can offer some guidance as we traverse the maze of complexities and uncertainties in age-related health policy. If we cannot be certain about the future, we can nonetheless make informed choices as we seek to shape the future in beneficial ways.

Index